To Lea Simonds,
whose consistent support,
intellectual enthusiasm, and
artistic sensitivity have kept us
going and growing

In Fact

. .

In Fact

THE BEST OF CREATIVE NONFICTION

EDITED BY LEE GUTKIND

INTRODUCTION BY ANNIE DILLARD

W · W · Norton & Company

New York   London

Manufacturing by The Haddon Craftsmen, Inc.
Book design by Margaret M. Wagner
Production manager: Amanda Morrison

Library of Congress Cataloging-in-Publication Data

In fact : the best of Creative Nonfiction / edited by Lee Gutkind; introduction by Annie Dillard.—1st ed.
    p. cm.
  ISBN 0-393-32665-9 (pbk.)
  1. American essays. 2. American prose literature—20th century. 3. American prose literature—21st century. 4. Reportage literature, American. 5. Journalism—United States. I. Gutkind, Lee. II. Creative nonfiction (Urbana, Ill.)
  PS681.I5 2005
  814'.508—dc22   2004016506

W. W. Norton & Company, Inc.
500 Fifth Avenue, New York, N.Y. 10110
www.wwnorton.com

W. W. Norton & Company Ltd.
Castle House, 75/76 Wells Street, London W1T 3QT

6 7 8 9 0

Contents

. .

Contents

Introduction: Notes for Young Writers

ANNIE DILLARD

■ ■

Dedicate (donate, give all) your life to something larger than yourself and pleasure—to the largest thing you can: to God, to relieving suffering, to contributing to knowledge, to adding to literature, or something else. Happiness lies this way, and it beats pleasure hollow.

A great physicist taught at the Massachusetts Institute of Technology. He published many important books and papers. Often he had an idea in the middle of the night. He rose from his bed, took a shower, washed his hair, and shaved. He dressed completely, in a clean shirt, in polished shoes, a jacket and tie. Then he sat at his desk and wrote down his idea. A friend of mine asked him why he put himself through all that rigmarole. "Why," he said, surprised at the question, "in honor of physics!"

■ ■

ANNIE DILLARD is the Pulitzer Prize–winning author of *Pilgrim at Tinker Creek* and numerous other works of nonfiction, most recently *For the Time Being*. She is professor emeritus at Wesleyan University.

If you have a choice, live at least a year in very different parts of the country.

Never, ever, get yourself into a situation where you have nothing to do but write and read. You'll go into a depression. You have to be doing something good for the world, something undeniably useful; you need exercise, too, and people.

Read for pleasure. If you like Tolstoy, read Tolstoy; if you like Dostoevsky, read Dostoevsky. Push it a little, but don't read something totally alien to your nature and then say, "I'll never be able to write like that." Of course you won't. Read books you'd like to write. If you want to write literature, read literature. Write books you'd like to read. Follow your own weirdness.

You'll have time to read after college.

Don't worry about what you do the first year after college. It's not what you'll be doing for the rest of your life.

People in the arts, I read once, take about eight years just to figure out which art they're in! Notify your parents.

MFA and MA writing programs are great fun, and many are cheap or free.

Learn grammar. Get a grammar book and read it two or three times a year. (Strunk and White is classic.)

Learn punctuation; it is your little drum set, one of the few tools you have to signal the reader where the beats and emphases go. (If you get it wrong, any least thing, the editor will throw your manuscript out.) Punctuation is not like musical notation; it doesn't indicate the length of pauses, but instead signifies logical relations. There are all sorts of people out there who know these things very well. You have to be among them even to begin.

Check the spelling; proofread. Get someone else to proofread, too.

Don't use passive verb constructions. You can rewrite any sentence.

Don't misspell dialect. Let the syntax and words suggest the pronunciation.

Don't use any word for "walk" or "say" except "walk" or "say." I know your sixth-grade teacher told you otherwise. She told me otherwise, too, and is still telling her sixth graders otherwise.

Always locate the reader in time and space—again and again. Beginning writers rush in to feelings, to interior lives. Instead, stick to surface appearances; hit the five senses; give the history of the person and the place, and the look of the person and the place. Use first and last names. As you write, stick everything in a place and a time.

Don't describe feelings.

The way to a reader's emotions is, oddly enough, through the senses.

If something in your narrative or poem is important, give it proportional space. I mean, actual inches. The reader has to spend time with a subject to care about it. Don't shy away from your big scenes; stretch them out.

Writing in scenes doesn't mean in television scenes. No dull dialogue: "Honey, I'm home! Where's the beer?" "In the refrigerator!" (I think most fiction contains far too much dialogue.)

Capturing the typical isn't a virtue. Only making something new and interesting is. If you find life dull and people hateful, keep thinking until you can see it another way. Why would any reader pick up a book to read a detailed description of all that is most annoying in his daily life?

Don't use any extra words. A sentence is a machine; it has a job to do. An extra word in a sentence is like a sock in a machine.

Buy hardback fiction and poetry. Request hardback fiction and poetry as gifts from everyone you know. Give hardback fiction and poetry as gifts to everyone. No shirt or sweater ever changed a life. Never complain about publishing if you don't buy hardcover fiction and poetry regularly.

Buy books from independent booksellers, not chain stores. For complicated reasons, chain stores are helping stamp out literary publishing.

(Similarly, register and vote. If you don't vote, don't complain.)

Write for readers. Ask yourself how every sentence and every line will strike the reader. That way you can see if you're misleading, or boring, the readers. Of course it's hard to read your work when you've just written it; it all seems clear and powerful.

Put it away and rewrite it later. Don't keep reading it over, or you'll have to wait longer to see it afresh.

Don't write about yourself. Think of books you like. Isn't it their subjects you like best? Boring people talk about themselves.

The work's unity is more important than anything else about it. Those digressions that were so much fun to write must go.

Usually you will have to rewrite the beginning—the first quarter or third of whatever it is. Don't waste much time polishing this; you'll just have to take a deep breath and throw it away anyway, once you finish the work and have a clearer sense of what it is about. Tear up the runway; it helped you take off, and you don't need it now. This is why some writers say it takes "courage" to write. It does. Over and over you must choose the book over your own wishes and feelings.

Ignore your feelings about your work. These are an occupational hazard. If you are writing a book, keep working at it, deeper and deeper, when you feel it is awful; keep revising and improving it when you feel it is wonderful. When you are young and starting out, often it is better, however, to write something else than to labor over something that was a bad idea in the first place. Write something else; then write something else; then write something else. No matter how experienced you are, there is no correlation, either direct or inverse, between your immediate feelings about your work's quality and its actual quality. All you can do is ignore your feelings altogether. It's hard to do, but you can learn to do it.

When you are writing full-time (three to four hours a day), go in the room with the book every day, regardless of your feelings. If you skip a day it will take three painful days to get to believing in the work again. Have a place where you can leave the work out and open so you don't have to get it all out and spread before you can start again.

The more you read, the more you will write. The better the stuff you read, the better the stuff you will write. You have many years. You can develop a taste for good literature gradually. Keep a list of books you want to read. You soon learn that "classics" are books that are endlessly interesting—almost all of them. You can keep rereading them all your life—about every ten years—and various ones light up for you at different stages of your life.

Don't find an interesting true story—a life, say, or a historical incident—and decide to turn it into a novel instead of a biography or a historical account. The novel based on fact is a muddy hybrid; readers can't tell what's true. Publishers won't touch these. Write it as nonfiction if you want to write it.

If you want to write novels (and if you buy hardcover novels regularly), go ahead and write novels. Publishing has changed, however, and novels are very difficult to publish. If you want to improve the odds that people will read what you write, write nonfiction narrative.

For fiction, poetry, or nonfiction, the more research you do, the more materials you will have to play with. You are writing for readers—a very educated bunch in this country. It's hard and interesting to tell them something they don't know. The more you read, the better you will know what they know.

No one can help you if you're stuck in a work. Only you can figure a way out, because only you see the work's possibilities. In every work, there's an inherent impossibility which you discover sooner or later—some intrinsic reason why this will never be able to proceed. You can figure out ways around it. Often the way around it is to throw out, painfully, the one idea you started with.

Publication is not a gauge of excellence. This is harder to learn than anything about publishing, and very important. Formerly, if a manuscript was "good," it "merited" publication. This has not been true for at least twenty years, but the news hasn't filtered out to change the belief. People say, "Why, Faulkner couldn't get published today!" as if exaggerating. In fact, Faulkner certainly couldn't, and publishers don't deny it. The market for hardback fiction is rich married or widowed women over fifty (until you all start buying hardback books). The junior editors who choose new work are New York women in their twenties who are interested in what is chic in New York that week, and who have become experts in what the older women will buy in hardcover. Eight books of nonfiction appear for every book of fiction. The chance of any manuscript coming into a publishing house and getting published is one in three thousand. (Agents send in most of these manuscripts. Most agents won't touch fiction.)

When a magazine rejects your story or poem, it doesn't mean it wasn't "good" enough. It means that magazine thought its particular readers didn't need that exact story or poem. Editors think of readers: what's in it for the reader? There is a cult of celebrity, too, in this country, and many magazines publish only famous people, and reject better work by unknown people.

You need to know these things somewhere in the back of your mind, and you need to forget them and write whatever you're going to write.

The Creative Nonfiction Police?

LEE GUTKIND

. .

I am giving a reading at St. Edward's University in Austin, Texas. It is a Thursday evening after a day of classes and questions about essay writing, but now, in the auditorium, the audience is sparse, perhaps sixty or so in a space that seats nearly two hundred and fifty. My host is embarrassed; she informs me that a popular Latino poet is reading on campus at the same time, so the potential audience is divided. I have a feeling that I am the lesser of the two. This is a city with a high percentage of Mexican-American residents. And poetry is written to be read aloud, unlike nonfiction, supposedly, which is factual and informative and which, students might assume, can be tedious and boring.

Of course, I am a *creative* nonfiction writer, "creative" being indicative of the style in which the nonfiction is written so as to make it more dramatic and compelling. We embrace many of the techniques of the fiction writer, including dialogue, description, plot, intimacy and specificity of detail, characterization, point of view; except, because it is nonfiction—and this is the difference—it is true.

But writing nonfiction so that it reads like fiction is challenging and extraordinarily difficult, unless, as some critics have pointed out, the author takes certain "liberties" which then may corrupt the nonfiction—making it untrue, or partially true, or shading the meaning and misleading readers. A comment from John Berendt, the author of *Midnight in the Garden of Good and Evil,* is frequently cited as indicative of this danger. Berendt made up transitions in order to move from scene to scene in his book. Most creative nonfiction writers will refrain from imagining and reporting that which did not happen, even in transitions, but Berendt was making the experience easier for himself and more enjoyable for his readers, a process he called "rounding the corners."

This, then, is the subject we are discussing in the auditorium after my reading—what writers can or can't do, stylistically and in content, while walking that thin, blurred line between fiction and nonfiction. If you are encouraged to use "literary techniques," straying from the literal truth for the sake of a more vitalized narrative can be easy and not necessarily an ethical violation. But how to be sure you are on safe ground? The questions pile up, one after another; the audience is engaged. "How can you be certain that the dialogue you are remembering and recreating from an incident that occurred months ago is accurate?" asks one audience member. Another demands, "How can you look through the eyes of your characters if you are not inside their heads?"

I am answering as best I can. I try repeatedly to explain that such questions have a lot to do with a writer's ethical and moral boundaries and, most important, how hard writers are willing to work to achieve accuracy and believability in their narratives. Making up a story or elaborating extemporaneously on a situation that did in fact occur can be interesting but unnecessary. Truth is often more compelling to contemplate than fiction. But the dialogue goes on and on. After a while, I throw up my hands and say, "Listen, I can't answer all of these questions with rules and regulations. I am not," I announced, pausing rather theatrically, "the creative nonfiction police!"

There is a woman in the audience—someone I had noticed earlier during my reading. She is in the front row—hard to miss—older than most of the undergraduates, blond, attractive, in her late thirties, maybe. She has the alert yet composed look of a nurse, a person only semirelaxed, always ready to act or react. She has taken her shoes off and propped her feet on the stage; I remember how her toes wiggled as she laughed at the essay I had been reading.

But when I announce, dramatically, "I am not the creative nonfiction police!" although many people chuckle, this woman suddenly jumps to her feet, whips out a badge, and points in my direction. "Well I am," she announces. "Someone has to be. And you are under arrest."

Then she scoops up her shoes and storms barefoot from the room. The Q and A ends soon after, and I rush into the hallway to find the woman with the badge. I had many questions, beginning with "Who the hell are you? Why do you have a badge? And how did you know what I was going to say, when I didn't have any idea?" I had never used the term "creative nonfiction police" before that moment. But she is gone. My host says the woman is a stranger. We ask around, students and colleagues. No one knows her. She is a mystery to everyone, especially me.

The bigger mystery, however, then and now, is the debate that triggered my symbolic arrest and the set of parameters that govern or define creative nonfiction—the concepts writers must consider while laboring in or struggling with what we call the literature of reality, beginning with the difference between fiction and nonfiction.

Most fiction, on some level, *is* true. How much doesn't matter, since fiction must be believable—but not necessarily true.

But how, exactly, is the truth in nonfiction determined? How much of what is being told should be true? And who is the final arbiter of truth—that "policing" figure I had referred to? The line between fiction and nonfiction is often debated, but is there a single dividing point or an all-encompassing truth a writer is supposed to tell?

A difficult question, to be sure. Truth is neither universal nor verifiable. The editors at *Creative Nonfiction*, the journal from which all of these essays have been selected, will fact-check controversial or litigious essays before publication. "Notes from a Difficult Case" by Ruthann Robson was among a few essays that delayed for nearly six months the publication of the issue in which they initially appeared, a special issue about health care in America. Our editorial board had to work with attorneys to determine what could be said about this dicey debate between a patient and her doctors, what names and places could be legitimately disguised and what names and places should be omitted. The danger here, of course, was building such a strong wall of protection against litigation by disguising detail that the essay becomes what the writer has been trying to avoid: fiction.

And then there's the idea that we all actually own our own truth. Although we are pretty certain that the information provided in "Notes from a Difficult Case" is factually accurate, we also know that Robson's truth, which is about almost dying from cancer treatment and suffering the arrogance of her physicians, might be different from her doctors' truth. Her doctors' stories may reveal an entirely different and legitimate spin on the same situation.

Does this sound fair, to only present one side of a complicated story? Traditional journalists might not think so. But Robson and the other writers appearing in this collection, such as Andrei Codrescu, whose essay reveals the bigotry of his father-in-law, or Terry Tempest Williams, who lambastes ranchers and lawmakers for their disregard of the value and rights of the prairie dog, are not in any way attempting to achieve balance or objectivity. This is a significant way in which creative nonfiction differs from journalism. Subjectivity is not required in creative nonfiction, but specific, personal points of view, based on fact and conjecture, are definitely encouraged.

Another point: journalists (and historians, anthropologists, attorneys, etc.) rely on sources—documents and interviews and testimonies to assure truth and accuracy—but how do they know if the documents are accurate or the witnesses' perceptions valid? Witnesses in court will usually tell what they see or remember as the truth—but how many innocent people have been convicted based on the testimony of a sincere and objective bystander who is, unwittingly, mistaken? In *All the President's Men*, Woodward and Bernstein insisted on the corroboration of two sources before they published anything in the *Washington Post* or, subsequently, in their book, but who is to say two sources are enough? A good historian or social scientist exhausts the available sources, but sooner or later must make decisions about which to accept or reject.

And why, I wonder, are critics and journalists always questioning the ethics and parameters of creative nonfiction writers? Are there no ethical boundaries in poetry and fiction? Are we more deceived by Truman Capote, who supposedly relied on memory to retell the horrible story of the murder of the Clutter family in *In Cold Blood*, or Michael Chabon, who disguised real characters and situations in his novel *Wonder Boys*? Many writers in Pittsburgh knew the facts of the story Chabon dramatized as intimately as Chabon, perhaps more so, but considered it improper and potentially hurtful to the characters and their families to write about it. David Leavitt's career was significantly damaged when, in his novel *While England Sleeps*, he described the esteemed poet Sir Stephen Spender, masked by another name and body, in a way that endangered his reputation. Spender initiated litigation in England, successfully, to halt the distribution of Leavitt's book.

The ethical boundaries of the narrative are not, however, a new dilemma or debate. Henry David Thoreau lived for two years on Walden Pond while documenting only one year. Which part of the two years did he choose, and how often, in his painstaking process of revision, did he combine two or three days—or even four weeks—into one? This technique that Thoreau evidently employed, by the way, is called "compression"—meaning that multiple incidents or situations are combined or compressed in order to flesh out the narrative—allowing a writer to build a more compelling, fully executed three-dimensional story.

In her book about Jeffrey Moussaieff Masson, *In the Freud Archives*, Janet Malcolm combined a series of conversations about the same subject or incident into one. Malcolm did not admit to altering the facts of the conversations—only to the act of disguising when and how the conversations occurred. Does this violate some sort of ethical or moral bond with the reader or subject? Probably not, as long as the information is not manufactured—which is the question that allowed Masson's suit against *The New Yorker* and Malcolm to climb all the way to the U.S. Supreme Court. Masson was initially contending that Malcolm manufactured quotes; he may not have been aware of the use of compression or would not have been disturbed by it had his attorneys not questioned the technique while investigating information subpoenaed from Malcolm. Compression was not the issue that concerned the court, however. Some of the quotations, it turned out, were not accurately reported. Malcolm was scolded, but eventually she and *The New Yorker* were absolved of guilt and responsibility for damages.

But recently a number of journalists have been discovered and disgraced for fudging the truth. In 1997, Stephen Glass admitted to fabricating parts of twenty-seven articles for the *New Republic*, the *New York Times*, *George*, and *Harper's* magazine. He even provided fake supporting material, including self-created Web sites, to outfox his fact-checkers. And we've all read too much about the exploits of Jayson Blair of the *New York Times* and Jack Kelley, *USA Today*'s star reporter, who allegedly bribed people to confirm stories—or pretend to be part of stories—that he had fabricated.

Despite its own problems—or perhaps because of them—the media remains skeptical of creative nonfiction—not only because of the potential to fudge but also because of the kind and depth of fact and truth that some creative nonfiction writers choose to tell. Recently *Harper's* magazine, *Poets & Writers* magazine, and Salon.com published articles critical of the genre. But the most heated attack took place a few years ago in *Vanity Fair* magazine. In "Me, Myself and I," James Wolcott called creative nonfiction "confessional writing" and took to task as "navel gazers" nearly any nonfiction writer who had been the least bit self-revelatory in their work. "Never have so many [writers] shared so much of so little," Wolcott wrote. "No personal detail is too mundane to share." He referred to me as "the Godfather behind creative non-fiction," because of the journal I founded and my many activities supporting the genre, a label I have enjoyed exploiting.

While Wolcott's attack was ill conceived and may well provide a certain insight into his own discomfort concerning self-revelation, his basic assessment of creative nonfiction— that it was or could be narrative of a very personal (maybe too personal?) nature—was on the mark. Creative nonfiction encourages personal reflection about events and ideas that affect our lives in a number of universal ways—not necessarily as therapy for writers, but so that more readers might understand and relate to the larger issues which connect to the personal stories.

Lauren Slater's essay, "Three Spheres," is an example of how a personal story, vividly and candidly revealed, can shed light on a more complex societal problem. And Meredith Hall's memoir, "Shunned," in which a small town in New Hampshire humiliates and rejects a teenage girl because she is pregnant, is taut with tragedy and suspense and illustrates a sense of isolation and rejection with which all readers can empathize. In Judyth Har-Even's "Leaving Babylon," a woman living in Israel petitions for a get— a divorce from her husband under primitive Orthodox Jewish law. The story is deeply personal and self-revelatory, yet journalistic in its informational quality: a perfect combination of style and substance—which is the driving force of the best creative nonfiction in this collection.

To tell her story, Judyth Har-Even devoted many hours to research, as did John Edgar Wideman and Sherry Simpson in "Looking at Emmett Till" and "Killing Wolves," respectively. The same applies to the essays of Philip Gerard, Ntozake Shange, Francine Prose, Gerald Callahan, Mark Bowden, and Madison Smartt Bell. These essays burst with narrative and read like fiction, yet their styles are vehicles through which ideas and information are dramatically, vividly revealed.

Which doesn't mean that "Shunned" is devoid of fact because it is so personal—only that the facts in this situation are somewhat redefined. The nonfiction or informational part of "Shunned" (and many of the other essays in this collection, including "The Brown Study" by Richard Rodriguez, "Mixed-Blood Stew" by Jewell Parker Rhodes, and "Delivering Lily" by

Phillip Lopate) is personal and anecdotal. It is the fact of a life lived in New England during an age of denial.

The information in "Shunned," although not retrieved through interview or unearthed in an encyclopedia, opens a window of enlightenment onto a time and place in America and a particularly painful point of view, bolstered by an intimate and rare interpretation. "Shunned," "Mixed-Blood Stew" and "The Brown Study," among others, provide a higher or three-dimensional truth—a deeper truth—that simple fact and reportage sometimes doesn't allow. Or as Gay Talese described the "new journalism" in the introduction to his landmark collection, *Fame and Obscurity:* "Though often reading like fiction, it is not fiction. It is, or should be, as reliable as the most reliable reportage, although it seeks *a larger truth* [my italics] than is possible through a mere compilation of verifiable facts, the use of direct quotation and the adherence to the rigid organizational style of the older form."

While Talese and Tom Wolfe are equally responsible for the popularity of the "new journalism," nobody actually knows who coined the term "creative nonfiction" or when exactly it came into vogue. Since the early 1990s there has been an explosion of creative nonfiction in the publishing and academic world. When I started teaching in the English Department at the University of Pittsburgh in the 1970s, the concept of an "artful" or "new" nonfiction was considered, to say the least, unlikely. My colleagues snickered when I proposed teaching a "creative" nonfiction course, while the dean of the College of Arts and Sciences proclaimed that nonfiction in general—forget the use of the word "creative"—was at its best a craft, not too different from plumbing. As the chairman of our department put it one day in a faculty meeting while we were debating the legitimacy of the course: "After all, gentlemen [the fact that many of his colleagues were women often slipped his mind], we're interested in literature here—not writing." That remark and the subsequent debate had been precipitated by a contingent of students from the school newspaper who marched on the chairman's office and politely requested more nonfiction writing courses—"of the creative kind."

One colleague, aghast at the prospect of this "new thing" (creative nonfiction), carried a dozen of his favorite books to the meeting—poetry, fiction, and nonfiction—gave a belabored mini-review of each, and then, pointing a finger at the editor of the paper and pounding a fist, stated: "After you read all these books and understand what they mean, I will consider voting for a course called creative nonfiction. Otherwise, I don't want to be bothered." Luckily, most of my colleagues didn't want to be bothered fighting the school newspaper, so the course was approved—and I became one of the first, if not the first, to teach creative nonfiction on a university level, anywhere. This was 1973.

When I started *Creative Nonfiction* in 1993, twenty years later, it was to provide a literary outlet for those journalists who aspired to experiment with fact and narrative. I wrote an editorial statement, put out a call for manuscripts, and waited for the essays to pour in. Which they did. Many dozens of nonfiction pieces arrived in our mailbox over the first few weeks, more and more as the word spread, and our first few issues were published.

And this was as I had expected. I had been confident that there were great creative nonfiction writers everywhere waiting for the opportunity to liberate themselves—all they needed was a venue. But I soon began to realize, as I spread the essays out on the floor in my office, as I tended to do when selecting and choreographing an issue, that most of the best essays were not written by journalists, but by poets and novelists. Writers crossing genres seems to be another significant hallmark of the creative nonfiction genre and a reason for its popularity. Half of the writers in this collection, including Madison Smartt Bell and Charles Simic, along with some I have already named, made their mark in other genres first.

The first issue of *Creative Nonfiction* featured a rare interview with John McPhee by Michael Pearson, who was surprised and challenged when McPhee made him put away his tape recorder and just take notes, like a regular old-fashioned reporter—a detail that captured the spirit of the journal as I had first conceived of it: good old-fashioned reporting—facts, plus story and reflection or contemplation.

It took eight issues over a period of three years to persuade McPhee to contribute an original piece to the journal, and surprisingly, when it happened, it was uncharacteristically personal. McPhee is obliged by contract to offer all work to *The New Yorker* first, and when then-editor Tina Brown saw "Silk Parachute," a story about teenaged McPhee's relationship with his mother, she grabbed it and published it immediately. Now, a half dozen years later, with help from McPhee, we are finally publishing the McPhee "Album Quilt" segment with "Silk Parachute" included, as originally intended. Because the profile of McPhee anchored our inaugural issue more than ten years ago, it is especially satisfying to feature McPhee in *In Fact*.

And the fact that McPhee, a Pulitzer Prize-winning author, perhaps *The New Yorker*'s most prominent and respected reporter, is writing a memoir, is indicative of the inroads and the impact of the new genre of creative nonfiction, introduced and championed over those ten years in the pages of *Creative Nonfiction*. To this point, McPhee has pretty much kept himself and his life out of the narratives. As an example, in his 60,000-word book *The Deltoid Pumpkin Seed*, he uses the word "I" (in reference to himself) twice. McPhee's work is distinguished by his ability to see the world through the points of view of other people and communicate them intimately and intricately. But he also recognizes the compelling nature of personal history and the insight into character and the human condition it can provide.

I said at the beginning that I wasn't the creative nonfiction police or the literary judiciary. But I am "the Godfather behind creative nonfiction," after all, according to *Vanity Fair*. I have been doing this for a long time: through more than a dozen published books and twenty-five years of teaching—and then the groundbreaking journal. So I would like to recommend a code for creative nonfiction writers—kind of a checklist. The word "checklist" is carefully chosen. There are no rules, laws, or specific prescriptions dictating what you can or can't do as a creative nonfiction writer. The gospel according to Lee Gutkind doesn't and shouldn't exist. It's more a question of doing the right thing, following the golden rule: Treat others with courtesy and respect.

First, strive for the truth. Be certain that everything you write is as accurate and honest as you can make it. I don't mean that everyone who has shared the experience you are writing about should agree that your account is true. As I said, everyone has his or her own very precious and private and shifting truth. But be certain your narrative is as true to your memory as possible.

Second, recognize the important distinction between recollected conversation and fabricated dialogue. Don't make anything up and don't tell your readers what you think your characters are thinking during the time about which you are writing. If you want to know how or what people are or were thinking, then ask them. Don't assume or guess.

Third, don't round corners—or compress situations or characters—*unnecessarily*. Not that rounding corners or compressing characters or incidents is absolutely wrong, but if you do experiment with these techniques, make certain you have a good reason. Making literary decisions based on good narrative principles is often legitimate—you are, after all, writers. But stop to consider the people about whom you are writing. Unleash your venom on the guilty parties; punish them, as they deserve. But also ask yourself: Who are the innocent victims? How have I protected them? Adults can file suit against you, but are you violating the privacy or endangering the emotional stability of children? Are you being fair to the aged or infirm?

Fourth, one way to protect the characters in your book, article, or essay is to allow them to defend themselves—or at least to read what you have written about them. Few writers do this because they are afraid of litigation or ashamed or embarrassed about the intimacies they have revealed. But sharing your narrative with the people about whom you are writing doesn't mean you have to change what you say about them; rather, it only means you are being responsible to your characters and their stories. I understand why you would not want to share your narrative; it could be dangerous. It could ruin your friendship, your marriage, your future. But by the same token, this is the kind of responsible action you might appreciate if the shoe was on the other foot.

I have on occasion shared parts of books with people I have written about—with positive results. First, they corrected my mistakes. But, more important, when you come face to face with someone in your story, you are able to communicate on a different and deeper level. When you show them what you think and feel, when they read what you have written, they may get angry—a reaction in itself that is interesting to observe and even to write about.

Or they may feel obliged to provide their side of the situation—a side you have been hesitant to listen to or interpret. With the text in the middle, as a filter, it is possible to discuss personal history as a story somewhat disconnected from the reality you are universally experiencing. It provides a way to communicate as an exercise in writing—it filters and distances the debate. Moreover, it defines and cements your own character. The people about whom you have written may not like what you have said—and may in fact despise you for saying it—but they can only respect and admire the forthright way in which you have approached them. No laws govern the scope of good taste and personal integrity.

The creative nonfiction writer must rely on his or her own conscience and sensitivity to others and display a higher morality and a healthy respect for fairness and justice. We all harbor resentments, hatreds, and prejudices, but that doesn't necessarily mean that because we are writers, we are being given special dispensation to behave in a way that is unbecoming to ourselves and hurtful to others. This rationale sounds so simple, yet it is so difficult. The moral and ethical responsibility of the creative nonfiction writer is to practice the golden rule and to be as fair and truthful as possible—to write both for art's sake and for humanity's sake. In other words, we police ourselves.

By saying this, I do not feel that I am being overly simplistic. As writers we intend to make a difference, to affect someone's life over and above our own. To say something that matters—this is why we write, after all. That's the bottom line: to have an impact on society, to put a personal stamp on history, to plant the seed of change. Art and literature are our legacies to other generations. We will be forgotten, most of us writers, but our books and essays, our stories and poems will always, somewhere, have a life.

Wherever you draw the line between fiction and nonfiction, remember the basic rules of good citizenship: Do not re-create incidents and characters who never existed; do not write to do harm to innocent victims; do not forget your own story, but while considering your struggle and the heights of your achievements, think repeatedly about how your story will affect and relate to your reader. Over and above the creation of a seamless narrative, you are seeking to touch and affect someone else's life—which is the goal creative nonfiction writers share with novelists and poets. We all want to connect with another human being—or as many people as possible—in such a way that they will remember us and share our legacy with others.

Someday I hope to connect with the woman with the badge and the bare feet, face to face—the person who actually inspired this essay. But the truth is I have never forgotten her. She has, in some strange way, become my conscience, standing over me as I write, forcing me to ask the questions about my work that I have recommended to you. Perhaps she is here today, as I write this introduction to *In Fact*. I hope we all feel her shadow over our shoulder each time we sit down, address our keyboard, and begin to write.

Acknowledgments

..

We have received approximately ten thousand manuscripts, mostly unsolicited, over the past ten years, publishing about three hundred of those essays and excerpts—about 3 percent of the total. The twenty-five selected for *In Fact* represent the best and most memorable of the three hundred.

The writers represented here are some of the most prestigious in the world. From the prominence of John McPhee and Diane Ackerman to the newly discovered genius of Meredith Hall and Brian Doyle—and to all of those who have submitted work to us over the years—*Creative Nonfiction* is most appreciative of your confidence in our judgment and your loyalty as readers and contributors. We intend to keep going for another ten years, expanding our readership and opening our pages to a broader spectrum of ideas and voices.

A magazine or journal is a reflection of the editors who choose and help shape the essays to be published while spearheading the editorial direction of each issue. Jessica Mesman, managing editor, assisted me in putting this collection together by helping to select the essays, by soliciting and/or editing many of the author's personal statements, and by securing missing permissions and brainstorming our title.

Leslie Aizenman, Rachael Crossland, Tracy Ekstrand, Kate Radkoff, Michael Rosenwald, Rebecca Skloot, and Kathleen Veslany have served in various editorial and production capacities with skill, insight, and dedication.

Members of our honorary editorial advisory board, Diane Ackerman, Annie Dillard, Tracy Kidder, Richard Rodriguez, and Gay Talese, have graciously lent their names and support.

And over the years, from the very beginning, the *Creative Nonfiction* editorial board—Patricia Park, Laurie Graham, and Lea Simonds—have worked tirelessly to read the vast majority of the manuscripts submitted to us. They have devoted thousands of hours of angst and concern, meeting and debating, helping us to maintain the highest and most consistent editorial standards.

In Fact
..

Three Spheres

LAUREN SLATER

. .

Linda Whitcomb: Initial Intake Notes

*Ms. Whitcomb is a 37-year-old SWF who has had over 30 hospital-
izations, all for suicide attempts or self-mutilation. She scratches her
arms lightly when upset. Was extensively sexually abused as a child. Is
now requesting outpatient therapy for bulimia. Ms. Whitcomb says
she's vomiting multiple times during the day. Teeth are yellowed and
rotting, probably due to stomach acids present during purges.*

*Client has been in outpatient therapy with over 70 (!) social
workers, psychologists, and psychiatrists. She has "fired" them all
because she cannot tolerate their limit setting. She has threatened to
sue "at least eight, maybe more," because "they never gave me what I
needed. They were a menace to the profession." Please note: Client
has never carried through with any of her threats to sue. She does,
however, demand complete access to her health care providers. Has a*

. .

LAUREN SLATER is a psychologist and the author of *Opening Skinner's
Box*, *Welcome to My Country*, and *Lying: A Metaphorical Memoir*. She
lives in Somerville, Massachusetts.

history of calling her therapists in the middle of the night, screaming that she needs to see them right away, and self-mutilating when her requests are refused.

During her intake and evaluation appointment, client presented as teary and soft-spoken. She wore large hoop earrings and much makeup. She said she believes she has gout and asked to be prescribed medication for it. Became belligerent when refused. Possibly this client is delusional, although she was fully oriented to all three spheres—person, place, and time—knowing who and where she was, and demonstrating capacity to locate historical figures in their appropriate periods. Proverb interpretation: somewhat concrete. Serial sevens: intact. RECOMMENDATION: psychological testing; 1x weekly behavioral therapy to address eating disorder; possible admission as an inpatient if she cannot get bulimia under control.

"So who wants to take the case?" Dr. Siley, the director of the outpatient portion of the unit where I work, asks. He folds the initial intake evaluation from which he's been reading back into its green file.

None of the other clinicians offer. A woman as outrageously demanding and consistently suicidal as this one is would add a lot of pressure to anyone's job. Ellen looks away. Veronica busies herself with the pleats on her skirt. The staff room stays quiet.

"What about you?" Dr. Siley says, looking in my direction. He knows my numbers are down. My job description states I'm responsible for seeing at least twenty outpatients, in addition to the chronic schizophrenics in the residential program.

"Well," I say, "she sounds like a lot of work."

"Who isn't?" Veronica says.

"Why don't you take her then?" I say.

"I'm full," Veronica says.

"And you aren't," Dr. Siley adds, pushing the file across the table toward me.

The phone rings six, maybe seven times, and then I hear a tiny voice on the other end—"Hello," it whispers, and I announce myself, the new therapist, let's make an appointment, look forward to meeting you, here's where the clinic is, in case you forgot—

"Can't," the voice weeps. "Can't can't." I hear the sound of choking, the rustle of plastic. "Ten times a day," the voice says. "Into thirty three-gallon bags. I've spent"—and sobbing breaks out over the line—"I've spent every last penny on frozen pizzas. There's blood coming up now."

"You need to be in a hospital then," I say.

"Oh please," the voice cries. "Put me in a hospital before I kill myself. I'm afraid I'm going to kill myself."

I tell her to sit tight, hang on, and then I replace the receiver. I know the routine by heart. I call 911, give the ambulance company her name and address, tell them there's no need to commit her because she said she'd go willingly. Next they'll take her to an emergency room and after that she'll be placed on an inpatient unit somewhere in this state. She can't come into our own program's inpatient unit because she's neither schizophrenic nor male, the two criteria for admission. She'll stay wherever she is put anywhere from three days to four weeks, enough time, probably, for her to forget I ever called, to forget she ever wandered into the clinic where I work. At the hospital they'll likely set her up with an after-care psychologist affiliated with their own institution, and he, or she, will have to deal with what sounds like her enormous neediness. And I, lucky I, will be off the case. Or so I think.

Two days later a call comes through to my office. "Ms. Linda Whitcomb tells us you're her outpatient therapist. Could you come in for a team meeting next Monday afternoon?"

"Well, I don't even know her, actually. I was assigned the case but before I could meet her she had to be hospitalized. Where is she?"

"Mount Vernon. I'm her attending psychologist here. Would you be willing to meet with us regarding her after-care plans?"

Mount Vernon, Mount Vernon. And suddenly, even though it's been years, I see the place perfectly all over again, the brick buildings, the green ivy swarming the windows. The nurses who floated down the halls like flocks of seagulls, carrying needles in their beaks. My heart quickens; a screw tightens in my throat.

"Mount Vernon?" I say. Of all the hundreds of hospitals in Massachusetts, why did it have to be *this* one? And another part of me thinks I should have been prepared, for eventually past meets present; ghosts slither through all sealed spaces.

"Look, I don't know the woman at all," I repeat, and I hear something desperate in my voice. I try to tamp it down, assume a professional pose. "I mean," I say, "the patient, although technically assigned to me, has not begun a formal course of psychotherapy under my care."

A pause on the line. "But *technically*," the voice retorts, "she is under your care, yes? You have some sort of record on her? Your clinic agreed to take the case?"

"Yes," I say. "Well . . . yes."

"Next Monday then, one o'clock, Wyman—"

"Two," I interrupt bitterly. "Wyman Two."

"Good," she says. "We'll see you then."

What else can I do? Technically, I *have* been assigned the case. But this isn't any longer about the case; my hesitations now don't have to do with Linda Whitcomb and her stained teeth, but with ivy on the brick, the shadow of a nurse, a needle, the way night looked as it fell beyond the bars and the stars were sliced into even segments. I remember looking out the windows on Wyman Two; I remember Rosemary swallowing her hidden pills, how she danced the Demerol onto her tongue and later sunk into a sleep so deep only the slamming cuffs of a cardiac machine could rouse her. Liquid crimson medicines were served in plastic cups. The rooms had no mirrors.

But the reflections came clear to me then, come still in quiet moments when past meets present so smoothly the seams disappear and time itself turns fluid. Sometimes I wish time stayed solid, in separable chunks as distinct as the sound of the ticking clock on my mantel right now. In truth, though, we break all boundaries, hurtling forward through hope and backward on the trail made by memory.

But what else can we do except reach, except remember? What else can I do, having been assigned this case? I will go in, go down. Go back.

American culture abounds with marketplace confessions. I know this. And I know the criticisms levied against this trend, how such open testifying trivializes suffering and contributes to the narcissism polluting our country's character. I agree with some of what the critics of the confessional claim. I'm well aware of Wendy Kaminer's deep and in part justified scorn for the open admissions of Kitty Dukakis, who parades her alcoholism for all to observe, or for Oprah, who extracts admissions from the soul like a dentist pulls teeth, gleefully waving the bloodied root and probing the hole in the abscessed gum while all look, without shame, into the mouth of pain made ridiculously public. Would it not be more prudent to say little, or nothing, to hold myself back like any good doctor, at most admitting some kind of empathic twinge? For what purpose will I show myself? Does it satisfy some narcissistic need in me—at last I can have some of the spotlight? Perhaps a bit, yes? But I think I set aspects of my own life down not so much to revel in their gothic qualities as to tell you this: that with many of my patients I feel intimacy, I feel love. To say I believe time is finally fluid, and so are the boundaries between human beings, the border separating helper from the one who hurts always blurry. Wounds, I think, are never confined to a single skin but reach out to rasp us all. When you die, there's that much less breath to the world, and across continents someone supposedly separate gasps for air. When—Marie, Larry, George, Pepsi, Bobby, Harold—when I weep for you, don't forget I weep as well for me.

I have to drive out of the city to get there, down forty miles of roads I've avoided for the past eight years. Where there was once farmland, horses spitting sand as they galloped, wide willow trees I sat under when the nurses let me out on passes, there are now squat square houses dotting the hills. But the building's bubbled dome rises unmistakably over a crest as I round the corner, floating there in the distance like a glittering spaceship, looking exactly the same as it did almost a decade ago. Walking back from passes, I would see that domed bubble, that silver blister bursting against a spring sky, and I would count *one, two, three,* getting closer, my heart hammering half with fear, half with relief. Safe again. Trapped again. Safe again. Trapped aga—

And I have the same heart in the same socket of chest, and it hammers like it used to and I find myself thinking the same words *safe again, trapped again.* My palms sweat on the steering wheel. I remind myself: I am *not* that girl. I am *not* that girl. I've changed. I've grown. I am now a psychologist who over the years has learned to give up her Indian print sundresses and bulky smocks for tailored skirts, who carries a black Coach leather briefcase. How often, though, I've marveled at the discrepancy between this current image of me and the tangled past it sprang from. Sometimes I've imagined shouting out in staff meetings, in front of all my colleagues who know me as a spunky, confident doctor, how often I've wanted to say, *Once I too* . . .

And what I would tell them goes something like this. On five separate occasions, spanning the ages from fourteen to twenty-four, I spent considerable portions of my life inside the very hospital whose graveled drive I am now turning into. Until what could be called my "recovery" at twenty-five or so, I was admitted to this institution on the average of every other year for up to several months. And even today, at thirty-one years old, with all of that supposedly behind me, with chunks of time in which to construct and explain the problems that led me to lockup, I find myself at a loss for words. Images come, and perhaps in the images I can illuminate some of my story. I am five years old, sitting under the piano, as my mother, her face a mask of manic pain, pummels the keys. Beneath the bench I press the golden pedals, hold them all down at the same time so our house swells with raw and echoing sounds, with crashing crescendos and wails that shiver up inside my skin, lodging there a fear of a world I know is impossible to negotiate, teetering on a cruel and warbling axis. And later, lying in my bed, she murmurs Hebrew while her fingers explore me and a darkness sprouts inside my stomach. A pain grows like a plant and when I'm twelve, thirteen, I decide to find the plant, grasping for its roots with a razor blade. Stocked solid with the romance of the teenage years, with the words of the wounded Hamlet and the drowned Virginia Woolf, whom I adored, I pranced on the lawn of my school, showing off the fresh gashes—Cordelia, a dwarf, a clown, Miss Haversham. I loved it all. I wept for the things inserted into me, the things plucked out of me. And I knew, with the conviction of adolescence, that pain confers a crown. I was removed to the hospital, then a foster home, then the hospital, again and again. Later on, in my late teens and early twenties, I starved myself, took pills to calm me down, wanted a way out. And finally I found one, or one, perhaps, found me.

I am not that girl any longer. I tell that to myself as I ride up the hospital's elevator. I *found* some sort of way into recovery. But I know, have always known, that I could go back. Mysterious neurons collide and break. The brain bruises. Memories you thought were buried rise up.

I rise up in the elevator and the doors part with a whisper. Stepping off, I find myself face to face with yet another door, this one bolted and on it a sign that says: ENTER WITH CAUTION. SPLIT RISK.

And now I am standing on the other side of that door—the wrong, I mean the right, side of the door, and I ring the buzzer. I look through the thick glass window and see a nurse hustle down the hall, clipboard in hand. I recognize her. Oh my God, I recognize her! I hunch, dart back. Impossible, I tell myself. It's been over eight years. Staff turnover in these places is unbelievably high. But it could be her, couldn't it? And what happens if she recognizes me? My mouth dries and something shrivels in my throat.

"Dr. S?" she asks, opening the door. I nod, peer into her eyes. They're the blue of sadness, thickly fringed. Her lips are painted the palest sheen of pink. "Welcome," she says, and she steps back to let me pass. I was wrong, I've never seen this woman in my life. I don't know those eyes, their liquid color, nor the voice, in whose tone I hear, to my surprise, a ring of deference. Doctor, she actually calls me doctor. She bends a bit at the waist, in greeting, acknowledging the hierarchies that exist in these places—nurses below psychologists, psychologists below psychiatrists. Patients are at the bottom of the ladder.

With a sudden surge of confidence, I step through. The reversal is remarkable, and for a second makes me giddy. I'm aware of the incredible elasticity of life, how the buckled can become straight, the broken mended. Watch what is on the ground; watch what you step on, for it could contain hidden powers and, in a rage, fly up all emerald and scarlet to sting your face.

And here I am, for the briefest moment, all emerald, all scarlet. "Get me a glass of water," I imagine barking to her. "Take your pills or I'll put you in the quiet room."

Then the particular kind of dense quiet that sits over the ward comes to me. Emerald goes. Scarlet dies down. I am me again, here again. I grip my briefcase and look down the shadowy hall, and it's the same shadowy hall, loaded with the exact same scents, as it was so many years ago. The paint is that precise golden green. The odor is still undefinable, sweet and wretched. Another woman comes up, shakes my hand. "I'm Nancy," she says, "charge nurse on the unit."

"Good to meet you," I say. And then I think I see her squint at me. I've the urge to toss my hair in front of my face, to mention a childhood in California or Europe, how I've only been in this state for a year.

"We're meeting in the conference room," Nancy says. Clutching my briefcase, I follow her down the corridor. We pass open doors and I hold my breath as we come to the one numbered 6, because that was my bedroom for many of the months I stayed here. I slow down, try to peer in. Heavy curtains hang, just as they used to, over a large, thickly meshed window. *There are the stars*, I want to say, for in my mind it's night again, and someone is rocking in a corner. Now, in the present time, a blond woman lies in what used to be my bed. On that mattress swim my cells, the ones we slough off, the pieces of ourselves we leave behind, forever setting our signatures into the skin of the world. As she sleeps, my name etches itself on her smooth flesh, and my old pain pours into her head.

And just as we are passing her by completely, the woman leaps out of bed and gallops to the door. "Oh Nancy," she keens. "I'm not safe, not safe. Get my doctor. I want my doctor."

"Dr. Ness will be up to see you at four," Nancy says.

Suddenly the woman snarls. "Four," she says, "Dr. Ness is always late. Always keeps me waiting. I want a new doctor, someone who'll really care. A new doctor, a new—"

Her voice rises and she sucks on her fist. "Stop it, Kayla," Nancy says. "Take your fist out of your mouth. You're twenty-nine years old. And if you want a new doctor, you'll have to bring it up in community meeting."

Kayla stamps her foot, tosses her head like a regal pony. "Screw you," she mutters now. "Screw this whole fucking place," and then she stomps back into her bed.

When we're a few feet beyond the scene, Nancy turns to me, smiles conspiratorially. I feel my mouth stretched into a similar smirk, and it relieves yet bothers me, this expression toward a patient. "Borderline," Nancy says matter-of-factly, giving a crisp nod of her head.

I sigh and nod back. "They're exhausting patients, the ones with borderline personalities." I pause. "But I prefer them to antisocials," I add, and as I say these words I feel safe again, hidden behind my professional mask. I am back on balance, tossing jargon with the confidence of a Brahmin in a village of untouchables. There is betrayal here, in what I do, but in betrayal I am finally camouflaged.

Of all the psychiatric illnesses, borderline personality disorder may be the one professionals most dislike to encounter. It's less serious than, say, schizophrenia, for the borderline isn't usually psychotic, but such patients are known for their flamboyant, attention-getting, overly demanding ways of relating to others. Linda, according to her intake description, is surely a borderline. Such patients are described with such adjectives as "manipulative" and "needy," and their behaviors are usually terribly destructive, and include anorexia, substance abuse, self-mutilation, suicide attempts. Borderlines are thought to be pretty hopeless, supposedly never maturing from their "lifelong" condition. I myself was diagnosed with, among other things, borderline personality disorder. In fact, when I left the hospital for what I somehow knew would be the very last time, at twenty-four years of age, I asked for a copy of my chart, which is every patient's right. The initial intake evaluation looked quite similar to Linda's, and the write-ups were full of all kinds of hopeless projections. "This young woman displays a long history marked by instability in her interpersonal and intrapsychic functioning," my record read. "She clearly has had a long career as a mental patient and we will likely encounter her as an admission again in the future."

I recall these words now, as we enter the conference room, where several other nurses and doctors sit around a table with a one-way mirror on the far wall. I scan their faces quickly, praying I look as unfamiliar to them as they do to me. I don't recognize any of the people in here, and I'm hoping against hope they don't recognize me. Still, even if we've never met, I feel I know them somehow, know them in a deep and private part of me. "Ta-da," I have the angry urge to shout out, bowing to the bearded psychiatrist at the oval's head, standing arms akimbo, twirling so my skirt swells out. "Here I am," I'd like to yell, "yes sireee, encountered again. Guess who you're looking at; guess who this is. The Borderline! And sure enough, folks, I *did* mature out, at least a little. . . ."

But of course I won't say such a thing, wouldn't dare, for I would lose my credibility. But the funny thing is, I'm supposedly in a profession that values honesty and self-revelation. Freud himself claimed you couldn't do good analytic work until you'd "come clean" with yourself in the presence of another, until you'd spoken in the bright daylight your repressed secrets and memories. Freud told us not to be so ashamed, to set loose and let waltz our mothers and fathers, our wetness and skins. Training programs for psychologists like me, and the clinics we later work in, have as a credo the admission and discussion of countertransference, which by necessity claims elements of private conflict.

At the same time, though, another more subtle yet powerful message gets transmitted to practitioners in the field. This message says, *Admit your pain, but only to a point. Admit it but keep it clean. Go into therapy, but don't call yourself one of us if you're anything more than nicely neurotic.* The field transmits this message by perpetuating so strongly an *us* versus *them* mind-set, by consistently placing a rift between practitioners and patients, a rift it intends to keep deep. This rift is reflected in the language only practitioners are privy to, in words like *glossolalia* and *echolalia* instead of just saying *the music of madness,* and then again in phrases like *homicidal ideation* and *oriented to all three spheres* instead of *he's so mad he wants to kill her* or *he's thinking clearly today, knows who, what, and where he is.* Along these same lines, practitioners are allowed to admit their *countertransference* but not the *pain pain pain the patient brings me back to, memories of when I was five, your arms my arms and the wound is one.* No. To speak in such a way would make the rift disappear, and practitioners might sink into something overwhelming. We—I—hang on to the jargon that at once describes suffering and hoists us above it. Suddenly, however, here I am, back in an old home; lowered.

I recognize the conference room as the place where, when I was fourteen, I met with my mother and the social worker for the last time. My father had gone away to live in Egypt. My mother was wearing a kerchief around her head and a heavy bronze Star of David wedged between the hills of her breasts. Years later, seeing the mountains of Jerusalem, cupping the scathing sand of the desert, hearing the primitive wails of the Hasidim who mourned the Temple's destruction, I would think of my mother's burning body, a pain I could never comprehend.

This is the conference room where she, unstable, prone to manic highs and depressive lows, shot through with a perpetual anxiety that made her hands shake, this is the same conference room where she told me she was giving me over to the care of the state, giving me up to become a foster child. "I can't handle you anymore," she'd said to me, spit at me. "I no longer want you with me."

I bow my head in deference to something I cannot name, and enter the room. Things are screaming inside me and my eyes feel hot. Nancy introduces me all around and I take a seat, pull out a notebook, try to act as calm and composed as possible. "The patient Ms. Whitcomb," the bearded psychiatrist begins, "is not able to make good use of the hospital. She's an extreme borderline, wreaking havoc on the unit. We suspect her of some factitious posturing as well." He pauses, looks at me, clears his throat. I smile back at him but my mouth feels uncoordinated, tightness at its corners. I won't cry, won't cry, even though in the one-way mirror, in the crisscrossing of the creamy branches beyond the ward's windows, I see my mother again, her face coming to me clearly, her eyes haunted with loneliness and rage. I feel her fingers at my breasts and flinch.

"We think," a social worker named Miss Norton continues, "that we'll be discharging her in a matter of days, as soon as we get her stabilized on some meds. We take it you'll be picking up her case on an outpatient basis. Any ideas of how you'll work with her?"

I nod, pretend to make some notes on the pad. As my voice rises through my throat, I'm surprised at how smooth it sounds, a sleek bolt of silk. "Lots of limits," I say. "We know borderlines do well with lots of limits. This is the only context in which a workable transference can begin."

The bearded doctor nods. In the tree, my mother tongues her teeth and wind lifts her lovely skirt, embroidered with fragile flowers. And then she is not my mother anymore, but a little girl whose legs are white, a single ruby scar on scrubbed knee. And while part of me sits in the conference room, part of me flies out to meet this girl, to touch the sore spot, fondling it with my fingers.

For I have learned how to soothe the hot spots, how to salve the soreness on my skin. I can do it so no one notices, can do it while I teach a class if I need to, or lead a seminar on psychodiagnosis. I can do it while I talk to you in the evenest of tones. "Shhhh," I whisper to the hurting part, hidden here. You can call her borderline—call me borderline—or multiple, or heaped with post-traumatic stress—but strip away the language and you find something simple. You find me, part healthy as a horse and part still suffering, as are we all. What sets me apart from Kayla or Linda or my other patients like George, Marie, Pepsi—what sets me apart from these "sick" ones is simply a learned ability to manage the blades of deep pain with a little bit of dexterity.

Mental health doesn't mean making the pains go away. I don't believe they ever go away. I do believe that nearly every person sitting at this oval table now has the same warped impulses, the same scarlet id, as the wobbliest of borderlines, the most florid of psychotics. Only the muscles to hold things in check—to channel and funnel—are stronger. I have not healed so much as learned to sit still and wait while pain does its dancing work, trying not to panic or twist in ways that make the blades tear deeper, finally infecting the wounds.

Still, I wonder. Why—how—have I managed to learn these things while others have not? Why have I managed somehow to leave behind at least for now what looks like wreckage, and shape something solid from my life? My prognosis, after all, was very poor. In idle moments, I still slide my fingers under the sleeves of my shirt and trace the raised white nubs of scars that track my arms from years and years of cutting. How did I learn to stop cutting and collapsing, and can I somehow transmit this ability to others? I don't know. It's a core question for me in my work. I believe my strength has something to do with memory, with that concept of fluid time. For while I recall with clarity the terror of abuse, I also recall the green and lovely dream of childhood, the moist membrane of a leaf against my nose, the toads that peed a golden pool in the palm of my hand. Pleasures, pleasures, the recollections of which have injected me with a firm and unshakable faith. I believe Dostoevsky when he wrote, "If man has one good memory to go by, that may be enough to save him." I have gone by memory.

And other things too. Anthony Julio wrote in his landmark study, *The Invulnerable Child*, that some children manage to avoid or grow out of traumatic pasts when there is the presence in their lives of at least one stable adult—an aunt, a neighbor, a teacher. I had the extreme good fortune to be placed in a foster home where I stayed for four years, until I turned eighteen, where I was lovingly cared about and believed in. Even when my behavior was so bad I cut myself in their kitchen with the steak knife, or when, out of rage, I swallowed all the Excedrin in their medicine cabinet and had to go back to the unit, my foster parents continued to believe in my abilities to grow, and showed this belief by accepting me after each hospital discharge as their foster child still. That steady acceptance must have had an impact, teaching me slowly over the years how to see something salvageable in myself. Bless those people, for they are a part of my faith's firmness. Bless the stories my foster mother read to me, the stories of mine she later listened to, her thin blond hair hanging down in a single sheet. The house, old and shingled, with niches and culverts I loved to crawl in, where the rain pinged on a leaky roof and out in the puddled yard a beautiful German shepherd, who licked my face and offered me his paw, barked and played in the water. Bless the night there, the hallway light they left on for me, burning a soft yellow wedge that I turned into a wing, a woman, an entire army of angels who, I learned to imagine, knew just how to sing me to sleep.

At a break in the conference, a nurse offers me a cup of coffee. "Sure," I say, "but first the ladies' room." And then I'm off, striding down the hallway I know so well, its twists and turns etched in subterranean memory. I go left, then right, swing open the old wooden ladies' room door, and sit in a stall.

When I come back, the nurse is ready with a steaming Styrofoam cup. She looks at me, puzzled, as she hands me my hot coffee. "You've been here before?" she asks.

My face must show some surprise, for she adds, "I mean, the bathrooms. You know where they are."

"Oh," I say quickly. "Right. I've visited some of my patients on this ward before, yes."

"You don't have to use the patient bathroom," she says, smiling oddly, looking at me with what I think may be suspicion. "We don't recommend it," she adds. "Please use the staff bathroom, through the nurses' station."

"Okay," I say. I bend my face into the coffee's steam, hoping she'll think the redness is from the rising heat. Of course. How stupid of me. What's she thinking? Can she guess? But in a way I *am* one of the patients, and she could be too. I'm not ready to say it yet, though, weak one. Wise one. This time, memory has led me astray.

The conference resumes. I pay little attention. I'm thinking about the faux pas with the bathroom, and then I'm watching the wind in the tree outside the window. I am thinking about how we all share a similar if not single pain, and the rifts between stalls and selves is its own form of delusion. And then I hear, through a thin ceiling, wails twining down, a sharp scream, the clattering of footsteps. I sit up straight.

"Delivery rooms," the social worker says, pointing up. "We're one floor under the maternity ward."

I smile and recall. That's right. Wyman Two is just one floor of what is an old large public hospital. The psychiatric unit we're on has always been wedged between labor rooms upstairs and a nursery downstairs. When I was a patient I could often hear, during group therapy or as I drifted into a drugged sleep, the cries of pushing women as their muscles contracted and in great pain their pink skins ripped, a head coming to crown.

"Why don't you meet with Linda now?" the psychiatrist says, checking his watch and gathering his papers. Everyone stands, signaling the end of the conference. "You can take one of the interview rooms," Nancy, the charge nurse adds. "They're nice places for doing therapy, comfortable."

I nod. I've almost forgotten about Linda and how she is the reason for my return here today. Now I walk with the rest out of the conference room and Nancy points down the long hall. "There," she says, her finger aiming toward a door on the left. "The third room. We'll bring Linda to you." And then, to my surprise, Nancy fishes deep into her pocket and pulls out a large steel ring of keys, placing them in my hand. They're the same keys, I know, from all those years ago, keys I was not allowed to touch but which I watched avidly whenever I could, the cold green gleam and mysterious squared prongs opening doors to worlds I didn't know how to get to. Keys, keys, they are what every mental patient must dream of, the heart-shaped holes keys fit into, the smart click as they twist the secret tumblers and unlatch boxes, velvet-lined and studded with sea jewels. Keys are symbols of freedom and power and finally separateness. For in a mental hospital, only one side has the keys; the others go to meals with plastic forks in their fists.

Slowly, I make my way down the hall to the interview room, stand outside the locked door holding the key ring. It feels cool, and I press it to my cheek. A hand there once, feeling me for a fever, stroking away my fear. Bless those who have helped.

A woman who looks far older than her thirty-seven years is now making her way down the hall. Stooped she is, with tired red ringlets of hair. As she gets closer I see the dark ditches under her eyes where years of fatigue and fear have gathered. I would like to put my finger there, sweep away the microscopic detritus of suffering.

"Linda," I say, and as she comes close to me, I extend my

hand. "Hello," I say, and I can hear a gentleness in my voice, a warm wind in me, for I am not only greeting her, but myself.

We stand in front of the locked interview room and I fumble for the correct key. I start to insert it in the lock, but then, halfway done, I stop. "You," I say to my new patient, Linda. "You take the key. You turn the lock."

She arches one eyebrow, stares up at me. Her face seems to say, *Who are you, anyway?* I want to cry. The hours here have been too long and hard. "You," I say again, and then I feel my eyes actually begin to tear. She steps forward, peers closely, her expression confused. Surely she's never seen one of her doctors cry. "It's okay," I say. "I know what I'm doing." And for a reason I cannot quite articulate at the moment, I make no effort to hide the wetness. I look straight at her. At the same time, for the first time today, my voice feels genuinely confident. "Take the keys, Linda," I say, "and open the door."

She reaches out a bony hand, takes the keys from me, and swings open the door. The interview room is shining with sun, one wall all windows. I've been in this room, too, probably hundreds of times over the years, meeting with the psychiatrists who tried to treat me. I shiver with the memory. Ultimately it was not their treatments or their theories that helped me get better, but the kindness lodged in a difficult world. And from the floor above comes the cry of a protesting baby, a woman ripped raw in birth. She is us. We are her. As my mother used to say, rocking over the Shabbat candles, chanting Jewish prayers late, late into the night, "Hear, O Israel. The Lord is God, The Lord is one, and so are we as a people."

She would pause then, her hands held cupped over the candlesticks. "We are one," she would repeat to me after a few moments, her strained face peering at me through shadows. "As a people we are always one."

Sometimes I miss her.

My patient and I sit down, look at each other. I see myself in her. I trust she sees herself in me.

This is where we begin.

On *"Three Spheres"* by Lauren Slater

" 'Three Spheres' was one of those pieces that was pushing at me and pushing at me, and when I finally allowed its exit from the interior of my head to the white light of the page, it was pretty much fully formed. That's always a treat, a rare occurrence," writes Lauren Slater.

First published in *Creative Nonfiction* 3, Emerging Women Writers, "Three Spheres" became the final essay in *Welcome to My Country*, Slater's first collection of essays. It is the most self-revealing of those essays: the others tell the story of Slater's practice as a psychologist in Boston, but in "Three Spheres" Slater directly addresses her own recovery from a debilitating psychological illness and the impact her recovery has had on her practice of psychology.

Slater thinks "Three Spheres" emerged in such a polished form because of the urgency of questions she had been asking herself for quite some time about her recovery. Writing "Three Spheres" helped her formulate answers and taught her that there's more where "Three Spheres" came from. "I have learned, from the writing of this piece, that there are questions about myself yet to be answered, scenes yet to be rendered," she said.

When she began writing "Three Spheres," Slater was not conscious that she had so many questions; she just wanted to write a story about her illness and recovery.

"In the original conception of the essay, I wanted to capture the complexity of my own 'mental illness,' its niches and caverns, the twists of its corridors," she said. She discovered while confronting "the white light of the page" that she wanted to be more specific about some aspects of her own story, more general about others.

"The essay is a bit more general when it comes to the detailing of my own personal history—my relationship with my mother, the trajectory that led me into foster homes—than I originally intended. However, the subjects of my own illness and the routes I have traveled toward health are broad and in many ways still mysterious to me, a subject sheathed still in some fog. I'm not sure a twenty-page piece could accommodate so large a topic as this one might be were I to fully unravel it."—Lee Gutkind

Looking at Emmett Till

JOHN EDGAR WIDEMAN

for Qasima

A *nightmare of* being chased has plagued my sleep since I was a boy. The monster pursuing me assumes many shapes, but its face is too terrifying for the dream to reveal. Even now I sometimes startle myself awake, screaming, the dream's power undiminished by time, the changing circumstances of my waking life.

I've come to believe the face in the dream I can't bear to look upon is Emmett Till's. Emmett Till's face, crushed, chewed, mutilated, his gray face swollen, water dripping from holes punched in his skull.

Warm gray water on that August day in 1955 when they dragged his corpse from the Tallahatchie River. Emmett Till and I both fourteen the summer they murdered him. The nightmare

JOHN EDGAR WIDEMAN is a professor of English at the University of Massachusetts at Amherst and the author of numerous books. His articles on Malcolm X, Spike Lee, Denzel Washington, Michael Jordan, Emmett Till, Thelonius Monk, and women's professional basketball have appeared in *The New Yorker*, *Vogue*, *Esquire*, *Emerge*, and the *New York Times Magazine*.

an old acquaintance by then, as old as anything I can remember about myself.

Yet the fact that the nightmare predates by many years the afternoon in Pittsburgh I came across Emmett Till's photograph in *Jet* magazine seems to matter not at all. The chilling dream resides in a space years can't measure, the boundless sea of Great Time, nonlinear, ever abiding, enfolding past, present, and future.

I certainly hadn't been searching for Emmett Till's picture in *Jet*. It found me. A blurred, grayish something resembling an aerial snapshot of a landscape cratered by bombs or ravaged by natural disaster. As soon as I realized the thing in the photo was a dead black boy's face, I jerked my eyes away. But not quickly enough.

I attempted to read *Jet's* story about the murder without getting snagged again by the picture. Refusing to look, lacking the power to look at Emmett Till's face, shames me to this day. Dangerous and cowardly not to look. Turning away from his eyeless stare, I blinded myself. Denied myself denying him. He'd been fourteen, like me. How could I be alive and Emmett Till dead? Who had killed him? Why? Would I recognize him if I dared look? Could my own features be horribly altered like his? I needed answers, needed to confront what frightened me in the murdered black boy's face. But Emmett Till just too dead, too gruesomely, absolutely dead to behold.

Years afterward during college I'd recall how it felt to discover Emmett Till's picture when one of my summer jobs involved delivering towels and sheets to the city morgue, and the booze-breathed old coroner who got his kicks freaking out rookies lifted a kettle's lid to prove, yes, indeed, there was a human skull inside from which he was attempting to boil the last shreds of meat.

Now when I freeze-frame a close-up shot of Emmett Till's shattered face on my VCR, am I looking? The image on the screen still denies its flesh-and-blood origins. It's a smashed, road-killed thing, not a boy's face. I'm reminded of the so-called "nail fetishes," West African wood sculptures, part mask, part freestanding head, that began appearing when slaving ships criss-crossed the Atlantic. Gouged, scarred, studded with nails, glass, cartridge shells, stones, drools of raffia, hunks of fur and bone, these horrific creatures police the boundary between human and spirit worlds. Designed to terrify and humble, they embody evil's power to transcend mere human conceptions of its force, reveal the chaos always lurking within the ordinary, remind us the gods amuse themselves by snatching away our certainties.

Whether you resided in an African-American community like Homewood, where I spent half my early years, or in white areas like Shadyside, with a few houses on a couple of streets for black people—my turf when we didn't live in my grandparents' house in Homewood—everybody colored knew what was in *Jet* magazine. *Jet*'s articles as much a part of our barbershop, pool-room, ball field, corner, before- and after-church talk as the *Courier,* Pittsburgh's once-a-week newspaper, aka the *Black Dispatch.* Everybody aware of *Jet* and the *Courier* even though not everybody approved or identified to the same degree with these publications, whose existence was rooted in an unblinking acknowledgment of the reality of racial segregation, a reality their contents celebrated as much as protested.

Jet would arrive at our house on Copeland Street, Shadyside, in batches, irregularly, when Aunt Catherine, who lived down the block and never missed an issue, finished with them and got around to dropping some off. Aunt Catherine was my father's sister, and they were Harry Wideman's kids and inherited his deep brown, South Carolina skin, while my mother's side of the family was light, bright, and almost white, like my other grandfather, Daddyjohn French, from Culpepper, Virginia.

Skin color in my family, besides being tattletale proof segregation didn't always work, was a pretty good predictor of a person's attitude toward *Jet* magazine. My mother wouldn't or couldn't buy *Jet*. I've never asked her which. In pale Shadyside, *Jet* wasn't on sale. You'd have to go a good distance to find it, and with neither car nor driver's license and five kids to care for 24/7, my mother seldom ranged very far from home. Tight as money was then, I'm sure a luxury like subscribing to *Jet* never entered her mind. If by some miracle spare change became available and Brackman's Pharmacy on Walnut Street had begun stocking *Jet*, my mother would have been too self-conscious to purchase a magazine about colored people from old, icy, freckle-fingered Brackman.

Although apartheid stipulates black and white as absolutely separate categories, people construct day by day through the choices they make and allow to be made for them what constitutes blackness and whiteness, what race means, and Mr. Brackman presided over one of the whitest businesses on Walnut Street. Clearly he didn't want folks like us in his drugstore. His chilliness, disdain, and begrudging service a nasty medicine you had to swallow while he doled out your prescriptions. White kids permitted to sit on the floor in a corner and browse through the comic-book bin, but he hurried me along if he thought I attempted to read before I bought. (I knew he believed I'd steal his comics if he turned his back, so in spite of his eagle eye, I did, with sweet, sweet satisfaction every chance I got, throwing them in a garbage can before I got home to avoid that other eagle eye, my mom's.)

Though copies reached us by a circuitous and untimely route, my mother counted on *Jet*. Read it and giggled over its silliness, fussed at its shamelessness, envied and scoffed at the airs of the "sididdy folks" who paraded through it weekly. In my grandparents' house in Homewood, when my mom got down with her sisters, Geraldine and Martha, I'd eavesdrop while they riffed on *Jet*'s contents, fascinated by how they mixed Homewood people and gossip into *Jet*'s features, improvising new stories, raps, and sermons I'd never imagined when I'd read it alone.

By the time an issue of *Jet* reached me, after it had passed through the hands of Aunt Catherine, Uncle Horton, my mother, my father when he was around, the pages were curled, ink-smeared, soft and comfortable as Daddyjohn French's tobacco-ripe flannel shirts. I could fan the pages, and the widest gaps opened automatically at the best stories.

With its spatters, spots, rings from the bottom of a coffee cup, smudges of chocolate candy or lipstick, pages with turned-down corners, pages ripped out, torn covers, *Jet* was an image of the black world as I understood it then: secondhand, beat-up, second-rate. Briar patch and rebuke.

But also often truer and better than the other world around me. Much better. *Jet*, with its incriminating, renegade, embarrassing, topsy-turvy, loud, proud focus on colored doings and faces expanded my sense of possibility. Compared to other magazines of the fifties—*Life, Look, House & Garden, Redbook*—*Jet* was like WAMO, the radio station that blasted rhythm and blues and gospel, an escape from the droning mediocrity of *Your Hit Parade*, a plunge into versions of my life unavailable elsewhere on the dial, grabbing me, shaking me up, reminding me life could move to a dance beat.

In 1955, the year Emmett Till was murdered, I, like him, had just graduated from junior high. I'm trying to remember if I, like him, carried pictures of white girls in my wallet. Can't recall whether I owned a wallet in 1955. Certainly it wouldn't have been a necessity since the little bits of cash I managed to get hold of passed rapidly through my hands. "Money burns a hole in your pocket, boy," my mom said. Wanting to feel grown up, manly, I probably stuffed some sort of hand-me-down billfold in my hip pocket, and carrying around a white girl's picture in it would have been ocular proof of sexual prowess, proof the color of my skin didn't scare white chicks away or scare me away from them. A sign of power. Proof I could handle that other world, master its opportunities and dangers. Since actual romances across the color line tended to be rare and clandestine then, a photo served as evidence of things unseen. A ticket to status in my tiny clan of Shadyside brown boys, a trophy copped in another country I could flaunt in black Homewood. So I may have owned a wallet with pictures of white girlfriends/classmates in it, and if I'd trav-eled to Promised Land, South Carolina, with my grandfather Harry Wideman one of those summers he offered to take me down home where he'd been born and raised, who knows? Since I was a bit of a smart-aleck like Emmett Till, I might have flashed my snapshots. I liked to brag. Take on dares like him. *Okay. Okay, Emmett Till. You so bad. You talking 'bout all those white gals you got up in Chicago. Bet you won't say boo to that white lady in the store.*

Two years before Emmett Till was beaten and murdered, when both Emmett Till and I were twelve, a stroke killed my mother's father, John French. I lapsed into a kind of semicoma, feverish, silent, sleeping away whole days, a little death to cope with losing my grandfather, my family believed. Grieving for Daddy-john was only part of the reason I retreated into myself. Yes, I missed him. Everybody was right about that, but I couldn't confide to anyone that the instant he died, there was no room for him in my heart. Once death closed his eyes, I wanted him gone, utterly, absolutely gone. I erected a shell to keep him out, to protect myself from the touch of his ghostly hands, the smells and sounds of him still lurking in the rooms of the Homewood house where we'd lived for a year with my mother's parents and her sisters after my father left our house on Copeland Street.

Losing my grandfather stunned me. He'd been my best friend. I couldn't understand how he'd changed from Daddyjohn to some invisible, frightening presence I had no name for. He'd stopped moving, speaking, breathing. For two interminable days, his body lay inside a coffin on a spindly-legged metal stand beside the piano in the living room, the dark polished wood of one oblong box echoing the other. Until we had to sell the piano a few years later, I couldn't enter the room or touch the piano unless someone else was with me. Sitting on the spinning stool, banging away for hours on the keys had been one of my favorite solitary pastimes, as unthinkable suddenly as romping with my dead grandfather, chanting the nonsense rimes he'd taught me—"Froggy went a-courting, and he did ride/Uh-huh, uh-huh."

Stunned by how empty, how threatening the spaces of my grandfather's house had become, I fought during the daylight hours to keep him away, hid under the covers of my bed at night. Stunned by guilt. By my betrayal of him, my inability to remember, to honor the love that had bound us. Love suddenly changed to fear of everything about him. Fear that love might license him to trespass from the grave. I'd never understood the dead. Shied away from talk of death, thoughts of the dead. The transformation of my grandfather the instant he became one of the dead confirmed my dread. If I couldn't trust Daddyjohn, what horrors would the rest of the dead inflict upon me? Given the nightmare's witness, am I still running, still afraid?

Emmett Till's murder was an attempt to slay an entire generation. Push us backward to the bad old days when our lives seemed not to belong to us. When white power and racism seemed unchallengeable forces of nature, when inferiority and subserviency appeared to be our birthright, when black lives seemed cheap and expendable, when the grossest insults to pride and person, up to and including murder, had to be endured. No redress, no retaliation, no justice expected. Emmett Till's dead body, like the body of James Byrd just yesterday in Texas, reminded us that the bad old days are never farther away than the thickness of skin, skin some people still claim the prerogative to burn or cut or shoot full of holes if it's dark skin. It's no accident that Emmett Till's dead face appears inhuman. The point of inflicting the agony of his last moments, killing and mutilating him, is to prove he's not human.

And it almost works. Comes close to working every time. Demonized by hot-blooded or cold-blooded statistics of crime, addiction, disease, cartooned, minstrelized, criminalized, eroticized, commodified in stereotypical representations, the black body kidnapped and displayed by the media loses all vestiges of humanity. We are set back on our collective heels by the overwhelming evidence, the constant warning that beneath black skin something *other*, something brutal lurks. A so-called "lost generation" of young black men dying in the streets today points backward, the way Emmett Till's rotting corpse points backward, history and prophecy at once: This is the way things have always been, will always be, the way they're supposed to be.

The circle of racism, its perverse logic remain unbroken. Boys like Emmett Till are born violating the rules, aren't they? Therefore they forfeit any rights law-abiding citizens are bound to respect. The bad places—ghettos, prisons, morgue slabs— where most of them wind up confirm the badness of the boys. Besides, does it hurt any less if the mugger's a product of nurture, not nature? Keeping him off your streets, confining him in a world apart, is what matters, isn't it?

But what if the disproportionate numbers of African-American males in prison or caught in the net of economic marginality are not a consequence of inborn black deviancy? What if incarceration and poverty are latter-day final solutions of the problem of slavery? What if the dismal lives of so many young black people indicate an intentional, systematic closing off of access to the mainstream, justified by a mythology of race that the closing off simultaneously engenders and preserves?

Nearly five hundred years ago, European ships began transporting captive Africans to the New World. Economic exploitation of the recently "discovered" Americas provided impetus for this slave trade. Buying and selling African bodies, treating them as property, commodities, livestock, produced enormous profit and imprinted a model for ignoring the moral and ethical implications of financially successful global commerce we continue to apply today. The traffic in human bodies was also fueled by a dream, a utopian dream of escape from the poverty, disease, class, and religious warfare of Europe, a dream of transforming through European enterprise and African slave labor the wilderness across the sea into a garden of wealth and prosperity, with the European colonist cast as the New Adam exercising divinely sanctioned dominion over all he surveyed.

Racism and genocide were the underside of this Edenic dream, persist today in the determined unwillingness of the heirs of the dream to surrender advantages gained when owning slaves was legal.

During its heyday slavery's enormous profit and enormous evil sparked continuous debate. Could a true Christian own slaves? Do Africans possess souls? Because it licensed and naturalized the subjugation of "inferior" Africans by "superior" Europeans, the invention of the concept of "race"—dividing humankind into a hierarchy of groups, each possessing distinct, unchangeable traits that define the groups as eternally separate and unequal—was crucial to the slaveholder's temporary victory in these debates. Over time, as slavery gradually was abolished, a systematic network of attitudes and practices based on the concept of race evolved across all fields and activities of New World societies with a uniquely pervasive, saturating force. The primary purpose of this racialized thinking was, under the guise of different vocabularies, to rationalize and maintain in public and private spheres the power European slave owners once held over their African slaves.

Emmett Till was murdered because he violated taboos governing race relations in 1955 in Money, a rural Mississippi town, but his killers were also exercising and revalidating prerogatives in place since their ancestors imported Emmett Till's ancestors to these shores. At some level everybody in Money understood this. Our horror, our refusal to look too closely at Emmett Till reside in the same deep, incriminating knowledge.

Perhaps an apartheid mentality reigns in this country because most Americans consciously hold racist attitudes or wish ill on their neighbors of African descent. I don't think so. Emmett Till dies again and again because his murder, the conditions that ensure and perpetuate it, have not been honestly examined. Denial is more acceptable to the majority of Americans than placing themselves, their inherited dominance, at risk.

Any serious attempt to achieve economic, social, and political equal opportunity in this nation must begin not simply with opening doors to selected minorities. That impulse, that trope, that ideology has failed. The majority must decide to relinquish significant measures of power and privilege if lasting transformations of self and society are to occur. There have always been open doors of sorts for minorities (emancipation, emigration, education, economic success in sports or business, passing as white). What's missing is an unambiguous, abiding determination declared in public and private by a majority of the majority to surrender privileges that are the living legacy of slavery. Begin now. Today. Give up walls, doors, keys, the dungeons, the booty, the immunity, the false identity apartheid preserves.

A first step is acknowledging that the dangerous lies of slavery continue to be told as long as we conceive of ourselves in terms of race, as black or white.

Emmett Till and the young victims of drug and territory wars raging in African-American neighborhoods today are signs of a deeply flawed society failing its children. Why do we perceive the bodies of dead *black* boys, imprisoned *black* men, homeless *black* people, addicted *black* people as *black* problems? Why do we support cynical politicians who cite these *black* problems as evidence for more brutal policing of the racial divide?

In 1955, one year after the Supreme Court's *Brown v. Board of Education* school-desegregation decision, a great struggle for civil rights commenced. The lynching of Emmett Till should have clarified exactly what was at stake: life or death. As long as racialized thinking continues to legitimize one group's life-and-death power over another, the battered face of Emmett Till will poison the middle ground of compromise between so-called "whites" and so-called "blacks." His face unmourned, unburied, unloved, haunting the netherworld where incompatible versions of democracy clash.

It was hard to bury Emmett Till, hard, hard to bury Carole Robertson, Addie Mae Collins, Denise McNair, and Cynthia Wesley, the four girls killed by a bomb in a Birmingham, Alabama, church. So hard an entire nation began to register the convulsions of black mourning. The deaths of our children in the civil rights campaigns changed us. The oratory of great men like Martin Luther King Jr. pushed us to realize our grief should be collective, should stir us to unify, to clarify our thinking, roll back the rock of fear. Emmett Till's mangled face could belong to anybody's son who transgressed racial laws; anyone's little girl could be crushed in the rubble of a bombed church. We read the terrorist threat inscribed upon Emmett Till's flesh and were shaken but refused to comply with the terrorists' demands.

Martin Luther King Jr. understood the killing of our children was an effort to murder the nation's future. We mourned the young martyrs, and a dedicated few risked life and limb fighting with ferocity and dignity in the courts, churches, and streets to stop the killing. Young people served as shock troops in the movement for social justice, battling on the front lines, the hottest, most dangerous spots in Alabama and Mississippi. And though they had most to gain or lose (their precious lives, their time on this earth), they also carried on their shoulders the hopes of older generations and generations unborn.

Now there seems to be in our rituals of mourning for our dying children no sense of communal, general loss, no larger, empowering vision. We don't connect our immediate trials— drugs, gang violence, empty schools, empty minds, empty homes, empty values—to the ongoing historical struggle to liberate our- selves from the oppressive legacies of slavery and apartheid.

Funerals for our young are lonely occurrences. Daily it seems, in some ghetto or another somewhere in America, a small black congregation will gather together to try to repair the hole in a brother's or mother's soul with the balm of gospel singing, prayer, the laying on of dark hands on darkened spirits.

How many a week, how many repetitions of the same, sad, isolated ceremony, the hush afterward when the true dimensions of loss and futility begin to set in? A sense of futility, of powerlessness dogs the survivors, who are burdened not only by the sudden death of a loved one but also by the knowledge that it's going to happen again today or tomorrow and that it's supposed to happen in a world where black lives are expendable, can disappear, *click*, in a fingerpop, quick like that, without a trace, as if the son or sister was hardly here at all. Hey, maybe black people really ain't worth shit, just like you've been hearing your whole life.

Curtis Jones, a cousin who accompanied Emmett Till on the trip from Chicago, Illinois, to Money, Mississippi, in August 1955, relates how close Emmett Till came to missing their train, reminding us how close Emmett Till's story came to not happening or being another story altogether, and that in turn should remind us how any story, sad or happy, is always precariously close to being other than it is. Doesn't take much to alter a familiar scene into chaos. Difficult as it is to remember what does occur, we must also try to keep alive what doesn't—the missed trains, squandered opportunities, warnings not heeded. We carry forward these fictions because what might have been is part of what gives shape to our stories. We depend on memory's capacity to hold many lives, not just the one we appear to be leading at the moment. Memory is space for storing lives we didn't lead, room where they remain alive, room for mourning them, forgiving them. Memory, like all stories we tell, a tissue of remembering, forgetting, of *what if* and *once upon a time*, burying our dead so the dead may rise.

Curtis Jones goes on to tell us about everybody piling into Grandpa Wright's automobile and trundling down the dusty road to church. How he and his cousin Emmett Till took the car into Money that afternoon while Moses Wright preached.

A bunch of boys loafing outside Bryant's General Store on Money's main drag. Sho 'nuff country town. Wooden storefronts with wooden porches. Wooden sidewalks. Overhanging wooden signs. With its smatter of brown boys out front, its frieze of tire-sized Coca-Cola signs running around the eaves of its porch, Bryant's the only game in town, Emmett Till guessed.

Climbing out of Moses Wright's old Dodge, he sports the broad smile I recall from another photo, the one of him leaning, elbow atop a TV set, clean as a string bean in his white dress shirt and tie, his chest thrust out mannishly, baby fat in his cheeks, a softish, still-forming boy whose energy, intelligence, and expectations of life are evident in the pose he's striking for the camera, just enough in-your-face swagger that you can't help smiling back at the wary eagerness to please of his smile.

To Emmett Till the boys in Money's streets are a cluster of down-home country cousins. He sees a stage beckoning on which he can perform. Steps up on the sidewalk with his cousin Curtis, to whom he is *Bo* or *Bobo*, greets his audience. Like a magician pulling a rabbit from his hat, Emmett Till pulls a white girl from his wallet. Silences everybody. Mesmerizes them with tales of what they're missing, living down here in the Mississippi woods. If he'd been selling magic beans, all of them would have dug into their overalls and extracted their last hot penny to buy some. They watch his fingers slip into his shirt pocket. Hold their breath waiting for the next trick.

Emmett Till's on a roll, can't help rubbing it in a little. What he's saying about himself sounds real good, so good he wants to hear more. All he wants really is for these brown faces to love him. As much as he's loved by the dark faces and light faces in the junior high graduation pictures from Chicago he's showing around.

He winks at the half dozen or so boys gathered round him. Nods. Smiles like the cat swallowed the canary. Points to the prettiest girl, the fairest, longest-haired one of all you can easily see, even though the faces in the class picture are tiny and gray. Emmett Till says she is the prettiest, anyway, so why not? Why not believe he's courted and won her, and ain't you-all lucky he come down here bringing you-all the good news?

Though Emmett Till remains the center of attention, the other kids giggle, scratch their naps, stroke their chins, turn their heads this way and that around the circle, commence little con-versations of eye-cutting and teeth-sucking and slack-jawed awe. Somebody pops a finger against somebody's shaved skull. Some-body's hip bumps somebody else. A tall boy whistles a blues line, and you notice someone's been humming softly the whole time. Emmett Till's the preacher, and it's Sunday morning, and the ser-mon is righteous. On the other hand, everybody's ready for a hymn or a responsive reading, even a collection plate circulating, so they can participate, stretch their bones, hear their own voices.

You sure is something, boy. You say you bad, Emmett Till. Got all them white gals up North, you say. Bet you won't say boo to the white lady in the store.

Curtis Jones is playing checkers with old Uncle Edmund on a barrel set in the shade around the corner from the main drag. One of the boys who sauntered into the store with Emmett Till to buy candy comes running. *He did it. Emmett Till did it. That cousin of yours crazy, boy. Said, "Bye-bye, baby," to Miss Bryant.*

The old man gets up so fast he knocks over the crate he's been sitting on. *Lor' have mercy. I know the boy didn't do nothing like that. Huhuh. No. No, he didn't. You-all better get out here. That lady come out that store blow you-all's brains off.*

Several months later, after an all-white jury in the town of Sumner, Mississippi, had deliberated an hour—*Would have been less if we hadn't took time for lunch*—and found Roy Bryant and J. W. Milam not guilty of murdering Emmett Till, the two men were paid four thousand dollars by a journalist, William Bradford Huie, to tell the story of abducting, beating, and shooting Emmett Till.

To get rid of his body, they barb-wired a fifty-pound cotton-gin fan to Emmett Till's neck and threw him in the Tallahatchie River. The journalist, in a videotaped interview, said, "It seems to a rational mind today—it seems impossible that they could have killed him."

The reporter muses for a moment, then remembers, "But J. W. Milam looked up at me, and he says, 'Well, when he told me about this white girl he had, my friend, well, that's what this war's about down here now, that's what we got to fight to protect, and I just looked at him and say, *Boy, you ain't never gone to see the sun come up again.*'"

To the very end, Emmett Till didn't believe the crackers would kill him. He was fourteen, from Chicago. He'd hurt no one. These strange, funny-talking white men were a nightmare he'd awaken from sooner or later. Milam found the boy's lack of fear shocking. Called it "belligerence." Here was this nigger should be shitting his drawers. Instead he was making J. W. Milam uncomfortable. Brave or foolhardy or ignorant or blessed to be already in another place, a place these sick, sick men could never touch, whatever enabled Emmett Till to stand his ground, to be himself until the first deadly blow landed, be himself even after it landed, I hope Emmett Till understood that Milam or Bryant, whoever struck first with the intent to kill, was the one who flinched, not him.

When such thoughts come to me, I pile them like sandbags along the levees that protect my sleep. I should know better than to waste my time.

In another dream we emerge at dawn from the tree line. Breeze into Money. Rat-tat. Rat-tat-tat.Waste the whole motherfucking ville. Nothing to it. Little hick town 'bout same today as when they lynched poor brother Emmett Till.

Some the bitches come rubbing up against us after we lined 'em up by the ditch. Thinking maybe if they fuck us they won't die. We let 'em try. You know. Wasn't bad pussy, neither. But when the time come, you know, they got to go just like the rest. Rat-tat-tat. Uh-huh.

Money gone. Burnt a hole in its pocket.

I asked a lover, a woman whose whiteness made her a flesh-and-blood embodiment of the nightmare J. W. Milam discovered in Emmett Till's wallet, what she thinks of when she hears "Emmett Till."

"A black kid whistling at a white woman somewhere down South and being killed for it, is what I think," she said.

"He didn't whistle," I reply. I've heard the wolf-whistle story all my life and another that has him not moving aside for a white woman walking down the sidewalk. Both are part of the myth, but neither's probably true. The story Till's cousin Curtis Jones tells is different. And for what it's worth, his cousin was there.

Something Emmett Till said to a white woman inside a store is what started it.

She wants to know where I heard the cousin's version, and I launch into a riff on my sources—*Voices of Freedom*, an oral history of the civil rights movement; Henry Hampton's video documentary, *Eyes on the Prize*; a book, *Representations of Black Masculinity in Contemporary American Art,* organized around a museum exhibit of black male images. Then I realize I'm doing all the talking, when what I'd intended to elicit was her spontaneous witness. What her memory carried forward, what it lost.

She's busy with something of her own, and we just happened to cross paths a moment in the kitchen, and she's gone before I get what I wanted. Gone before I know what I wanted. Except standing there next to the refrigerator, in the silence released by its hum, I feel utterly defeated. All the stuff spread out on my desk isn't getting me any closer to Emmett Till or a cure. Neither will man-in-the-street, woman-in-the-kitchen interviews. Other people's facts and opinions don't matter. Only one other person's voice required for this story I'm constructing to overcome a bad dream, and they shut him up a long time ago, didn't they?

Here is what happened. Four nights after the candy-buying and "Bye-bye, baby" scene in Money, at 2 a.m. on August 21, 1955, Roy Bryant, with a pistol in one hand and a flashlight in the other, appears at Moses Wright's door. "This is Mr. Bryant," he calls into the darkness. Then demands to know if Moses Wright has two niggers from Chicago inside. He says he wants the nigger done all that talk.

When Emmett Till is delivered, Bryant marches him to a car

and asks someone inside, "This the right nigger?" and somebody says, "Yes, he is."

Next time Moses Wright sees Emmett Till is three days later when the sheriff summons him to identify a corpse. The body's naked and too badly damaged to tell who it is until Moses Wright notices the initialed ring on his nephew's finger.

Where were you when JFK was shot? Where were you when a man landed on the moon? When Martin Luther King Jr. was shot? Malcolm shot? When the Rodney King verdict announced? Where were you when Emmett Till floated up to the surface of the Tallahatchie River for *Bye-bye, baby*ing a white woman?

A *white man* in the darkness outside a tarpaper cabin announcing the terror of his name, gripping a flashlight in his fist, a heavy-duty flashlight stuffed with thick D batteries that will become a club for bashing Emmett Till's skull.

An old black man in the shanty crammed with bodies, instantly alert when he hears, "You got those niggers from Chicago in there with you?" An old man figuring the deadly odds, how many lives bought if one handed over. Calculating the rage of his ancient enemy, weighing the risk of saying what he wants the others in his charge to hear, Emmett Till to hear, no matter what terrible things happen next.

"Got my two grandsons and a nephew in here."

A black boy inside the cabin, a boy my age whose name I don't know yet, who will never know mine. He rubs his eyes, not sure he's awake or dreaming a scary dream, one of the tales buried deep, deep he's been hearing since before we were born about the old days in the Deep South when they cut off niggers' nuts and lynched niggers and roasted niggers over fires like marshmallows.

A man in my own warm bed, lying beside a beautiful woman rubbing my shoulder, a pale, blond woman whose presence some-times is as strange and unaccountable to me as mine must be to her, as snow falling softly through the bedroom ceiling would be, accumulating in white drifts on the down comforter.

Why am I telling Emmett Till's story this way, attempting the miracle or cheap trick of being many people, many places at once? Will words change what happened, what's missing, what's lost? Will my nightmare dissolve if I cling to the woman almost asleep now next to me, end if I believe this loving moment together might last and last?

The name Emmett is spoiled for me. In any of its spellings. As big a kick as I get from watching Emmitt Smith rush the football for the Dallas Cowboys, there is also the moment after a bone chattering collision and he's sprawled lifeless on the turf or the moment after he's stumbled or fumbled and slumps to the bench and lifts his helmet and I see a black mother's son, a small, dark, round face, a boy's big, wide, scared eyes. All those yards gained, all that wealth, but like O.J. he'll never run far enough or fast enough. Inches behind him the worst thing the people who hate him can imagine hounds him like a shadow.

Sometimes I think the only way to end this would be with Andy Warhol-like strips of images, the same face, Emmett Till's face, replicated twelve, twenty-four, forty-eight, ninety-six times on a wall-sized canvas. Like giant postage stamps end to end, top to bottom, each version of the face exactly like the other but different names printed below each one. Martin Luther Till. Malcolm Till. Medgar Till. Nat Till. Gabriel Till. Michael Till. Huey Till. Bigger Till. Nelson Till. Mumia Till. Colin Till. Jesse Till. Your daddy, your mama, your sister, brother, aunt, cousin, uncle, niece, nephew Till . . .

Instead of the nightmare one night, this is what I dream.

I'm marching with many, many men, a multitude, a million men of all colors in Washington, D.C., marching past the bier on which the body of Emmett Till rests. The casket, as his mother demanded, is open. *I want the world to see what they did to my baby.* One by one from an endless line, the men detach themselves, pause, peer down into the satin-lined box. Pinned inside its upright lid a snapshot of Emmett Till, young, smiling, whole, a jaunty Stetson cocked high across his brow. In the casket Emmett Till is dressed in a dark suit, jacket wings spread to expose a snowy shroud pulled up to his chin. Then the awful face, patched together with string and wire, awaits each mourner.

My turn is coming soon. I'm grateful. Will not shy away this time. Will look hard this time. The line of my brothers and fathers and sons stretches ahead of me, behind me. I am drawn by them, pushed by them, steadied as we move each other along. We are a horizon girding the earth, holding the sky down. So many of us in one place at one time it scares me. More than a million of us marching through this city of monumental buildings and dark alleys. Not very long ago, we were singing, but now we march silently, more shuffle than brisk step as we approach the bier, wait our turn. Singing's over, but it holds silently in the air, tangible as weather, as the bright sun disintegrating marble buildings, emptying alleys of shadows, warming us on a perfect

October day we had no right to expect but would have been profoundly disappointed had it fallen out otherwise.

What I say when I lean over and speak one last time to Emmett Till is *I love you. I'm sorry. I won't allow it to happen ever again*. And my voice will be small and quiet when I say the words, not nearly as humble as it should be, fearful almost to pledge any good after so much bad. My small voice and short turn, and then the next man and the next, close together, leading, following one another so the murmur of our voices beside the bier never stops. An immensity, a continuous, muted shout and chant and benediction, a river gliding past the stillness of Emmett Till. Past this city, this hour, this place. River sound of blood I'm almost close enough to hear coursing in the veins of the next man.

In the dream we do not say, *Forgive us*. We are taking, not asking for, something today. There is no time left to ask for things, even things as precious as forgiveness, only time to take one step, then the next and the next, alone in this great body of men, each one standing on his own feet, moving, our shadows linked, a coolness, a shield stretching nearly unbroken across the last bed where Emmett Till sleeps.

Where we bow and hope and pray he frees us. Ourselves seen, sinking, then rising as in a mirror, then stepping away.

And then. And then this vision fades, too. I am there and not there. Not in Washington, D.C., marching with a million other men. My son Dan, my new granddaughter Qasima's father, marched. He was a witness, and the arc of his witness includes me as mine, his. So, yes, I was there in a sense but not there to view the face of Emmett Till because Emmett Till was not there, either, not in an open casket displayed to the glory of the heavens, the glories of this republic, not there except as a shadow, a stain, a wound in the million faces of the marchers, the faces of their absent fathers, sons, and brothers.

We have yet to look upon Emmett Till's face. No apocalyptic encounter, no ritual unveiling, no epiphany has freed us. The nightmare is not cured.

I cannot wish away Emmett Till's face. The horrific death mask of his erased features marks a site I ignore at my peril. The site of a grievous wound. A wound unhealed because untended. Beneath our nation's pieties, our self-delusions, our denials and distortions of history, our professed black-and-white certainties about race, lies chaos. The whirlwind that swept Emmett Till away and brings him back.

JOHN EDGAR WIDEMAN ON *"Looking for Emmett Till"*

The thoughts and feelings this essay prompted continue to grow as I add, subtract, and discover new places in my writing where the material the essay excavated and invented fits. Young black boys are still being cut down as relentlessly as Till's murderers cut short his life—nobody's fault, everybody's fault, a deep, deep fault that remains in our national psyche.

The writing, or exploration, or examination, or mourning, was precipitated by turning the pages of *Jet* magazine and being confronted by Emmett Till's face, the face that has haunted me since I was fourteen, and saw myself reflected in the dead—horribly transformed, suddenly mortal, suddenly vulnerable, mutilated by my age, my color.

The writing developed more or less like the action of a basketball game—a spontaneous call-and-response process in which anticipation and reaction are indistinguishable. Improvisation is key—improvisation that's both innocent and steeped in conscious preparation, all the practice, the games played and imagined and observed, the internalization of traditions and patterns, the work of readying the body so it rises to the occasion, forgetting the moment, the possibility (necessity) of failure, risking the flow, living it no matter the outcome.

Writing is writing and I employ every new trick and technology I'm able to muster in whatever kind of writing I'm attempting. The lines between fiction and nonfiction, for me, are more and more arbitrary, blurred, problematic. In many senses, the distinctions are nonexistent. Does a photo document or fabricate an event? Is life composed of facts or a constructed fiction? Both. Always. I think biographers and historians are fiction writers who haven't come out of the closet. It's probably important to share with readers my intentions—is this piece fact or fiction?—but those intentions may include a desire not to share my intentions—fact or fiction. Good work seizes the reader's attention, enforces its unique version of reality. The best work changes the shape, the definitions of the genre, explodes traditional codes that translate/confine reality.

Language performs functions that identify communities and cultures. The collective effort of writing should be to keep the language alive as a medium for imaginative truth-telling, for communication that gives the lie to language as fact. All information includes a point of view, intention, and author. Facts pretend this isn't so. Good writing reminds us everyone's responsible for dreaming a world, and the dream, the point of view embodied by it, within it, is as close to fact, to reality, as we ever get.

Read the classics, go back in time as far as you're able—Egyptians, Greeks, cave painting—and then creep forward, trying always to stay aware of how much you're missing. This sort of foundation should be helpful as you read yourself and read your peers, your contemporaries. Don't forget what's going on in other

countries, other languages—translations are better than total ignorance—and what's happening in the margins, whether it's silence
or scary babble or scorn or insult or madness. Persevere with some
writing that you may not like at first—especially when the writing
is highly recommended by somebody you respect. Study your own
writing always against this background of ongoing reading, this
project of listening and learning, this understanding that the best
anybody can achieve will fail, will open rather than close doors.

Shunned

MEREDITH HALL

. .

Even now I talk too much and too loud, claiming ground, afraid that I will disappear from this life, too, from this time of being mother and teacher and friend. That It—everything I care about, that I believe in, that defines and reassures me—will be wrenched from me again. Family. Church. School. Community. There are not many ways you can get kicked out of those memberships. As a child in Hampton, New Hampshire, I knew husbands who cheated on their wives. Openly. My father. I know men and women who beat their children. We all knew them. We all knew men who were too lazy to bring in a paycheck or clean the leaves out of their yards, women who spent the day on the couch crying while the kids ran loose in the neighborhood. We knew who drank at the Meadowbrook after work each day and

. .

MEREDITH HALL lives in Maine. Her work has appeared in *Creative Nonfiction*. She received the 2004 Pushcart Prize and was also awarded the 2004 Gift of Freedom Award from A Room of Her Own Foundation, allowing her to take an eighteen-month sabbatical from her teaching at the University of New Hampshire to write her book, a collection of essays titled *Without a Map*.

drove home to burn SpaghettiOs on the stove for the children. We even knew a witch. We called her Goody Welsh, as if her magic had kept her alive since the Salem days. But this was 1966. All these people were tolerated. More than tolerated; they were the Community. The teachers and ministers' wives and football players and drugstore owners. They lived next to me on Leavitt Road and Mill Road and High Street. They smiled hello when I rode my bike past their clean or dirty yards, their sunny or shuttered houses.

Then I got pregnant. I was sixteen. Family, church, school— each, which had embraced me as a child—turned its back. Shunning is supposed to keep bad things from happening in a community. But it doesn't correct the life gone wrong. It can only expose the transgression to a very raw light, use it as a measure, a warning to others that says, "See? That didn't happen in our home. Because we are Good. We're better than that." The price I paid seems still to be extreme. But I bet it was a while again before any girl in Hampton let herself be fucked in the gritty sand by a boy from away who said love.

A friend once told me that when he was in seventh grade, he and his best friend, Nathan, fought. Nathan got everyone in school to ignore my friend the next day, incited them to the silent treatment. It only lasted until noon. One by one my friend drew his friends back, outmaneuvering Nathan. But still my friend remembers the impotent shame he felt for those four hours. The injustice. It didn't last because my friend was a boy, a boy who knew how to fight back, a boy who believed that he could interrupt the current and draw his world back into order. It didn't work because he felt powerful, after all, worthy of those friends and their loyalty.

And it didn't work because there was no moral to be exalted, no messy failure to be feasted upon. But pregnant in 1965: if this could happen to Bobbie's daughter, then, like contagion, it could happen to anyone's girl. Unless we scared them so much they would never spread their legs again. Injustice. It had to be unjust. It had to be electrifying to work.

I have often wondered whether the grown-ups I went to church with, who had made sandwiches for me and their children on dreamy summer days, who praised me year after year for my A's and my manners and my nice family, who paid me extra for watching their babies so well—I have wondered if they had to tell their children to shun me, or if the kids slid into it on their own. The motives of the grown-ups seemed quite different from those of my peers. When Diane and Pepper and Debbie and John and Stephen stopped speaking to me, when they started to cross the street in tight, hushed groups, when they left Tobey's Rexall, their cherry Cokes unfinished, because I walked in—had they been told to steer so clear of me? Did they understand that if shunning is to work, it must be absolute? No soft heart to undermine the effect? Or did they find their own reasons to cast me out? "I never liked her, anyway" or "She thinks she's so smart." "Her father left, you know." Maybe I was simply too dangerous. If they did not abruptly turn away, they would be judged, by association, for being as dirty as I was.

This sort of shunning has the desired effect of erasing a life. Making it invisible, incapable of contaminating. I suddenly had no history with these kids. I had started school with them at Mrs. Winkler's kindergarten, in the basement of her husband's dental office. First grade, fifth, eighth, tenth—Mrs. Bean and Mrs. Marcotte and Mr. Cooper—twenty-four kids moving together year after year. We all knew each other's parents and brothers and sisters and whether they went to the Congregational or the

Methodist or the tiny Episcopal church. We knew who practiced piano after supper and who lived with a grandmother and who read secretly in the field behind Pratt's barn.

No one in our class was bad. We believed we were good children, and were. The 1950s still breathed its insistent, costly calm through our childhoods. When we said, "I'm in sixth grade," we meant, I belong with these boys and girls; we are bound in inevitable affection. The grown-ups reinforced for each of us this sense of our lives being woven together, sticky strands of a resilient web. We liked each other as a matter of course; idiosyncrasies and conflicts, like broken rays of the whole, were quickly corrected, the flaw made invisible and forgotten.

I still can tell you that Kenneth had a funny, flat head. That fat Jimmy surprised us in eighth grade by whipping out a harmonica and playing country ballads. That he also surprised us that year by flopping on the floor in an epileptic fit. That Jill, an only child, lived in a house as orderly and dead as a tomb. That I coveted her closetful of clothes. That Patty's father had to drag our muddy, sagging dog back every few weeks from hunting in the marshes; that he apologized politely every time to my mother, as if it were his fault. That in kindergarten Jay wanted to marry me and that I whipped him a year or two later with thorny switches his father had trimmed from the hedge separating our yards. That his father called me Meredy-My-Love, and I called him Uncle Leo. That Heather's grandmother, Mrs. Coombs, taught us music once a week, the fat that hung from her arms swinging wildly just offbeat as she led each song.

I still can tell you that Linda wouldn't eat the crusts. I thought she was spoiled. That Sharon smelled and was supposed to be pitied, not ostracized. That Bonnie wore my old skirts and dresses, found in the Clothes Closet in the church vestry, and I was never to mention anything to her, as though everyone had not seen those same clothes on me all the previous year. That Bev was Mr. Fiedler's pet, that her mother made cookies for the Brownies every Wednesday when we sat like grown women, gossiping while we sewed aprons and washcloth slippers for our mothers and grandmothers at Christmas. That Johnny was a flirt and liked to kiss girls, and he would come to no good, although he came to something better than I did. That Sheila's mother sold us eggs. That Bill was almost as smart as I was, but he was a boy and never got all A's. That I followed the rules and craved praise, that I was cheerful and a pleaser, a leader who was headed somewhere.

These are myths, of course. We children touched ourselves in the dark and stole money from our mothers' purses and listened at night to our parents screaming obscenities. But the myths worked; none of those secrets were visible. There was a silent hierarchy based in part on social class but also on something less tangible—an unswerving sense of who came from a "good" family. They didn't need to have money. But the good family must protect its secrets. No grandparent could be a public drinker or an atheist. If Dad walked out, Mother must become a saint.

Lucky for me I came from just such a family. I was a good girl, the darling of teachers and chosen as a friend by these twenty-four kids I knew as if we were cousins.

I have a very small box containing everything that survives that childhood—a perfect-attendance pin from Sunday school; my Brownie sash; a jet-and-rhinestone pin given to me by a crazy old woman up the street; my toe shoes, the pink satin worn through; one Ginny doll, her hair half gone, and a few clothes my mother and I sewed for her; a silver dollar my first boyfriend gave me for

Christmas my sophomore year; my prayer book, signed in the front by my mother, "To my beloved daughter"; and a class picture, titled "My Class," from tenth grade.

I don't ever look at this photo and should throw it out. I loved My Class. I loved belonging. I loved the promise I thought I heard, that they would become my past, my history. It is as if there was a terrible death and they were all lost to me, abruptly and all at once. But nobody died. The loss was only mine, a private and interior devastation.

Robin and I walked to school together every day until the day I was kicked out. I heard from her suddenly ten years ago— twenty-four years after I walked home alone at eleven-thirty in the morning with the green slip of expulsion in my book bag, my secret let loose and starting its zinging trip mouth to mouth— when her mother, my mother's best friend, Margie, was dying of Alzheimer's. Now when Robin and I get together, she tells me the stories of my own life that I have had to forget. Like an artist painting in the details of a soft charcoal sketch, she fills in the forgotten, the high school years that I cannot afford to carry. She says, "You remember, Meredy. MaryAnn lived on the corner of Mill Road. You used to spend the night at her house a lot." I don't remember. Maybe a certain flip of dark hair or a faint laugh. But I vanished in my own mind, along with all the comfortable, small facts of my life, on that day of expulsion in 1965. Shunned, made invisible, I became invisible to myself. The photo of "My Class" is a record of the history I do not share.

I suppose they all get together every few years for a reunion. They were the class of 1967. I am certain that the space I occupied in the group for sixteen years closed in as fast as the blooms on a shrub when one flower dies or is pinched out. I wonder what they would say if my name came up. I wonder if they ever think of me. I sometimes imagine that I will somehow find out where they will meet for the next reunion. I will arrive looking clean and successful and proud. But what would I say to them? That this thing, this shunning, this shaming is an eraser, a weapon that should never be wielded?

Last year I had a student from Hampton in my writing class at the state university. I knew from her last name that she must be the daughter of Timmy Keaton. I told her that I had known her father all through my childhood. I didn't tell her that we weren't really friends, that I was important in class and he was one of those peripheral members no one ever really noticed. She came back the next Monday for a conference. To make conversation— or maybe, thirty years later, to reclaim some of my purged identity—I asked if she had mentioned my name to her father. She looked embarrassed, and I realized right away my misstep: I could not have a student knowing my dark and secret past. But she said, squirming in her chair, "He couldn't really remember your name. I tried to describe you, but he couldn't remember you."

Mrs. Taccetta played the small organ softly as I followed my mother and sister to seats up front. My shy brother was lighting candles on the altar with a long wand, his face shiny with embarrassment. This used to be Johnny Ford's house, a big colonial gone to seed, between my house and uptown. The Episcopal church had originally met upstairs in the Grange hall, my mother and Mrs. Pervier and Mr. Shindledecker setting up folding metal chairs and restacking them each Sunday morning for six years. Finally those pioneers, seeing some crucial and mysterious distinction between themselves and the Congregationalists and Methodists, raised the funds to buy Johnny's house and turn his living room and dining room into a chapel. The kitchen stayed, but my mother donated our old refrigerator; I could still smell our potatoes in the old-fashioned flip-out drawer in the bottom. The fridge gave me a sense of ownership in the church. So did my mother's role as president of the women's auxiliary. Exotic, deeply embroidered stoles and altar cloths hung in her closet, carefully washed, starched, and ironed and laid over my absent father's wooden coat hangers. My mother walked up to the church each Saturday afternoon to set up, arranging flowers and replacing the grape juice and communion wafers.

I felt important there, and loved. I heard every Sunday as we walked into church, "Oh, Bobbie, you have raised such wonderful children." My mother told us we were special, a family united by the trauma of my father's going, and made stronger for it. Church allowed us to parade our family's bravery and fortitude. Smiling, slim and tan, and absolutely capable, my mother led us into the gaze of our congregation. I was proud. When Mrs. Palmer and Mrs. Zitrick and Mr. Keniston and Crazy Lulu and Reverend Andrews nodded and smiled their hellos, I felt the light of adoration shine on me. In the pew, in the little chapel she had helped to build, my mother held my hand, and I was a child of grace.

I was kicked out of school on the day we returned from Christmas vacation. I was a junior, sixteen years old. My mother had watched me with cool suspicion as I refused to eat breakfast. Five months pregnant, a slim dancer, I had zipped my wool skirt over my hard, round belly and prayed for one more day of hiding.

In gym class that morning, we had used the mats for tumbling. Over and over, Miss Millett had made us practice running somersaults, kips, and splits. When my turn came to do a move called the fish-flop—a backward somersault, legs held high for a pause in the follow-through, and an arched-back slide down onto the chest and belly—I balked. I was starting to understand that what had ended my periods, what made my belly grow, was not just a terrifying threat, an ominous messenger telling me that I was doomed; it was becoming a life—a child, curled inside me in, perhaps—why not?—the same dread and fear of its future that I carried every minute. Suddenly, watching the girls ahead of me slamming back down onto the mats, I felt a confused and ferocious protectiveness and a giving-in, two of us too tired to hide anymore. The class watched as I ran out of the gym into the girls' locker room.

My best friends, Kathy and Chris, followed me. "What's wrong?" they asked earnestly. I hadn't showered after gym class for a month, but they had bought my excuses about not having time before biology class. This time I turned and faced them in the clammy room. "I'm pregnant," I said. I remember now that they both visibly drew back, sucking in air, suspended. Maybe not. Maybe they just stared for a minute. Maybe they looked at me and considered how to react. But I was surprised, after all the months of rehearsing the scene in my mind, to see them turn silently to their lockers, fumble with their clothes, and leave together without saying a word to me. If I hadn't understood during those five terrified months that everything I had ever been, everything I had ever believed in and dreamed of, was gone, I understood it at that moment.

Miss Millett may have called Mrs. Zitrick, the school nurse and my mother's helper on the women's auxiliary at church. Or maybe Mrs. Zitrick watched me one day too many as I ran up the steps of the cafeteria into the bathroom to vomit lunch, my skirt stretched tight. Maybe she saw the change in my face, the darkness of fear and aloneness underlying the charade of walking and talking and sitting. She called me to her office. She was surprisingly tender as she handed me the expulsion slip.

"Do you want me to call your mother at work?" she asked.

"No, thank you," I answered. "How will I take my midterms?"

Mrs. Zitrick sat back in her chair. "You understand that you may not return to this school?"

I left my books, left my notes, my notebooks, with my childish penmanship of looping phrases and doodles and who-loves-whom, on her desk. I walked down the silent, polished hallway to my locker, put on my jacket and mittens, and walked alone through the White wing, past the office staff staring at me through the big window, and out the door. The first phase of outcasting was done.

"Well," my mother said that night after work, sitting on the couch across the room in her trim wool dress and heels. "Well. You can't stay here."

The second phase.

I was supposed to move to my father's house the next morning. I asked my mother if I could wait until Sunday so I could go to church. She looked surprised. "Haven't you figured anything out?" she asked. "You can't go to church like that. They won't want us anymore." I don't believe my mother ever went to church again. When she died my brother and sister and I argued about whether she would want a minister at her grave. I believed that she would; I knew my own ambivalent heart. Finally we asked a nice man from the Unitarian church to come, a neutral voice who was delicate in referring to a benevolent God.

No one from church ever called or wrote to me after I left Hampton. The silence made me feel as if I had never been part of their Christian body. The beloved smells of leather prayer books and wax and old women's perfume, the swish of Mr. Andrews' robes, the sweet wheeze of the organ, Mrs. Taccetta's tiny feet in stubby black heels pumping the pedals; the voices of the church rising together, proclaiming God's mercy and forgiveness; the refrigerator humming in the kitchen; my mother's hand wrapped around mine while we stood to sing and knelt to pray; Mr. Spellacy or Miss St. Germaine smiling at me during the long sermon; the permanence and comfort of the affection of grown-ups. The radiant, bored peace of church. All this evaporated when word got out.

Last Easter I finally succeeded in getting my grown sons to accompany me to a service in the local Episcopal chapel. They had never been in a church, and I had not been in one, except for funerals, since I was sixteen. "Come," I said. "Easter is a joyous time in the church. Let's go sing about the rebirth of the earth." They liked it. I sang by heart every word of "Christ the Lord Is Risen Today" and gave the responses to the Nicene Creed like a believer. I wasn't. But I was home—the sublime faces and the murmurings and the music and the candles and the lilies. The warmth felt deceptive, though, and seductive. Dangerous. My old defenses rose up again instinctively, and I defied the beautiful place and the pious hearts and the father on the altar to catch me again.

I hadn't spent time with my father since he had remarried six years before. He and Dorothy lived in a large old colonial in Epping, fifteen miles from home. They were renovating the house themselves, and Dorothy was a terrible housekeeper, so it was crowded with Sheetrock panels and five-gallon buckets of plaster and boards and crushed boxes of nails and screws and tiles for the bathroom and old magazines and piles of mail and clothes strewn over chairs. The kitchen was greasy, and mounds of dirty dishes filled the sink. My father and Dorothy both traveled for their jobs and were seldom home. Dorothy told me to keep the thermostats at sixty-four; she bought cottage cheese and pineapple so I would stay thin and not "lose my shape." I had never slept alone in a house before.

I was not formed yet, not a decision maker about my life. I was not yet born to consciousness. But here, suddenly, I was facing the results of being in the world. In those empty, slow, lonely days, I had to be born into my next life, as I lost my old self in a kind of death.

My stepsister, Molly, was still on her winter vacation from Deerfield Academy. The morning before I arrived, she was moved from her home to her grandmother's house in western New Hampshire. We were told to stop writing letters to each other; my father explained that Molly was still only fifteen and they didn't want her exposed to "things like this." I was forbidden to go outside because no one in town was told that I was there and pregnant. Once, after a deep, comforting snow, I shoveled the driveway and walks, thinking that my father and Dorothy would be happily surprised when they came home the next day. They were angry and reiterated that I must never go outside again.

I spent long, silent days and nights in the house. When my father and Dorothy were home, they often had dinner parties. I was sent up to my room early with a plate of food and told not to make any noise. I didn't dare go to the bathroom down the hall, afraid that someone would come up the stairs. So I lay under the covers in my frosty, gloomy room, holding my pee, waiting. The laughter rose in bursts from the room below, voices from lives lived on another planet.

The winter was very long and very cold and very gray. The house, my room were large and cold and gray. I waited for calls from Karen and Chris, from friends at school who would be missing me, and then stopped waiting. Once I got a letter from a boy named Bill, a kind letter referring obscurely to my trouble and asking me to write back. It was a moment of tenderness that threatened to break my new, tough heart. I could not afford to cry and could not figure out what I—a dirty pregnant girl hiding upstairs in a cold, lonely house—could say to a handsome boy who still went to history class and shoveled driveways on Saturday mornings. I never wrote back.

I know now that what happened that winter was a deep and scarring depression. Despair and a ferocious, watchful defiance saturated my young life. I was formed largely in those four months, those months that isolated me from any life, from any belief, from any sense that I belonged to anyone. I was alone. My fear and grief burned like wildfires on a silent and distant horizon. I watched the destruction day after day, standing by my bedroom window, staring out over the snow-covered fields that belonged to my father.

My mother finally called in March. My birthday was coming, and she wanted to bring me home for dinner. I was pushed to excitement. I missed my mother badly, the mother of my childhood. I missed my bedroom and my cat. I missed that life, that girl, and wanted to reclaim her for a day.

I was exchanged between my parents' cars on the Route 101 overpass at noon. My mother stared at my large belly and didn't hug me. We drove in silence to Hampton; I wished I had not agreed to come. Being near her, being in our car, which belonged now to before, approaching my town on roads as familiar as my own body had once been, all agitated the deep, deep sense of loss that I had struggled so hard to kill. When we turned onto Lafayette Road near town, my mother told me to get down on the floor of the car. I didn't move. "We might see someone," she explained. I squeezed my baby and me onto her floor and watched my mother's faraway face staring straight ahead as we drove home.

My bedroom was a museum of another life. It was pink and soft and sunny and treacherous. I sat all afternoon on my bed, fingering the white chenille bedspread and stroking my purring black cat. I called up my numbness. A white lace cloth, one I had ironed when I was a child in this house, covered the bureau. The blue plastic clock whirred quietly. Cars slid silently down High Street, carrying people I knew: Mrs. Shindledecker and Corky Lawrence and Sally and Mr. Palmer. They were in a movie, and I watched from beyond the screen.

I don't remember my birthday dinner, at seventeen years old and seven months along. I am sure my mother gave me something nice. I hid on the floor of the car in the dark and was relieved to return to the empty obscurity of my father's house.

I had a keen sense of my baby and me being outcasts together. My father and mother had decided immediately that "we" would give the baby up for adoption. I didn't fight; I understood with absolute clarity that I would have no one helping me, that I had held one summer job in a candy store at the beach, that I could never return to high school. That we would be loved and protected nowhere. My sister and brother "knew," but no one else in the family had been told. I still don't know where my grandparents thought I was that year. I do know they were not there telling me that families don't give babies away.

The sense that I had a foreign and threatening force inside me had given way to an intense feeling of connection, of being lost together. We spent the dead-quiet hours alone, our heartbeats measuring together the passage of time, the damage, the unexpressed grief. We would be separated forever in two more months. We shared time in a strange and intense and encompassing sorrow.

My sister, six years older and longing since she was ten to have a baby of her own, said to me, "This is a baby. A baby is growing inside you." I could not afford it with her.

"I hate this baby," I said to her, scaring her away.

I could feel his small heel or an elbow pressing hard against the inside of my belly as he rolled. I spent the days doing nothing but thinking, learning to live in my head, my arms wrapped under my belly, my baby absorbing my stunned sadness. He had hiccups in the night. I lay in the deep, cold emptiness of the house, the night shared with another living being. My blood flowed through him. Tenacious threads joined us outside the world. I could not feel loved by him, ever. But we were one life, small and scared and alone.

"*You have got* to let this baby go!" the doctor roared at me. He smelled of cigarettes. We had been there a very, very long time. "You cannot hold this baby inside you," he said angrily. "Push!" My baby was born on Memorial Day, 1966.

Four days after the birth, my mother drove me to High Mowing, a small boarding school on a mountaintop in western New Hampshire, for an interview to enter in the fall. That morning she had found me crying as I squeezed milk from my impacted breasts into the bathroom sink.

"Oh, sweetheart," she had said. "My poor sweetheart."

I whipped around and hissed at her, "Get out." They were the first and only tears I had shed throughout the pregnancy and birth and the terrible, terrible drive away from the hospital. We had moved beyond mother and daughter forever. Whatever she felt, watching me cry, could not help me now.

She was cheerful and talkative on the way to the school. "This is a time to regroup," she told me, "to get back on track." She didn't look at me as she drove. "You need to forget these difficult months and make a new start," she said.

My belly was empty and soft. I had stuffed handkerchiefs in my bra to soak up the milk that spilled and spilled from my breasts. I felt old. The fierce sense of aloneness intensified. My other being, my baby who shared life with me, who was alive in me when everything else had died, was left alone someplace on the third floor of the hospital, the absolute outcast, a castaway.

"I'm relieved," my mother said, "that this whole ordeal is over." She reminded me again that some of her friends had dropped her when they heard about me; she had paid a big price, she said. I was lucky she had found this school, the only one that had agreed to consider me. She talked on and on while we drove toward my next life.

Mrs. Emmet met us in the living room of the old farmhouse. She was eighty-three, a wealthy eccentric and educator who carried her ideas from Germany and Austria. I felt at home; this was a world away from Hampton and Epping and my school friends, who had become cardboard cutouts from someone else's past. If I did not get in here, I would have to go to work without a diploma. I had always imagined I would go to Smith or Wellesley, the first generation. Now I hoped this old woman would let me finish high school in her strange little school for fuckups.

She said I could come, even though I had "run amok." I had to promise I would never talk to any of the girls about what I had done; I would have the only single room, to isolate me from the possibility that the need to talk would compromise my promise. In September, ancient and so diminished I barely felt alive, I joined eighty children for a final year of school. I graduated in 1967, the same year my old class finished up in Hampton.

For several years after that, I occasionally went "home." I slowly grew bold and defiant and would walk uptown and into the familiar stores. I always saw someone I knew. Inevitably they stared and then turned away abruptly. If two were together, they bent together in whispers and walked away from me. Patty, who had been for six years the only other member, with me, of an experimental, accelerated class, refused to sell stamps to me at the post office. Mrs. Underwood stayed busy in the back of the five-and-ten, folding and refolding clothes until I left. Once, as I got out of the car in my mother's driveway, Diane drove by with three girls from my class. They whipped around in the next driveway and stopped in front of my house. Diane leapt out of the car, smiling at me. "Is it true—" she asked loudly, grinning back at my old friends. "Is it true you got knocked up?"

I have not been to my father's house for thirty years. There are many things and many places that speak to me of what has been lost. I long, in an odd way, for my gray and forsaken bedroom in that lonely house, where someone lay close to my heart.

There are other truths, of course, behind this history, glimmers and flickers of understanding that underlie these memories. I was not the do-good child I thought myself to be. For example I know now that I hated school. I was bored and arrogant, clamoring for more from better teachers. I once told the principal to go to hell. I offered to replace Mr. Belanger as French teacher when he couldn't answer my questions. My brother was a day student at Phillips Exeter, and I was jealous.

I think I was a skeptic—actually a cynic—by the time I was in high school. I was outspoken, with strong opinions—even defiant. I was intolerant of ignorance or injustice. I read the daily paper and *Atlantic Monthly* and knew that people suffered terrible inequities. I laid blame passionately around me—the battle was between the haves and have-nots. I believed in the Truth, in what was Right, and must have been righteous. I tended to be a loner; I had lots of friends, but they knew, I think, that I always reserved some elemental piece of myself. I imagined myself always on the outside, by choice on the days I felt loved and by some fated flaw on those other days. I carried a deep sadness, a melancholy that belied my cheerfulness.

I did love my church. But when at fourteen I attended confirmation class, I grew increasingly frustrated with the lack of answers to my questions. I perceived this as a failure on the part of the minister and the church to own up to its limitations and hypocrisies. I challenged Mr. Andrews; he appeared to tolerate my confrontations, but I left confused and agitated each Wednesday evening. Two years before my expulsion, I realize now, my beliefs in God and my church had already started to fray.

It is true that my mother might not have continued in the church after I left. But she had met Paul the year before. He was a jazz musician, a writer, a thinker. I remember going to church alone for a while, probably during that year of tumultuous changes in my mother's own life. She became a radical, started keeping a journal, sketched faces on the phone pad. She worked for Paul at a new job with a small, artsy magazine. After work they joined friends at the house Paul rented at the beach for long nights of drinking and talk and cigarettes and music. That was the summer I got pregnant. Leaving the church may actually have happened for my mother months before my outcasting. Of course I believed completely that she was a nearly perfect mother and any trouble I found was born in my own reckless, selfish heart.

It is true that my shunning was a message from our community to my mother, also: Bobbie Hall thought she was so high and mighty, but she couldn't keep her husband, and now she hangs out with beatniks at the beach. And don't even mention her youngest. You get what you deserve. Her rejection of me was a measure of the humiliation she felt. She believed until her death that I caused her to lose her friends and her stature in our town.

I struggle to reckon with my own silence, my lack of fight. I allowed my family and community to abandon me while I was drowning. Worst of all, I allowed my baby to be abandoned. I abandoned my baby. I never said a word. Sometimes my own failure of courage feels like the most hideous kind of cowardice, a flaw in me that confirms my unworthiness for love. Sometimes, rarely, I get a flicker of understanding about other realities and feel a powerful protectiveness of that stunned and desperate girl.

These various truths sometimes collide with memories I have used to reconstruct the puzzle, but they cannot alter the perfect truth I carry of having been turned out.

It is a function of shunning that it must eliminate the shunned completely. It feels like a murder and is baffling because there is no grave. No hymns were sung to ease my going or to beg for God's blessing on my soul. Shunning is as precise as a scalpel, an absolute excision, leaving, miraculously, not a trace of a scar on the community body. The scarring is left for the girl, an intense, debilitating wound that weeps for the rest of her life. It's quite a price to pay for having sex, scared sex, on a beach on a foggy Labor Day night.

The shunning has created a deep shame that infuses my life. It makes me feel wildly vulnerable. I struggle still to claim a permanent space, an immutable relationship to those around me. It negates forever the ability to have a real friend. To speak in a room with confidence. To walk anyplace without believing that I have no right to be there and that I am in danger. In response I have built a formidable tenacity; my grandmother, never knowing its source, called me her "little Rock of Gibraltar." I sometimes meet women and recognize in them an instinct to run, to be gone before harm can come again, mixed with a ferocious recklessness because nothing else can be taken. I wonder what they could have done to be paying such a price.

MEREDITH HALL ON *"Shunned"*

I have a friend who is a blacksmith. He roams around Maine in his pickup looking for scrap iron. Our farms are derelict now, all the work that men and women and children once did lying hidden in encroaching grass and sumac. Robert spends long afternoons behind barns with sagging roof ridges and broken-out windows that let flocks of swallows into the silent dusty cathedrals of beams and lofts. He rakes his bare hands through the tangle of weeds, pulling out long heavy pieces of iron, parts from horse-drawn plows and tedders and hay loaders. From piles scattered in the unmown grass, he digs out casings and axles and shafts. Robert feels reverence for these iron scraps, tools that were themselves forged by working hands generations ago, tools cleverly imagined to serve a specific function and artfully crafted with the unnecessary, the beautiful— a fine groove running along the haft, a bead edging the tine. He drags them back to his barn—old stories waiting to be forged again, reimagined, recontextualized, made his own.

Fire, oxygen, sweat, and water: the alchemy of forged iron, elemental, endlessly transmutable. Robert rakes the clinkers—impurities in the fuel which settle out—from yesterday's fire and lays new coal in the bed of his forge. The fire slowly takes; Robert pulls the cord of the huge bellows slowly, once, twice. Oxygen fuels the fire to 2,000 degrees, a seething sea of orange currents. Robert lays the old iron—a short, thick section from a harrow—into the coals, turning it occasionally, drawing it out to size up its heat, settling it again into the fire. He knows when the iron becomes malleable. Now he is the maker. He positions the glowing iron on the anvil and drops his heavy hammer. A solid, ancient *tonk* and sparks fly. Again, and again, into the fire and onto the anvil, Robert turning the iron a bit each time, *tonk, tonk,* finding in the old story his own: harrow becomes bracket, or hinge pin, or hasp. When the form is right, when the iron becomes his imagined structure, scheme, configuration, Robert dips it, red-hot and nearly molten, into the barrel of cold water. The iron hisses, the water boils around the new form. This is the quenching. The old story is transformed, redescribed, and fixed again in time.

But this is the real wonder: the farmer's hands, his early mornings and tidy shed and love or not for his children and wife, his work-tired or guiltless sleep, the soft green of spring and the sear of late August spreading across his fields—all of this is within the memory of the forger's new piece. The iron holds the substance of that earlier life. Robert's story and the farmer's, and the story of the person who will someday find Robert's hinge pin in the overgrown grass, galvanize; the universal story is forged as his own.

"*Shunned*" is a story that moves beyond the events in my own young life. Girls have been cast out throughout time for insults to their community. Mothers have lapsed, lost in their own unfilled hearts, leaving daughters adrift. Babies have been left behind. Women have floundered, struggling to construct a life around that gaping hole. Loneliness is an old story which belongs to all of us. Shame comes in degrees. In the end, love—withheld or offered, lost and sought after—is the story, again and again. I make my stories from all the interwoven bits, my own, those of the people I love, those of people before me, people I never knew who live like ghosts within me. The events in "Shunned" are inextricable from those lives, and may be recognizable to others no matter what they have known of love.

The final truths are never evident before I start writing. As I took these old stories—my life, others' lives—and began to write "Shunned," my material was simply a series of images embedded in my memory. In the writing, I discovered the girl I once was, scared and alone. I met her then, although she has been me all this time. My children carry her, as I carry my mother and her mother. That terrified and isolated girl becomes part of the ongoing story. Children sit in church still; cars drive by houses in which girls hide. Stories arise from the overgrown grass.

An Album Quilt

JOHN McPHEE

It has somehow become 1978 and for ten or fifteen years I have
been intending to attempt a piece of writing called "Six Princetons"—the school as it has variously appeared to someone who
was born in Princeton and has lived in Princeton all his life. It
would begin with the little kid who knew the location of every
pool table and Hajoca urinal on the campus, the nine best ways
to sneak into the gym, the gentlest method of removing a
reunion costume from a sleeping drunk. Princeton through the
eyes of a student in Princeton High School. Princeton from the
20/20 omnicomprehensive undergraduate perspective. Princeton
from the point of view of a commuter absorbed with other
worlds. (Once, in that era, I found myself saying to my wife,
"What are all these young people doing on Nassau Street?") The

JOHN McPHEE is the Pulitzer Prize–winning author of more than
twenty-five books of creative nonfiction, most recently *The Founding
Fish*. He lives in Princeton, New Jersey.

Princeton University library and campus studied from across the street by an incarcerated freelance who stares out an upstairs office window all through the day. (My next-door neighbor is the Swedish Massage Studio, a legitimate business which darkens at 5 p.m. Later in the evening, the Swedish Massage's unwanted customers see my light and come tapping on my door. When I open up, their faces fall. "Is this the Swedish Massage?" they say incredulously, their disappointment all too apparent at the sight of the hoar in the beard.) Princeton a fixed foot, as it appears after long stays elsewhere. Princeton as witnessed by a perennial, paradoxical "visiting professor" who is neither visiting nor a professor, but in spring semester after spring semester is given tonic by a roomful of writing students who yield as much as they receive.

"Six Princetons" will never be written, though, because new Princetons keep coming along. "Dear Parent: We are pleased to inform you that your daughter has succeeded you as an editor of the *Nassau Literary Review,* and, incidentally, that her room-board-tuition for the academic year 1978–79 has been raised *quinque* per centum to $2,500,000."

As I write this, in 1983, one of my daughters is somewhere in India, another is believed to be in Egypt, another is skating on a north Italian pond, and the oldest is working as a writer in Pittstown, New Jersey. There is a moral in this tale.

My children have always thought me mildly eccentric for living my whole life in one town, yet there is no need to move away from Princeton to get a change of scene. You stay here all your life and you get a new town every five years.

When you are young and getting married, or your daughter is getting married and your own youth is silt in the river, you turn to Nature for instruction and example. And so Laura and I, one truly fine day, went a couple of hundred kilometers into Iceland's interior for the ritual purpose of consulting Nature to see what we might learn.

Along the way we stopped at Geysir, where a great hole in the ground is the world's eponymous geyser. The old geyser is no longer forthcoming. It is full of water but not of action. It had literally been roped off. Close at hand was a young geyser. At five-to seven-minute intervals—no more than that—it swelled tumescently, let forth a series of heavy grunts, and into the sky shot a plume of flying steam. Meanwhile, the old geyser just sat there—boiling. We learned how—on special occasions—Icelanders make the old geyser do its thing. They throw soap into it, and it erupts.

Moving on, we passed a waterfall the size of the American Niagara, and then we drove for an hour or two on the gravels of an outwash plain that was covered with rounded boulders and no vegetation, not so much as a clump of grass. Eventually, the car could go no farther, so we left it behind and proceeded north on foot. There was a stream to ford. Laura had running shoes, and I had boots. She got onto my back, and I carried her across. We then walked a couple of miles, also on rounded rocks, and up onto a high moraine, where, coming over the crest, we looked down into a lake backdropped by cliffs of blue ice. This was the edge not of a valley glacier but of an ice cap covering nearly 500 square miles. Above the lake, the ice wall rose about 150 feet, and was sheer. There came sounds like high-powered-rifle shots, as huge bergs calved away from the ice cap and plunged into the water. There was no going farther. On the way down the moraine and back toward the river ford, I attempted to increase my credit line by mentioning that glacial rivers grow in the afternoon with the day's melt from the sun, and this time we could expect a larger river when I carried her across it. But this time she was having none of me. Apparently, she had forded her last river on her father's back. She took off her shoes and negotiated the stream.

Idaho Springs, Colorado, dawn. A white rented car. Alone, I toss my gear into the trunk and get going early. After a couple of miles, I note in the rearview mirror that the back window is fogged over. "Condensation," I tell myself. "Car dew. It will soon evaporate." I get up onto Interstate 70 and head west. Now and again, I look in the mirror. Visibility zero. Evaporation has not yet kicked in. Twenty miles. Twenty-five. Climbing. Eventually, I realize that when I put my gear in the trunk I did not close the lid. I don't know whatever else I was once. Now I'm a little, gray-bearded, absentminded professor. With events like this one in mind, my daughter Jenny has long called me Lefty. I don't think I'm going to recover. I don't think I'm going to go backwards.

In the late 1970s and early 1980s, I collected material in Wyoming for a book about the geology there. Almost without exception, those journeys were made in the company of John David Love, of the United States Geological Survey, who had started life in 1913 on a solitary ranch in the center of the state and had long since achieved a reputation of preeminence among Rocky Mountain geologists. My intention was to try to present the natural history of his region through his eyes and his experi-ence. It is not uncommon for a geologist to reflect in the style of his science the structure of his home terrain.

We had been making field trips together for a couple of years when he reached into a drawer in his office in Laramie and handed me a journal that had been started by his mother long before she was married—when she had first come to Wyoming. She had been born more than a hundred years before I saw her manuscript, and needless to say I never met her, but, as I have noted elsewhere, the admiration and affection I came to feel toward her is probably matched by no one I've encountered in my professional life. This was not merely because she had the courage to venture as a young teacher into very distant country, or because she later educated her own bright children, or because she was more than equal to the considerable difficulties of ranch subsistence, but also because she recorded these things—in her journals and later writings—with such wit, insight, grace, irony, compassion, sarcasm, stylistic elegance, and embracing humor that I could not resist her.

Her unpublished journal was a large gift to me, and with the permission of her son and daughter I used fragments from it to help re-create her family's world. My work, though, did not include a hundredth part of what was there. My presentation could only suggest her. In years that have followed, two of her granddaughters have sifted through attics and other archives to discover packets of letters to and from her, various forms of writing by and about her, and another journal. Their work in arranging, annotating, and editing what they found has not only been loving in nature but restrainedly skillful in accomplishment. In *Lady's Choice*, they have elected to present her between 1905, when she began her first journal, and 1910, when she decided to marry John Galloway Love, a cowboy from Scotland who, in the Wind River Basin of Wyoming, had presented his credentials to her seemingly within moments of her arrival. The boundaries of this volume (another will follow) are deliberate and significant, for they enclose a young American woman of nearly a century ago in something like a complex of competing magnets. Self-possessed, cool, detached, she clearly knows that this is her time, and she takes it. As this chronological flow of journal entries, letters, and poems progresses, she is not only wooed by the cowboy but also importuned by a Wyoming mother who sees the young schoolteacher as a match for her own son, and who attempts to assassinate the character of John Love by referring to him as a gossip. Possibly she helps to effectuate a marriage she hopes to prevent. Letters are arriving all the while from Wellesley friends who are now in places like medical school and Paris. She experiments with teaching jobs in other states, in one instance at a sort of nunnery in Wisconsin, with macabre, humorous results. Always, she is writing—an incidental skill that would later become an ambition. Always, as well, John Love is writing to her. Indirectly, she is being asked to choose between a very isolated family life and the realm of other possibilities easily within

reach of (as someone puts it in a letter to John Love) "her combination of strength and the gentlest charm—welded by that
flashing mind."

Recently, when her granddaughters sent to me the annotated
manuscript of this volume, I raced through the innumerable letters and the later journal that I had never seen, looking for that
flashing mind and the person I felt I knew. When she described
one of the faculty members at the school in Wisconsin as "a
square prunes-and-prisms lady with a mouth like a buttonhole," I
was reassured that I had found her.

Elsewhere, when a difficult woodstove at last began to function properly, she wrote, "The stove has developed a conscience."

When she taught Latin and Greek for a time at Central High
School in Pueblo, Colorado, and lived in the home of one Mrs.
Butler, she wrote to John Love:

Mrs. Butler . . . is a little war-horse of a woman with a long,
thin husband. I'm telling you about her, because she has
been improving him for about 20 years, and it is beginning to
tell on him.

Reading again the journal that she kept when she was
twenty-three, I found everywhere the sense of landscape that
resembled her touch with people:

The dampness had brought out the darkness of the red soil,
and the blackness of the green cedars. The sagebrush, too,
along the way, was as black about the branches as if a fire had
passed over the hills. The bluffs loomed dark and moody
against the gray sky, but far away at the Big Bend the hills
were the color of pale straw. The mountain looked yellowish

green, softened by a sifting of snow. It is strange how the whole face of the country will be changed by a little dampness, like the face of a person intensified but softened by tears.

It should be said that while this lady's choice was a classic dilemma, John Love's side of it was something close to an all-or-nothing gamble. He was thirty-five years old when he fell in love with her. He lived in a place so far from community that he did not glimpse a woman for months at a time. He presented himself to her without guile, and she dealt in kind with him. For five years, he took no for an answer but never changed his question. When his letters developed closing salutations that were unacceptably intimate—for example, "Ever Yours"—and she verbally rapped his knuckles for it, thereafter he said, "Sincerely." Abidingly, he carried within him the heart and the humor, not to mention the brain, of the Scots. He was a match for her. Evidently, she knew it.

As this volume ends, she accepts him, his ranch, and a fulfillable vision of their life together. Her granddaughters quote from something she wrote years later, describing an embroidered sampler that existed only in her imagination and depicted the ranch and its hands and her family and certain symbols of a time in the Wind River Basin.

I will wait impatiently for the sampler. Meanwhile, these distinct themes from her single life will more than do.

I used to go to New Hampshire in the summertime with a stack of *New Yorkers* a foot and a half high. I would paddle straight over the lake until I was twenty-seven yards out of earshot, and then I would lie down and go through those magazines like a drill bit, looking for things I particularly remembered, looking for things I'd missed on journeys during the year. Trillin in Provence fighting bulls in water—*Taureaux Piscine!* Mark Singer and the Puerto Rican rooster in the window of the Israeli locksmith shop on Seventh Avenue. Ackerman and the albatross, Iglauer and the salmon, Frazier's metaphysical bears. Barich up, in the eighth at Santa Anita, wearing our silks. Updike on the eighth, parring. Angell in the eighth, relieving.

Finished with the animals, I started on the vegetables, and once in a while I paddled ashore and called up the *New Yorker* library. Hello, Helen, in what issue did Whiteside tee up the American-latex tomato? Whose was the thing about the grass at Wimbledon? When was Kahn in the rice paddy? Helen Stark knew everything, but her line was often busy with calls from other canoes.

Speaking of libraries: A big open-stack academic or public library is no small pleasure to work in. You're, say, trying to do a piece on something in Nevada, and you go down to C Floor, deep in the earth, and out to what a miner would call a remote working face. You find 10995.497S just where the card catalog and the online computer thought it would be, but that is only the initial nick. The book you knew about has led you to others you did not know about. To the ceiling the shelves are loaded with books about Nevada. You pull them down, one at a time, and sit on the floor and look them over until you are sitting on a pile five feet high, at which point you are late home for dinner and you get up and walk away. It's an incomparable boon to research, all that; but it is also a reason why there are almost no large open-stack libraries left in the world.

When your mother is ninety-nine years old, you have so many memories of her that they tend to overlap, intermingle, and blur. It is extremely difficult to single out one or two, impossible to remember any that exemplify the whole.

It has been alleged that when I was in college she heard that I had stayed up all night playing poker and wrote me a letter that used the word "shame" forty-two times. I do not recall this.

I do not recall being pulled out of my college room and into the church next door.

It has been alleged that on December 24, 1936, when I was five years old, she sent me to my room at or close to 7 p.m. for using four-letter words while trimming the Christmas tree. I do not recall that.

The assertion is absolutely false that when I came home from high school with an A-minus she demanded an explanation for the minus.

It has been alleged that she spoiled me with protectionism, because I was the youngest child and therefore the most vulnerable to attack from overhead—an assertion that I cannot confirm or confute, except to say that the facts don't lie.

We lived only a few blocks from the elementary school and routinely ate lunch at home. It is reported that the following dialogue and ensuing action occurred on January 22, 1941:

"Eat your sandwich."

"I don't want to eat my sandwich."

"I made that sandwich, and you are going to eat it, Mister Man. You filled yourself up on penny candy on the way home, and now you're not hungry."

"I'm late. I have to go. I'll eat the sandwich on the way back to school."

"Promise?"

"Promise."

Allegedly, I went up the street with the sandwich in my hand and buried it in a snowbank in front of Dr. Wright's house. My mother, holding back the curtain in the window of the side door, was watching. She came out in the bitter cold, wearing only a light dress, ran to the snowbank, dug out the sandwich, chased me up Nassau Street, and rammed the sandwich down my throat, snow and all. I do not recall any detail of that story. I believe it to be a total fabrication.

There was the case of the missing Cracker Jack at Lindel's corner store. Flimsy evidence pointed to Mrs. McPhee's smallest child. It has been averred that she laid the guilt on with the following words: " 'Like mother like son' is a saying so true, the world will judge largely of mother by you." It has been asserted that she immediately repeated that proverb three times, and also recited it on other occasions too numerous to count. I have absolutely no recollection of her saying that about the Cracker Jack or any other controlled substance.

We have now covered everything even faintly unsavory that has been reported about this person in ninety-nine years, and even those items are a collection of rumors, half-truths, prevarications, false allegations, inaccuracies, innuendos, and canards.

This is the mother who—when Alfred Knopf wrote her twenty-two-year-old son a letter saying, "The readers' reports in the case of your manuscript would not be very helpful, and I think might discourage you completely"—said, "Don't listen to Alfred Knopf. Who does Alfred Knopf think he is, anyway? Someone should go in there and k-nock his block off." To the best of my recollection, that is what she said.

I also recall her taking me, on or about March 8, my birthday, to the theater in New York every year, beginning in childhood. I remember those journeys as if they were today. I remember *A Connecticut Yankee.* Wednesday, March 8, 1944. Evidently, my father had written for the tickets, because she and I sat in the last row of the second balcony. Mother knew what to do about that. She gave me for my birthday an elegant spyglass, sufficient in power to bring the Connecticut Yankee back from Vermont. I sat there watching the play through my telescope, drawing as many guffaws from the surrounding audience as the comedy onstage.

On one of those theater days—when I was eleven or twelve—I asked her if we could start for the city early and go out to LaGuardia Field to see the comings and goings of airplanes. The temperature was well below the freeze point and the March winds were so blustery that the windchill factor was 40 below zero. Or seemed to be. My mother figured out how to take the subway to a stop in Jackson Heights and a bus from there—a feat I am unable to duplicate to this day. At LaGuardia, she accompanied me to the observation deck and stood there in the icy wind for at least an hour, maybe two, while I, spellbound, watched the DC-3s coming in on final, their wings flapping in the gusts. When we at last left the observation deck, we went downstairs into the terminal, where she bought me what appeared to be a black rubber ball but on closer inspection was a pair of hollow hemispheres hinged on one side and folded together. They contained a silk parachute. Opposite the hinge, each hemisphere had a small nib. A piece of string wrapped round and round the two nibs kept the ball closed. If you threw it high into the air, the string unwound and the parachute blossomed. If you sent it up with a tennis racquet, you could put it into the clouds. Not until the development of the ten-megabyte hard disk would the world

---

know such a fabulous toy. Folded just so, the parachute nev
failed. Always, it floated back to you—silkily, beautifully—to
start over and float back again. Even if you abused it, whacked it
really hard—gracefully, lightly, it floated back to you.

On "An Album Quilt" by John McPhee

John McPhee admits that he starts the first line of an essay or book
with absolutely "no confidence." He procrastinates. Just because he
is laboring in his Princeton University office day after day "certainly doesn't mean I am working. . . . I just walk around, make a
cup of coffee or tea, look out the windows, inventing ways to avoid
writing. . . . Until 4 or 5 p.m. comes along, and it is really getting
late, and then I'll get going. If I have a good day, I might actually
be writing only two or three hours."

But "writing begets writing," says McPhee. "You feel yourself
growing as a result of the writing you do." Normally he will write
four drafts of his essays, and he reads everything he writes aloud
before the final draft. McPhee's objective at the beginning of each
essay or book "is to find a good way into the piece, a lead that
works, a lead that isn't cheap, a lead that shines down into the subject and illuminates it. Almost always I know the last line of the
piece before I know anything else."

A few years ago, McPhee began putting together a collection
of his writing that had never been published in book form—or
published at all. This included articles from his earliest days at
Time magazine and a number of unsigned pieces written for the
"Talk of the Town" section of *The New Yorker*. It also included random, unpublished notes, about 250,000 words in all, which
McPhee refined into about 75,000. His aim was to "present a mon-
tage of patches and fragments of past work that I have picked out

and cut and trimmed (and edited and touched up in the minor
ways that I would edit and touch up the final draft of any new piece
of writing) and sewn together as if it were an album quilt." Developed in Baltimore in the 1880s, album quilts were custom-made for
individuals and often commemorated technological innovations,
but also dealt with personal histories. This is an excerpt from
McPhee's *Album Quilt.*—*Lee Gutkind*

Dinner at Uncle Boris's

CHARLES SIMIC

■ ■

Always plenty of good food and wine. The four of us at the table take turns uncorking new bottles. We drink out of water glasses the way they do in the old country. "More bread," somebody yells. There's never enough bread, never enough olives, never enough soup. We are eating through our second helping of thick bean soup after having already polished off a dozen smoked sausages and a couple of loaves of bread.

And we argue with mouths full. My Uncle Boris would make Mother Teresa reach for a baseball bat. He likes to make big pronouncements, to make the earth tremble with his political and artistic judgments. You drop your spoon. You can't believe your

■ ■

CHARLES SIMIC is a poet, essayist, and translator. He teaches American literature and creative writing at the University of New Hampshire. He has published sixteen collections of his own poetry, five books of essays, a memoir, and numerous books of translations. He has received many literary awards for his poems and translations, including the MacArthur Fellowship and the Pulitzer Prize. *The Voice at 3 A.M.,* his selected and new poems, was published by Harcourt in 2003.

ears. Suddenly, you are short of breath and choking as if you swallowed a big fly.

"Is he kidding?" I hear myself say, my voice rising to a falsetto.

I am the reasonable type. I try to lay out the pros and cons as if I were a judge making a summation to the jury. I believe in the calming effect of an impeccable logical argument. Before I can get very far, my brother interrupts to tell me that I'm full of shit. His philosophy is: The more reasonable it sounds, the less likely it is that it's true. My father, on the other hand, always takes the Olympian view. "None of you know what the fuck you're talking about," he informs us, and resumes slurping his soup.

Before we can all gang up on him, the pork roast is served. The skin is brown and crusty with a bit of fat underneath. There are potatoes and onions in the pan soaked in the drippings. We are in heaven. The new bottle of wine is even better. Nuits-Saint-Georges is my father's favorite wine since his name is George. That's the only one he buys when he is flush.

For a while we don't say anything. We just grunt with our faces in our plates. My aunt is carving more meat while my uncle runs into the kitchen to get those hot little red Mexican peppers he forgot all about.

Unfortunately, one of us starts on politics. Immediately, we are arguing again. In the last few years Boris has become very conservative. He loves Barry Goldwater. He loves Nixon. As for Bobby Kennedy, he's a Russian agent, if you ask him. Boris even warned the *New York Times* about that, but they didn't print the letter, of course. Tonight he shouts that I am a Communist, too. He has suspected it for years and now has had his final proof just two minutes ago.

I have no idea what I said to make him think that, so I ask him to please repeat it. He's appalled. "No guts," he says. "Feigning innocence, backtracking. Jesus Christ!" He calls on the heavens to witness.

"It's what you said about Hoover," my brother says, guffawing. Both he and my father are enjoying themselves, while I'm debating whether to punch Boris in the mouth. He's really pissed, too. He says I even look like Trotsky with my wire-rim glasses. "Get me the FBI on the phone," he yells to my aunt. He's going to speak to J. Edgar personally about me.

It's hard to tell with Boris if he's entirely serious. He loves scenes. He loves opera. It's the third act, we are all dead on the stage, and he is caterwauling. Without histrionics life is boring. This is bliss, as far as he's concerned.

Watching him rant like that, I get an inspiration. I rise from the table, walk over, and solemnly kiss him on the top of his bald head. He's stunned speechless. It takes him some time to collect himself. Finally, he smiles sheepishly and embraces me in turn.

"Forget about the FBI," he yells to my aunt in the kitchen.

She comes out with enough different cheeses to open a store. We eat and drink and converse politely. The old guys are reminiscing about the war.

Is it true that one grows nostalgic even about the horrors as one grows old? Probably. I'm nostalgic about an August afternoon after the war. My mother, brother, and I were being escorted at gunpoint and on foot from one prison to the other. At some point we walked past an apple orchard, and our guard let us stop and pick apples. Not a care in the world. Munching the apples and chatting with the guard.

As for my father and Boris, it seems, when they were in Trieste they used to pull this stunt. My father would invite friends to a fancy restaurant, but when the time came to pay the bill, he'd send Boris to break the news to the unsuspecting owner that they were completely broke.

"You were very good at it," my father assured him.

Boris, when he's not raving, looks like an English gentleman and has the appropriate clothes and fine manner to go along with his face. The owner of the restaurant would accept his apologies and his promise to settle the bill expeditiously, and would even permit his financially strapped guests to order another round of brandies before going off into the night.

"It's his smile," we all agree. Boris has the sweetest, shiest smile when he's happy. Old ladies, especially, adore him. Nobody knows how to bow and kiss their hands like he does. It's hard to believe he was once a guard in a maximum security penitentiary in Australia. Come to think of it, none of us, individually or collectively, make much sense. We are all composite characters, made up of a half dozen different people, thanks to being kicked around from country to country.

Boris, for instance, right now is singing. He studied opera singing for years, tried to make a career of it, and failed. Now he sings only when he's happy. He has a huge, beautiful tenor voice, but no ear. When he starts hitting the high notes, you have to run for your life. It's no use. He can be heard across the street. He has the world's loudest voice, and it's off-key.

He sings for us an aria from *Otello*. We survive that somehow, but he's not through yet. We are going to hear Tristan's death scene. Across the table my father looks grim. My brother has vanished. I am lying on the floor at Tristan's feet, trying my best to keep a straight face. Boris paces up and down conducting the Berlin Philharmonic as he sings. From time to time he stops to translate for us. "Tristan is going mad," he whispers. No doubt about that. This Tristan is ready for the loony bin. His tongue is lolling, and his eyes are popping out of his head. He's standing on the sofa and leaning against the wall, arms spread, as if he is about to be crucified.

"Verflucht wer dich gebrant!" he shrieks.

"Stop it, Boris," my aunt says calmly, coming in from the kitchen with the cake.

"Please let him sing the death scene, Auntie," I say, and now even my father has to grin.

You have to admire the man's love of the music. Boris confessed to me once that he could never sing in the real opera house. He'd get so excited on the stage, he'd jump into the orchestra pit at the conclusion of his aria.

Now we applaud him. We are thirsty and hungry again, and so is he, luckily. My brother has reappeared.

"I'm going to bed," my aunt announces after she brings back the cheese and cold cuts. She knows this is not going to end soon. We are on our favorite topic, the incredible stupidity of our family.

I don't know if all large families indulge in such orgies of self-abuse, but we make a specialty of it. I don't think it's pretense either. I mean, it's not like we believe secretly we are really superior and this is just talk. Our family is a story of endless errors of judgment, of bad situations made even worse by bickering.

"Imagine this," my father says. "There's a war on, the Nazis, the Ustashi, the Hungarians, the Romanians, the Chetniks, the Italians, the Bulgarians, the Communists are killing us, and even the English and the Americans are dropping bombs. So, what do we do to make things really interesting? We all take different sides in that war so we can really make life miserable for each other."

We are silent with the weight of our drunkenness and the sad truth of my father's last remark. Finally, Boris looks up and says, "How about a really great bottle of wine?"

We all look at Boris, puzzled, but he explains that this wine is supposed to be very special, very old, very expensive.

"What is it?" we want to know.

He's not telling. He's going to decant it in the cellar so we can blind-taste it and guess its origins.

Very well. Off he goes, and he's gone so long we are beginning to think the bastard sneaked off to bed. Instead, he returns with an air of mystery, carrying a bottle wrapped in a towel. The last time Boris had a bottle of expensive wine he had us sip it from a teaspoon. He went around the table pouring drops of a fine old Margaux into a spoon and making us all in turn say "Aaaaaahh" like a baby doctor.

This time we just get clean glasses, and he pours everybody a little taste. It's red wine. There's no doubt about that even at three in the morning. We twirl it in our glasses, sniff it like real pros, and take a sip. I think it's a Chianti, my father says it's a Burgundy, my brother mentions Spanish wine, but is not sure.

Boris is triumphant! Here's the final proof! Serbs as a people, and the members of this family, especially, are all know-nothings, show-offs, and the world's biggest phonies.

Then, to rub it in, he tells us how he found out recently that the Sicilian who pumps his gas in Brooklyn makes his own wine. "Probably in the same bathtub where he washes his ass," he adds for effect. Anyway, the man gave him a bottle for Christmas and this is what we are drinking.

It still tastes pretty good, but on second thought, we have to admit, we made complete fools of ourselves. Of course, we can barely keep our eyes open. The day is breaking. For the moment we have run out of talk. We just look at each other, yawning occasionally. The house is quiet. The city is quiet. Even the cops are catching forty winks in their patrol car on the corner.

"How about some ice cream?" Boris asks.

CHARLES SIMIC ON *"Dinner at Uncle Boris's"*

"Dinner at Uncle Boris's" conveys a sense of what our family gatherings were like. As for my original goals for this essay, I don't remember what they were. I'm in the dark. It's been a dozen years since I wrote this, and since I don't keep drafts, I have no idea. I'm a poet. I like to move quickly, make collages of different realities and not spell everything out.

Personal essay has always been a part of American literature. I was just reading some of Hawthorne's sketches and had that view confirmed. Some experience cannot be done properly in either poetry or fiction, so this kind of writing will always be around.

My advice for new writers: Read a lot of books, and keep your eyes and ears open.

Prayer Dogs

TERRY TEMPEST WILLIAMS

■ ■

Prairie dogs. Prairie gods. Pleistocene mammals standing on their hind legs in the big wide open.

What do they see?

What do they smell?

What do they hear?

What they hear is the sound of a truck coming toward their town, the slamming of doors, the voices, the pressure of feet

■ ■

TERRY TEMPEST WILLIAMS'S most recent book, *The Open Space of Democracy* (Orion Society, 2004), reflects her thoughts on America in these times of war and terror. These essays focus on the power of deep listening and how engagement within our own communities becomes its own form of prayer. *Red: Patience and Passion in the Desert* (Pantheon, 2001) traces her lifelong love of and commitment to the desert, inspiring a soulful return to "wild mercy" and the spiritual and political commitment of preserving the fragile red-rock wilderness of southern Utah, where she lives with her husband. She is the recipient of both a John Simon Guggenheim Fellowship and a Lannan Literary Award in creative nonfiction.

walking toward them. What they see now inside their burrow is the well-worn sole of a boot, now the pointed toe of the boot kicking out the entrance to their burrow, blue Levi's bending down, gloved hands flicking a lighter, the flame, the heat, then the hands shoving something burning inside the entrance. Something is burning. They back up farther down their tunnel, smoke now curling inside the darkness as the boot is kicking dirt inside, closing their burrow, covering their burrow, tamping the entrance shut. They are running down, down, down, around. They cannot see. What they smell is fear, fear in the form of gas. They cough and wheeze, their eyes burning, their lungs burning, tightening, cramping. They try to run, try to turn, nowhere to turn, every one of them scurrying to escape, to flee, but all exits have been kicked closed. The toxic smoke is chasing them like an invisible snake promising an agonizing death, suffocation, strangulation, every organ in spasm, until they collapse into each other's bodies, noses covered in blankets of familiar fur, families, young and old, slowly, cruelly gassed to death.

The truck drives away. The American flag is waving, the red-white-and-blue banner in the American West that says the rights of private landowners take precedence over the lives of prairie dogs who are standing in the way of development.

Above ground, all quiet on the Western front.

Below ground, a massacre.

Nearly four hundred Utah prairie dogs disappeared in the summer of 1999 at the Cedar Ridge Golf Course. It is believed they were murdered, gassed to death. Two federal agents have been investigating the crime. This is a federal criminal offense. Penalties for killing or attempting to kill the federally protected animals range from fines of up to $100,000 to one year in prison. Some say the locals know who did it and are glad they did. Other locals are outraged. Both sides have offered rewards. One group has agreed to post bail for the offender; the other has offered a reward for the offender's arrest.

Gone. The prairie dogs are gone. Praise the Lord. Say it again with the Utah accent, "Praise the Lard." Fat. Fat Cats. Money. Money in the bank. The golf course, emerald green, with perfectly cropped lawn, is the crown jewel of the town in desert country.

Almost two years have passed. Nothing has been resolved. No one is talking. The Incident at Cedar Ridge has been all but forgotten. Cedar City takes pride in being a clean, wholesome town.

Utah prairie dogs, *Cynomys parvidens*, numbered more than 95,000 in the 1920s. By the 1960s their distribution was greatly reduced, the result of intensive poison-control campaigns administered by the Department of Agriculture, indiscriminate shooting, disease, and loss of habitat. By the 1960s it was estimated that only 3,300 Utah prairie dogs in thirty-seven separate colonies remained and that the species would be extinct by the year 2000. Because of the dramatic decline in its numbers and distribution, the species was classified as endangered on June 4, 1973. In the year 2000, the Utah prairie dog did not become extinct, but it continues to be threatened. Their numbers now are estimated at 4,582 individuals. Sixty-five percent of the population lives in Iron County, Utah. Eighty-six percent of all Utah prairie dogs live on private lands. The situation grows increasingly contentious between ranchers in southern Utah who want them exterminated because "the dogs are ruining the range," outside developers who want to cash in on the value of these open lands, and the federal agencies who must administer the Endangered Species Act. The hostile environment is fueled even further by the fact that southern Utah is one of the fastest-growing areas in the American West.

Iron County commissioner Gene Roundy said, "I think it's a crime against society that a prairie dog can move into your front yard and you can't take care of it."

Whose society?

The South African poet Breyten Breytenbach writes, "The real revolutionary question is 'What about the Other?' "

There is a lion with his mouth open. I walk through it and enter TOTE-EM-IN, a roadside attraction off Carolina Beach Road in Wilmington, North Carolina. We are on vacation. Having worked in a natural history museum for over a decade, I am eager to learn what they may house inside. The interstate zoo boasts of having "over one hundred exotic animals in a Dr. Dolittle atmosphere where you can 'talk with the animals.'"

The list is impressive: alligator, snapping turtle, painted turtle, box turtle, cottonmouth, king snake, corn snake, green rat snake, copperhead, spur-thighed tortoise, squirrel monkey, weeper capuchin, mandrill, jaguar, binturong, peccary, palm civet, kinkajou, python, black leopard, golden spider monkey, black spider monkey, Himalayan bear, Siberian tiger, Bennett's wallaby, Sitka deer, nilgai, camel, Patagonian cavy, zebra, aoudad, prairie dogs— my eye stops at a hometown species as the list continues.

"Where are your prairie dogs?" I ask the woman behind the counter of the gift shop inside.

"Out in back," she says. "We had two of our own and took two others in that belonged to someone else. We tried to slowly introduce them to one another, but it didn't work out."

"What do you mean?" I ask.

"I mean there are a lot of people who love prairie dogs, but they are more than they can handle; they're wild, after all. Some college students had them in their apartment, and the prairie dogs got out and made new tunnels in the heating ducts between apartments and escaped. They eventually found them and brought them to us, but they didn't get along with ours." She pauses. "It didn't work out—they died."

The woman is Sherrie Brewer. She and her husband, Jerry, run TOTE-EM-IN Zoo—bought it several years ago from George Tregemo, who started the zoo in 1952. Sherrie has kind eyes. Bucket in hand, she is on her way to feed the animals. "Come on out," she says. "I'll take you to the prairie dogs."

Wearing an orange knitted cap and a camouflage jacket, she pours the contents of the bucket into a yellow wheelbarrow, then lifts the wheelbarrow and steers it down the gravel aisle lined with cages on either side.

We walk past the squirrel monkeys and two black panthers pacing back and forth.

"Some weather we've had," she says. "Record snowstorms for North Carolina this month, after a siege of hurricanes last summer."

Sherrie stops at a hay-lined cage on wheels, six feet tall, maybe four feet wide, and makes kissing sounds with her lips.

"Where you at, little guy? You're hidden real good now, aren't you?"

We wait.

"It doesn't say much for us that we spread out so much and ruin all their natural habitat, and this is where these animals end up, does it?" she says.

The guinea hens are crying for more food. Peacocks in the background are yelling, *Halp! Halp!*

"There he is," she says. "Hi, little guy."

We bend down and I see a prairie dog peeking out from a garbage can that is turned on its side and covered with hay. He scurries back in.

"How old do you think he is?" I ask.

"Probably two years."

We wait a few more minutes.

He comes out again, walks toward me, sniffing, stands upright, nose twitching, tail vibrating like a metronome. A tractor comes toward the cart. The prairie dog runs back into the can and turns his back.

"I'll leave you alone. If you need anything, I'll be over by the cats."

In time the prairie dog comes back out and climbs the side of the cage, his fingers with long black nails grasping the chain links. I move closer and crouch down, eye to eye. This is the closest I have ever been to a prairie dog. It is also the only one I have seen in captivity.

My first impulse is to offer him something, anything. Without thinking, I click my tongue and offer my finger, which he takes. He just keeps staring. Eyes. His eyes. Black, unwavering eyes, like dark suns rising.

The characteristic mask is faded, a slight dusting of brown against beige. The black tip on his tail gives the species away. This is not a Utah prairie dog but a black-tailed prairie dog indigenous to the plains.

Suddenly he jumps down and begins chewing on hay, holding a piece in both hands. He is the color of dry grasses in the prairie, the desert, perfectly camouflaged, even in the hay.

Another visitor arrives. "How's my boy? How's my little boy, my little prairie-dog boy?"

The prairie dog climbs back up the side of the cage, and the man, obviously a regular, pokes his fingers inside to pat his stomach.

"Yes, that feels good, doesn't it? What a good boy. What a sweet boy, yes, yes. You don't get your belly rubbed every day, do you? Oh yeah, yeah, that's my sweet prairie-dog boy."

The prairie dog puts his cheek against the chain link and closes his eyes as the man continues to rub his stomach.

"I come here a lot," the man says.

Prairie dogs out—standing on mounds all along I-70 from Grand Junction, Colorado, to Cisco, Utah, just twenty-five miles from home. It's been a mild winter.

Sentinels. Up on their haunches. Arms folded. Some barking. Some foraging. Some running from mound to mound, their bodies rippling through the grasses. Others standing guard. Eagles may be near.

Today I am surprised by how large they seem. I keep thinking of the little one in North Carolina, held captive, his willingness to have his belly rubbed, his shy sociability, the brightness and intelligence of his eyes in spite of his surroundings, a cart of straw and a garbage can turned sideways.

Lewis and Clark wrote in 1804, during their journey west, that this "wild dog of the prairie . . . appears here in infinite numbers." Naturalist Ernest Thompson Seton estimated that prairie dogs numbered 5 billion in North America in the early 1900s. The largest prairie dog colony on record, in Texas, measured 100 miles wide and 250 miles long and contained an estimated 400 million prairie dogs.

Today the headlines in the *Rocky Mountain News* read: LITTLE HELP FOR PRAIRIE DOGS. In Colorado 98 percent of the prairie dog population is gone, as Colorado's Front Range is being developed from Boulder to Colorado Springs at an alarming rate. The U.S. Fish and Wildlife Service wants to list the black-tailed prairie dog as threatened, but they have no money for enforcement. Meanwhile developers of subdivisions and shopping malls are buying up land containing prairie dog towns as fast as possible, having them removed by companies such as Dog Gone (*dog suckers*, they are called, who come and vacuum the prairie dogs up into the back of an enclosed truck with padded walls, then release them outside of town or sell them as ferret food) and starting to build immediately, before any protective measure might make any further development against the law.

What the spotted owl is to the old-growth forests in the Pacific Northwest, the prairie dog is to the grasslands and prairies of Middle America. The prairie dog has become another "indicator species," sounding the alarm for a disappearing ecosystem. The difference, however, between the owl and the prairie dog is the difference of perception: owls are symbols of wisdom; prairie dogs are varmints.

There are five species of prairie dogs in North America: black-tailed, white-tailed, Gunnison's, Mexican, and the Utah prairie dog. All of them are sociable creatures. All of them are seriously threatened.

Prairie dogs evolved in the Pleistocene era and now represent the last of the Great Frontier. Historically, prairie dog towns followed the bison, aerating the soil after the great stampedes. These towns could range in size from one to one thousand acres. Many in the Great Plains seemed to spread as far as the horizon. Within these communities are family units called *coteries*. A coterie, consisting of a single adult male, one to four adult females, and offspring up to two years old, can occupy a territory up to about an acre.

As above, so below. One could consider the double life of prairie dogs.

Above ground, prairie dog colonies literally change the land. Mounds created from the excavation of burrows may be two feet high and ten feet in diameter. These serve as lookout posts and will keep the burrows dry from rain. Their communication system is sophisticated. Biologists have identified twelve different vocalizations and a variety of postures and behavioral displays. One researcher studying a Utah prairie dog population near Bryce Canyon National Park noted specific calls, distinguishing between the calls made when a truck versus a coyote crossed into their territory. When danger is near, a series of barks occur in a prairie dog chorus, often led by sentinel dogs guarding the periphery of the colony. The word spreads. They quickly scramble and scurry across the desert and disappear into nearby holes. When danger seems to have passed, a prairie dog will carefully emerge, look in all directions, then stand on its mound and throw back its head, with its hands raised in what looks like a gesture of prayer, and give what has been called a *jump-yip* call that the coast is clear.

It is also common to see prairie dogs engage in what looks like kissing. The "kiss" is used to distinguish one coterie member from another. When prairie dogs recognize each other, they will participate in elaborate grooming behavior. If one of the prairie dogs is an intruder, teeth may be bared, territory fought over, claimed, or reclaimed by dominant males. In most cases the outsider flees.

Below ground, a burrow will typically be three to six feet deep and about fifteen feet long, although the size varies tremendously, depending on the landscape. Prairie dogs will often dig small chambers to the side of the main burrow where they can listen to what is going on above. Deeper inside the burrows, they make nests out of grasses they have pulled under, where they will sleep, give birth, and care for their young (four is the norm) in spring, with the babies usually not emerging until June. Native grasses make up 70 to 95 percent of their diet during the summer, changing to seeds and insects, even roots, as fall and winter approach. Unlike other members in the ground squirrel family, prairie dogs do not hibernate but rather lie dormant inside their network of burrows.

Prairie dogs create habitat not only for themselves but also for other grassland species. With their mounds and extensive burrowing systems (black-tailed prairie dogs typically have thirty to fifty burrow entrances per acre, while Gunnison's and white-tailed prairie dogs have fewer than twenty), their underground world is not simply the haunt of prairie dogs but home to myriad other creatures as well. One study of black-tailed prairie dogs identified more than 140 species of wildlife associated with prairie dog towns, including bison, pronghorn antelope, burrowing owls, pocket mice, deer mice, ants, black widow spiders, and horned larks, and many predators, such as rattlesnakes, golden eagles, badgers, bobcats, weasels, foxes, coyotes, and black-footed ferrets. In a grassland community historically tamped down by the weight of stampeding bison, burrowing prairie dogs loosen and aerate the soil, keeping the land supple. In the spring and summer, they also spend most of their time foraging above ground. A single prairie dog may consume two pounds of green grasses and forbs per week. Their hunger alters the landscape.

Prairie dogs' digging and scratching stimulates the soil, creating greater opportunities for seeds to germinate. With heightened water drainage due to the tunnels, plants grow. Plant diversity follows. Animal diversity follows the plants. Meadowlarks appear with an appetite for grasshoppers. Grasshopper sparrows appear in the abundance of seeds. Vacant or abandoned prairie dog burrows become the homes of cottontails, kangaroo rats, and deer mice. Burrowing owls, with their long, spindly legs, stand on the former mounds of prairie dogs with an eye for the multiplying mice. One successful life inspires another, creating the strength of a grassland community. If the prairie dog goes, so goes an entire ecosystem, including the black-footed ferret and burrowing owl, which now are endangered and threatened species.

Prairie dogs create diversity. Destroy them, and you destroy a varied world.

On my desk I have a small constellation of bones bleached by the sun. They belong to a prairie dog: a skull with the jaw intact, two femur bones about the length of my little finger, and two tibia, one broken in half. Alkaline sand from the Cisco desert still shakes out of the tiniest pores and teeth.

What is distinctive about this skull is the size of the eye socket. It is enormous in proportion to the rest of the skull. What does this vulnerable and venerable being see?

Niles Eldredge, a curator at the American Museum of Natural History, writes:

> We are living amid a sixth extinction, one that, according to the Harvard biologist E. O. Wilson, is costing the earth some 30,000 species a year. Biologists estimate that there are at least 10 million species on earth right now. At this rate, the vast majority of the species on earth today will be gone by the next millennium.

What are we to do?

The prairie dog is not a charismatic species, not a grizzly bear or wolf or whale. It is a rodent. We have gassed prairie dogs, poisoned them, and used them as targets. My own family calls them pop guts, which is what happens when you shoot them in the stomach. Their bodies are left to rot. They are expendable, despised, a lowly caste of animals, "the untouchables."

A headline in the March 7, 2001, edition of the *Denver Post* reads: JUDGE LIMITS KILL TO PRAIRIE DOG. The article explains that a district judge has issued a temporary restraining order halting the extermination of a prairie dog colony because of the danger to other animals. A state law protects all animals except rodents and birds from poisoning and trapping.

The issues circling the Utah prairie dog are the same ones shaping politics and culture in the American West. How do we define justice? How do we view progress? What kind of world do we want to maintain, and what kind of world do we want to create? Is economics the only standard by which we measure society's values? Or is it possible to adopt another ethical structure that extends our notion of community to include a compassion toward all species?

The fate of the prairie dog is caught in the middle of an ethical war: traditional farming and ranching practices, continued growth and sprawl versus ecological sustainability. Bull's-eye. Hit or miss?

What will we miss?

In 1950 government agents proposed to get rid of prairie dogs on some parts of the Navajo reservation in order to protect the roots of the sparse desert grasses and thereby maintain some marginal grazing for sheep. The Navajo elders objected, insisting, "If you kill all the prairie dogs, there will be no one to cry for the rain."

The amused officials assured the Navajo there was no correlation between rain and prairie dogs and carried out their plan. The outcome surprised only the federal officials. The desert near Chilchinbito, Arizona, became a virtual wasteland with very little grass. Without the ground-turning process of the burrowing animals, the soil became solidly packed, unable to accept rain. Hardpan. The result: fierce runoff whenever it rained. What sparse vegetation there was, was carried off by flooding waters.

J. M. Coetzee, in *The Lives of Animals*, creates a character named Elizabeth Costello, a novelist, who defends the rights of animals before a skeptical university audience. She says, "There is no limit to the extent to which we can think ourselves into the being of another."

A professor of philosophy, Dr. Thomas O'Hearne, responds, "We may certainly wish for there to be community with animals, but that is not the same thing as living in community with them. It is just a piece of prelapsarian wistfulness."

Readers familiar with Coetzee's work as a South African writer know the passionate stance against apartheid, racism, and specism that appear in such novels as *Waiting for the Barbarians* and *Disgrace*. Coetzee writes of a dream:

> *In the dream I stand again in a pit. The earth is damp, dark, water seeps up, my feet squelch, it costs me a slow effort to lift them. I feel under surface, searching for the bones. My hand comes up with the corner of a jute sack, black, rotten, which crumbles away between my fingers. I dip back into the ooze. . . . A dead bird, a parrot: I hold it by the tail, its bedraggled feathers hang down, its soggy wings droop, its eye sockets are empty. When I release it, it falls through the surface without a splash. "Poisoned water," I think. "I must be careful not to drink here. I must not touch my right hand to my mouth."*

A poisoned world. We are living in an increasingly toxic world, not just physically but emotionally. It is not a comfortable connection to make for most people: the ill-treatment of human beings and the mistreatment of animals. Both responses belong to arrogance, a lack of respect for life in all its diversity and complexity. We would rather not think too much about "what is being done to those outside the sphere of the favored group," yet I believe we can make a strong case for the extension of our empathy toward "the Other."

Schopenhauer writes:

> *Boundless compassion for all living beings is the firmest and surest guarantee of pure moral conduct, and needs no casuistry . . . May all living beings remain free from pain.*

I think about my encounters with prairie dogs, both inside a cage and in the wild. I think about what they know in their bodies that has nothing to do with morals or ethics or any manner of abstractions, how they sing and chatter, kiss and caress and groom each other's fur, the interactions within their own families and the community at large, all this in the high desertlands of Utah, where eagles stand watch and coyotes skirt the periphery of prairie dog towns. They are surviving, and given half a chance, they will survive us.

I believe prairie dogs know joy and fear and love and pain and that it is communicated within their tribe from every muscle and multiplying cell. All one has to do is stand on a bluff and listen to prairie dogs call back and forth to one another—this midday chatter, alongside meadowlarks and grasshoppers. Prairie dogs respond with their bodies, not with reason. It is a kinetic encounter, not an abstract one.

Call it instinct.

Call it "embodied knowledge."

Call it survival.

Prairie dogs know when they are safe, and they know when they are in danger.

Do we?

The Incident at Cedar Ridge haunts me. That boot, that hand, that hand that lit the cartridge of gas and shoved it inside the burrow of the prairie dog town and allowed them to "disappear," is my own hand if I choose to do nothing in the wake of those murders.

I want to live and love in a varied world. I want to encounter Prairie Dog People, Bear People, Raven People, Deer People, too, in the wild and near our homes and not be embarrassed by feelings of kinship that in our cynical world are viewed as sentimental.

"One sort of love does not need to block another," Mary Midgley writes in *Animals and Why They Matter*, "because love, like compassion, is not a rare fluid to be economized, but a capacity which grows by use."

I cannot imagine the loneliness and cultural isolation we will suffer if we choose to live only in a world of our own making.

Without the diversity of the other-than-human world, without the individual intelligences and grace of other animals, our own intelligence and imagination are diminished.

We, too, are animals. We have evolved together. We evolved even with prairie dogs during the Pleistocene era. Can we not continue our shared evolution, even the evolution of our own compassion? To deny our own animalness is to deny our both humble and powerful place in the scheme of life.

How do we wish to live, and with whom?

Once when I was walking the land near my home, a neighbor

came up to me and said, "Have you seen any of them prayer dogs lately?"

"No," I said. "Not here."

"Damn if they didn't used to be a nuisance."

ON *"Prayer Dogs"* BY TERRY TEMPEST WILLIAMS

Describing the work of Edward Abbey, Terry Tempest Williams wrote, "He is always reminding us that 'sentiment without action is the ruin of the soul.'" We might say the same of Williams' own essays. Her work fits squarely in the Abbey tradition, for she writes lyrically, spiritually about landscape, but she also writes with conscience, and with an urgency to act.

"Prayer Dogs," a perfect fusion of Williams' roles as author, naturalist, and activist, first appeared in *Creative Nonfiction* 19, Diversity Dialogues. As she famously did in her now-classic 1991 book, *Refuge*, Williams writes with a deeply personal voice about an urgent ecological crisis. In *Refuge*, it is the destruction of a migratory bird habitat at wetlands near Great Salt Lake in northern Utah. In "Prayer Dogs," it is the extermination of the white-tailed prairie dog.

While writing the essay, Williams joined with conservation groups to petition the U.S. Fish and Wildlife Service to list the white-tailed prairie dog under the Endangered Species Act. She also helped to formally petition the Bureau of Land Management to designate key white-tailed prairie dog colonies—in Utah, where Williams lives, and in Wyoming and Colorado—as Areas of Critical Environmental Concern. After publishing "Prayer Dogs" in *Creative Nonfiction*, Williams reworked the piece as an op-ed in the

New York Times ("In the Shadow of Extinction," February 2, 2003). "Prairie dogs have a great deal to teach us about the nature of communities," she writes. "When asked to write an essay on diversity, I could think of no greater example than a prairie dog colony to illustrate this point. Over 140 species of wildlife have been associated with prairie dog towns, including bison, pronghorn antelope, burrowing owls, pocket mice, deer mice, ants, black widow spiders, horned larks, and predators such as rattlesnakes, golden eagles, badgers, bobcats, weasels, foxes, coyotes, and specifically black-footed ferrets. . . . Prairie dogs create community. Destroy them and you destroy a varied world."—*Jessica Mesman*

What Is It We Really Harvestin' Here?

NTOZAKE SHANGE

▪ ▪

We got a sayin', "The blacker the berry, the sweeter the juice," which is usually meant as a compliment. To my mind, it also refers to the delectable treats we as a people harvested for our owners and for our own selves all these many years, slave or free. In fact, we knew something about the land, sensuality, rhythm, and ourselves that has continued to elude our captors—puttin' aside all our treasures in the basement of the British Museum, or the Met, for that matter. What am I talkin' about? A different approach to the force of gravity, to our bodies, and what we produce: a reverence for the efforts of the group and the intimate couple. Harvesttime and Christmas were prime occasions for

▪ ▪

NTOZAKE SHANGE was born Paulette Williams. In 1971 she changed her name to Ntozake Shange, which means "she who comes with her own things" and "she who walks like a lion" in Xhosa, the Zulu language. She has written plays, poetry, novels, and essays. She has taught at California State College, the City College of New York, the University of Houston, Rice University, Yale, Howard, and New York University. Among her many awards are an Obie, a *Los Angeles Times* Book Prize for Poetry, and a Pushcart Prize.

courtin'. A famine, a drought, a flood, or Lent do not serve as inspiration for couplin', you see.

The Juba, a dance of courtin' known in slave quarters of North America and the Caribbean, is a phenomenon that stayed with us through the jitterbug, the wobble, the butterfly, as a means of courtin' that's apparently very colored, and very "African." In fact we still have it and we've never been so "integrated"—the *Soul Train* dancers aren't all black anymore, but the dynamic certainly is. A visitor to Cuba in Lynne Fauley Emery's *Dance Horizon Book* described the Juba as a series of challenges.

> A woman advances and commencing a slow dance, made up of shuffling of the feet and various contortions of the body, thus challenges a rival from among the men. One of these, bolder than the rest, after a while steps out, and the two then strive which shall tire the other; the woman performing many feats which the man attempts to rival, often excelling them, amid the shouts of the rest. A woman will sometimes drive two or three successive beaux from the ring, yielding her place at length to some impatient belle.

John Henry went up against a locomotive, but decades before we simply were up against ourselves and the elements. And so we are performers in the fields, in the kitchens, by kilns, and for one another. Sterling Stuckey points out, in *Slave Culture*, however, that by 1794 "it was illegal to allow slaves to dance and drink on the premises . . . without the written consent of their owners," the exceptions being Christmas and the burials, which are communal experiences. And what shall we plant and harvest, so that we might "hab big times duh fus hahves, and duh fus ting wut growed we take tuh duh church so as ebrybody could hab a pieces ub it. We pray over it and shout. Wen we hab a dance, we use tuh shout in a rinig. We ain't have wutyuh call a propuh dance tuday."

Say we've gone about our owners' business. Planted and harvested his crop of sugarcane, remembering that the "ration of slaves/sugar was ten times that of slaves/tobacco and slaves/cotton." That to plant a sugar crop we have to dig a pit three feet square and a few inches deep into which one young plant is set. Then, of course, the thing has to grow. A mature sugarcane plant is three to nine feet tall. That's got to be cut at exactly the right point. Then we've got to crush it, boil it, refine it, from thick black syrup to fine white sugar, to make sure, as they say in Virginia, that we "got the niggah out." Now it's time to tend to our own gardens. Let's grow some sweet potatoes to "keep the niggah alive."

SWEET POTATOES

Like everything else, we have to start with something. Now we need a small piece of potato with at least one of those scraggly roots hanging about for this native Central American tuber. This vegetable will stand more heat than almost any other grown in the United States. It does not take to cool weather, and any kind of frost early or seasonal will kill the leaves, and if your soil gets cold the tubers themselves will not look very good. Get your soil ready at least two weeks before planting, weeding, turning, and generally disrupting the congealed and solid mass we refer to as dirt, so that your hands and the tubers may move easily through the soil, as will water and other nutrients.

Once the soil is free of winter, two weeks after the last frost, plant the potato slips in 6-to-12-inch ridges, 3 to 4.5 feet apart. Separate the plants by 9 to 12 inches. If we space the plants more than that, our tubers may be grand, but way too big to make good use of in the kitchen. We should harvest our sweet potatoes when the tubers are not quite ripe, but of good size, or we can wait until the vines turn yellow.

Don't handle our potatoes too roughly, which could lead to bruising and decay. If a frost comes upon us unexpectedly, take those potatoes out the ground right away. Our potatoes will show marked improvement during storage, which allows the starch in them to turn to sugar. Nevertheless, let them lie out in the open for 2 to 3 hours to fully dry. Then move them to a moist and warm storage space. The growing time for our crop'll vary from 95 to 125 days.

The easiest thing to do with a sweet potato is to bake it. In its skin. I coat the thing with olive oil, or butter in a pinch. Wrap it in some aluminum foil, set it in the oven at 400 degrees. Wait till I hear sizzling, anywhere from 45 minutes to an hour after, in a very hot oven. I can eat it with my supper at that point or I can let it cool off for later. (One of the sexiest dates I ever went on was to the movies to see El Mariachi. My date brought along chilled baked sweet potatoes and ginger beer. Much nicer than canola-sprayed "buttered" popcorn with too-syrupy Coca-Cola, wouldn't you say?)

MUSTARD GREENS

No, they are not the same as collards. We could say they, with their frilly edges and sinuous shapes, have more character, are more flirtatious, than collards. This green can be planted in the spring or the fall, so long as the soil is workable (not cold). It's not a hot weather plant, preferring short days and temperate climates. We can use the same techniques for mustard greens that we use for lettuce. Sowing the seeds in rows 12 to 18 inches apart, seedlings 4 to 8 inches apart. These plants should get lots of fertilizer to end up tender, lots of water, too. They should be harvested before they are fully mature. Now, you've got to be alert, because mustard greens grow fast, 25 to 40 days from the time you set them in the soil to harvest. When it comes time to reap what you've sown, gather the outer leaves when they are 3 to 4 inches long, tender enough; let the inner leaves then develop more or wait till it's hot and harvest the whole plant.

Now we cook the mustard greens just like the collards, or we don't have to cook it at all. This vegetable is fine in salads or on sandwiches and soups. If you shy away from pungent tastes, mix these greens with some collards, kale, or beet greens. That should take some of the kick out of them. I still like my peppers and vinegar, though. If we go back, pre-Columbus, the Caribs did, too. According to Spanish travelers, the Caribs, who fancied vegetables, added strong peppers called aji-aji to just about everything. We can still find aji-aji on some sauces from Spanish-speaking countries if we read the labels carefully. Like "La Morena." So appropriate.

WATERMELON

The watermelon is an integral part of our actual life as much as it is a feature of our stereotypical lives in the movies, posters, racial jokes, toys, and early American portraits of the "happy darky." We could just as easily been eatin' watermelon in D. W. Griffith's Birth of a Nation as chicken legs. The implications are the same. Like the watermelon, we were a throwback to "African" prehistory, which isn't too off, since Lucy, the oldest Homo sapiens currently known, is from Africa, too.

But I remember being instructed not to order watermelon in restaurants or to eat watermelon in any public places because it makes white people think poorly of us. They already did that, so I don't see what the watermelon was going to precipitate. Europeans brought watermelon with them from Africa anyway. In Massachusetts by 1629 it was recorded as "abounding." In my rebelliousness as a child, I got so angry about the status of the watermelon, I tried to grow some in the flower box on our front porch in Missouri. My harvest was minimal to say the least.

Here's how you can really grow you some watermelon. They like summer heat, particularly sultry, damp nights. If we can grow watermelons, we can grow ourselves almost any other kind of melon. The treatment is the same. Now, these need some space, if we're looking *for a refrigerator-sized melon or one ranging from 25 to 30 pounds. Let them have a foot between plants in between rows 4 to 6 feet apart. They need a lot of fertilizer, especially if the soil is heavy and doesn't drain well. When the runners (vines) are a foot to a foot and a half long, fertilize again about 8 inches from the plant itself. Put some more fertilizer when the first melons appear. Watermelons come in different varieties, but I'm telling you about the red kind. I have no primal response to a golden or blanched-fleshed melon. Once your melons set on the vines and start to really take up some space, be sure not to forget to water the vines during the ripening process.*

When is your watermelon ripe? You can't tell by thumping it nor by the curly tail at the point where the melon is still on the vine. The best way to know if your melon is ready is by looking at the bottom. The center turns from a light yellow to deep amber. Your melon'll have a powdery or mushy tasteless sorta taste if you let it ripen too long.

Surely you've seen enough pictures or been to enough picnics to know how to eat a watermelon, so I won't insult you with that information. However, there is a fractious continuing debate about whether to sprinkle sugar or salt on your watermelon slice. I am not going to take sides in this matter.

Some of us were carried to the New World specifically because we knew 'bout certain crops, knew 'bout the groomin' and harvestin' of rice, for instance.

Plantation owners were perfectly aware of the superiority . . . of African slaves from rice country. Littlefield [a journalist] writes that "as early as 1700 ships from Carolina were reported in the Gambia River". . . . In a letter dated 1756, Henry Laurens, a Charleston merchant, wrote, "The slaves from the River Gambia are prefer'd to all others with us save the Gold Coast." The previous year he had written: "Gold

Coast or Gambias are best; next to them the Windward Coast are prefer'd to Angolas."

These bits of information throw an entirely different, more dignified light on "colored" cuisine for me. Particularly since I was raised on rice and my mother's people on both sides are indefatigable Carolinians, South, to be exact, South Carolinians. To some, our "phrenologically immature brains" didn't have consequence until our mastery of the cultivation of "cargo," "patna," "joponica," and finally Carolina rice, "small-grained, rather long and wiry, and remarkably white," was transferred to the books and records of our owners. Nevertheless, our penchant for rice was not dampened by its relationship to our bondage. Whether through force or will, we held on to our rice-eatin' heritage. I repeat, I was raised on rice. If I was Joe Williams, insteada singin' "Every day, every day, I sing the blues," I'd be sayin', "Oh, every day, almost any kinda way, I get my rice."

My poor mother, Eloise, Ellie, for short, made the mistake of marrying a man who was raised by a woman from Canada. So every day, he wanted a potato, some kinda potato, mashed, boiled, baked, scalloped, fried, just a potato. Yet my mother was raising a sixth generation of Carolinians, which meant we had to eat some kinda rice. Thus, Ellie was busy fixing potato for one and rice for all the rest every day, until I finally learnt how to do one or the other and gave her a break. I asked Ellie Williams how her mother, Viola, went about preparing the rice for her "chirren"—a low-country linguistic lapse referring to offspring like me. Anyway, this is what Mama said.

MAMA'S RICE

"We'd buy some rice in a brown paper bag (this is in the Bronx). Soak it in a bit of water. Rinse it off and cook it the same way we do now."

"How is that, Ma?" I asked. "Well, you boil a certain amount of water. Let it boil good. Add your rice and let it boil till tender. Stirring every so often because you want the water to evaporate. You lift your pot. You can tell if your rice is okay because there's no water there. Then you fluff it with a fork. You want every kind, extra, extra, what you call it. No ordinary olive oil will do.

"Heat this up. Just a little bit of it. You don't want no greasy rice, do you? Heat this until, oh, it is so hot that the smoke is coming quick. Throw in 3 to 4 cloves garlic, maybe 1 cup chopped onion too, I forgot. Let that sizzle and soften with 1/2 cup each cilantro, pimiento, and everything. But don't let this get burned, no. So add your 4 cups water and 2 cups rice. Turn up the heat some more till there's a great boiling of rice, water, seasonings. The whole thing. Then leave it alone for a while with the cover on so all the rice cooks even. Now, when you check and see there's only a small bit of water left in the bottom of the pot, stir it all up. Turn the heat up again and wait. When there's no water left at all, at all. Just watch the steam coming up. Of course you should have a good pegau by now, but the whole pot of your rice should be delicioso, ready even for my table. If you do as I say."

For North Americans, a pot with burnt rice on the bottom is a scary concept. But all over the Caribbean, it's a different story entirely. In order to avoid making asopao—a rice moist and heavy with the sofrito or tomato-achiote mixture, almost like a thick soup where the rice becomes one mass instead of standing, each grain on its own—it is necessary to let the rice on the bottom of the pot get a crustlike bottom, assuring that all moisture has evaporated. My poor North American mother, Ellie, chastises me frequently for "ruining" good rice with all this spice. Then I remind her that outside North America we Africans were left to cook in ways that reminded us of our mother's cooking, not Jane Austen's characters. The rice tastes different, too. But sometimes I cheat and simply use Goya's Sazón—after all, I'm a modern woman. I shouldn't say that too loudly, though. Mathilde can hear all the way from her front porch any blasphemous notion I have about good cooking. No, it is her good cooking that I am to learn. I think it is more than appropriate that we know something about some of the crops that led to most of us African descendants of the Diaspora, being here, to eat anything at all.

But rather than end on a sour note, I am thinking of my classes with the great Brazilian dancer, choreographer, and teacher Mercedes Baptista at the now-legendary Clark Center. We learned a harvest dance, for there are many, but the movements of this celebratory ritual were lyrical and delicate, far from the tortured recounts of Euro-Americans to our "jigaboo" gatherings; no gyrations, repetitive shuffling that held no interest. Indeed, the simple movement of the arms, which we worked on for days until we got it, resembled a tropical port de bras worthy of any ballerina. Our hip movements, ever so subtle, with four switches to the left, then four to the right, all the while turning and covering space. The head leaning in the direction of the hips, the arms moving against it, till the next hip demanded counterpoint.

A healthy respect for the land, for what we produce for the blessing of a harvest, begot dances of communal joy. On New Year's Eve in the late fifties, we danced the Madison; today it's a burning rendition of "the Electric Slide." Eighty-year-olds jammin' with toddlers after the weddin' toast. No, we haven't changed so much.

ON *"What Is It We Really Harvestin' Here?"*
BY NTOZAKE SHANGE

Ntozake Shange, playwright, novelist, poet, and young adult author, crosses genres freely in her work, often within the same piece. *for colored girls who have considered suicide/when the rainbow is enuf,* combined poetry and ritual for the theater; it was performed on Broadway and won an Obie Award in 1977. "What Is It We Really Harvestin' Here?" which originally appeared in *Creative Nonfiction* 9, The Universal Chord, is a cookbook, cultural history, and memoir in less than ten pages.

"I used to have boundaries up all the time, which is limiting," she told an interviewer. "I never want to feel limited. If anything is life-changing, being the descendant of a slave is. I went into therapy ten years ago because I needed to work that out. I've gotten better. Everything about me is more fluid, much less rigid. I'm gonna do everything I can, feel everything I can, until it hurts. Then I'll stop. All they did was buy us—it's not an honor, it's just something that happened. Our gifts belong to us."

"What Is It We Really Harvestin' Here?" was excerpted from *If I Can Cook/You Know God Can,* a history, in food, of the African Diaspora. It's also a damn good cookbook, even for beginners, with useful recipes for "collard greens to bring you money" and *asopao—* a Caribbean rice dish that is even better when you burn the bottom of the pot.—*Jessica Mesman*

The Brown Study

RICHARD RODRIGUEZ

. .

Or, as a brown man, I think.

But do we really think that color colors thought? Sherlock Holmes occasionally retired to a "brown study"—a kind of moribund funk; I used to imagine a room with brown wallpaper. I think, too, of the process—the plunger method—by which coffee sometimes is brewed. The grounds commingle with water for a time and then are pressed to the bottom of the carafe by a disk or plunger. The liquid, cleared of sediment, is nevertheless colored, substantially coffee. (And *coffee-colored* has come to mean coffee-and-cream-colored; and coffee with the admixture of

. .

RICHARD RODRIGUEZ is an editor at Pacific News Service and a contributing editor for *Harper's* magazine, *U.S. News & World Report*, and the Sunday "Opinion" section of the *Los Angeles Times*. He has published numerous articles in the *New York Times*, the *Wall Street Journal*, the *American Scholar*, *Time*, *Mother Jones*, and the *New Republic*, as well as other publications. He has also written three books: *Brown: The Last Discovery of America*, *Hunger of Memory*, and *Days of Obligation: An Argument with My Mexican Father*, as well as two BBC documentaries. He lives in San Francisco.

cream used to be called *blond*. And vanilla has come to mean white, bland, even though vanilla extract, to the amazement of children, is brown as iodine, and *vanilla-colored*, as in Edith Sitwell's "where vanilla-coloured ladies ride," refers to Manila and to brown skin.) In the case of brown thought, though, I suppose experience becomes the pigment, the grounds, the mise-en-scène, the medium of refraction, the speed of passage of otherwise pure thought.

In a fluorescent-lit jury room attached to a superior court in San Francisco, two jurors were unconvinced and unmoving. I was unconvinced because of the gold tooth two bank tellers had noticed. The other juror was a man late in his twenties—rather preppy, I thought on first meeting—who prefaced his remarks with, "As a black man, I think . . . "

I have wondered, ever since, if that were possible. If I do have brown thoughts.

Not brown enough. I was once taken to task—rather, I was made an example of—by that woman from the *Threepenny Review* as the sort of writer, the callow, who parades his education. I use literary allusion as a way of showing off, proof that I have mastered a white idiom, whereas the true threepenny intellectual assumes everybody knows everything, or doesn't, or can't, or shouldn't, or needn't, and there you are. Which makes me a sort of monkey-do.

Well, you see, I thought I was supposed to. I wasn't decorating my remarks. Was I too eager to join the conversation? It's only now I realize there is no conversation. Allusion is bounded by spell-check.

After such a long education, most perceptions authentically "remind." And I'm not the only one. The orb Victoria held in her hand has passed to her brown children, who, like Christ children in old paintings, toy with the world a bit, and then, when no one is looking, pop it into their mouths. The only person I know for whom the novels of Trollope are urgent lives in India.

It is interesting, too, to wonder whether what is white about my thought is impersonation, minstrelsy. Is allusion inauthentic, Ms. Interlocutor, when it comes from a brown sensibility? My eyes are brown. *Cheeks of tan?*

Most bookstores have replaced disciplinary categories with racial identification, or sexual. In either case I must be shelved Brown. The most important theme of my writing now is impurity. My mestizo boast: as a queer, Catholic, Indian Spaniard at home in a temperate Chinese city in a fading blond state in a post-Protestant nation, I live up to my sixteenth-century birth.

The future is brown, is my thesis—is as brown as the tarnished past. Brown may be as refreshing as green. We shall see. L.A., unreal city, is brown already, though it wasn't the other day I was there—it was rain-rinsed and as bright as a dark age. But on many days, the air turns fuscous from the scent glands of planes and from Lexus musk. The pavements, the palisades—all that jungly stuff one sees in the distance—are as brown as an oxidized print of a movie—brown as old Roman gardens or pennies in a fountain, brown as gurgled root beer, tobacco, monkey fur, catarrh.

We are accustomed, too, to thinking of antiquity as brown, browning. Darkening, as memory darkens, as the Dark Ages were dark. They weren't, of course; they were highly painted and rain-rinsed. We just don't remember clearly. I seem to remember the ceiling, how dark it was. How tall it seemed. The kitchen ceiling. And how frail we are! What used to be there? A shoe store? A newsstand? I seem to remember it, right about here . . . a red spine, wasn't it? Have I felt that before? Or is this cancer?

At last, the white thought, the albin pincer—pain—an incipient absence, like a puddle of milk or the Milky Way. *The glacier knocks in the cupboard*. Why is cancer the white ghost? Why are ghosts white? And what year was that? Which play? Well, obviously it's Shakespeare. *Lear? Cymbeline? Golden lads and girls all must* . . . Death is black. Coffee may be black, but black is not descriptive of coffee. Coffee is not descriptive of death. Can one's life be brown? My eyes are brown, but my life? Youth is green, and optimism; Gatsby believed in the green light.

Whereas there is brown at work in all the works of man. By the eighteenth century, the majority of Mexico was mestizo, neither "pure" Indian nor "pure" Spaniard—brown. Time's passage is brown. Decomposition. Maggots. Foxing—the bookman's term—reddish brown, reynard. Manuscripts, however jewel-like, from Dark Ages, will darken. Venice will darken. Celluloid darkens, as if the lamp of the projector were insufficient sun. College blue books. Fugitive colors. My parents!

If we wish to antique an image, to make memory of it, we print it in sepia tone—sepia, an extract from the occluding ink of the octopus, of the cuttlefish, now an agent for kitsch. Whereas the colors, the iridescent Blakes at the Tate, are housed now in perpetual gloom, lest colors be lifted from the page by the cutpurse sun. The Kodachrome prints in your closet—those high-skied and hopeful summer days—are dimming their lights, and the skies are lowering. Would we be astounded by the quality of light in 1922?

> *Unreal City*
> *Under the brown fog of a winter dawn,*
> *A crowd flowed over London Bridge, so many,*
> *I had not thought death had undone so many.*

The prince had always liked his London, when it had come to him. And it had come to him that morning with a punctual, unembarrassed rap at the door, a lamp switched on in the sitting room, a trolley forced over the threshold, chiming its cups and its spoons. The valet, second floor, in alto, Hindu Cockney—and with a startled professionalism (I am browner than he)—proposed to draw back the drapes, brown, thick as theater curtains.

Outside the hotel, several floors down, a crowd of blue- and green-haired teenagers kept a dawn vigil for a glimpse of their Faerie Queene. Indeed, as the valet fussed with the curtain, they recommenced their chant of "Mah-don-ahh. Mah-don-ahh."

Madonna was in town and staying at this hotel. All day and all night, the approach or departure of any limousine elicited the tribute.

Mah-don-ahh was in town making a film about Eva Perón (both women familiar with the uses of peroxide. Not such a bad thing to know in the great brown world, Oi, mate?).

I was in London because my book had just come out there. My book about Mexico. Not a weight on most British minds.

Did I ever tell you about my production of *The Tempest*? I had been at the theater the previous evening. Not *The Tempest* but the new Stoppard, and I watched with keener interest as the Asian in front of me leaned over to mouth little babas into the be-ringed ear of his Cockney hire. One such confidence actually formed a bubble. Which in turn reminded me of my production of *The Tempest*. (South Sea Bubble.) I would cast Maggie Smith as Miranda—wasted cheeks and bugging eyes—a buoyant Miss Haversham, sole valedictorian of her papa's creepy seminary. Caliban would be Johnny Depp. No fish scales, no seaweed, no webbed fingers, no claws, no vaudeville. No clothes. Does anybody know what I'm talking about? Ah, me. I am alone in my brown study. I can say anything I like. Nobody listens.

Will there be anything else, sir?

No, nothing else, thank you.

Brown people know there is nothing in the world—no recipe, no water, no city, no motive, no lace, no locution, no candle, no corpse that does not—I was going to say descend—that does not become brown. Brown might, as well, be making.

My little Caliban book, as I say, bound in iguana hide, was about Mexico. With two newspapers under my arm, and balancing a cup of coffee, I went back to my bed. I found the book section; I found the review. I knew it! I read first the reviewer's bio: a gay Colombian writer living in London.

What the book editor had done—dumb London book editor of the *Observer* had done, as Kansas City does and Manhattan does—is find my double, or the closest he could find, in Greater London. It's a kind of doppelgänger theory of literary criticism and it's dishearteningly fashionable among the liberal-hearted. In our age of "diversity," the good and the liberal organize diversity. Find a rhyme for orange. If one is singular or outlandish, by this theorem, one can't be reviewed at all. Worse than that, if one is unlike, one will not be published. Publishers look for the next, rather than the first, which was accident. But the *Observer* wasn't even within bow-range. Their gay gaucho was clueless.

The liberal-hearted who run the newspapers and the university English departments and organize the bookstores have turned literature into well-meaning sociology. Thus do I get invited by the editor at some magazine to review your gay translation of a Colombian who has written a magical-realist novel. Trust me, there has been little magical realism in my life since my first trip to Disneyland.

That warm winter night in Tucson. My reading was scheduled for the six-thirty slot by the University of Arizona. A few hundred people showed up—old more than young, mostly brown. I liked my "them," in any case, for coming to listen, postponing their dinners. In the middle of a paragraph, a young man stood to gather his papers, then retreated up the aisle, pushed open the door at the back of the auditorium. In the trapezoid of lobby light thus revealed, I could see a crowd was forming for the eight o'clock reading—a lesbian poet. Then the door closed, silently sealing the present. I continued reading but wondered to myself, Why couldn't I get the lesbians for an evening? And the lesbian poet serenade my Mexican-American audience? Wouldn't that be truer to the point of literature?

Well, what's the difference? I do not see myself as a writer in the world's eye, much less a white writer, much less a Hispanic writer, much less "a writer" in the 92nd Street Y sense. I'd rather be Madonna. Really, I would.

The Frankfurt Book Fair has recently been overrun with Koreans and Indians who write in English (the best English novelist in the world is not British at all but a Mahogany who lives in snowy Toronto and writes of Bombay). Inevitably, the pale conclusion is that brown writers move "between" cultures. I resist *between*, prefer *among* or *because of*. You keep the handicap. After all, it has taken several degrees of contusion to create a jaundice as pervasive as mine. It has taken a lifetime of compromises, the thinning of hair, the removal last year of a lesion from my scalp, the assurance of loneliness, the difficulty of prayer, an amused knowledge of five-star hotels—and death—and a persistence of childish embarrassments and evermore prosaic Roman Catholic hymns, to entertain a truly off-white thought. Here comes one now. *Un marron!*

No, I guess not. There's a certain amount of "So what?" that comes with middle age. But is that brown thought?

Thus did literary ambition shrivel in my heart, in a brown room in a creamy hotel in London, constructed as a nineteenth-century hospital and recently renovated to resemble a Victorian hotel that never existed except in the minds of a Hispanic author from California and a blond movie star from New Jersey.

Eve's apple, or what was left of it, quickly browned.

"Christ! A white doorway!" was Bukowski's recollection of having taken a bite of the apple. When Eve looked again, she saw a brown crust had formed over the part where she had eaten and invited Adam's lip. It was then she threw the thing away from her. Thenceforward (the first Thenceforward), Brown informed everything she touched.

Don't touch! Touch will brown the rose and the Acropolis, will spoil the butterfly's wing. (Creation mocks us with incipient brown.) The call of nature is brown, even in five-star hotels. The mud we make reminds us that we are: *In the sweat of thy face shalt thou eat bread, till thou return into the ground; for out of it wast thou taken. . . .*

Toil is brown. Brueghel's peasants are brown, I remember noting in a Vienna museum.

In his book *Abroad,* Paul Fussell reminds us how, early in the 20th century, the relative ease of modern travel and boredom allowed moneyed Americans and Europeans to extrude the traditional meaning of the laborer's brown and to make of it a glove of leisure. What the moon had been for early nineteenth-century romantics, the sun became for bored twentieth-century romantics. The brown desired by well-to-do Europeans was a new cure altogether: tan.

There is another fashionable brown. An untouchable brown. Certain shrewd, ancient cities have evolved an aesthetic of decay, making the best of necessity. Decrepitude can seem to ennoble whomever or whatever chic is placed in proximity—

Anita Ekberg, Naomi Campbell. The tanned generation, aka the Lost Generation, gamboled through the ruins of the Belle Époque. The *cardinali* of postwar drug culture—Paul Bowles, William Burroughs—found heaven in North Africa, mansions white. It's a Catholic idea, actually—that the material world is redeemed; that time is continuous; that one can somehow be redeemed by the faith of an earlier age or a poorer class if one lives within its shadow or its arrondissement, breathes its sigh. And lately fashion photographers, bored with Rome or the Acropolis, have ventured further afield for the frisson of syncretism. Why not Calcutta? Why not the slums of Rio? Cairo? Mexico City? The attempt is for an unearned, casual brush with awe by enlisting untouchable extras. And if the model can be seen to move with idiot stridency through tragedy, then the model is invincible. Luxury is portrayed as protective. Or protected. Austere, somehow—"spiritual." Irony posing as asceticism or as worldly-wise.

One of the properties of awe is untouchability. *Silenzio*, the recorded voice booms through the Sistine Chapel at five- or 10-minute intervals. *Do not speak. Do not touch.* Even resurrected Christ—the white doorway himself—backed away from Mary Magdalene's dirty fingernails. Don't touch! I would have expected a Roman Catholic understanding of time to accommodate centuries of gaping mouths, respiration, prayer, burnt offerings—and reticence—offering the exemplum of a clouded ceiling to twentieth-century pilgrims. After all, we live in time. Our glimpse of the Eternal must be occluded by veils of time, of breath, of human understanding.

The human imagination has recently sustained a reversal.

One would have expected the pope, as the preeminent upholder of the natural order, to have expressed reservations about the cleaning of the Sistine ceiling. The pope, however, in a curiously puritanical moment, gave his blessing to a curator's blasphemy, which was underwritten by the Japanese fetish for the cleaning of history. The blasphemy was to imagine that restoring the ceiling might restore the Vatican's luster. The blasphemy was to imagine that time might be reversed. The blasphemy was to believe that time should be reversed.

The human imagination has recently sustained a reversal. We have cleaned the ceiling. Michelangelo's *Creation* and *Judgment*, the first and the last and the pride of centuries—a vault over the imagination of the world—have been cleaned, have been restored, unhallowed, changed and called "original," though no one has any idea what that might mean. (What was the light of day in 1540?) Nile greens and rose-petal pinks, tangier oranges and the martyred saints—what supernal beaver-shots. Well, we want them preserved, of course we do. And we are keen to see them as *they*, the dead, saw them, as Michelangelo painted them. The very Tree of Knowledge has been restored, each leaf rinsed and all the fruit polished, the fruit and the sin repolished. Having seen, we also want them back the way they were.

We want what Eve wanted. . . . *Just curious.*

We had become accustomed to an averted eye, to seeing darkly, as old men see. It required many thousands of Q-tips, many thousands of gallons of distilled water, which is to say, merely a couple of years, to wipe away the veil of tears, the glue from awakened eyes, to see born-again Adam touched by the less complicated hand of God. Now our distance from the representations, both alpha and omega, has been removed. And with it all credibility.

Blind John Milton—*brown all!*—dictating *Paradise Lost* to his aggrieved daughter in the dark, understood that what changes after Adam's sin is not creation but our human relationship to creation. (We cannot be content, even on a warm winter day in L.A., but we must always carp about a white Christmas.)

Maybe Milton, in this sense, in his preoccupation with the Fall, was more an ancient, swarthy Catholic than a true, ready Protestant. (Protestantism was also an attempt to clean the ceiling.) Those famous religious refugees from Restoration England were (like Milton) Puritans who believed they had entered a green time and were elected by God to be new Adams, new Eves (as old John Milton could not, with the scabs of Europe grown over his eyes, and painted tropes of angels plaguing his memory—*brown all, brown all*).

Let us speak of desire as green. In the Roman church, green is the color of Ordinary Time, a prosaic pathway. For American Puritans, green was extraordinary. They supposed themselves remade by their perilous journey to a new world they were determined to call green, proclaiming by that term their own refreshment. They had entered a garden ungardened and felt themselves free of history, free to reenact the drama of creation.

Green became the founding flag of America; and so it would remain for generations of puritans to come, whatever our religion or lack. American optimism—our sense of ourselves as decent, naive, primary people (compared to those violet, cynical races); our sense of ourselves as young, our sap rising, our salad days always before us, our belief that the eastern shore the Europeans "discovered" and the fruited plain beyond were, after all, "virgin"—all this would follow from an original belief in the efficacy of green.

Thus did the Dutch sailors in F. Scott Fitzgerald's *Great Gatsby* spy the sheer cleft of an approaching "fresh green breast." That same green breast is today the jaded tip of Long Island, summer home to New Amsterdam investment bankers and other rewarded visionaries who do not resemble their portraits. And the tragic hustler's ghost:

> *Gatsby believed in the green light, the orgiastic future that year by year recedes before us. It eluded us then, but that's no matter—tomorrow we will run faster, stretch out our arms farther. . . . And one fine morning . . .*

We—I write in the early months of the twenty-first century—we are now persuaded by Marxist literary critics to god-damn any green light, to hack away at any green motif. Someone offstage has suffered, and no good can come of it. We are a college of victims, we postmoderns; we are more disposed to notice Fitzgerald's Dutch sailors were not alone upon the landscape (we easily pick out chameleon Indians hidden among the green tracery) than we are to wonder at the expanding, original iris: how the Indians must have marveled at those flaxen-haired Dutchmen.

Well, most likely the Indians were too terrified to morphologize or eroticize on the spot. *What happens next?* Watch, as the Indians did watch—with darker dread and puzzlement—what cargo these pale sailors unloaded. From below deck emerged Africa in chains, the sun in thrall to the moon.

Thus, perceiving Europeans having only just arrived, the Indians already saw. Indians saw Original Sin. The dark ceiling. The stain spreading like oil spill. Rumor, too, must have spread like wildfire across the Americas—making green impossible from that moment except as camouflage or tea.

Forgetting for the moment the journeys of others and the lateness of the hour, considering only the founding triad of our clandestine exhibit—Indian, European, African—we see (as well as the Founding Sin) the generation of the erotic motif of

America. A brown complexity—complexity of narrative and of desire—can be foretold from the moment Dutch sailors and African slaves meet within the Indian eye.

I think I probably do. (Have brown thoughts.)

RICHARD RODRIGUEZ ON *"The Brown Study"*

The very difficulty some readers of this essay complain about, I find most agreeable. I intended an essay dense with allusion and filled with a despair for the entire literary enterprise (this brown, gay, "ethnic" writer, shelved in some remote section of the bookstore). Time was, there were readers in this world who enjoyed difficulty and density in books. Now simplicity is all, the flat horizon. Too bad for me. Too bad for the reader. And to answer your last question: No, the essay did not fall short of my original goals. Just the reverse.

I intended this essay to be the first chapter in my book called *Brown*. I intended the essay to work as an overture for that book, to introduce its many themes, but also to raise the question: What should a brown voice sound like?

As it turned out, the essay became too baroque and elaborate to work as an introductory essay. In fact, the essay wanted to become more difficult, even comically so, each time I revised it. This essay required that I portray the writer (myself, sitting in the Lanesborough Hotel in London, on the same day Madonna is in residence) caught by rage for critics as well as deliciously inclined to celebrate the brown world that literature provides.

I have never writtten for the theater, but have always been very much interested in the possibilities of the stage. I think my interest in drama informs this essay. For, in the end, it reads like a dramatic monologue, as do many other essays of mine. In fact, on two occasions I have heard actors perform this essay from upon a darkened stage. I yearned only for the prop of a bed from a five-star hotel.

Literary essays have always required creative energies. I certainly use all the possibilities of the pen when I write—narrative, poetry, drama. So I really don't distinguish among literary enterprises. My essays are stories. My essays are poems. My essays are dramatic monologues. Even jazz compositions.

I think the new writer should not assume that there are going to be readers of her work. There are many writers of value today who are barely read and may turn to video games for their living. On the other hand, there are writers, in our nonliterate culture, who manage to seduce some portion of the reading world or, at least, Oprah Winfrey. In short, the writer should be strong. But to those who are crazed by the enterprise, and need to write, as they need to pee or eat or sleep, my advice will not console them or help them get published or read.

Killing Wolves

SHERRY SIMPSON

. .

At *the Goldstream* General Store just down the road from my house, three creamy wolf pelts dangle from the log beam above the dog food section. Their paws brush my cheeks as I walk the

. .

SHERRY SIMPSON teaches creative nonfiction writing as an assistant professor at the University of Alaska at Anchorage. She is the author of an essay collection, *The Way Winter Comes*, which won the Chinook Literary Prize. She contributed the essays for a photographic book, *Glacier Bay National Park*, which won the national Benjamin Franklin Award in the travel/essay category. Her essays and articles have appeared in such magazines, newspapers, and journals as *Sierra*, *Summit*, the *Alaska Quarterly Review*, the *San Francisco Chronicle*, the *Washington Post*, *nidus*, *Backpacker*, and *Newsday*. Her essays have been anthologized in numerous collections, including the *American Nature Writing* series, *On Nature: Great Writers on the Great Outdoors*, *Alaska Travelers' Tales*, and the forthcoming *Going Alone*. She is the recipient of the Andres Berger Nonfiction Award and was a Bakeless Nonfiction Scholar at Bread Loaf Writers' Conference. She recently completed a collection of essays tentatively titled *A Nuisance to Myself and Others*.

narrow aisle, the wood floor creaking beneath my feet. My fingers drift across the fur. A single paw covers my entire hand.

When it's cold, as it often is in Fairbanks, I wear a dark blue felt hat trimmed with toffee-colored muskrat, and a down parka thinly ruffed with coyote. The plain animal softness warms and comforts me in the harshness of winter. Sometimes I covet thicker, more beautiful furs—the flaming fox hats and luxurious wolverine ruffs that others wear. I bought a glossy black fox hat in Vladivostok once, but it's too fancy for everyday use. It hangs in my closet and tickles my arms when I reach for my more sensible hats.

Usually I try not to dwell on how these animals died, or who killed them. Even though I was raised in Alaska, I was also raised on Disney, in that fantasy world where creatures sing and talk, foxes and hounds play together, and only mean people kill animals. I cried the first time I saw Bambi's mother die. I was twenty-nine. In the real world, of course, nothing is that simple. I acknowledge my own contradictory notions. I don't hunt, but I enjoy a tender moose roast. I dislike state-sponsored wolf control, but I'm irritated by people from Outside telling Alaskans what to do. I want to wear fur, but I don't want to kill animals for it, least of all the appealing, doggish wolf. Deep in this ambivalence, I recognize a moral blind spot, a deliberate turning away from the way life and death proceed.

I know I will never kill a wolf. Still, I wonder what goes on out there in the wilderness, where wolves kill moose and caribou, and men kill wolves, where something happens that is more cruel and honest and frightening than most of us can bear.

Ben Hopson Jr. stands on the frozen lake thirty miles northeast of Fairbanks and sweeps his hand across the scene. "Pretend this is a wolf trail," he says, gesturing to a snow-machine track waffling the snow. A Nunamiut Eskimo from Anaktuvuk Pass, he wears snowpants, a wool hat pulled over a baseball cap, and a white anorak ruffed with wolf. His eyeglasses darken as the wan morning light of February seeps through the trees and washes away the blue shadows. In the ten-below chill, our breath frosts.

We shuffle closer, our boots squeaking in the feathery snow, and strain to hear Hopson's soft voice as he points beyond the fringe of black spruce and birch trees. "There's a herd of caribou ten miles that way," he says. Now we're trying to picture the Brooks Range country he knows near his village, where constant wind lathes the snow into a hard crust and the wolves grow long, silky coats.

Just when I think I've fixed the picture—the line of wolves loping against the snow, moving as silently as smoke—Hopson drops a 750 Helfrich trap on the snow. To me, it is a clanking, rusty contraption, a metal puzzle that will somehow resolve into something that can seize a 100-pound wolf by the leg and hold it fast. With his feet, Hopson carefully spreads the square steel jaws apart and sets them into an instrument of kinetic desire that cannot be satisfied until it springs free and claps shut.

We are learning how to catch imaginary wolves, here at Wolf Trapping School. Everyone else is catching them better than I am, because they are trappers and I am not. Going to Wolf Trapping School is like attending graduate school in catching animals, the organizers tell me. A certain level of outdoor skill is presumed here; you cannot simply saunter into the woods and expect to hoodwink the fabled Alaska wolf, a clever and elusive animal with more claim to the territory than we have.

Our instructor, Ben Hopson, learned what he knows from his wife's brother and uncles, and from all his time on his Arctic trapline. As he shows us how to catch phantom wolves with a blind, or concealed, set, he moves and speaks deliberately, as if first considering every act and word. First, he anchors the trap's chain by freezing it into the snow with steaming hot water poured from a Thermos. Scooping a trap-sized hollow into the trail, he lines the bottom with six-inch lengths of slender willow branch to prevent the trap from freezing to the bed.

With a few hundred caribou nearby, he says, wolves will circuit through his traps once a week, following the same trail, often stepping in their own tracks.

"Sure, it's like going to the store," someone says.

The men laugh. "7-Eleven for caribou," someone says.

Gripping a long knife in his bare hands, Hopson begins paring snow from a rectangular slab until he's shaped a square pane an inch or two thick. Gently, he lays the snow pane across the trap. "A lot of times I have to do this four or five times when the snow conditions are too soft. While I'm shaving these I've had them fall apart right on me," he says with a slow smile, acknowledging all the things that can go wrong. Hopson trims the lid until it drops evenly across the trap, flush with the trail surface. He scrapes his fingers across the snow until the edges blend, then with the knife tip grooves the surface to match the snowmachine track.

Now the trap lies unseen, waiting. Trappers describe the situation like this: Out of 365,000 square miles in Alaska, the wolf must step onto a four-inch circle. I start to understand something about wolves and trappers, the intricacy of effort that leads to their encounters.

As the sun tops the trees and illuminates the snow, Hopson demonstrates other techniques. How to disguise a trap with moss common to his area. Where to set traps around a caribou kill— here he uses a partial carcass to demonstrate. What scent lures to use—"Bear fat. Puppies really like it. You'll have them all lined up in your traps there." (I blanch until I realize he means full-grown but inexperienced wolves, not little puppies.)

My mind lingers on the trap cloaked beneath the snow. When the session ends for lunch, Hopson presses his foot carefully against the surface and then slides it back quickly. The trap erupts from below with a metallic gulp, spraying bits of snow and moss into the air.

There have always been trappers in Alaska, beginning with the Natives who caught furbearers for clothing, meat, and a score of vital needs. In the old days, Inupiat Eskimos wrapped fat around sharpened and bent pieces of whalebone; when the bait thawed in the wolf's stomach, the bone sprang open and pierced the animal's gut. Once whites moved into the country, wolves were generally considered vermin that ate up all the game that men desired. Trappers were often solitary men like old Oscar Vogel, who guided and trapped in the Talkeetna Mountains for decades and wrote things like, "Time and suffering mean nothing to wolves," and "Intelligence and compassion go hand in hand, and wolves are without compassion," never recognizing his own lack of compassion for a fellow predator.

Beginning in the 1920s, the Territory of Alaska paid a bounty on wolves, first ten dollars, then fifteen, then twenty. Trapping wasn't the only way to kill a wolf. Some bounty hunters poisoned them. Others bludgeoned pups in dens. Somehow, despite episodic pogroms—aerial wolf shooting, state-sponsored predator control—the wolves survived. Today, biologists guess that between 6,000 and 7,000 wolves exist in Alaska, swallowed up somewhere between the mountainous southern coasts and the tundra plains of the North Slope.

Hardly ever does anyone see a living wolf in the wild. I have a friend who grew up in Ruby, a Native village on the Yukon River. He trapped marten and other animals to put himself through college, though, as he says, it's a helluva way to make a living, relying on what rich women in Paris and New York feel like wearing that year. One winter he called to tell me something about wolves. He'd been sleeping in his trapline cabin when a stirring outside awakened him. Peering through the single small window, he saw a pack of wolves slipping through the trees and circling the cabin before they disappeared again. From his mystified but pleased tone, he could have been telling me about a dream he'd had, a dream that might signify nothing, or everything.

The unknowable wolf hunts along the edge of our vision, never allowing a clear view of itself. Imagination, fear, and longing fulfill what experience cannot. And so a wolf is no longer just a wolf. It's a vicious, wasteful predator. Or it's the poster child of the charismatic mammals, the creature that stands for all that's noble, wild, and free. A wolf is social, family-oriented, intelligent, and communicative—like humans. A wolf kills because it can, for the sheer pleasure of it—like humans. It's either-or, the sacred or the profane. Inevitably, the wolf becomes a distorted reflection of the human psyche, a heavy burden for one species to carry. We can hardly bear the burden of being human ourselves.

In Alaska, people are always fighting about wolves, and I knew the trappers wouldn't be happy when I asked to attend their school and write a newspaper story about it. Pete Buist, the head of the Alaska Trappers Association, is deeply suspicious of reporters, mostly because he regards the Anchorage newspaper that hired me as a stronghold of liberal greenies who have never written one true word about trapping. But the trappers understand how bad they'll look if they refuse, and so they agree with false cheer. Nevertheless, when Buist addresses the gathered students before we begin, he warns them that I am present with a photographer. "I have no reason to distrust Sherry Simpson," he announces loudly in his blustering voice. "But don't feel you have to talk to her if you don't want to." I try to look trustworthy and sympathetic, even though I know and they know they probably won't like what I write.

Luckily, trapping interests all kinds of Alaskans, most of them individualists who don't care about party lines. They want to look good in the newspaper, but more than that, they want to be understood. Nearly three-quarters hail from south-central Alaska. Among them are weekend trappers from Anchorage and Fairbanks, bush trappers from Coldfoot, Bettles, and Nabesna, a chiropractor and a commercial pilot, a father and son, middle-aged and young men. Trappers are mostly just guys, guys who hunt and fish and like doing what they want when they want.

My group includes Mike Johnson, a friendly fellow who traps alone along the southern edge of the Brooks Range. He figures if he learns one trick that catches him one wolf, the $125 fee will be worth it. Jim Farrell, a lean, bearded guy with a Western drawl, comes right out and announces he's a novice at wolf trapping, though until he moved to Wasilla a couple of years ago he trapped coyotes as part of Wyoming's predator-control program. Phil Rogers of North Pole is burly and talkative; he traps marten, wolverine, wolf, and other furbearers to earn money in the winter. A Delta River man, he hardly says anything, not even his name, but he pays close attention to the instructors and lets me drive his snow machine. He wears a beaver hat the same coppery shade as his mustache; I never see his hair because he never takes off his hat. Two young Norwegian exchange students from the

University of Alaska came because they're just interested in trapping, or so they say. They scribble notes and snap photographs and speak to each other in low voices, and some of the hard-core trappers regard this warily, as if the handsome youths might actually be animal rights infiltrators.

It's hard to imagine the mountain men of yore registering for seminars in killing and skinning. When I signed up, organizer Steve Potter told me that for many years wolf trapping in Alaska waned as trappers concentrated on easier, more lucrative furbearers such as marten and lynx. The body of lore gathered by old-time wolfers began fading away, like many skills of northern living. But in recent years, interest has grown as pelt prices began to improve and wolf populations increased. The Alaska Trappers Association founded the wolf trapping school to encourage new trappers and teach them the right way to go about it. In most parts of the country, people want to preserve wolves. In Alaska, some believe in preserving wolf trappers.

It's not an easy life. Fur prices and market demands can be fickle. The weather can work against you. Animal populations fluctuate. The European Union threatens to ban imports of fur caught in leghold traps. Trappers don't get rich. And people who regard wolves as symbols of the wild don't appreciate seeing their symbols shot, trapped, and strangled in snares. Against all this, the trapper struggles to hold on to something that seems almost as elusive as the wolves they pursue: the chance to make a life out of wilderness.

Smart wolves and smart trappers share certain traits. Both must be exceptionally cautious and alert to the world around them. To outsmart the other, each relies on natural attributes—the wolf its superior sense of smell, the trapper his opposable thumbs and large brain. Technology is not enough to catch wolves. Instinct is not enough to evade trappers. Among wolves and trappers alike, the most successful individuals learn from their mistakes. But as instructor Jim Masek reminds us, wolves risk far more than people do.

"Humans—we take lots of lessons to learn things," he says, unloading his trapping gear from his snow machine. "Wolves, it's life or death for them. If they don't learn it once, it'll be something that kills them."

Masek, thirty-nine, is not much interested in educating wolves. Long acknowledged as an expert trapper, he earned legendary status among his fellows in February 1994 by capturing a dozen wolves in one set of snares and traps on the Minto Flats near Fairbanks. This act prompted the editor of the *Alaska Trapper* to suggest establishing a new unit of measure: a "Masek" of wolves. I remember feeling dismay and anger when I studied the newspaper photograph of Masek kneeling within a semicircle of dead wolves laid out like trout. It seemed so excessive and unnecessary. The article included Masek's account of how he lured the pack toward a booby-trapped moose kill. The young, inexperienced wolves stepped into traps first; the others panicked, bolting away from the scene and into other snares. Masek figured eventually he'd catch the few who escaped, since they were deprived of their leaders.

Now that I see his boyishly rosy cheeks, blue eyes, and strawblond hair, Masek seems less like a bloodthirsty killer and more like what he is, a country boy who hails from Nebraska and South Dakota. His face, other trappers joke, is probably enshrined in wolf dens throughout Minto Flats. Masek is consumed by the hard work, the contest of wits, the outdoor life. This is a man who buys snare cable in 10,000-foot rolls, who owns a hundred wolf traps, who learned the feeding call of ravens so he can locate wolf kills. He lives alone out on Minto Flats, northwest of Fairbanks, in a log cabin he built on the Chatanika

River. In winter, he rides his snow machine thirty miles to the nearest road, and then drives another twenty miles to reach Fairbanks. In summer, he works for a big construction company, but you can see that the trapline embraces his true existence.

On this snow-bright afternoon along the icebound Chena River, we double up on snow machines and skim along the river for a mile or so before stopping here. Sundogs hover in the hazy sky above us. Spruce and birch trees crowd the riverbanks, some of them tipping gradually into the river. Once we left the road, we entered a largely unpeopled wilderness that stretches east for thousands of miles to the other side of the continent. The keen air reddens our cheeks and noses, and we try not to step off the hard-packed snow-machine trail into deep snow, where we'll flounder and sink.

A successful trapper not only understands wolf behavior but uses the wolf's own nature against it. Anything unnatural troubles a wolf, and trappers take advantage of this to manipulate or distract the animals. A trapper, for example, might hang a ribbon of surveyor's flagging to scare a wolf off the trail and into a trap or snare. A wolf's tendency to step over a twig planted in the trail can direct its foot into a trap.

Masek chose this place because wolves tend to relax a bit when they can see clearly around them. As he unloads his gear from his snow-machine sled, he compresses some of what he's learned in two decades of trapping into a few hours. Lesson No. 1: The slightest sign of anything unnatural can spook a wolf, especially the reek of humans. Wolves have, as one biologist describes it, "a big honking nose and they really know how to use it."

So don't spit, don't smoke, don't pee on the trail, Masek says. Keep clothing, gear, and equipment scrupulously free of disturbing scents. Use only clean, dry cotton work gloves. Prepare snares and traps by washing them in solvent or boiling them in water fragrant with local plants. Dye them black with logwood crystals to eliminate a distracting shine. Hang them outdoors away from human smells. Try not to contaminate them with sweat, fuel, and other scents while handling them. Make yourself null, a sensory void in the olfactory landscape.

Setting a trap in exactly the same spot where a wolf will step is a more challenging problem. Fortunately for trappers, wolves and other animals prefer trotting dead center along the trail of snow-machine tread. Human tracks, however, worry them, and snowshoe prints simply scare them off. (The trappers speculate about this more than once: Some lingering smell? An inbred association between snowshoes and traplines?) In the field, Masek works off the back of his snow-machine sled, standing on a rectangle of plywood to avoid disturbing the trail.

Masek holds up a trap, a No. 9 Manning that costs about a hundred dollars. The offset jaws spread into a nine-inch circle. When the jaws clamp shut, a three-eighths-inch gap remains between the steel arcs. The mechanism acts like a handcuff by grasping a knob above the foot rather than pinching the toes or cutting into the paw, causing less damage and pain to the wolf.

In his shop, Masek modifies his traps in various ways. He laminates an extra layer of steel along the jaws to strengthen and spread the holding surface, which is easier on the animal's leg. He also bolsters various parts so that wolves can't destroy them. "I've got traps that are almost mangled, with the pan crushed down, the trigger dog bent, tooth marks in the steel," he says. "Wolves have tremendous force in their jaws so they can crush moose bones."

Trappers are always fooling with gear, trying to build a better mousetrap, so to speak. Masek's been inventing. He holds up what he jokingly calls a "bedpan," a round section of galvanized stovepipe that has been modified into a pan that can hold a No. 9 trap. The pan works like a cookie cutter in the snow, outlining the trap bed. The trap fits inside the pan, and Masek inserts the device into a small white garbage bag to prevent snow from clogging the jaws. He settles the pan into the trail bed and lightly brushes snow over the plastic cover with a small hand broom. "Usually you want to be able to see a gray shadow," he says, straightening to study the way the trap barely darkens the snow.

The pan allows a snow machine to drive across the trap without triggering it or pushing snow into the jaws. The trap lies concealed beneath the snow-machine track, with no visible sign to any wolf that lopes down the path. "Out on an open trail, they're bobbing around, enjoying the view, looking for a moose, and they'll step right into it and, poof, get nailed," Masek says.

Sometimes, something goes wrong. The wolf plants a foot on the trap, takes a few steps, and then the trap fires. "You've just educated one wolf," Masek says flatly.

A trap can be used as a kind of trigger for snaring a pack. The first wolf along the trail steps into a leghold trap, causing the others to explode off the trail and bolt through the trees, where a score or more of wire snares fill most of the gaps and openings. Masek shows us how to hang the handmade snares by wrapping the stiff end of the holding wire around a sturdy small tree. Each snare falls open about knee high above the snow, opening into a 72-inch loop. From a few feet away, we can't even see the snares dangling among the branches. The idea is that as the wolf's head enters the snare, its forward motion slips the loop closed. A small locking device prevents the snare from reopening. When it works right, the wolf's struggle pulls the loop tighter, and the animal dies quickly from suffocation as its trachea collapses.

Everything doesn't always work right, though. Sometimes a snowfall will raise the snowpack so that the snares no longer hang 18 inches above the ground. Instead of naturally thrusting their heads through the loops, the wolves charge through them or step into them and become entangled. Sometimes wolves snared by the leg chew off their own limbs.

Masek knows many other ruses. He points out a piece of driftwood that would make a natural scent post, a place where wolves might stop and mark their territory. At such a spot he would set a trap beneath a paw print and then re-create the track. He's studied the way male dogs lift their legs—where they stand, how high they spray. He takes out a duct-tape-wrapped bottle of dog urine and splashes it like canine graffiti into the snow, where it will attract the attention of passing wolves. Friends gather chunks of frozen urine from their dog yard; Masek warms it in the field by storing the bottle next to his snow-machine manifold.

He also saves wolf urine from the trail, sometimes distracting and exciting one pack by marking their urine posts with scent from a different pack. Sometimes, if he catches an alpha female, he uses her urine to confuse her puppies; they sniff around, thinking she's nearby, and often blunder into traps.

This wrenching picture makes me imagine that when one wolf is caught, the others stick around, trying to figure out what's happening. Sometimes they do, Masek says, and sometimes they don't. "If an adult gets caught they may mill around. Half the time if it's a puppy, they might not even look back. If you get the adult, you may have caught the killer, the breeder, the smart one. Clip him and the rest have to work harder to live," he says.

Someone asks what happens when the trapper returns to his line and finds a wolf waiting in a trap. "Some adults might howl and snap and lunge at you," Masek says, his face revealing nothing. "A puppy tends to cower. It won't make eye contact with you."

I make myself think about this scene. I wonder what it's like to shoot a wolf that is looking at you with its amber eyes, rage or fear in its heart. But I don't ask. It seems too personal, something between trappers and wolves. Part of me recoils from knowing, too, as if the explicit knowledge of death will make it my fault as well.

Because I don't know wolves, I first think the black animal lying on the floor of the meeting hall that night is a sleeping dog. A large sleeping dog. I realize my mistake when I see its leaden stillness.

Fairbanks trappers Greg and Mike Chapin discovered the wolf this morning in one of their blind-set traps on the Chena River. A pair of wolves had followed the trail on and off for about four miles. They stepped over two traps before this wolf planted its foot into the third one, a No. 9 Manning leghold. For perhaps thirty-six hours, it waited in the trap before the brothers arrived. Greg Chapin killed it by shooting once with his .22-caliber rifle crosswise through its chest. "It stood about three seconds and fell over," he says.

The wolf is a young female, a yearling or a two-year-old. About the size of a German shepherd, she weighs 65 or 70 pounds. Ripples of silver highlight her black fur. She's still slightly warm. Greg, thirty-one, holds up a broad front paw, the one caught in the leghold, and says, largely for my benefit, "Not a broken tendon. The skin's not broken, nothing."

The woodstove warms the room, and the trappers chat and joke while Greg begins skinning the wolf as it lies on a table. He's a beefy man with receding red hair that makes him look like a tonsured monk. He handles the wolf straightforwardly, not as if it were something revered or reviled but simply a dead animal.

Every winter he and his brother run their eleven-mile trapline along the upper reaches of the Chena River; they've taken as few as four wolves and as many as fourteen in a season.

"I always start with the mouth," he says, picking up a small, wickedly sharp knife and making short slicing strokes around the wolf's black lips. He peels back the snout; as soon as the nose flops loose, the animal loses some part of its wolf identity. I see the trappers looking at me sideways; they're wondering if I might start crying, or run outside, or throw up. But I can be as detached as they are, and so I simply sit taking notes, and soon they forget I'm there.

Chapin slits the hide from the paws up along the wrist, then breaks the joint at all four paws. A few men step forward to help him hoist the animal by its rear leg from a gambrel so that it hangs head down, blood pooling on the floor beneath it. After a while, Chapin stuffs a wad of newspaper in its mouth to slow the blood.

Slowly he works off the hide, exposing the blue-red flesh and sinew, the stretch and compression of muscle and tendon. A wolf's thick fur sheathes the sleek architecture of something meant to run, to kill, to survive.

The talk turns to the uncanny nature of wolf senses. Chapin recalls a wolf he caught three months ago that was moving about a hundred yards in front of the pack. From the tracks, he saw that after the lead wolf was trapped, the others stopped, left the trail, and headed into the brush. A couple of weeks later, three wolves that he believes belonged to a different pack traveled down the same trail. When they arrived at the spot where the first group departed, they also suddenly stopped and abandoned the trail, as if they knew something dangerous and disturbing awaited them. "So in their standing and dancing around, they communicated something," Chapin says of the original pack.

The trappers spend a lot of time this weekend exchanging similar wolf lore, mulling over what it all means. Ben Hopson leaves skinned wolf carcasses near his traps to attract other wolves. Mike Johnson says such carcasses spook wolves in his part of the Brooks Range. Some believe that wolves notice stepping sticks placed in trails as clearly as if they were little signs that announce "Trap Ahead." Others are convinced they work. Different wolf packs learn different things; the experiences of their leaders shape the group intelligence. This is how the trappers learn, too, by sharing knowledge difficult to come by.

"Another thing I know is that it's a lot easier to catch wolves in a bar than it is out on a river," Chapin says, and others laugh knowingly.

Somebody asks Chapin about the fur's value. He studies the black hide, silver gleaming in it like light upon water, and says, "I wouldn't sell it for less than two hundred and probably two and a half." When Fairbanks fur buyer Dean Wilson eyeballs it the next day, he pegs it at $300; it would be worth more if the neck pile was deeper.

Chapin takes care with skinning because the demand for taxidermy mounts creates much of the wolf market. For some, the fur is not enough to evoke the wolf; it must be draped over a form and posed realistically with cold marbles for eyes. People also covet wolves as wall hangings and especially as trim for parkas, mitts, and other winter garments. Nearly three-quarters of wolf sales remain within Alaska, where it is not considered shameful but practical to wear animal fur.

Several factors determine the value of a wolf pelt, most importantly size and color. Taxidermists love an Alaska wolf that's seven feet long or more, Wilson says; it just sounds good. This particular wolf stretches to about seven feet, four inches. Color matters, too. Of all the wolf shades—gray, blue, red, white, black—white is the rarest. Also important are the fur's depth and texture, particularly to parka makers. They want a ruff thick enough to swallow a prodding finger up to the second knuckle.

Chapin shares a cleaning tip with his fellow trappers. "When you got grays with a brown cast, wash 'em. Take 'em to a laundromat. It's amazing how much of that is dirt."

"What happens if you do that and they catch you?" someone calls out.

"They ask you not to come back," Chapin answers, his grin hinting at personal experience in this breach of etiquette.

Conversations eddy as the hide slacks off the wolf. A raw, meaty smell and the hot stove make the room close and stuffy. The trappers stand around talking guy talk with their hands shoved deep in their pockets, their hats tipped back on their heads. They jaw about the merits of various snow machines, the trapper's iron dog. They compare the amount of fur in their parts of the country.

"Here's a trivia question," Chapin announces. "How many toenails are there on an entire wolf?"

People shout out guesses. Eleven. Fourteen. Twenty. Never counted 'em.

The answer is eighteen. "Sixteen and two dewclaw nails," says Masek, who leans against the wall with arms crossed. Masek knows everything there is to know about wolves, it seems.

"How do you turn a fox into a wolf?" a trapper yells. "Marry her!" Gusts of laughter.

"Instead of a No. 9, it was a wedding ring, eh?" someone says. Guy talk.

"How many trappers does it take to make popcorn?" No answer. "Three—one to hold the pan and two to shake the stove!"

Chapin finishes unpeeling the wolf, stripping it to a lean,

whippet-like shape. The hide remains intact through the belly and chest. He pushes the wolf's ears inside out with the blunt end of a broomstick so they will dry into their alert shape. Then he pulls the hide through itself, until the meaty side faces outward. Now comes the most tedious task of all, fleshing the hide. Chapin drapes the fur over a fleshing beam, a hinged log attached to a stand. The butt of the beam rests against Chapin's leg as he scrapes away gobbets of meat with long knife strokes, trying to avoid nicking the pelt.

"You got to be really careful on the belly," he warns. "The skin is really tender on the belly."

The wolf's paws rest on the table behind him, the long, elegant bones ruddy with blood. Each foot is worth $1.50; the penis bone brings another buck and a half. Indians use them to make breastplates that sell for $10,000. An intact wolf skull brings $25, more for a large one. Scent glands from the feet, ears, tail, and anus, and such organs as the bladder, brains, and gallbladder are saved to age in a jar and use later as lure. Lure, I hear someone explain to the Norwegian students, is like "perfume on a woman"; the scent intrigues and draws wolves to trap sets.

The young black she-wolf has been transformed into an assemblage of products and possibilities: ornaments and fur, essences and emblems. She has literally been dismantled, and even examining her piece by bloody piece, I feel no closer to understanding the enigma of wolves. Something tightens in me when I think of her terrible beauty, the lovely sharpness of her teeth, the predatory brilliance of her gaze. But that is only what I see. The trappers see a pelt, a paycheck, a trickster outwitted by a human. We're the ones who write the stories, and so what else can a wolf be except a symbol for everything good and bad about us, everything we want, everything we've lost?

Nearly three hours after beginning, Chapin makes his last

fleshing strokes. He slips the hide, still inside out, over a stretching plank shaped like a surfboard. The hide needs to dry for a day or so before it's ready to be tanned commercially. "Come in with three or four of these, you'll be up all night," Chapin says, wiping his forehead with the back of his gory hand. To earn his $300, he's spent perhaps thirty hours checking the trap, killing the wolf, and skinning the hide. It's not just the money he's after, he says. But when he tries to explain, all he can do is telegraph clichés: "The challenge. Being outdoors. The wilderness."

That night, most of us sleep in the same room, spreading our sleeping bags across couches and mattresses thrown on the floor. Here's another thing about trappers: they snore. The room seems to swell and toss on the waves of their long, shuddering breaths, the snores of the innocent, of men at peace with themselves. Someone talks to himself in the urgent dialect of sleep.

In the corner, the wolf hide dries, shaped more rigidly than the wolf itself ever was. Sleep comes to me slowly in the hot, noisy room. I see the wolf running in a black ripple through the snow. I see the lustrous pelt hanging on my wall, where I can touch the shining fur every day. I could climb into it, peer through the eyeholes, wear the wolf's face like a mask. Embraced in a wolf skin, I could run for miles through the forest, searching for the smell of living blood. But I would wear death, too. I would look out into the world through the eyes of death.

In winter the flat, frozen surface of the upper Chena River becomes a boulevard for wildlife, where tracks inscribe the snow in a calligraphy of motion. Everything is going somewhere. I ride behind trapper Phil Rogers on his Tabasco-red snow machine, clinging to his stout midriff. The long ivory hairs of his wolf ruff tickle my nose as I press my face against his back. Rogers shouts out track identifications as we skim across the snow: Moose. Marten. Fox. Wolf.

The wolf tracks emerge from the forest and dip onto the river, gradually curving across the channel. The trail arrows toward a downed spruce tree jutting across the river. Yellow snow around the tree indicates the wolves' interest; they've made it into a scent post. Several hundred yards later, the tracks separate around an overflow spot on the river, revealing three animals, probably young ones by the print size. Fur between their footpads dragged as they walked, grooving the snow between tracks. The tracks seem so clear that I exclaim about their freshness, but Rogers points out the hoarfrost blurring the outlines.

"The wolf makes his living with his feet," is how state biologist Mark McNay had described it the night before. Packs travel continuously as they search for game, often using the same routes year after year as they cover distances that average 600 to 700 square miles. "To do that they really got to pick 'em up and put 'em down," McNay told us. Jim Masek once trapped a mangy wolf on the Minto Flats that had been radio-collared on the Kenai Peninsula, a good 500 miles by air to the south.

We follow the wolf tracks as if they were a story, and not far up the river, we come upon the climax. All that remains of the moose calf are scattered bits of fur and bone, and a jagged ridge of ribs. Ravens, foxes, and other animals trampled the snow, sharing the bounty. The experienced trappers speculate about where the cow's carcass lies—perhaps off the river, in the forest.

"You hear a lot about wolves killing the old, sick, weak, and young, and there's some truth to that," McNay explained. "A better and more accurate view is that wolves prey on vulnerable animals, old, young, middle-aged. . . . Any animals can be vulnerable if the wolves catch them in the right situation. Generally wolves don't." Winter is all about vulnerability; in the deep

Interior snows, moose find it difficult to move about on their willowy legs.

After hearing McNay's talk, I find it easier to imagine what happened here on the river. Killing is usually an exhausting, bloody business for the wolf and the moose. Generally, only the most experienced animals in the pack attack first, searching for a hold on the rump or nose, wearing away the moose's strength until they can force it down and feast on all the rich, nourishing blood and meat. Usually the prey of wolves do not perish from anything as merciful as a crushed trachea; most die from shock and blood loss. More than one trapper remarks on the gruesome and often lengthy death of moose and caribou, but McNay pointed out the enormous size difference between a 100-pound wolf and a 1,000-pound moose. "I don't want to give the impression that wolves are somehow ruthless, abnormally aggressive killers," he said. "That's the only way they can kill. If you had to kill a moose with your mouth, you'd do it, too."

The wolf does not automatically prevail, either. Moose can charge, fling off a wolf that's hanging by its jaws, kick viciously. Wolf autopsies commonly show fractured ribs, cracked skulls, even broken and rehealed legs. A moose can even throw jabs like a boxer, McNay noted, adding that he once saw a moose coldcock another moose. "But that's another story," he said.

Trappers don't always find kills so well devoured as this calf. "This is responsible in part for the idea that wolves are killing and 'wasting' meat," McNay told us. "In many cases they kill, eat, and then travel and come back." But the trappers do not seem entirely convinced that wolves subscribe to a philosophy of "waste not, want not." During the weekend, I hear these characterizations, which I suspect are really justifications:

"When you see these wolves cruising down a river running, you realize they're nothing but a stomach and a set of jaws."

"I've seen moose with their guts pulled out, and nothing eaten."

"Wolves are the biggest killers of wolves. It's not uncommon that they eat each other in traps. You can come back and find only the head."

"Last winter there was a tendency to kill for the fun of it. That's what they are—a killing machine."

Now that this moose is dead, it represents a natural bait site for wolves, which tend to return again and again to kills, even if only to chew nostalgically on a few bones. The trappers discuss where they would place their snares, the proper arrangement of traps. A raven flies overhead, and a veteran trapper from Tok turns his head to follow the black motion, his eyes as quick as a marten's. "If we could follow that raven, we'd find that cow," he says mostly to himself. There are things about this killing place that I don't see, signs I can't decipher.

We return the way we came as the milky winter sky dims and the forest darkens around us. I try to identify the tracks we cross by their gait and size. The wolf trail, I see, makes the steadiest, deepest path through the snow. Wolves don't wander like dogs. They know where they're going. Sometime soon, they'll be back; they are always circling their world with their feet.

All weekend, I puzzle over Mike Johnson, the Brooks Range trapper, who wears a T-shirt portraying an Alaska wolf, the kind of romanticized shirt a tourist might buy. At first I wonder if the shirt is some kind of joke, like the T-shirts sold by the Alaska Trappers Association that say "PETA: People for the Eating of Tasty Animals." This is a poke at the animal rights group People for the Ethical Treatment of Animals. I wonder if Johnson is indulging in irony, wearing that shirt blazing with the silvery face of a wolf.

He answers my questions openly, with none of the shyness you might expect from a man who's just emerged from a winter in his cabin on the Arctic Circle, along the flanks of the Brooks Range. He resembles a jovial Mennonite with his mustache-less beard and his wide, toothy smile. Unlike many trappers, Johnson works alone, living on his trapline five months out of the year. To do that, a person must not mind his own company, nor the constant presence of winter. "I tell myself jokes out loud," Johnson confides.

Johnson, fifty-four, came to Alaska in 1971 coveting the same things most Alaskans desire—wilder country, a different kind of life. Eight years ago, after his marriage dissolved, he bought his trapline and moved north to live the way he had always wanted. In the summers, he runs halibut charter boats out of Homer.

"I don't know anybody who works harder than trappers for the money," Johnson says. Trappers are people who cannot stand idleness, he tells me, and I can see this in him. This afternoon he explained to his colleagues how he survives on the trapline alone. He showed off the come-along winch he added to his snow machine to hitch it out of bad spots, the complicated engine modifications, the hip boots he fashioned out of giant inner tubes so he won't freeze his feet in overflow. He painted his ax and the butt of his rifle fluorescent orange so he can find them against the snow. To lose them would be disastrous.

This winter, Mike Johnson is going broke. He can't find enough marten, the trapper's bread-and-butter fur. He sold one snow machine to make payments on the other. Johnson relates all this in the same cheerful tone he uses when he talks about why he loves trapping: "It's the attraction of the wild. It's the lifestyle. The challenge of doing what I'm doing." The same words we all use, but he's the one curled in the dark bosom of the Brooks Range in January. When he visits his family in Indiana, they talk mostly about the price of corn, which is a foreign tongue he used to know, and he looks out the window and thinks about coming home.

Thinking about the T-shirt, I ask him what he thinks about wolves.

"All the things you hear are probably true, good and bad," he says, and then he considers. "I love wolves. It would be a sad day if there were not wolves in this country." He lowers his voice a little, as if he's telling a secret. "I'd rather have too many than not enough, to tell you the truth. I want there always to be wolves. Always, always."

If trappers do not regard the wolf as a symbol of wilderness, perhaps it's because people who spend so much time working in the wilderness don't need symbols. Steve Potter is a large, good-natured man who can hardly find the words to describe the way he feels sometimes out there in the woods, under the innocent sky. He struggles to tell me the feeling that took him once as he watched a flock of snowy ptarmigan sweep across the black-green expanse of forest. After tangling himself in awkward words and long pauses, he finally gives up. You had to be there, is all he can say. But I know what he means. Being there means seeing all of it—what's beautiful and impossible to express, what's painful and hard to watch.

Trappers believe that if anyone understands nature, it's them, not the city folks who hang photographs of wolves on their cramped city walls and listen to recordings of wolf howls to drown out the sound of traffic and other kinds of emptiness. Greg Chapin rejects as well-meaning but misguided the notion that animals can and should die painlessly. "It would be neat if you could get the fur and let wolves go—like sheep," he says. "But we can't." If the wolf is just another animal out there trying to hustle up a living, well, then, so is the trapper. "I would never kill the last wolf. I don't hate wolves," he says. "But [trapping] is no more cruel, no less cruel than anything that happens in nature. It's no less natural than the wolf killing the moose. The wolf kills the moose to eat it, and I kill the wolf."

I envy his certainty; everything has its place in the world, including him. Anyone who hunts or traps must come to some similar reconciliation. Alaska's Native cultures encompass a complicated relationship with the animals they kill, because their own survival—spiritual and physical—depends on a respectful attitude toward their fellow creatures. Most trappers employ less formal and articulate relationships, but what seems like callousness is often, I believe, something closer to affection. In the *Alaska Trapper* magazine, a young man writes of a lonely winter working his trapline on the Black River, two hundred miles northwest of Fairbanks and as far from anywhere as you'll find. For months a lone gray wolf shadowed his cabin. "It was just he and I here on the Black, and I felt an affinity growing between us," the trapper wrote. In January, the trapper discovered his "befriended wolf" in a No. 9: "Soon he was sharing a ride in my sled with a marten. Now I was alone on the Black." As I read this account I wonder which seems worse, to kill an animal you feel a kinship with, or to kill an animal you feel nothing for?

I worry over this problem during the weekend, returning to it again and again, the way wolves return to a killing place. First I think of animals I ate during the weekend that I didn't kill: Moose. Black bear. Cow. Pig. Northern pike. I didn't even say grace beforehand. Even as a vegetarian, I could shed the conceit of guilt only if I didn't know that my mere presence in Alaska requires space, habitat, resources that animals depend on. And if I didn't wear fur, I would wear manufactured gear: petroleum-based, nonrecyclable, nonrenewable garments. A trapper tells me, "Fur is organic. It doesn't ruin one thing in the woods to use it." Except the animal itself, of course.

Eventually I ask Steve Potter, in a circuitous and abstract way, about killing wolves. He explains without hedging, as if this is something he's thought about a lot. After all, he's been trapping since he was a kid, and now he's teaching his own eleven-year-old son to catch marten and beaver. "The way I feel is, there's no difference between a wolf and a mouse," he says. "They're each a life, and you can't take any life lightly. When you come on an animal alive, you want to dispatch it as quickly as you can."

It sounds right that a person shouldn't distinguish between the value of a mouse and the value of a wolf. Still, I can't shake the sense that killing a wolf is different somehow. Does the wolf recognize impending death, having delivered it so often?

Delicately, I ask again, this time a coworker who traps recreationally. Once, Norm says, looking away, he found a wolf alive in a trap. But he didn't have a gun to kill it. So he attached a Conibear trap used for killing wolverines to a stick and poked the contraption at the wolf. The wolf snapped at the trap and the trap snapped back, catching the wolf's jaw and immobilizing it. Then Norm smashed the wolf's skull with a stick, shattering the ridge above its eye and killing it instantly. "It was a messy death," he says, regret shading his voice. "It was beneath its dignity."

Norm's story makes me feel a little weak inside, because he's saying wolves do require a separate honor. It's true that I can also think of worse fates for an animal. Zoos, for example, and the way all wild animals go blank in cages, as if some part of them is not there. Neglected dogs chained in suburban yards. Cats abandoned to pounds. A thousand kinds of death await animals, none easy. It's the deliberateness of killing an animal, whether for food or for fur, that seems like a barbaric throwback, something humans used to do until we evolved into the kind of creature that doesn't need to kill to survive. Yet anyone who eats a Big Mac or an Easter lamb or a slab of salmon prepared by a fancy chef has simply delegated the killing to others. We want to believe a wolf has more intrinsic value than a chicken raised in an industrial coop. A wolf means more to us because we've made it something more; we believe it lives the life we want to live. But most wolves perish no more nobly than chickens. Biologist David Mech has said that a wolf usually dies in one of two ways: it starves to death, or another wolf eats it.

Still, some would argue, people have no place within these events; what happens in nature is none of our business. I used to feel this way myself, that the mere presence of a human in the wilderness was enough to taint it forever. That a wolf would kill a wolf seemed acceptable because it was "natural"; that a man would kill a wolf, unforgivable. I've used the same tone other nature lovers do as they talk about "the natural circle of life" in hushed and reverent tones, as if it were a church we could never attend but only stand outside, listening to the godly and mysterious harmonies issuing from within. The circles of life and death wheel about each other in great concentric spirals. Humans, like wolves, have never been anything else but killers.

When trapping school is over and the trappers have all returned to town or to their traplines, I cross the frozen lake just past nightfall and wait by the narrow road for my ride home. The temperature floats into the thirties, and the air seems impossibly warm, comforting. Behind thin clouds, the moon blurs.

I think about wolves. In these two days of talking about

trapping, the only thing missing was the wolf itself. I have seen the deliberate pace of its tracks, the scattered remains of its meals, the stripped cipher of its carcass. Harder to picture is the elusive, living creature, the shape of its eyes, the heat of its breath, the way its tail plumes behind as it runs.

I've seen a wolf only once, during a fall drive through Denali National Park. The wolf was the color of a clouded sky. A radio collar ringed its neck, a constant insult to its supple motion. The wolf padded steadily down the middle of the road, as if it had a long way to walk. People yanked their cars to the roadside to let the animal pass and then hung their heads from windows, following with their eyes. A man standing outside his car closed the door against himself, like a shield.

We all looked hungrily at the wolf, because not often will a wolf pass a few feet away from you without intervening bars or fences. My first thought—what a big dog—evaporated the moment I glimpsed its eyes—not the color, which I don't remember, but the inner, private light. The wolf glanced neither right nor left, but only ahead, as if none of us were there. Down the road it walked for miles, and we all looked and looked.

Not far from where I wait this night, wolf tracks course down the frozen Chena River. Somewhere out there, wolves lope through the dark, or sleep, or kill. Somewhere out there, a wolf waits in a trap, anchored to approaching death. The wolf is a predator. The wolf is prey.

All those who care about nature fashion a private covenant with it. Some people love wilderness best from a distance; it's the easiest way, this unconditional love. Totems of wildness substitute for wildness itself. Put a poster of a wolf on the wall and admire it like a movie star, like someone you wish you were. Whatever happens in the wild happens without you, because you are not part of it.

Some people draw near to wilderness, into a harder but truer place. They kill animals to eat them or wear them or sell them, never looking away from what they are about to do. By acknowledging the death that arrives through their own hands, surely they secretly wonder if they can't somehow master the way death will come to them.

And some people, like me, want to look. We want so much to belong to nature, to be kin to every part of its difficult beauty, but in the end, we turn away. All we can do is follow the tracks, knowing that someday, the wolf will circle around to us.

SHERRY SIMPSON ON *"Killing Wolves"*

A wolf pelt hangs on my wall at home. The fur is black and silky, tinged with silver. Sometimes I bury my face in it, trying to smell something of the wild animal it once was.

This is the very wolf described in this essay, the one we watched being skinned at Wolf Trapping School. The trappers tried to give me the pelt after my piece was published. "It wasn't complimentary, but it was fair," one man said. Of course, I bought the wolf instead. I wanted to avoid the conflict of interest but not the conflicting emotions the pelt still represents: regret, respect, fear, longing.

Writing this essay changed the way I thought about wolves, trapping, our ideas of nature, and even death. It also changed the way I think about writing creative nonfiction. Like many writers, I didn't know what I thought before I started writing. I recognize now that the process of "essaying" began long before I sat at the computer. The most important part of the process turned out to be listening to the trappers, not only to record quotes and details but to work hard at understanding their ideas and their passions. The reporting and writing forced me to resist easy conclusions and flat judgments. I had to interrogate myself—what do I believe, and why do I believe it? Above all, I had to reconcile myself to the tangle of complexity that is life itself.

Wolves are the subject of much journalism, particularly in Alaska, but creative nonfiction offered me a way to deal with many related ideas: what people mean by "wilderness" and "nature," what we're willing to face, what we look away from. Because I could report on my own reactions and emotions without allowing them to dominate the essay's intentions, I could be honest and reflective in a way that straight journalism doesn't usually allow. My ideal reader for this piece is someone who disagrees with the trappers and with me. I hope very much that the style and the approach convince readers to finish the piece and perhaps even reconsider their own notions.

Probably I would never trap a wolf or even buy a wolf pelt as a decoration. I wanted the wolf pelt because it reminds me that the world is exciting, painful, beautiful, and difficult—just like writing.

Being Brians

BRIAN DOYLE

. .

There are 215 Brian Doyles in the United States, according to a World Wide Web site called "Switchboard" (www2.switch board.com), which shows telephone numbers and addresses in America.

We live in forty states; more of us live in New York than in any other state. Several of us live on streets named for women (Laura, Cecelia, Chris, Nicole, Jean, Joyce). A startling number of us live on streets and in towns named for flora (Apple, Ash, Bay, Berry, Chestnut, Hickory, Maple, Oak, Palm, Poinsettia, Sandlewood,

. .

BRIAN DOYLE is the editor of *Portland Magazine* at the University of Portland, in Oregon—twice named the best university magazine in America. He is the author of four essay collections, most recently *Leaping: Revelations & Epiphanies*, and the editor of *God Is Love*, a collection of the best spiritual essays from *Portland Magazine*. Doyle's own essays have appeared in the *American Scholar*, the *Atlantic Monthly*, *Harper's*, *Orion*, *Commonweal*, and the *Georgia Review*, among other periodicals, and in the *Best American Essays* anthologies of 1998, 1999, and 2003. He is a contributing essayist for *The Age* newspaper in Melbourne, Australia.

and Teak) or fauna (Bee, Bobolink, Buck, Buffalo, Bull, Deer, Fox, Gibbon, Hawk, Pine Siskin, Salmon, Swift, Wildcat).

Some of us live on streets named in the peculiarly American fashion for a bucolic natural place that doesn't exist, a pastoral Eden of the imagination, the sort of name that has become de rigueur for housing developments: Bellarbor, Greenfield, Greenridge, Cresthaven, Cricklewood, Knollwood, Pleasant Hill, Shady Nook, Skyridge, Ridgewood, Spring Winds, Trailwood.

And there are Brian Doyles in uncategorizable but somehow essentially American places (Vacation Lane, Enchanted Flame Street, Freedom Road, Sugar Land) and in some places that seem to me especially American in their terse utility: Main Street, Rural Route, United States Highway, Old Route, New Road.

One of us is paralyzed from the chest down; one of us is eighteen and "likes to party"; one of us played second base very well indeed for the New York Yankees in the 1978 World Series; several of us have had problems with alcohol and drugs; one of us is nearly finished with his doctorate in theology; one of us is a nine-year-old girl; one of us works for Promise Keepers; one was married while we were working on this article; one welcomed a new baby; one died.

The rest of us soldier on being Brian Doyle.

"Tell me a little bit about yourself," I wrote us recently:

How did you get your name? What do you do for work? What are your favorite pursuits? Hobbies? Avocations? Have any of us named our sons Brian? What Irish county were your forebears from? Where were you born? Where did you go to college? What's your wife's name?

Brian, the doctoral student in theology at the Catholic University of America:

I ride my bike and search for new microbrews. No children. We still have family in County Kerry. They live on a dairy farm and moved out of the thatched-roof cottage about fifteen years ago, but it still stands on the property.

Brian, the New England field representative for Promise Keepers, "a Christian ministry dedicated to uniting men in vital relationships so that they might be godly influences in their world":

My wife and I are committed to honoring Jesus Christ in our lives, marriage, and in all that we do. He is Central to our daily living.

Brian of Waltham, Massachusetts, in a handwritten note:

I am a union iron worker in Boston and have been iron working for twenty-three years. I am pretty much a free spirit.

Brian, the undergraduate at the University of Kansas:

Hiked 700 miles of the Pacific Crest Trail. Biked from Newport, Oregon, to San Francisco down Highway 101. I don't know much about my name, but now you got me curious.

Brian of Red Hook, New York, eighteen years old:

Being eighteen really is not bad. It is cool for the first couple of months but the novelty wears off after a while. I am a junior at Red Hook High School where in my class there is only about 150 kids. Red Hook is a very small hick town (in the countryside). I have two jobs one at a place called Beverage Way, a beer and soda warehouse, and my second job is at Bard College where I do cater-

ing for parties. It is not much, but it pays the bills. Since I am only eighteen I am not married yet, but I have a high school sweetheart named Heather. My hobbies include basketball, quadding (four wheeling), taking care of my car, and partying as any teenager loves to do. Besides that there is not much more to do up here.

Brian in Denver, Pennsylvania:

Our clan came from Kerry around the turn of the century. One of my uncles became chief of police in New York City.

Brian of Leicester, Massachusetts:

I never realized that there are that many of us. I am forty-nine years old and was injured in the military back in 1969. I was wounded three times in Vietnam and got to walk off the plane, but within two months I was involved in a motor vehicle accident while home on leave and I became paralyzed from the chest down. I have worked as a police dispatcher and clerk/dispatcher for my local highway department. In the last three years I have been spending the winter months in Florida and the summer months here in Massachusetts, and eventually I will be spending all my time in Florida as there is so much more to do and a lot easier to get around. I am currently retired as I decided a few years ago that it was time to enjoy life right now as I grow older I will not be able to get around as easy as I can now. My wife Shirley is legally blind with a degenerative eye disease. So let's go for the gusto and enjoy while we can. I do not know what county my Irish forebears came from. I wish I did. I went to work at our local highway department after my one year in college and was drafted into the Army in 1968. Hope to hear back from you.

I write back to Brian of Leicester and tell him that I am grateful for his courteous note. I think about him in his wheelchair and his wife who cannot see very well and the days and months he must have spent on his back after his car crash thinking about the irony of surviving warfare only to be savagely injured on a highway, and by then it is time to put my sons and daughter to bed, which I do with the sharp flavor of gratitude in my mouth.

Brian in Livonia, Michigan:

I have four daughters—Nicole, Meghan, Adrienne, and Stephanie. Sons? What are sons?

Brian of Livonia adds a genealogical note about our surname, which is an English translation of the Gaelic word *dubghaill,* or *dark stranger,* a word often used in early times to denote a Dane. Doyle is now the twelfth most common name in Ireland. Brian of Livonia also points out that the name Brian hails from the last Irish high king, or *ard righ,* Brian Boru, slain in 1014 in the battle of Clontarf.

Brian Doyle in Poughkeepsie, New York:

I know of a few other Brian Doyles—a plumbing supply salesperson, a local restaurateur, and an IBM public relations official—but have met none of them. I have been asked several times if I played second base for the New York Yankees in 1978. Of course, I confess that I am this same person who nearly won the 1978 World Series MVP Award—but later confess to this lie.

Brian from Chicago, who turns out to have been a year behind me in college, to our mutual astonishment:

A Doyle anecdote. Our Doyles originally settled in Brooklyn, New York. My great-grandfather started a business making men's dress shirts, the kind without the collar, as was the custom then. Doyle and Black was a good name in dress shirts. Black, the partner, died early on, but the name was retained as Doyle and Black. The business failed during the Depression, but during its early years of prosperity, my great-grandfather gave rings to his sons. The rings, plain gold bands with a ruby, diamond, and sapphire—red, white, and blue, to remind us of how good this country has been to us—are handed down from Doyle father to Doyle son. I received my father's ring when I turned twenty-one and will give it to my son Trevor. My father's uncle Ed passed away without heirs, so I will have his ring also to pass on to my son Jay.

Brian Doyle in Baton Rouge, Louisiana:

Please forgive me for not responding sooner, but I, like most Brian Doyles, am extremely important and in constant demand. I work as a probation and parole agent, but consider it a ministry. I was born again in 1983 and attended Trinity Bible College in Ellendale, North Dakota, and became credentialed with the Assemblies of God. Evangelism is my call and my heartbeat. Baseball is my passion. I write as a hobby. My wife and I were actors in Manhattan for over a decade, and she's a published Christian playwright. I specialize in smart-aleck letters. I've never been to Ireland other than in drunken fantasies, back before I got sober in 1979. I know I'm part Irish (the sentimental, poetic, occasionally morose part), part English (the self-righteous, self-important, frequently overbearing part), part German (just ask my son about my "Gestapo tactics"), and part French (the part of me that instinctively wants to immediately surrender when I face a battle). I entered AA in NYC in 1979 where I met my lovely and *wonderful wife, Christy. She was an actress; I was an actor; we were both drunks; what else could we do but get married? Which is what we did in 1982. We're still having a great time together.*

Brian of Naples, Florida:

I was also named after the great Brian Boru. Recently divorced, though very much in love again with a wonderful woman. Early life at home was very confusing, and I took refuge in hiding in mind and mood alterers, i.e., alcohol and drugs. I have not indulged in such behavior in over seven years. I have taken up long-distance running and have run ten marathons and countless other races. I was in the air-conditioning field for fifteen years, but as I became more aware it just didn't feel right.

Next morning I count up the number of letters that have come back stamped UNDELIVERABLE or NO LONGER AT THIS ADDRESS or UNDELIVERABLE AS ADDRESSED or that have the new resident's angry, scrawled HE DOESN'T LIVE HERE ANYMORE!!!! on them in large, annoyed block letters: forty-three. Where are those Brian Doyles? The Lost Brian Doyles, addresses gone bad, addresses rotten, addresses thrown out on the compost heap, moldering.

Denise Doyle, of Saltillo, Pennsylvania, in a handwritten letter:

We thought your letter was very neat! Brian is self-employed in the carpenter field: building, remodeling, etc. He loves to fish and hunt. We have a daughter, Brianne, named after her daddy, age nine. Brian is a layed back sort of guy and has a lot of care for other people.

Calm, compassionate, caring—it's a Brian Doyle thing.

Brian in Houston, Texas: Likes cold beer.

Brian in Braintree, Massachusetts: Named for Brian Boru. Parents: Francis and Frances, both Irish natives. Brian was the goalkeeper on the University of Lowell's 1979 national championship hockey team, had a cup of coffee with the National Hockey League's Phoenix Coyotes, and once played in a high school hockey game where both goalies were named Brian Doyle.

Brian of Valley Cottage, New York: Father called him Boru as a boy. Appalachian Trail nut:

I've hiked the trail from Maine to Georgia, and I guess you could say that I'm a woodsman, eastern style.

Remembers with affection his cousin Brian Doyle who died a few years ago in Pittston, Pennsylvania, where his father's people, fleeing *An Gorta Mor*, the horrendous Irish famine of 1845–51, landed in America to work the coal mines.

Not unlike some of my father's ancestors, who fled Wicklow and Cork from what my grandmother called "the Horror" and became bartenders, bricklayers, cigar dealers, steelworkers, die cutters, freight clerks, and bookkeepers in the Tenth, Eighteenth, Twentieth, and Thirty-fourth Wards of Pittsburgh, this line eventually producing my grandfather, James Aloysius Doyle, who with Sophia Holthaus produced another James Aloysius Doyle, my father, who with Ethel Clancey produced another James Aloysius Doyle, my brother, nicknamed Seamus, who died as a baby, my mother discovering him seemingly asleep in his stroller on a bright April morning in New York in 1946, which discovery plunged my parents into a great blackness, but eventually they recovered, as much as possible, and they made a daughter and four more sons, one of whom is named for Brian Boru, high king of Ireland until his last day at Clontarf.

Obituary notice in the *Oregonian*, Thursday, May 22:

Brian Doyle, died May 16, age 42. Veteran, United States Army; spent last 15 years of life working as mail handler for United States Postal Service. Accomplished figure skater, competed for U.S. Olympic teams in 1976 and 1980. Gifts in his memory are to be sent to the St. Vincent de Paul Society, a Catholic organization that collects food and clothe. for the poor.

What Brian died of, the article does not say. Nor, for all the facts, does it say who he was. It doesn't say who or how he loved. It doesn't report the color of his eyes. It doesn't show the shape of his ambition, the tenor of his mind, the color of his sadness, the bark of his laugh. It doesn't say with what grace or gracelessness he bore his name, how he was carved by it, how his character and personality and the bounce in his step were shaped and molded by its ten letters, how he learned slowly and painstakingly to write

$$B R I A N$$
$$D O Y L E$$

as a child and so saw himself on paper, how he learned to pick the quick song of *Brian* out of the soup of sound swirling around him as an infant, how he sat in the first row in school because his surname began early in the alphabet, how other schoolchildren tried to edit and mangle and nick his name—Brian the Lion, Lying Brian, Oily Doyle, Lace Doyley—how he was fascinated as a small boy sitting at his grandmother's knee and watching her sew a lace doily, the word doily squirming in his mouth, his tongue tumbling over *Doyle* and *doily* for days afterward. Probably as a boy he added up the letters and admired the symmetry of his first and last names, as I did. Probably he spent a few moments, once, late on a rainy summer afternoon, bored, writing Mrs. *Brian Doyle* to see what it looked like, to hold the dangerous idea of a wife on paper for a moment, as I did. Probably he saw and heard his name misspelled, as we all did, on applications and reports and documents and certificates and letters and envelopes and phone calls: Brain Doyel, Brian Dooley, Bryan Doyle, Brien Doyle, Brian Dalkey, even Brian Dahlia once, the woman at the other end of the scratchy phone doing her best to spell what she so dimly heard, to make real the faraway sound of a name.

BRIAN DOYLE ON *"Being Brians"*

Aw, what pleases me about this piece is that it went off in unexpected directions and twists and turns, and it went deeper than I expected into the heart, and it was sometimes hilarious and sometimes sad, like life, like good essays do—they take off through the woods their own damned selves to go wherever they are going and the author, if he is not a complete dolt, follows after, interested to find out what it is he has to say.

E. M. Forster: "How do I know what I think until I see what I say?"

It fell short of my dreams for it only in that I didn't talk to all of the Brian Doyles—I only connected to about half of them. Us. Nor did I ever connect to the most famous American Brian Doyle, who played for the Yankees in the World Series, though I did have many a fun talk with his secretary Nancy, who is a gracious soul with a memorable drawl. "Briiiiiiiiiiian's not heeeah," she'd say politely.

Though I did hear from many Brian Doyles round yon globe afterward: Canada's best-selling young adult author Brian Doyle, and Australia's famous comedian Brian Doyle, and a Brian Doyle in Sligo, and . . .

I didn't expect, in pulling this thread to see what stories would pour out shining and singing, to find Brian Doyles who were female. That was a startlement.

To write creative nonfiction is really only to write stories; and stories all begin with paying attention and listening and asking questions; and then you pull the grinning thread to see what will happen; and after you pour it all down you feel for the bones of the story, and make it lean and taut and clean; and very often I find that the essay is about something else utterly than I thought. Which is a delight and perhaps the prime reason writers write. Along with catharsis and beer money.

I do think that creative nonfiction is the great burgeoning genre of modern America post-world war; the boom in "nature writing," for example, is a boom in telling true stories about people and the world; which is what all literature is, of course; but the best and widest form in which to tell it is, to me anyway, small true odd interesting unusual voice-laden funny poignant detailed musical sweet sad stories. Creative nonfiction is really the coin of our lives and discourse; along with the lies we tell each other, we tell many small true creative stories. So we have essayettes in our mouths all day long, and trade them like kisses.

My advice for new writers is the same advice my dad, a newspaperman, gave me many thousands of years ago:

1. learn to type sixty words a minute or better
2. write something every day: letter, rant, journal, poem, prayer, whatever
3. learn to listen
4. get a job to pay the bills

When you are pretty sure a piece is done, get it off your desk and onto an editor's.

Language at Play

DIANE ACKERMAN

. .

All language is poetry. Each word is a small story, a thicket of meaning. We ignore the picturesque origins of words when we utter them; conversation would grind to a halt if we visualized flamingos whenever someone referred to a *flight* of stairs. We clarify life's confusing blur with words. We cage flooding emotions with words. We coax elusive memories with words. We educate with words. We don't really know what we think, how we feel, what we want, or even who we are until we struggle "to

. .

DIANE ACKERMAN was born in Waukegan, Illinois. She received an MA, MFA, and PhD from Cornell University. Her works of nonfiction include, most recently, *Cultivating Delight: A Natural History of My Garden; Deep Play*, which considers play, creativity, and our need for transcendence; *A Slender Thread*, about her work as a crisis-line counselor; *The Rarest of the Rare* and *The Moon by Whale Light*, in which she explores the plight and fascination of endangered animals; *A Natural History of Love; On Extended Wings*, her memoir of flying; and the best-seller *A Natural History of the Senses*. In June 2004, Scribner published her book *An Alchemy of Mind*, a poetics of the brain based on the latest neuroscience.

find the right words." What do those words consist of? Submerged metaphors, images, actions, personalities, jokes. Seeing themselves reflected in one another's eyes, the Romans coined the word *pupil*, which meant "little doll." Orchids take their name from the Greek word for testicles. Pansy derives from the French word *pensée*, or "thought," because the flower seemed to have such a pensive face. "Bless" originally meant to redden with blood, as in sacrifice. Hence, "God bless you" literally means "God bathe you in blood."

We inhabit a deeply imagined world that exists alongside the real physical world. Even the crudest utterance, or the simplest, contains the fundamental poetry by which we live. This mind fabric, woven of images and illusions, shields us. In a sense, or rather, in all senses, it's a shock absorber. As harsh as life seems to us now, it would feel even worse—hopelessly, irredeemably harsh—if we didn't veil it, order it, relate familiar things, create mental cushions. One of the most surprising facts about human beings is that we seem to require a poetic version of life. It's not just that some of us enjoy reading or writing poetically, or that many people wax poetic in emotional situations, but that all human beings of all ages in all cultures all over the world automatically tell their story in a poetic way, using the elemental poetry concealed in everyday language to solve problems, communicate desires and needs, even talk to themselves. When people invent new words, they do so playfully, metaphorically—computers have *viruses*, one can *surf* the Internet, a naive person is *clueless*. In time, people forget the etymology or choose to disregard it. We dine at chic restaurants from *porcelain* dinner plates without realizing that when the smooth, glistening *porcelain* was invented in France long ago, someone with a sense of humor thought it looked as smooth as the vulva of a pig, which is indeed what *porcelain* means. When we stand by our scruples, we don't think of our feet, but the word comes from the Latin *scrupulus*, a tiny stone that was the smallest unit of weight. Thus a scrupulous person is so sensitive he's irritated by the smallest stone in his shoe. For the most part, we are all unwitting poets.

When we create with words, in the literary arts, we raise the stakes. Then we stare straight at our inherently poetic version of life, make it even more vigorous and resourceful. Poetry, for example, speaks to everyone, but it cries out to people in the throes of vertiginous passions, or people grappling with knotty emotions, or people trying to construe the mysteries of existence. At a stage of life remarkable for its idealism, sensitivity, and emotional turbulence, students tend to respond for all three reasons.

Sometimes when I pass a basketball court I'm transported, thanks to the flying carpet of memory, back to my first real teaching job in the early eighties. At the University of Pittsburgh, I taught various undergraduate writing and literature courses, but I remember most dearly the graduate poets I taught. Not much older than most of them, younger than a few, I found their blue-collar enthusiasms a tonic. All the elements of their lives breathed with equal intensity. They played as hard as they worked as hard as they loved as hard as they wrote. It was typical of them to discuss Proust in the stands before a hockey game. They bought poetry, read poetry, wrote poetry in the seams between work and family, met at a bar after class to drink Iron City beer and continue talking about poetry.

After class one evening, we all went to a nearby basketball court so that one of the students could teach us "fadeaway jump shots," an image he had used beautifully in a poem. Sometimes I went with them to the Pitt Tavern after class, where we would continue talking late into the night. With an unself-conscious fervor that amazed me then, and in retrospect still does, they demanded to be well taught. They knew instinctively that words could change their lives. My job was to keep pace with their needs. I had no choice but to teach them everything I knew, learn with fresh energy, then teach them even more if I could.

At the end of one semester, in the closing hour of the final seminar, I asked if there was anything we hadn't talked about that needed to be addressed. One of the best writers raised his hand. "How to make love stay," he said simply. For the remaining hour, that is what we discussed. I can still see his soulful face. Smart, romantic, unpredictable—he was all poet. Even now, a dozen years later, I worry about him, hope he survived the intensity he craved but could not live with. I hope he continued writing. I see the faces of the others, too, and wonder how they've fared. Although I could not tell them so at the time, I knew where some of their emotional travels might lead them. They were intense young poets. In vital ways, we were similar. We shared a common currency—we understood the value of poetry.

When I was a freshman at Boston University in the late sixties, I used to stroll beside the Charles River with a copy of Dylan Thomas's poems in one pocket and Wallace Stevens's in another. I was drawn to the sensuous rigor of Thomas and the voluptuous mind of Stevens. Together they opened the door for me and many others into a realm of ideas, song, wordplay, idea play, discovery, and passion. What I loved about Thomas (and still do) is the ways his poems provide a fluid mosaic in which anything can lose its identity in the identities of other things (because, after all, the world is mainly, as he put it, a "rumpus of shapes"). By mixing language and category with a free hand, he seems to know the intricate feel of life as it might come to a drunk, or a deer, or a devout astronomer freezing to death at his telescope. His poems throb with an acute physical reality. No poet gives a greater sense of the *feel of life*.

Then he goes even further, to re-create the *process* of life through a whole register of intricate and almost touchable images and events. Working himself into a state of neighborly reverence, he invents metaphors that don't so much combine A and B as trail A and B through a slush of other phenomena. He ardently weds himself to life's sexy, sweaty, chaotic, weepy, prayerful, nostalgic, belligerent, crushing, confused vitality in as many of its forms as he can find, in a frenzy that becomes a homage to creation. In this way, he seems to create a personal physics to match his ideas, so that the language of his best poems echoes the subject matter, and both suggest the behavior deep in our brains, hearts, and cells. He really does nibble the oat in the bread he breaks, intuit the monkey in the newborn baby, see the shroud maker in the surgeon sewing up after an operation. Sometimes he's cryptic, as when he writes: "Foster the light nor veil the manshaped moon." Sometimes a clear-eyed observer, as when he refers to: "the mousing cat stepping shy,/The puffed birds hopping and hunting." Sometimes he's lyrically emphatic: "The hand that signed the paper felled a city." Sometimes he's a maker of schoolboy jokes, sometimes a celebrant seer. But above all, he can transform the Saturday afternoon reputation of the planet—a couple of imposing-sounding topics, its being called a "star," the Pyramids, Jesus, Adam, illness, birth, death, sex—into something sacramental. Not neat. Not well behaved. Not explicit. Not always argued or even structured. But bold, wild, and tenderly voluptuous. How could I resist all that?

Other poets took my fancy, too. I loved the way poets illuminated life like a holy text, drawing my attention to how dreams were made, and to the beauty at the heart of the most commonplace dramas and things. Poetry had a way of lifting a feeling or idea out of its routine so that it could be appreciated with fresh eyes. In "the foul rag and bone shop of the heart," as Yeats called it, I knew words, and especially the charged reality of poetry, had everything to teach me about life.

Poetry was all I knew to write at eighteen. Much has happened in my writerly life since then. Although I still write poetry, I've learned to write prose, too, and that has brought its own frustrations and freedoms. In both genres, writing is my form of celebration and prayer, but it's also the way in which I inquire about the world, sometimes writing about nature, sometimes about human nature. I always try to give myself to whatever I'm writing about, with as much affectionate curiosity as I can muster, in order to understand a little better what a human being is, and what it was like to have once been alive on the planet, how it felt in one's senses, passions, and contemplations. In that sense, I use words as an instrument to unearth shards of truth.

These days, I do that more often in prose. But the real source of my creativity continues to be poetry. I've just published a new collection of poems. I read poetry regularly. My prose often contains what are essentially prose poems. Why does poetry, with its highly charged words, play such an important role in my life? For centuries poetry was vital to the life of nearly everyone. In the nineteenth century, poets such as Byron and Tennyson were superstars of Hollywood status. Movies and television may draw more viewers now, but poetry continues to inspire us, reveal us to one another, and teach us important truths about being human.

The reason is simple: poetry not only reflects the heart and soul of a people, it has a wisdom all its own. There is nothing like poetry to throw light into the dark corners of existence, and make life's runaway locomotive slow down for a moment so that it can be enjoyed. Science and technology explain much of our world. Psychology tells us more about human behavior; all three succeed by following orderly rules and theories. Poetry offers truths based on intuition, a keen eye, and the tumultuous experiences of the poet. Long ago in India, for example, Urdu poets writing in the verse form known as a *ghazal* were also trying to figure out the universe. A ghazal was the technology they used to make sense of their world, and no doubt they felt as sonneteers and composers of villanelles do, that there are truths only to be learned when you're dancing in chains.

The craft of writing poetry is a monklike occupation, as is a watchmaker's, tilting tiny cogs and wheels into place. It's ironic that poets use words to convey what lies beyond words. But poetry becomes most powerful where language fails. How can we express in words that are human-made emotions that aren't? How can we express all the dramas and feelings that are wordless, where language has no purchase? Words are small shapes in the gorgeous chaos of the world. But they *are* shapes, they bring the world to focus, they corral ideas, they hone thoughts, they paint watercolors of perception. Truman Capote's *In Cold Blood* chronicles the drama of two murderers who collaborated on a particularly nasty crime. A criminal psychologist, trying to explain the event, observed that neither one of them would have been capable of the crime, but together they formed a third person who was able to kill. Metaphors, though more benign, work in the same way. The chemical term for what happens is *hypergolic:* you can take two inert substances, put them together, and produce something powerfully different (table salt), even explosive (nitroglycerine). The charm of language is that, though it's human-made, it can on rare occasions capture emotions and sensations which aren't.

The best poetry is rich with observational truths. Above all, we ask the poet to teach us a way of seeing and feeling, lest one spend a lifetime on this planet without noticing how green light sometimes flares up as the setting sun rolls under, the unfurling of a dogwood blossom, the gauzy spread of the Milky Way on a star-loaded summer night, or the translucent green of a dragonfly's wings. The poet refuses to let things merge, lie low, succumb to habit. Instead the poet hoists events from their routine, plays with them awhile, and lays them out in the sunshine for us to celebrate and savor.

When a friend and I were cycling the other day, she mentioned that reading poetry frightens her.

"What if I don't get the real meaning?" she asked. "What if I read 'a ghostly galleon' and think it's referring to a ship, when it's really referring to the lost innocence of America?" I was dumbfounded. Someone had taught her (and nearly everyone else) that poems work like safes—crack the code and the safe opens to reveal its treasure.

"There are many ways to read a poem," I said. "After all, you don't really know what was going through the poet's mind. Suppose he was having a tempestuous affair with a neighbor, and once when they were alone he told her that her hips were like *a ghostly galleon*. He might have then used that image in a poem he was writing because it fit well, but also as a sly flirtation with his neighbor, whose hips would be secretly commemorated in verse."

"Do poets do that?" she asked, slightly scandalized that noble thoughts might be tinged with the profane.

"I've done it," I admitted with a grin. "I presume other poets do."

I went on to explain, as teachers of the writerly arts do, that poems dance with many veils. Read a poem briskly, and it will speak to you briskly. Delve, and it will give you rich ore to contemplate. Each time you look, a new scintillation may appear, one you missed before.

The apparent subject of a poem isn't always an end in itself. It may really be an opportunity, a way for the poet to reach into herself and haul up whatever nugget of the human condition distracts her at the moment, something that can't be reached in any other way. It's a kind of catapult into another metaphysical county where one has longer conceptual arms. The poet reminds us that life's seductive habits of thought and sight can be broken at will. We ask the poet to shepherd us telescopically and microscopically through many perspectives, to lead us like a mountain goat through the hidden, multidimensionality of almost everything.

We expect the poet to know about a lot of strange things, to babysit for us, to help us relocate emotionally, to act as a messenger in affairs of the heart, to provide us with an intellectual calling card, to rehearse death, or map escape routes. As many have pointed out, poetry is a kind of knowing, a way of looking at the ordinary until it becomes special and the exceptional until it become commonplace. It both amplifies and reduces experience, paradoxical though that may sound. It can shrink an event teeming with disorder to the rigorous pungency of an epigram. It can elasticize one's perspective until, to use an image of John Donne's, a drop of blood sucked by a single flea accommodates the entire world of two lovers. Few views of life are as panoramic as the one seen through John Milton's cosmological eye. Milton could write "all Hell broke loose" because he knew where (and what) Hell was; he had sent his wife and daughters there often enough, and his vision encompassed it, just as it did the constellations (many of which he introduces into *Paradise Lost*). He could write "Orion rose arm'd" because he'd observed Orion often enough when the arms weren't visible.

Poetry, like all imaginative writing, is a kind of attentiveness that permits one both the organized adventure of the nomad and the armchair security of the bank teller. Poetry reminds us of the truths about life and human nature that we knew all along but forgot somehow because they weren't yet in memorable language.

If a poet describes a panther's cage in a certain vivid way, that cage will be as real a fact as the sun. A poem knows more about human nature than its writer does, because a poem is often a camera, a logbook, an annal, not an interpreter. A poem may know the subtlest elisions of feeling, the earliest signs of some pattern or discord. A book of poems chronicles the poet's many selves, and as such knows more about the poet than the poet does at any given time, including the time when the book is finished and yet another self holds her book of previous selves in her hands. A poem knows a great deal about our mental habits, and about upheaval and discovery, loneliness and despair. And it knows the handrails a mind clings to in times of stress. A poem tells us about the subtleties of mood for which we have no labels. The voluptuousness of waiting, for instance: how one's whole body can rock from the heavy pounding of the heart. It knows extremes of consciousness, knows what the landscape of imagination looks like when the mind is at full throttle, or beclouded, or cyclone-torn. Most of all, it tells us about our human need to make treaties. Often a poem is where an emotional or metaphysical truce takes place. Time slow-gaits enough in the hewing of the poem to make a treaty that will endure, in print, until the poet disowns it, perhaps in a second treaty in the form of a poem. There is even a technical term for that: a *palinode*. A poem knows about illusion and magic, how to glorify what is not glorious, how to bankrupt what is. It displays, in its alchemy of mind, the transmuting of the commonplace into golden saliences. A poem records emotions and moods that lie beyond normal language, that can only be patched together and hinted at metaphorically. It knows about spunk, zealousness, obstinacy, and deliverance. It *accretes* life, which is why different people can read different things in the same poem. It freezes life, too, yanks a bit out of life's turbulent stream and holds it up squirming for view, framed by the white margins of the page. Poetry is an act of distillation. It takes contingency samples, is selective. It telescopes time. It focuses what most often floods past us in a polite blur.

We read poems in part, I think, because they are an elegant, persuasive form of reasoning, one that can glorify a human condition feared to be meaningless, a universe feared to be "an unloving crock of shit," as philosopher Henry Finch once said offhandedly. To make physical the mystery is in some sense to domesticate it. We ask the poet to take what surpasses our understanding and force it into the straitjacket of language, to rinse the incomprehensible as free of telltale ambiguity and absurdity as possible. That's not to say that we don't find nature ambiguous or life absurd, only that the temptation to play and land the mystery like a slippery salmon, to freeze it in vocabularic aspic, is irresistible. Surely this is not far afield from the hunting magic of the cave drawings at Lascaux.

We ask the poet to reassure us by giving us a geometry of living, in which all things add up and cohere, to tell us how things buttress one another, circle round and intermelt. Once the poet has broken life into shards, we ask him to spin around and piece it back together again, making life seem even more fluid than before. Now it is a fluency of particulars instead of a nebulous surging. We ask the poet to compress and abbreviate the chaos so we don't overload from its waterfall of sensations, all of which we nonetheless wish somehow to take in.

Every poem is a game, a ritual dance with words. In the separate world of the artwork, the poet moves in a waking trance. By its nature, poetry and all art is ceremonial, which we sometimes forget, except perhaps when we think of the Neolithic cave

painters in the *mysterium tremens* of their task. Intent on one feature of life, exploring it mentally, developing it in words, a poet
follows the rules of the game. Sometimes artists change the
game, impose their own rules and disavow everyone else's. Then
they become an ist among the isms. But there are always rules,
always tremendous concentration, entrancement and exaltation,
always the tension of spontaneity caged by restriction, always
risk of failure and humiliation, always the drumbeat of rituals,
always the willingness to be shaken to the core.

Once, after a lecture, a woman asked why accomplished scientists and prose writers (such as Loren Eiseley), who turned to
poetry late in life, were such poor poets. Is it easier to switch from
poetry to prose than from prose to poetry? she wondered. I don't
think the genre is what matters, but the time of life. If you read
the first book by famous scientists—J. B. S. Haldane, Werner
Heisenberg, Francis Crick, Fred Hoyle—you find minds full of
passion and wonder. Those books are thrilling to read because
mystery is alive in them, and they are blessed by a youthful, free-
flowing enthusiasm. But in later books these same people
become obsessed with politics and sociology; their books are still
of intellectual interest, but they've lost the sense of marvel.
Those who stay poets all of their lives continue to live in that
youthful state, as open and vulnerable and potentially damaging
as it can be.

I suppose what most people associate with poetry is soul-
searching and fiercely felt emotions. We expect the poet to be a
monger of intensity, to pain for us, to reach into the campfire so that
we can watch without burning ourselves. Because poets feel what
we're afraid to feel, venture where we're reluctant to go, we learn
from their journeys without taking the dramatic risks. We cher-
ish the insights that poets discover. We'd love to relish the
moment and feel rampant amazement as the seasons unfold. We

yearn to explore the subtleties, paradoxes, and edges of emotions. We long to see the human condition reveal itself with spellbinding clarity. Think of all the lessons to be learned from deep rapture, danger, tumult, romance, intuition—but it's far too exhausting to live like that on a daily basis, so we ask artists to feel and explore for us. Daring to take intellectual and emotional chances, poets live on their senses. In promoting a fight of his, a boxer once said: "I'm in the hurt business." In a different way, artists are too.

And yet, through their eyes—perhaps because they risk so much—we discover breathtaking views of the human pageant. Borrowing the lens of an artist's sensibility, we see the world in a richer way—more familiar than we thought, and stranger than we knew, a world laced with wonder. Sometimes we need to be taught how and where to seek wonder, but it's always there, waiting, full of mystery and magic. I feel that much of my own duty as a writer is to open those doors of vision, shine light into those dark corners of existence, and search for the fountains of innocence.

The world is drenched with color and nature is full of spectacles. You would think that would be enough. Yet we are driven to add even more sensations to the world, to make our thoughts and feelings available in words. We use words for many reasons. As a form of praise and celebration. To impose an order on the formless clamor of the world. As a magical intermediary between us and the hostile, unpredictable universe. For religious reasons, in worship. For spiritual reasons, to commune with others. To temporarily stop a world that seems too fast, too random, too chaotic. To help locate ourselves in nature and give us a sense of home. Words bring patterns, meaning, and perspective to life. We keep trying to sum life up, to frame small parts of it, to break it into eye-gulps, into word-morsels that are easier to digest.

Sometimes words allow us to put ourselves in harmony with the universe, to find a balance, however briefly, in life's hurricane. They make it possible not only to communicate with one another but to do it in a way that may change someone's life.

Isn't it odd that one big-brained animal can alter the course of another's life, change what the other sees when it looks at its reflection in a mirror, or in the mind's mirror? And do that by using the confection of *words*. What sort of beings are we who set off on symbolic pilgrimages, pause at mental towns, encounter others who—sometimes without knowing it—can divert or redirect us for years? What unlikely and magical creatures. Who could know them in a lifetime? When I start thinking like this, in *words*, wonder shoots its rivets into my bones. I feel lit by a sense of grace, and all my thoughts turn to praise.

Excerpted from *Deep Play* (Random House, 1999)

DIANE ACKERMAN ON *"Language at Play"*

Among the many kinds of nests writers create for the feathered mysteries that live inside them, I find poems more like nesting stones and prose more like woven mud-and-twig nests. But both are home. I alternate between writing books of nonfiction and poetry, and I'm always happiest with the most poetic sections of my prose books.

Poetry was all I knew to write until I was about twenty-two; so it was also the only way I could know the All. In graduate school, when I felt I needed more elbow room, I began learning to write prose, which didn't come naturally to me, and was a nightmare chore for years. Novelist Paul West tutored me and guided my progress. What also helped enormously was writing thirteen very short, densely poetic articles (about American heroes and landmarks that had grown stale in the imagination) for *Parade*, because it taught me how to balance a vast amount of research, observation, and response in a tiny space. I will always be grateful to its editor in chief, Walter Anderson, a tall man who casts a long shadow, for believing in me and setting me a challenge that would teach me priceless skills. How vividly I remember that first assignment from *Parade*—a thousand-word portrait of everything and everyone that happened at Ellis Island. It was dead summer and brutally hot. I'd tried for days to write it, and, crying, sat down beside a pool where Paul was swimming. I showed him the jumbled manuscript, and bawled about how I would never be able to fix it, that I was in over my head, that I had no job, no bank account, no future, and no hope. Holding on to the pool coping, he read the essay, praised its descriptive passages and intuitions, damned its organization, and reassembled it. "Put this here, and that there, and this bit at the end, and that bit at the beginning, and write a paragraph about those things here, and then it'll be fine!" he said. That's just what I did, and it worked. Structuring prose—whose rhythms, patterns, and architecture were so different from poetry's—was the hardest thing for me to learn. But at some point, after grueling years of struggle, for reasons I can't explain, something clicked and prose became a familiar country. Now I find it comfortable, fascinating, sometimes even thrilling to write. My muse has become highly miscellaneous. And I feel lucky indeed to have been able to use prose as a passport to some of the most astonishing subjects, people, and landscapes on earth.

Finders Keepers: The Story of Joey Coyle

MARK BOWDEN

▪ ▪

South Philadelphia does not call attention to itself. It is built low to the ground, in row after brick row; no house stands high above another. Brothers live across narrow streets from brothers, fathers from sons and nephews and grandsons. Down the alley folks can sometimes see in the awkward way a boy runs or squints or throws a ball the reflected image of his grandfather or great-uncle. When a man from South Philly says he knew a fellow "from the neighborhood," it means something more like family than acquaintance. A woman in South Philly might live two doors down from her most hated high school rival, who, after decades, children, dozens of pounds, and a lifetime of worries, has become like a sister. South Philly is Catholic. It is proud and superstitious, pragmatic and devout. It harbors hate that outlasts the grave, but knows more love than hatred. It has many stories to tell, but they are like stories told around the dinner table,

▪ ▪

MARK BOWDEN writes for the *Philadelphia Inquirer* and is the author of the nonfiction books *Black Hawk Down*, *Bringing the Heat*, and *Doctor Dealer*. He lives in Philadelphia.

stories not readily offered to outsiders, who lack the appropriate context and who might insist upon awkward detail.

Those who grow old in this world know more answers than they will give. For instance, there is an old expression in South Philly that a man uses when he comes into money that he would rather not explain. He says, "It fell off the truck."

It means: *Don't ask.*

Day One

Coming down made Joey Coyle feel desperate and confused. When he was high the drug filled his chest and head with gusts of power so great he could barely breathe or think fast enough. This was how Joey spent his nights. When he slept it was during the day.

It had been almost a month since the union had called to give Joey work on the docks. He made good money as a long-shoreman. It was where his father had worked and where his older brother worked. Joey had never finished high school, but he had an educated feel for machinery. On the docks they used him to repair the lifts, and he was good at it. He took pride in that. Engine grease colored gray the heavy calluses on his hands.

But for more than a year the economy had been bad in Philadelphia, and there were few chances to work. They had called him to fill in for a few weeks over the holidays. But that had been more than a month ago.

Shiftlessness weighed on Joey. He was twenty-eight, and he still lived in his mother's house. He was devoted to his mom. His father had died of a heart attack on a night after Joey had stormed out in anger after an argument. The old man didn't like the length of the boy's hair. His father had been gone six years, but in Joey the grief and guilt was still fresh. Staying with his mother had somehow helped. But now his mother was sick with liver disease, and he couldn't care for her anymore. She had moved just a few blocks away to his sister Ellen's apartment. Without reason, Joey blamed himself. He felt rejected and a failure, but would not have put those words on the feelings because he never looked inside himself long enough to figure them out. He couldn't. In the months since she left, his days blurred into nights in a speeding carousel of exhilarating highs and then crushing lows as he hustled to get money to buy more of the white powder called meth, which he called blow. It blew away all the demons of self-doubt and depression.

His home on Front Street was at the tattered edge of the tight weave of South Philly's streets, away from its strong, nurturing core. East of Front Street is a wasteland: weedy, trash-piled lots, junkyards, old brick warehouses defaced with graffiti, rusting hulks of old boxcars in forlorn rows alongside the newer cars that come and go, fenced-in lots around the trucking yards and dwindling industrial works along the Delaware River waterfront. Over this bleak expanse, the air is tinged gray and tastes of ash. Just behind the row of houses on Joey's block loomed the giant concrete underside of Interstate 95, which threw a perpetual shadow wider than a city block. When Joey was a little boy, he would leave the comfortable nest of his neighborhood and pass through the cool shadow of the great highway, the rush of its restless traffic roaring steadily overhead, and play on the grotesque junk heaps and boxcars beyond. It was a crude playground. He would search out clusters of rat holes, pour gasoline down all of them but one, and then touch a match to them. Joey would sit a few yards off from the one unburning hole and shoot at the fleeing rats with a bow and arrow. When he was older, he and his friends stealthily passed television sets from loaded boxcars to waiting arms, then ran to trade the loot for money to buy grass and beer.

For a boy, and then a young man, the wasteland beckoned as a lawless haven, training for streets seductive with vice. After Joey's father died, what little resistance he had to the lure of those streets was gone. Unlike his friends, Joey Coyle had not outgrown those years. He avoided the demons that troubled him in quiet moments and projected to the world a feckless, fun-loving style that was both frustrating and endearing to those who loved him. His complexion was pale pink, his hair so thin and blond you could hardly make out the mustache he had been growing for five years or the eyebrows over his small, deep-set blue eyes. Joey spoke in a gruff whisper that often turned into laughter and had no more of an interest in serious conversation than he had in hanging by his thumbs—which is something neighborhood bullies had actually once done to him. But trouble was immune to Joey's charm; it sought him out, and when it strayed, it seemed like Joey went looking for it. Like the time his car stalled and blocked a street. A man disputed Joey's placement of the vehicle and, in the ensuing brawl, drew a savage slice across the left side of Joey's face that had healed into a crooked gray scar from eye to earlobe. There was nothing funny about that scar, but Joey would tell the story in a way that would make people laugh, about how he finally got the man down just in time for the fuzz to arrive and spot him as the aggressor— which earned Joey another, official, beating. But bad luck just seemed to bounce off Joey. He would laugh and laugh even though the joke was on him. With bitter irony he would call it the luck of the Irish; he even had the word "Irish" tattooed on his upper right arm with a pipe and shamrock and shillelagh. His neck and chest and arms were broad and thick, and his hands seemed oversized—so swollen from all the times he had broken them working on engines that it was hard for him to close them into a fist. He could look tough, especially with that scar, but Joey was a danger to no one but himself. Meth had muddied his mind so that he could not think straight for more than a few sentences. His front teeth had all been knocked out and replaced by a row of fakes. Joey had the calloused look of someone who had been knocked down a lot on hard streets, and a smile that wouldn't quit.

But nothing in Joey Coyle's resilient history could have prepared him for the joke fate would play on him this day.

He woke well after noon with the realization that he had used the last of his meth the night before. He was still high, but he could feel the sick feeling gaining on him.

He awakened in his mother's big bed in the wood-paneled bedroom one story above Front Street. Joey rose and walked downstairs in his underpants to start a pot of coffee. He went back upstairs while the coffee was brewing and returned wearing worn jeans and a flannel shirt. He poured a cup of black coffee and walked outside to sit on his front steps and drink it. His pay-check for the holiday work was supposed to arrive in the mail any day now—about $700. Maybe his dealer would front him.

It was a cold afternoon. Joey scanned down the line of parked cars toward Spite's Bar at the corner. The block of two-story homes was empty. Above the telephone lines that draped lazily across the street, the sky was bright gray.

A few houses down, Johnny Behlau was out working on his father's car. It was a maroon boat of a Chevy, a 1972 Malibu. John had a coat of blue primer over the right front end that he had hammered back into shape. Behlau's friend, Jed Pennock, was just hanging out watching him work. Both John and Jed, like Joey, were unemployed. John was twenty-one. He was the taller of the two, a skinny blond-haired kid with a cocky, tough manner. Jed was short and stout. He had dark hair which enabled him, at twenty, to sport a heavier mustache than Joey. Jed wore glasses with heavy, dark frames and was, in contrast to his friend, introverted, mild, and unsure of himself. Both Behlau and Pennock were out of school, waiting long, idle days for the economy to improve so they could get regular work on the waterfront and resume a normal life.

Joey knew them just as kids in the neighborhood. He was going to make their day. He walked down and greeted them with an offer.

"I can cop some blow if you give me a ride," he offered.

Boredom being easy prey to controlled substances, the boys and Joey set out at once in the Chevy.

But the dealer wasn't in. John and Jed sat in the car while Joey knocked, paced the sidewalk in front of the house, and then knocked some more. For the boys, it was a minor disappointment, but they could see that it was more serious with Joey. He was frantic. He slumped back into the car.

"We can try him again later," he said.

On the way home, Behlau stopped to buy gas at the Shell station on Oregon Avenue. Then he took a shortcut home up Swanson Street.

Swanson Street is a back road on the western edge of the wasteland, almost under I-95. For trucks, it is an axle-jarring shortcut from waterfront loading docks to Oregon and Delaware Avenues. High in the distance to the south is the long approach ramp of the Walt Whitman Bridge.

As Behlau turned up this rugged back alley, Joey was slumped in the front passenger seat, depressed as the landscape. To the left were familiar mounds of black earth piled with tires, garbage, bedsprings, soggy, stained mattresses, and broken glass. To the right was the double fencing around the Purolator Armored Car Company grounds. It was habit for Joey to scan the curbs along

Swanson. It was amazing the things you could find. Sometimes people dumped things he could sell or use.

And, sure enough, up ahead toward the right curb of Swanson was a yellow metal tub with its wheels pointing up. Behlau had to slow down to steer the car around it.

"Might make a good toolbox," said Joey. Behlau stopped.

Joey opened the car door and leaned out to right the tub and take a better look at it. It had two lid flaps that joined at the center with holes for padlocks, but there were no padlocks, and as he pushed the tub upright the top fell open, and out onto the street spilled two big canvas bags. They were white with lead seals and yellow tags at the top. Black letters on the sides of the bags spelled out "Federal Reserve Bank."

Joey laughed loudly. "Holy shit!" he said. "To hell with the box!"

Both bags were heavy. Joey stepped out for leverage and yanked them into the car.

"Let's get out of here!" Joey shouted. "Move it! Let's roll!"

"Where?" shouted Behlau, who already had the car moving.

"My house! Go!"

Behlau stepped on it. The car flew over the railroad tracks as he turned left on Wolf Street. Joey pulled a ballpoint pen from Behlau's dashboard, poked a hole through the thick canvas of one bag, and tore it open. Behlau stopped the car momentarily by the curb between two warehouses to have a look. Pennock leaned over the front seat. Inside the torn bag on Joey's lap were tightly-wrapped cellophane bundles of what looked like . . . Sweet Jesus! . . . Hundred-dollar bills!

"Oh, man!" said Joey. "What am I into now?"

John and Jed whooped deliriously.

Wheels squealed as the Malibu sped into the shadow of I-95. Joey felt a rush like a jolt of the drug. The boys were shouting for joy and thumping him on the shoulders. He just stared at the money and shook with laughter. Joey laughed and laughed. He laughed so hard that the plate with his front teeth plopped in his lap.

Rumpled, steady Detective Pat Laurenzi was in his car at about 3 p.m. when he heard the report on his police radio. An armored car had dropped a bag of money somewhere near the vicinity of Front Street near the Purolator property. No information on the amount missing.

Laurenzi lived on street smarts, coffee, and hustle, a small man with a boyish face and muscular frame. He had wide brown eyes and straight brown hair that was cropped in a straight line high across the middle of his forehead, the haircut of a man with no time for barbers. There were places in the back where the hair stood upright. Reporting for his eight-hour shift, the detective looked more like an oversized Philly street kid than a man with a gold badge. His tight stretch sport shirt was tucked into the belt of light brown jeans, which he pulled high. Under his worn gray docksiders were white socks.

He was not surprised by the Purolator report. This sort of thing had happened before. It usually involved a couple thousand dollars, and the money usually didn't stay missing long.

But back at his South Philly precinct, a bulky gray stone fortress on a tree-lined block of South Twenty-fourth Street, Laurenzi learned immediately that this Purolator drop was far more serious. Two bags were missing. The company estimated they held a total of $1.2 million. And it was casino money, which meant that instead of being in numerical sequence, the way it comes from the Federal Reserve Bank, these were bundles of random hundred-dollar bills, untraceable, the cleanest money money could buy.

Of course, with $1.2 million missing you had to start with the drivers. So Laurenzi drove over to the Purolator building. First, he inspected the armored car in the Purolator yard. There were two doors in back. The left door had to be shut and padlocked before the right door could be closed, so that door was usually kept shut. The right door fastened above and below with two steel rods that fitted into slots by rotating the door handle first to the right and then to the left. Once closed, a button at the center of the handle could be pushed to lock it in place. Just for the hell of it, Laurenzi had one of the Purolator men lock him inside the back. He leaned forward with one broad shoulder to the double doors, and the right one gave a loud snap and popped open. There had been two metal tubs in the back end that afternoon, one with two money bags, the other empty. Both were missing.

Laurenzi asked to see the drivers. Poor Bill Proctor and Ralph Saracino had already been suspended indefinitely. Everybody was eyeing them suspiciously.

Proctor, who was forty-six, was visibly shaken. He had told his story over and over in the past two hours. He swore he had locked the door tightly when they left the Federal Reserve Bank on Arch Street that afternoon. He had placed the two money bags in one of the two empty wheeled tubs they were supposed to take down to Ventnor the next day. Saracino, the twenty-one-year-old partner, said that he had watched Proctor fasten the door, by the book. They had driven down Delaware Avenue, turned right on Wolf Street, and then left on Swanson down to the back entrance of Purolator. It was a trip they could make blindfolded. It took only about six minutes. Sure, the roads were bad and it had been a bouncy ride, but with the doors locked it couldn't have dropped out!

Their attention had been called to the open back door by a dispatcher at the second, interior gate into the Purolator yard.

Proctor said he had bounded out to see. The vertical steel bars of the right door were still in the locked postion, but the door had somehow swung open. When Proctor had leaned in the back end to look, both tubs were gone. He had run back to the front of the truck.

"Turn around," he shouted to Saracino. "We got to go back and retrace our route!"

Proctor took off on foot to ask the guard to reopen the first gate. Saracino backed the truck out, and Proctor jumped back in. Their panic eased briefly when they immediately saw the yellow tub up the street. Two men were standing over it. But as they approached the two men, one asked, "Was there anything in this?"

"There was," said Proctor, his hopes dashed.

Proctor got out to look. Inside, on the bottom of the tub, was the yellow receipt for two bags, one carrying $800,000, the other $400,000. There was nothing to say. They had driven past that same spot less than three minutes ago! Somehow, in the time it had taken them to drive down one hundred yards, pull through the first Purolator gate, discover the door was open, back out, and return, somebody had removed the bags from the tub. Proctor felt like someone had knocked the air out of him. He felt sick and nervous, and a little bit scared.

After talking to both Proctor and Saracino separately, Laurenzi was suspicious of their story. With that much money gone he had to be suspicious of everyone. Maybe the locked door had swung open when the heavy tub banged into it. But maybe not. Laurenzi didn't believe in the lie detector, but the company wanted the guards tested. He asked Proctor and Saracino if they would agree to it. The men were alarmed, but they agreed.

It is worth mentioning that while Detective Laurenzi was going through these essential first steps of his investigation, two FBI men in suits arrived. Often, it is reported in cases that might involve federal jurisdiction that the FBI is "standing by," or "following the case closely," or that it is "ready to provide assistance" to local police. Laurenzi was thirty-one, and he had been a city cop for one-third of his life, a detective for almost five years, yet this was the first time he had the chance to observe firsthand the FBI fulfilling this generous role. The men in suits stood nearby, observing but not commenting or getting involved. It began to get on the detective's nerves. Now, there's no denying that the FBI is good at what it does, and the detective with his Cardinal Dougherty High School/Philadelphia Police Academy diplomas certainly didn't want to make it appear as though he didn't appreciate the professional presence of these feds with college/ FBI Academy credentials, but Laurenzi called the men in suits aside and made it plain that if they weren't going to do anything but hover over his shoulder, maybe they could find something more useful to do uptown.

When the FBI men left, Laurenzi got back to work. He interviewed the other witnesses gathered in the Purolator Building, and by late afternoon he had come to the reluctant conclusion that the guards were telling the truth. Thomas Piacentino had been working at his father's junkyard just off Swanson Street where the one tub fell off the truck. He related the whole scene to Laurenzi: The yellow tub falls. In the minute or two that follow, one or two cars come down Swanson, ease around the obstacle, and drive on. Then this maroon Chevy Malibu with the right front fender painted blue stops suddenly, and a man looking to be in his late twenties or early thirties leans out, laughs loud enough for Piacentino to hear forty yards away, pulls two white things—they look like gunnysacks—out of the container, throws them into the car, jumps in, and it takes off fast around the corner. Curious now, Piacentino and his brother Charles walk out to have a look at the container. Just as they reach it, the armored truck comes barreling back up Swanson, and out jumps this guard, who looks real nervous.

It was dark when Laurenzi left the Purolator property that evening. His first working hunch was blown. He mulled over the problem as he twice retraced the route taken by the armored car from the Federal Reserve Bank to Swanson Street. The case was going to be hard. If somebody had just driven by and picked the money up, and that appeared to be what happened, how were you going to find them if they were intent on keeping it? Purolator was ready to put up a $50,000 reward. But it takes a special breed of honesty to trade $1.2 million for $50,000. The detective knew that if whoever had those money bags just stuck them in a closet for long enough, there was virtually no way of recovering them. Philadelphia is a city of five million people. The only way to make a mistake would be to start passing out a lot of hundreds right away. Nobody was that dumb. But Laurenzi knew that was his only chance.

Then again, Swanson Street was no main thoroughfare. It was a neighborhood shortcut. The only people who used it were those who worked along that stretch of waterfront . . . and those who lived nearby.

It takes effort to believe a stroke of luck so grand. Joey and the boys felt an immediate need to hold the cellophane bundles in their hands, tear off the packaging, and feel and smell the bills. Johnny Behlau turned south on Front Street and stopped his father's car in front of Joey's. Joey took the bigger of the two canvas bags and sprinted up four front stairs. Pennock carried the other bag. He and Behlau followed Joey inside.

They ran upstairs to Joey's room, tore open the second money bag, and dumped the contents on his bed. There the

three stood gaping at the treasure. There was bundle after compressed cellophane bundle of cash, more than a hundred of them.
Every one of the bundles was more money than they had ever
seen. Each was wrapped with a paper band that read $10,000. All
the bills appeared to be hundreds.

Joey was delirious with joy. He shouted, he leapt, he laughed.
He kept embracing and kissing John and Jed, who were equally
thrilled. Joey kept saying it was like a scene in a movie, like a
scene in a movie. He felt more excitement than he knew how to
express. Every time he looked down at the pile of bundles on his
bed it was almost like he expected it not to be there.

Of course, somebody was going to be looking for this money.
After the initial excitement, reality began to intrude. Joey, John,
and Jed stood around the big colonial-style bed and excitedly discussed their find. They figured the money belonged to the government, that it had fallen off one of the Purolator armored cars. The
cops were going to hear of anyone flashing hundred-dollar bills.
John and Jed wondered what kind of a reward there might be. But
if Joey had even one fleeting thought of returning this bounty it
was banished before it was fully formed. Finders keepers, man.

"It's mine," Joey told the boys. "I worked hard all my life. My
hands are all busted up. I got nothin'."

He was no fancy talker, so he had no words to express it, but
Joey felt at that moment like he had been touched by destiny, by
the hand of God. His father had smiled down from heaven on his
troubles. This was his chance. He had never felt more sure of a
thing in his life. It was perfect! He had done nothing wrong. No
crime had been committed. He hadn't hurt anyone. It was
money from heaven. It was money meant for him. Finders keepers—if he just didn't blow it.

Now Joey had to try to think clearly. He swore John and Jed
to silence. No, they could not even tell their parents.

"I'll take care of everything," he said.

If it worked out, they would get a share of the money, too. If it didn't, it was on him.

"Leave it to me," he said.

But the problem seemed overwhelming. He would have to find a way of breaking the hundreds into smaller bills. But how? Where? Joey knew he needed help. And the man who came first to mind was his friend Carl Masi.

Carl Masi had once been a prizefighter. After the war, he boxed as a lightweight for a few years before settling back in Philadelphia as a typesetter. At fifty-four, he was still a muscular man with square features and curly gray hair. But Masi's heart was failing. Surgeons had opened his chest twice from neck to belly to make repairs. The doctors were always cheerful and optimistic, but Masi didn't expect to live much longer. This had softened his manner, which was quiet anyway. It seemed there was no surprise or anger or fear that could overcome his will to savor what life he had left. His two daughters were grown; the older one was married. His wife, Dee, worked at Fidelity Bank. Since he couldn't hold a regular job anymore, Masi worked some nights as a bouncer for The Purgatory Club on Second Street, which was owned by a friend. In his condition, he could hardly be expected to mix it up with anyone, but the customers didn't know that.

Masi had known Joey Coyle and his family from the neighborhood. Over the years, he had taken a special liking to Joey. The kid had no father, and Carl had no son. Joey was trouble sometimes. He took drugs and drank too much and gave his poor mother fits, but Masi saw that he was a good-hearted kid. He got mad when he saw how other men took advantage of Joey whenever the kid came home from the docks with a big paycheck.

Joey had poor judgment and was easily misled. Send the kid out with a roll of cash in his pockets, and he would come home high, happy, bruised, and broke. But Masi was indulgent. He was past the point of being riled by failed expectations, his own or anyone else's. He never gave up on Joey. He had gotten the kid a job as a doorman for the Purgatory Club. And it was there that Joey observed that Masi knew personally some of the shadowy, serious men who were part of the Philadelphia/Atlantic City mob.

Once Carl Masi's name popped into Joey's head he clung to it like a lifeline. Leaving Pennock with the money, he and Behlau got back in the Chevy and drove to a Sunoco station on Oregon Avenue. From a pay phone, he called Masi's house. Masi's daughter answered.

"This is Joey. It's important."

"He's not home," she said. "You can call Mom at work."

So Joey dialed Dee Masi at the bank.

"Where's your old man?" he asked.

"He should be picking me up soon," she said. "What's wrong?"

"You comin' home now?"

"Yes."

"Good. I'll see you there," said Joey, and then teased her a little. "Got somethin' to show you."

Behlau drove Joey first to another dealer's house, where he at last copped some meth. As he rode back to his house, Joey impatiently fingered the plastic bag full of white powder in his jacket pocket.

At home, Joey prepared to inject himself in the kitchen. The ritual was a familiar one. Pour some powder on a spoon, add a few drops of water, hold the spoon over a flame until the powder was mixed well with the water, draw the white liquid up into a hypodermic needle, pick a vein in his right forearm—they were getting harder to find—and inject. Joey's need had grown so urgent that he performed this ritual every hour.

Fired up again, Joey returned to his bedroom and dragged two Bishop Newman schoolbags, small square suitcases of stiff black cardboard, from his closet. He stacked the bundles in the suitcases, then folded the canvas bags in on top of them. Then he and Behlau took the suitcases to Masi's rowhouse on South Twenty-ninth Street.

"He's connected," Joey told Behlau, which the younger man understood to mean Masi had ties to the mob. "Carl will know what to do with it."

Masi's daughter let them in. They took the suitcases to a front bedroom on the second floor. It was the biggest bedroom in the house, second floor front, with beige walls and standard, sixties-style department store furnishings. White curtains over the front windows allowed only a dim glow of light into the room. Joey set the black cases on the Masis' bed.

He removed the money in urgent fistfuls. Each of the $10,000 bands was marked with a set of three initials, for each of the tellers who counted it. Joey marveled at the rituals of procedure revealed by the money's packaging. The initials were repeated on each bundle in the same order, on the top hundred-dollar bill in each bundle, and then again on the tag at the top of the canvas bag. Joey began to remove the wrappers and tags. After he had accumulated a mound of cellophane and paper wrappers, he stuffed that and the lead seals from the tops of the torn canvas bags into a double paper grocery bag. He got a can of lighter fluid from Masi's daughter and took it out to the patio, no bigger than a driveway, behind Masi's house. He stuffed the bag inside a trash can, soaked it with lighter fluid, and set it on fire. Joey stood by until it smoldered and then squirted more fluid on it. He kept the inside of the can burning until all the paper was gone and the seals were molten disks of lead. When the lead cooled, he took the dull, smooth disks from the bottom of the can and dropped them in his pocket. He didn't want to leave a trace.

While Joey was doing these things, Behlau left to get Pennock. Back up in the bedroom, Joey piled the wrapped and unwrapped hundreds into neat stacks of $50,000 and set them in a bureau drawer. Then he went down to the kitchen to wait for Dee and Carl. John and Jed returned and flopped on the plastic-covered furniture in the Masis' living room.

Carl and Dee arrived at about 4 p.m. Joey met them at the door.

"Come on upstairs," he said. "I got somethin' for ya."

It looked to Masi like Joey was all cranked up again. The older man eyed suspiciously the two strange boys in his living room. Joey told John and Jed to wait for them downstairs. Then he and the Masis walked upstairs together. In the bedroom, Joey pulled open the drawer. Carl and Dee Masi stared at the money silently.

"Joey, did you kill anybody?" Masi asked.

"No!" Joey laughed.

"Did you hurt anybody?"

"No!"

Joey was impatient with his friend's subdued response. He drew the cash from the drawer and made a pile of it on the bed. Then he picked up Dee and dropped her on top of it. Dee laughed. Masi just looked on quietly. He didn't know where the money came from, but he knew it couldn't legitimately belong to Joey Coyle. Then he remembered. On the radio news in the car he had heard that more than a million dollars had fallen off the back of an armored truck.

"I heard about this," he said. "This is the money that fell off the truck this afternoon."

"Yeah," said Joey.

"Joey, you ought to get in touch with a lawyer and get in touch with Purolator and see what they'll give you for a reward."

"No way, Carl. It's mine. I found it."

"Joey, they're not going to let you keep it."

"How they gonna know?"

Masi knew Joey, and he knew there was no way he and these two kids downstairs were going to keep a secret like that. They were too excited, too young, too careless. He knew what Joey was like when he was all cranked up. It was going to be all over South Philly in a couple of days, no avoiding it.

"They already got a description of your car," Masi said. "I heard it on the radio coming over. Maroon Chevy with a blue front fender. There it is parked right outside. You're crazy."

Joey felt a touch of panic. It hadn't occurred to him that somebody might have seen them picking the money up.

"I come to you for help," Joey said. Joey explained that he had called Masi because he was connected. He wanted somebody from the mob to help him change the money into smaller bills. He would be willing to share it, he said.

"Could you get in touch with a few people? Get the money broke down from hundreds?"

Whatever they were going to do, first they would have to get rid of the car. It sat out in front like a red flag. It was past four-thirty. The evening news would be on in a few minutes. Then everybody in Philadelphia would be looking for a maroon 1972 Chevy with blue primer on the front fender.

So Joey and Carl went downstairs and explained to Behlau that they had to ditch his father's car. Behlau was alarmed. It was his father's! What could he tell him?

"What are you going to do with it?" he asked.

"Look, we're just going to take the car over the bridge and sit it over in Jersey for the time being," said Joey.

Behlau reluctantly went out to the car, removed some of his own things and some scraps of ID from the glove compartment, and handed over the keys. Joey drove the Chevy, and Masi followed in his own car. Joey held his breath as they crossed the Walt Whitman Bridge. His gaze swept from one rearview mirror to the other. He expected to get pulled over at any minute. He drove to the 200 block of Mercer Street in Gloucester, near the shipyard where his older brother Billy was a supervisor, and parked it. Then he and Masi drove to a bar for a few drinks. Pennock, Behlau, and Dee Masi and her daughter were waiting for them when they returned two hours later.

Many men talk of their willingness to take great risks to accomplish great things, but few are really ready for the challenge when it stares them in the eye. If it had taken an hour early that afternoon for John Behlau and Jed Pennock to believe they had really found more than a million dollars on the street, it took only a few minutes of that night's television news for the scale of their adventure to sink in. The Purolator boondoggle was that night's lead story. Something akin to stage fright fluttered in the boys' bellies. Then came second thoughts.

"What did you do with my father's car?" Behlau asked when Joey returned.

"Don't worry," said Masi.

"We should get it crushed down," said Joey.

Behlau freaked. "That's my father's car!"

"Okay, okay. Jesus! We'll buy him a new car. We'll get it repainted. Tell him you're having it repainted. You'll get it back in a couple of days. No," said Joey. "I got too much to think about. Just leave it where it is for now."

Joey had asked Masi to call someone to help out with the money. The group of six sat in the Masis' small living room before the television and discussed what they had learned on the news. Pennock told Joey that the money definitely belonged to Purolator. They had been a little surprised at how much attention the story was getting. They told Joey that maybe they ought to consider giving the money back.

"Don't worry about it, don't worry about it," said Joey, his gruff voice rising with impatience. "There's been no crime committed. If there's anything that goes down, it's their fault, not ours! Like, they're negligent for losin' the money. Nobody has said there's a reward or anything. We just gotta lay low. We're rich. They know it's gone, but they don't know we got it."

What happened next that evening is a part of the story that retreats into shadow. One of the abiding oddities of life in South Philly is the mob, a long-standing, hierarchical, neighborhood (in that meaningful sense) criminal organization. There are those who will smile and swear that such a thing does not exist. But several times a year, an otherwise healthy man is found on the sidewalk or in the trunk of a car with a belly full of pasta and a bullet hole in his head. Decent, patriotic folks who go to church every Sunday and wash their children's mouths out with soap for swearing will shrug their shoulders and turn their heads and fail with alacrity to summon any outrage over this. The shadow world of violence coexists with virtue in South Philly, just as in the hearts of even the best of men there is sin. It is not spoken of. Even those who would speak of it are silenced by fear. There are things said or seen that become secrets vaulted so securely that the truth stays locked beyond the reach of any truth serum, courtroom, or oath.

A man from these depths came that night to Carl Masi's house. He was called Sonny. He was a man in his mid-fifties, short and thick, with glasses and a balding forehead. He spoke with a deep, gruff voice. Joey believed the man was Mario "Sonny" Riccobene, younger brother of the bearded, hunchbacked Harry Riccobene, and one of the most notorious organized crime leaders in Philadelphia. Joey felt a chill of fear and pleasure to be with him in the same room. He and Masi and Sonny went upstairs, where the money was still in a big pile on the bed. The others waited downstairs.

"What's the matter? You got a problem?" asked the man called Sonny.

Joey showed the cash. He explained that it was the Purolator money. The money that had fallen off the truck, $1.2 million.

"You gonna give it back?"

"I figure there wasn't, like, no crime committed," said Joey. He had a tendency to stutter when he was too excited.

"Is there a reward?"

"Like, the money is being looked for—it was on radio and TV and all—but they ain't put up no reward. So, I figure, these people lose $1.2 million, and they ain't puttin' up no reward for it! And I got these stacks of money, and it's very real, and they're offerin', over there, like nothing, a row of zeroes, you know what I mean? Hey, it ain't greed, but show me something to show good faith."

"What are you gonna do with it?"

Joey had given this some thought. He spelled out his plan. "Look, I think it would be smart to take this money and split it in three directions. Four for you, four for me, four for Carl. Put it in three different places, right? That way, if they catch me, I still got eight hundred thousand dollars when I get out. And you take the four for you, and you give me back three in small bills. The other hundred thousand is for you. Whatever, you know what I'm saying? Like, just get me back the three hundred thousand in small bills as quick as you can, and you can keep a hundred thousand just for doin' it."

Sonny nodded slowly. Joey stood alone in the bedroom while the two older men conferred in the dark hallway. Then they returned.

"I think I could do that," said Sonny. "We could take it down to the casinos and play it. You win some and you lose some, but that way you pass as much of it as you can as fast as you can. We could do that. These aren't consecutive bills. It would take me a day or two."

Joey was delighted. It was more than merely getting the help he sought. It was a kind of recognition. They had bought his plan! Joey felt . . . well, honored. He sorted the money into three roughly equal piles. He put his cut back in one of the black cases. Masi and Sonny put theirs in brown paper bags. Then they came back downstairs. Before leaving the house, the man called Sonny turned to John and Jed. Silently, he put his forefinger to his lips and then, pointing toward them, held up his thumb like the hammer of a gun and let it fall. Both boys got the message.

Carl Masi would live much longer than he expected, but even in later years when he was asked to tell the story of Joey Coyle and the money that fell off the truck, long after the case was over and the police had lost interest in it, he would leave out the part about another man coming into his house that night.

"Wasn't there a man who visited that night?" he would be asked, because the story was well known.

"Here?"

"Yes. Others who were here have said that Sonny Riccobene came over that night."

"No way. Sonny Riccobene has never set foot in my house."

"No? Did anyone else come in?"

"Joey brought somebody in here, but it wasn't Sonny Riccobene. Those kids are crazy. I know Sonny Riccobene. Those kids are wrong. I bet you if you showed those boys Sonny Riccobene face to face they wouldn't even know him."

"Do you know who it was who came over that night?"

"Some guy. But it wasn't Sonny Riccobene. I wish those kids were here looking at me when they said that. Because they're wrong. They always said that it was Sonny Riccobene. They had the name 'Sonny.' And they said it was Sonny Riccobene. But they're full of shit. They are one hundred percent wrong. Do you think a guy like Sonny Riccobene would have let somebody like Joey Coyle keep two-thirds of that kind of money? They're crazy, spreading stories like that. Sonny Riccobene has never been in this house. That's the truth."

With his plan in motion, Joey Coyle felt like a man who had wrestled a giant opponent to the earth, and even though he knew the match was not over, he could take a deep breath again for the first time since finding the money that afternoon. Soon after the man called Sonny left, Masi drove Joey and John and Jed back to Front Street. They left the remaining $800,000 in the bureau drawer in Masi's bedroom. Joey and the boys felt unburdened.

Masi arranged for a friend to loan Joey a big boat of a car, a car sufficient to match Joey's prosperous mood. It was an emerald Cadillac El Dorado with a white convertible top and a white interior. It was . . . well, perfect.

Waiting for Joey at home was his nineteen-year-old girl-friend, a small, thin blond woman named Linda Rutter. Linda was seeing Joey somewhat on the sly. She had another boyfriend, a more respectable boyfriend, from whom she kept Joey secret. She and Joey had been seeing each other like this for about a year. At the house, in the mail, Linda had found Joey's $700 check. She had taken it right away to a check-cashing place in the neighborhood where they knew her and Joey, and they had cashed it for her. She knew Joey was hungry for that money, and she was looking forward to blowing some of it that night. But when Joey came in, he looked strung out. Without hesitation, Joey explained to Linda his remarkable and exhausting day. Linda was excited and a little scared.

An hour after returning home, at about nine-thirty, Joey and Linda went out to buy groceries at the Pathmark at Fourth and Oregon. They bought groceries and came home, where John and Jed were waiting for Joey.

Joey was in no mood to get into it with the boys again. He felt like he had bought into something bigger after the meeting with Sonny. John and Jed were out of their depth. He had to get rid of them. Joey knew that Sonny had scared them badly enough that they weren't going to tell anyone about the money. So he told them that he didn't want to talk in front of his girl-friend and that he would meet them in half an hour on the corner. John and Jed left. They waited down the street, and then watched angrily as Joey and Linda left the house, got back in the Cadillac, and drove off.

Joey drove to his sister Ellen's house on Darien Street. Ellen was ironing. She is a big, blond, articulate, outgoing woman of thirty-one who tried to mother Joey the way she did her own children. She saw her baby brother as a vulnerable, artistic boy who lacked the maturity or self-confidence to manage life on his own. Like the time Joey had worked out a mechanical device to keep drivers down on the docks from accidently blowing out transmissions on the lifts. Ellen had forced Joey to sit down and sketch the thing and sent him to a lawyer to see about getting a patent so he could get some profit out of it. Joey had drawn it and had gone to see the lawyer, but he had never pursued it. That was the way he was. People loved Joey, but the same boyish qualities that made him lovable made him maddeningly difficult. Ellen, on the other hand, was a rock. She was as sober and steady as Joey was addled and dissolute. Ellen had been especially worried about Joey ever since their mother was bedridden and had to leave the old house to move in with her. She knew he was using drugs heavily and that he wasn't working. She worried about him. When she looked at his battered body, scarred face, and wild eyes, she saw a little blond-haired boy in a suit on the day of his first communion. She prayed for him. But there was only so much she could do.

Leaving Linda in the car outside, Joey went upstairs to see his mom, who was watching television with Ellen's eight-year-old daughter, Katie. His mother was sitting up in bed. She looked bad. Katie was on the floor by the television. Joey spent about fifteen minutes with them, talking quietly. He offered to let his niece in on a big secret. He made her swear not to tell, and the little girl opened her eyes wide and swore it. Then he told her that he had come into a lot of money and that they were all going to be rich.

"You're my baby, don't worry about nothin'," said Joey. "I'm going to be leaving for a little while, but I'll be sending for everybody. We're going to fly Mama out of the city, get her to some really good doctors."

When he came back downstairs, Ellen thought Joey looked upset. She wanted to talk to him, so she offered him a cup of coffee.

"No thanks," said Joey. "I got to go." He was moving around the room, looking out the windows down the street.

"What's wrong, Joey?" Ellen asked.

"Nothing, nothing. Everything is all right."

He said goodbye and walked out the door.

Day Two

And who hasn't dreamed of finding a million dollars by the side of the road?

It might be argued that the Purolator Armored Car Company's misfortune was hardly as important to the lives and well-being of Philadelphia citizens as, say, President Reagan's visit to the British prime minister to discuss international trade, or the congressional debate over sending military aid to embattled Central American governments, but in white honor boxes on sunny street corners and folded on the front steps of hundreds of thousands of homes that Friday came the morning paper with this story stripped across the top: $1.2 MILLION FALLS OFF TRUCK; 2 FLEE WITH IT.

And as the city rose to sunny, warmer skies and the promise of a springlike weekend in late winter, and as the odors of coffee, eggs, and toast mixed in a million busy kitchens, readers skimmed reports of the world's weightier matters but read to the last line the story of the $1,200,000 that fell off the truck and then wondered aloud along Broad Street and on subways and trains and buses about what their next move would be. Very, very few of these fantasies began by giving the $1,200,000 back.

There was another story that day of particular interest to South Philly. Police had found the body of one Frank Stillitano, thirty, in a parking garage at Philadelphia International Airport. Stillitano, who was wanted at the time for questioning in another mob murder, had been shot once in the leg and once behind the left ear, packed in the trunk of a car, and parked in an airport lot for the long, long term. It was the latest in a series of mob killings—there would be a dozen in 1981—sparked by the 1980 assassination of longtime Philadelphia Mafia boss Angelo Bruno. News of the new mob killing had made its way around South Philly without benefit of modern media.

Joey Coyle and his girl, Linda, hadn't seen the newspaper. It was early morning over the blue Ben Franklin Bridge and over Alexander Calder's bright stainless-steel approximation of old Ben's kite and key, as Joey rolled his borrowed green and white El Dorado back from Jersey into Philadelphia and steered it south through rush-hour traffic. His secret $1,200,000 find was all over the morning airwaves. Linda kept punching the radio buttons. Joey wasn't really listening. He was so pumped up he was shaking. He had scored some meth the night before and had been injecting himself at intervals. It was all he could do to sit still behind the wheel of the car. He and Linda had spent most of the night celebrating at a series of Jersey watering holes and at the Admiral Wilson Motel, where they registered as Mr. and Mrs. Joey Coyle. But Joey could not sit still. All through Thursday night, he and Linda moved from the motel room to bar to bar to bar, and then back to the motel room. The combination of his excitement over the money and the rush of the drug swept him along in a whirl of energy that found expression only in sex and constant motion. He had no desire to eat or sleep. They had left the motel that morning because Joey told Linda he wanted to show her the money. Truth is, through all his confusion Joey had begun to worry that his friend Masi and this Sonny might not be content to just babysit his million. A worm of doubt had begun to creep into his thoughts.

Joey's fears were fed when he and Linda arrived at Masi's soon after sunrise to find Masi and the man he knew as Sonny huddled together in the kitchen. Sonny got up when they entered and quickly left.

"We want to take another look," said Joey.

So Masi escorted the couple upstairs to the bedroom. He showed Joey the black case filled with his third of the money. Joey asked Linda to unwrap more of the bundles and stack the bills on the bureau while he talked with Masi in the hall.

In the hall, Joey asked Masi where the rest of the bills were. The older man explained he had hidden his third, and that Sonny was leaving for Las Vegas that morning with his third. Masi could see how spooked Joey was.

"Stop worrying," he told him. Masi reminded Joey that the plan to split up the money had been his own. It took time to move that much money. He and Sonny had run into a few snags, but it was all going to be okay.

Joey trusted his friend, but the worry was hard to shake. The feeling had just started coming over him early that morning, and it was getting stronger. The drug just seemed to amplify it. He told Masi that he was going to take his third with him. When the older man left to drive his wife to work at the bank, Joey and Linda stuffed the remaining cash and loose wrappers into the black case and pointed the El Dorado back east toward Front Street.

Upstairs in his bedroom, Joey finished unwrapping the cash. He arranged the hundred-dollar bills into forty stacks, $10,000 in each stack, and fastened each bundle with a rubber band. He gave Linda a coffee can and told her to take the cellophane and paper wrappers to the bathroom, burn them, and flush the ashes down the toilet. She did.

Then Joey drove Linda over to her sister's house on Roseberry Street. He planned to spend the day alone at home, lying low. Joey told Linda he would get back in touch that night.

Back home on Front Street, Joey injected meth again into his right forearm. Over the years, the drug had ceased to give him anything that could be called pleasure. Addiction was like riding a devilish engine that worked double, triple time. At first it was fun and made Joey feel all-powerful, vibrantly potent, and so much happier than he felt normally. But then, as the drug's grip on him hardened, even though Joey's mind and body grew tired, they stayed strapped to the same frantic engine which ran on and on at its double, triple speed through day and night, dulling both pleasure and pain, until he was pinioned to it like some pathetic, wildy gesticulating marionette. It was here where the drug played its deadly trick. Instead of giving Joey a rush of energy and potency, he found he now needed the regular injections to calm himself down. After only a few hours without a boost, the engine threatened to career out of control, his senses reeling, his mind muddled and tormented by imagined terrors, his limbs shaking and in pain. The real devilish twist was that, in time, the only thing that hurt more than staying on the engine was getting off.

This time with the sudden surge of relief came another stronger surge of fear. Staring at all the green bundles, Joey felt suddenly overwhelmed by the challenge of hanging on to it. He expected the door to break down and the police to stomp in at any moment. Maybe he should have just left the cash with Masi. Joey got up and checked out the windows, just to make sure. Down the street in one direction he saw John Behlau and Jed Pennock out working on a pickup truck. In the other direction was a police car. It cruised slowly down the block, past Joey's house, and turned right on Wolf Street. The neighborhood was crawling with cop cars.

Joey paced and fidgeted. He had to find a safe place for the $400,000. But where? He gathered the bundles into a brown paper bag and took it down to the kitchen. Underneath the kitchen floor, Joey had long ago built a safe spot to hide his drugs. Twice, the police had searched his house looking for drugs, and both times they had missed the hiding place. Joey slid the bag of cash into the open space under the floor and covered it. At last, he could relax.

But only for a minute. Because right away the worry came back. Just because it had been a good hiding place for drugs, that didn't make it a good enough spot for $400,000. The cops would be looking a lot harder for the money than the drugs. A hiding place under the floor? No. They probably had dogs or something that could sniff out cash. Joey could almost smell the dogs in the house. He checked all the windows again. Then he returned to the kitchen, uncovered the hiding place, and removed the bag of money.

There had to be a better place. Joey walked down to the basement, looking for the perfect spot. He was poking around down there for about ten minutes, stumped, when he hit upon the idea of hiding the money inside his hot-water heater. He set down the bag and fetched his tools. After disconnecting the piping, Joey removed the top of the heater and pulled out the fiberglass insulation inside it. Then he stuffed the bag inside, replaced the fiberglass, and reconnected all the fittings. He worked up a sweat doing it. The whole job took about half an hour. Unburdened at last, Joey went upstairs to the kitchen and made a cup of instant coffee.

But the wheels kept turning. The hot-water heater was gas. It had a pilot light inside of it. What if the paper got too hot and caught on fire? It would all burn up! Leaving the coffee cup full on the kitchen table, Joey bolted back out for his tools and returned with them to the basement. Working methodically now, he disassembled the piping on top of the heater, removed the fiberglass again, and drew back out the bag of money. Then he put the heater back together.

Two hours had elapsed, and the money bag was still at Joey's feet. With his tools in one hand and the money bag in another, Joey walked up to the bathroom on the second floor. He had another idea. Getting down on all fours, he went to work on the toilet. He unbolted the toilet and, working with his plumbing tools, cut off the water connection. It felt good to be working with his tools; it calmed him. He tilted the bowl, and underneath, around the porcelain underbelly of the bowl, was a large enough empty space for him to stash the bag of money. The idea was appealing. Joey had known dealers who hid drugs there because the smell of the toilet bowl hid the stash from police dogs. He stuffed the bag up under the toilet bowl, reconnected the pipes, and bolted the toilet back to the floor.

Finally! Joey now felt relaxed enough to shower and change clothes. He made himself another cup of coffee and sat uneasily in the living room. Joey found lying low extremely difficult. Every few minutes he got up to check the windows, pulling back his mother's old curtains and peering out. He watched up and down the street. He paced. When the effects of the meth began to ease he would fix himself again. Taking a trip upstairs to urinate, Joey found himself no longer comfortable with the money inside the toilet bowl. It just didn't feel right to him. He couldn't explain it, even to himself, but Joey went straight for his tools again and began disassembling the toilet once more.

Before he had finished putting things back together, Joey thought of an even better hiding place. There was an empty space between the outside wall of the house and the plaster inside the walls. From inside the closet in his mother's bedroom he could climb up into the space between the ceiling and the roof beams, a tight squeeze, crawl the twenty feet across to the front of the house, and then lower the bag into the opening between the two front walls. It was a delicate task. His mother's bedroom had a dropped ceiling of tiles suspended on a fragile aluminum matrix. Joey carefully edged out along the wooden ceiling beams. He lowered the bag of money into the space behind the front wall. Perfect! Feeling more confident, he tried to back out faster than he had climbed in. Then, with a sudden terrific jolt, Joey found himself on the floor of his mother's bedroom. He was too cranked up to feel any pain. It took a few instants to figure what had happened. He had momentarily blacked out. Around him on the floor were several bent pieces of aluminum stripping and two of the large tiles from the ceiling. Overhead was a gaping hole. Crawling backwards, his knee had missed the two-by-four beam. Joey had been thrown suddenly off-balance, and his whole 175-pound frame had crashed through the ceiling and plunged eight feet down to the floor, where he now lay looking up.

It took Joey another hour to repair the dropped ceiling. He bent the aluminum strips back into shape and refastened them, and then replaced the tiles. When he finished, Joey paused to inject himself with meth again and decided that the money wasn't safe between the two walls, so he climbed back up into the crawl space, edged back over to the front of the house, and fished it out again. . . .

Detective Pat Laurenzi had gone home to Roxborough late Thursday night. He had written reports of his interviews at Purolator and sent out the following message to area police departments:

Wanted: theft, RSP, Comsp. 2-26-81 appx. 2:30 PM on the hwy. Swanson and Wolf St. committed by 2 W/M's #1 20 to 30 yrs. light brown hair thin NFD #2 male were in a Maroon Chevy Malibu 1969 to 72. with a right front blue fender.

males took from the Hwy. 2 canvas bags from a yellow container that fell from a Purolator Truck bags contained the
amount of appx. $1.2 million dollars in cash in used $100
bills Ser# unknown, money was picked up from the Federal
Reserve Bank at 6th Arch St. 2-26-81. Bags may have a tag
white in color with the name Atlantic National Bank of
Ventnor, N.J. Bags were tied by a rope-type tie and crimped
with lead. and further info contact F.B.I. or South Detective
Special Invest Unit Det. Laurenzi.

When he came back in to work at about eight the next
morning, there was a stack of telephone tips. Calls had started
dribbling in after the evening news Thursday night, and as public interest grew, the tips accelerated. Every hundred-dollar bill
in the region was suspect. People had seen the car in three states
going in five different directions. One caller had seen the car in
West Philadelphia by Drexel University. So Laurenzi got in his
car and spent a few hours cruising through that part of town.
Nothing. Then he drove back to precinct to take more calls.

He obtained a search warrant for the junkyard, in case the
brothers Piacentino had been less than forthcoming, but after
driving over and surveying the fantastic expanse of debris, the
detective realized that it would take weeks to conduct a proper
search—there were simply too many places where the money
could be hidden—and, besides, he tended to believe the brothers' story anyway.

Back at precinct again, Laurenzi knew he could do nothing
but wait for something else to happen. At his gray metal desk,
using a ruler as a straightedge, the detective drew a simple map of
Swanson Street between Oregon and Wolf. He labeled in small
squares the Purolator office and the junkyard, and drew a smaller
square in the center right of the road and wrote next to it

"TUB." He put other details in the drawing. A few yards up from the place where the tub had fallen there was a telephone pole, so he drew a small circle and next to that wrote "pole."

Through that afternoon, Laurenzi cruised the neighborhood, familiarizing himself with the layout of streets at that furthermost eastern edge of his beat. They had thrown a large number of uniformed units into the neighborhood, on foot, in cars, even a helicopter. They were looking for a Chevy Malibu with signs of bodywork on the front end, but short of that, anything in the ballpark. He figured the brothers Piacentino might have been mistaken about the make or even the color. But so far the search had turned up nothing.

Waiting for something else to happen had stretched the day to frustrating lengths for Laurenzi. But the detective was not disheartened. Despite all the crazy telephone tips, he felt sure that whoever had picked up the money bags lived right here in this network of narrow streets. And if that was true, then the secret was bound to come out. This was South Philly. Nobody in these rowhouse blocks was going to find more than a million dollars without confiding the discovery to somebody. And once that someone knew, somebody else would get the news, then someone else, and so on. Laurenzi knew he only had to stick around and be ready.

He drove slowly, in widening circles, until he was about ten blocks away from Wolf and Swanson, then he reversed direction and worked his way gradually back to the center in smaller circles. Then he started over again.

MARK BOWDEN ON *"Finders Keepers: The Story of Joey Coyle"*

My goal for this essay was to so thoroughly understand Joey Coyle's story that I could tell it with the intimacy and directness of fiction, and I'm happy with the way it turned out.

I was one of many reporters who worked on the story of the missing Purolator money during the frantic week Joey Coyle was on the run. The tale and its central character captivated Philadelphians. When I set out in the aftermath to piece the whole thing together, I saw the story as just a hilarious romp, with Coyle as a bumbling, lovably roguish Everyman.

I soon learned that Joey was a hopeless meth addict, and that the story, which had heretofore been strictly lighthearted, was colored from beginning to end by his addiction. At least one editor at the *Inquirer* wondered if I should just drop it at that point, since it wasn't the story we had all thought it was. But I came to see that the whole thing was about addiction. The money was just a slapstick symbol for Joey's true craving. I realized, as I sat down to write, that the story of Joey Coyle was a parable of addiction, of how hopeless and empty it is to assume success and happiness can be scooped up off the street or administered through a needle.

I started out with the ambition of writing creative nonfiction, inspired by writers like Tom Wolfe, Gay Talese, Norman Mailer, Truman Capote, and many others. My whole journalism career, including my two books, has been devoted to becoming a better reporter and writer, and I've been tackling more and more ambitious projects as I've gone along. I have now begun supplementing my nonfiction work with fiction, partly because it's a way of writing more about my own experience, but also because it enables me to sit down and write without investing the tremendous amount of time and energy it takes to do the reporting (it also frees me from depending on the goodwill and availability of my subjects).

I think creative nonfiction is the major literary innovation of the last half century. It proceeds directly from the revolution in communications technology. Writers have always drawn their material from real life, from stories long told, half-truths, and legends. Today, the "real story" is front and center before anyone has a chance to put it into words. TV, radio, newspapers, magazines, and even Hollywood package this "truth" in slick, highly proscribed ways. Readers look to writers of creative nonfiction for the same reason they looked to Shakespeare's histories and dramas, to flesh out and bring to compelling life the events and people we experience from a distance.

Take Tom Wolfe's *The Right Stuff*, for example. Few events in modern history had been more exhaustively documented by modern media than the early astronaut program. But it wasn't until Wolfe wrote his book that we learned what it was really like to be John Glenn, or Al Shepard, or the other original seven fliers.

On page after page we learned things we didn't know, or things we knew in faint outline but hardly understood. For instance, everyone knew that Gus Grissom's capsule sank at the end of his mission, and that he did not get another mission for a long time. It took Wolfe's reporting and writing to make us understand that Gus had "screwed the pooch," been found wanting at a critical moment. Our appetite for this kind of reporting and writing will only grow, and continues to be fed by highly skillful practitioners.

Another terrific example is Norman Mailer's *Executioner's Song*, which not only fleshes out intimately the middle-American nightmare of Gary Gilmore, it then turns and captures the media phenomenon Gilmore created by insisting that he be executed. In a world where we are all bombarded by facts, great nonfiction storytelling does what literature had always done—makes sense of things.

Scenes, dialogue, characters, plot, foreshadowing, metaphor, interior monologue . . . you name it. I use every technique I've ever read and admired. I use them to make my writing as interesting as I possibly can, because that's the point. No one was ever moved by something they didn't read. My goal is to keep the reader going, and the techniques of good storytelling are no secret.

My advice to young writers is to stop reading like readers and start reading like writers. Reread stories, books, and passages from books that work for you. Dissect the prose. Write it out yourself longhand. Get inside the mind of the writer. Figure out why it works. Then go forth and do the same.

Notes from a Difficult Case

RUTHANN ROBSON

■ ■

Almost everyone I know advised me to sue. Their advice was not casual, because almost everyone I know is an attorney. As am I.

At forty-two, I'd been an attorney almost half my life.

At forty-two, the doctors let it be known that I was far advanced into what would be the second half of my abbreviated life.

These were not just any doctors; these were the doctors at the world-famous cancer center.

If I'd been charged with a heinous crime, I would have retained the best criminal defense attorney I could find. Convicted of a rare cancer, I sought the best advocates for my appeal.

■ ■

RUTHANN ROBSON is a professor of law at the City University of New York School of Law and has written widely on lesbian legal theory, including *Sappho Goes to Law School*. She is also the author of several novels, including *AKA*.

The doctors at the famous cancer center pronounced mine a difficult case.

My tumor was inoperable, the cancer had metastasized to my liver, and the only possible treatment was a highly toxic regimen of chemotherapy. If the chemotherapy infusions were not successful, I had no chance of survival.

The doctors at the world-famous cancer center were correct in their prediction regarding the chemotherapy: it failed to shrink the twenty-pound tumor that distended my abdomen even more pronouncedly now that I had lost thirty pounds after four cycles of chemotherapy.

But they were incorrect about almost everything else.

My tumor was not inoperable.

My cancer had not metastasized to my liver.

Chemotherapy had never been successful on a cancer such as mine.

I turned forty-three. Forty-four. Forty-five.

The circumstances of my ordeal are both simple and complicated. They could be allegations on a complaint, numbered and neat, and augmented by specific dates and quotes from the defendants' own records:

1. On such and such a date, the patient plaintiff was seen by the chief sarcoma surgeon, who observed that the plaintiff had "a very large abdominal mass and lesions in the liver consistent with liver metastases."

2. On a date approximately a week later, the patient underwent a liver biopsy, for which the cytology report read "suspicious cells present" on "*scanty* evidence" [emphasis added].

3. On a date approximately another week later, the patient plaintiff was seen by the oncologist, who told her that she had an "extensive intra-abdominal, presumed soft tissue sarcoma, probable liposarcoma, with hepatic metastases" with no "curative potential," and "no role for surgical intervention at this time, given the presence of metastatic disease."

4. On yet another date yet another week later, the patient was ordered to have a biopsy of the *abdominal mass*, the surgical pathology report for which was *liver biopsy* [emphasis added] with the diagnosis of "well-differentiated lipoma-like sarcoma."

Meaning that within these four weeks, the patient was first diagnosed with liver metastases by the famous sarcoma surgeon, given a liver biopsy to confirm this judgment on "scanty evidence" that showed "suspicious cells," then told she was incurable by the oncologist because of liver metastases, and then given another biopsy of the abdominal tumor, which was mislabeled a biopsy of the liver.

In other words, the doctors screwed up their biopsies.

Later, the complaint would introduce the expert opinions from oncologists and oncology textbooks.

32. There has never been a case in which liposarcoma has metastasized to the liver.

33. Well-differentiated liposarcoma is a non-metastatizing lesion.

34. Chemotherapy is ineffective on well-differentiated liposarcoma.

In other words, the doctors screwed up more than the biopsies.

The doctors at the famous cancer center were wrong when they pronounced me hopeless, incurable, and inoperable because of liver metastases, not knowing that liposarcoma, in its well-differentiated state, does not metastasize. Even if it becomes poorly differentiated, liposarcoma does not metastasize to the liver. I was misdiagnosed and mistreated.

"Screwing up," translated into legal language, is a breach of the duty of care. "Deviation from the applicable standard of care" is one of the elements necessary to establish a cause of action for medical malpractice.

My complaint would omit facts that are not legally relevant: details that do not establish breach of the duty of care and that may not be objective or provable. I do not recall the dates of these occurrences, and if they appear at all in the medical records, those narratives would differ from mine. These are the legally irrelevant facts that subsume my complaint:

The surgeon's secretary called me and told me the liver biopsy confirmed metastasis. His secretary. Who could not answer my questions. Who did not have a soothing voice. Who was not a surgeon.

The oncologist, when questioned, repeatedly told me that of course she/they were correct that surgery was useless because she/they were at the world-famous cancer center. Though, perhaps, she admitted, I could find "someone off the street to do surgery."

The oncologist smirked—I swear—when I lost my previously waist-length hair.

Despite my protests, I was repeatedly advised to take tranquilizers, given prescriptions for Ativan, and referred to a psychiatrist to help me deal with "it."

A phlebotomist who stuck my emaciated arm with the needle too sharply, jabbing after he couldn't find a vein, told me I was being difficult and that I wasn't really hurt.

I had to carry the order for the CT scan to the technicians; an order on which my doctor wrote the diagnosis "*huge* abdominal tumor." "Huge" was underlined. Twice.

When I asked about the long-term effects of the chemotherapeutic agents with which I was being treated, my oncologist replied that "long-term effects" were really not the issue and—I swear it again—she smirked.

According to several studies, the decision whether to sue for medical malpractice is not necessarily related to the degree of the doctor's negligence or fault, or to the degree of the patient's injuries, including death.

Instead, the most consistent variable is something that is named as compassion, caring, or communication.

According to some of these same studies, only one person in thirty-five who suffers what the medical profession calls an "adverse event" decides to sue for medical malpractice.

I did not want to be the kind of person who sued.

By this I did not mean greedy, avaricious, money-hungry, gold-digging, grasping, or craven. I had become an attorney to work for the poor, turning down offers from large law firms which included bonuses of more money than I'd ever made in my life and yearly salaries that seemed to me obscene. Then I became a law professor, certainly not one of the most lucrative positions.

By this I did not mean vengeful, spiteful, savage, malicious. I knew I had the best revenge against their misdiagnosis: I had defied them and I was living and well.

By this I did not mean litigious. I admired people who sued, people who had the courage of their convictions, people who used the courts as social reform.

By this I meant damaged.

Damages are the key element in any cause for medical malpractice. It is not enough that the doctors have made mistakes; these mistakes must cause damages to the patient.

Although in some cases causation can be difficult to prove, in my difficult case causation is unquestionable.

Damages are my difficulty.

In the medical records, the doctors note that "the patient understands that her disease is incurable."

But I did not understand. I railed and sobbed and protested. I did not sleep and could not eat, even before I succumbed to chemotherapy. I was too young and too otherwise healthy to die, wasn't I?

I lived with my imminent death for months and months. Dark days and darker nights. There were no sunsets and no sunrises during all that time. I read books I can't recall. I cursed my career, devoted to constitutional law rather than molecular biology.

Simple phrases—"planning for retirement," "after my son graduates high school," "next summer"—constricted my throat.

Trivial possessions—my hair barrette from Australia, my fountain pen with the lifetime guarantee, my *Healthy Living Cookbook*—flooded my eyes.

Pain and suffering are incalculable.

In the medical records, the doctors note that "possible chemo-therapeutic options were outlined in detail. Toxicities from the chemotherapeutic agent doxorubicin/adriamycin include, but are not limited to, myelosuppression and the risk of infection, mucositis, diarrhea, nausea/vomiting, and hair thinning; and from the agent ifosfamide, hemorrhagic cystitis, renal failure, and neurotoxicity."

But they told me this was my only chance. A slim one, but the only one.

I suffered all the short-term side effects.

I weighed less than one hundred pounds and was so thin it hurt to sit on a chair. I had fevers that clawed at my bones. I was so weak I crawled down the hallway to the bathroom. I lost all my hair, even those sweet little hairs on my toes.

It's become mundane to lose one's hair.

Wear a scarf, tied jauntily. And tightly, so it doesn't slip off the slick skin.

Buy a wig; match your own color as closely as possible.

Or brave it bald and beautiful.

Don't admit to vanity.

But how to explain?

That I'd had hair to my waist for my entire life.

That the first time in my life I went to a hair salon was to get a short cut so that losing my hair would be less painful.

That it was part of my identity: "You'll recognize me at the airport. I have very long hair."

That when I was five years old, I swore I'd never cut my hair. And I didn't. Except for my annual spring split-end trim.

That I still dream of myself with long hair.

That when I see someone with hair as long as mine once was, I have to turn away.

There are long-term effects from the chemotherapy I should not have been given.

Adriamycin, an agent that is among chemotherapy's most toxic drugs, damages the heart muscle. My recent CT scans have revealed a new "pericardial effusion," liquid in the cavity around my heart. My regular blood tests proclaim severe and persistent anemia. My heart leaks its thinned blood as I battle to regain my balance.

Ifosfamide causes neurotoxity. Nerve damage. I have peripheral neuropathy that is so severe some days I cannot hold a pen or strike the correct key on the keyboard. My feet, to phrase it genteelly, tingle. Not so politely, I often crumple when I try to stand, hobble when I try to walk.

Excerpts from the transcript in my possible lawsuit for wrongful chemotherapy:

Q: And what was your experience after being administered the chemotherapeutic agent adriamycin, also known as doxorubicin?

A: Also known as the "red devil." My long hair began to fall out—not "thin"—and this was accompanied by a sensation of burning on my skin, my scalp, and everywhere else I had hair, as if I was being scorched with an iron set for cotton. It also produced an intense and sudden menopause with hot flashes that lasted for hours and combined with fever to make me feel as if I was on fire. I had to force myself to eat since everything tasted like the chemotherapy, which seemed to pool in my mouth even though it was administered intravenously. Nausea does not adequately describe the urge to vomit and then the vomiting. I felt as if I was being poisoned. Which I was.

Q: And what was your experience after being administered the chemotherapeutic agent ifosfamide?

A: There were many physical symptoms, nausea and intense constipation, but what was most difficult to bear was the loss of mental acuity. There seemed to be a great distance between my self and the outer world. Perhaps this is always true, but usually that distance is populated with the effluvia of daily life: a list of things to do, snatches of conversation, the last book I'd read, something I wanted to remember to say to a student or friend. But these things had evaporated, leaving a desert of immense vistas between me and the rest of the world. I struggled to be lucid, to connect, but I was intensely isolated. Everything existed on a mesa, far away and tinged with pink—

Q: (Interrupting) Thank you. Now, did you experience any side effects from the other drugs that were administered, drugs that were intended to curtail some of the side effects of the chemotherapeutic agents?

A: Yes. (Crying) Can we take a break?

But if anyone asks me how I am, I say I am fully recovered. After I found a surgeon to remove the large abdominal tumor, I was fine.

After I underwent the experimental procedure of cryosurgery to treat the liver metastases that did not exist, I was cured and in perfect health.

When I am dizzy, I wait a moment and put my head down, casually, as if I am looking at something. When my hands are too numb to type or write and my feet too numb to walk, I am possessed of a sudden urge to read in a warm bath.

If there is a mind-body connection, then I am determined to capitalize on it.

I feel great.

I am well.

Repeat ten times. Turn around and face the four directions.

If there is an opposite term for "malingerer," that would be me.

My damages are not only impaired by my refusal to be ill but substantially compromised by my own actions.

The day I decided to leave the oncologists at the famous cancer center and no longer follow their advice and endure their arrogance was the day I—or more correctly, my surviving family members—diminished the claim for damages.

If I had acceded to their (mis)diagnosis and (mis)treatment, I would have died. The tumor would have become so large it would have pushed against my other organs until they were dysfunctional. I would have been strangled from the inside out.

And if it were ever discovered that the lesions on my liver

were not metastases but simple hemangiomas, a condition which affects 40 percent of all women, and if those surviving me had learned of my nonmetastatic liver, there would have been a terrific multimillion-dollar suit for a wrongful death resulting from medical malpractice. Economists would have testified about the worth of my life, multiplying my projected life span by my yearly salary with expected increases and the occasional book and honoraria.

But because I disagreed, much too late in hindsight, but still soon enough to save my life, I mitigated the damages and made my case less valuable.

As the studies have shown, the decision to sue for malpractice is not necessarily motivated by money. Whether I could get one thousand dollars or ten million dollars is not the determinative factor, although it might be for any attorney I might hire, dependent as he or she would be on the contingent-fee percentage of recovery.

Financially, it would seem fair to be reimbursed for the fifty thousand dollars in needless chemotherapy treatments for which I and my insurance company paid the famous cancer center.

But no amount of money can compensate me for the months I had no appetites, no fun, no joy, no hope. There is no way to pay for the looks in the eyes of those who saw me: despair in the eyes of my partner, disbelief in my adolescent child, shock in my parents, the terrible pity in my coworkers and even strangers. Nothing can buy back the taste of chemical cremation that still smolders at the back of my throat.

Some studies demonstrate that the few people who choose to sue are often motivated by the altruistic desire to prevent the same fate from befalling someone else.

To save some unknown stranger.

But what are the odds that these same facts would coalesce again?

Slim to none, I assumed.

However, I later learn that a few months *before* I first went to the famous cancer center, a man a little older than I also consulted them, and was diagnosed with liposarcoma and liver metastasis. But for some reason he went to a different hospital and found that his liver lesions were hemangiomas.

When I wasn't crying in the examining room, I argued with my oncologist at the famous cancer center. The little notebook I now carried everywhere with my medical questions was more spotted than my liver. I'd had hepatitis as a college student, couldn't the lesions on my liver be a result of that? Especially since they weren't growing, while my abdominal tumor was?

As for symptoms, I was becoming so debilitated from the chemotherapy that I felt as if my liver as well as all my other organs were barely resisting an acute failure.

No, my oncologist insisted.

No. No. No. No. No.

There is no use in denying it: your cancer has metastasized to your liver.

Even as the contrary evidence was staring her in the face.

My face, to be precise.

My lip, to be more precise. Upper lip, left quadrant.

A hemangioma.

Something that looked to me like a blood blister had appeared after an accident a few years ago. It hadn't gone away, and then, after I consulted doctors, it hadn't responded to either conventional or laser surgery. When the plastic surgeon suggested plum lipstick, I decided I'd just live with a lesion on my upper lip.

Not knowing that I was also living quite fine with the same purpling on my invisible liver.

Did the oncologist even notice my face? What else did she fail to notice?

Or did she not even know what a hemangioma was?

Should I sue? Should I not?

The statute of limitations ticks like the metronome of my adriamycin-damaged heart.

All states limit the time in which a lawsuit for medical malpractice, or almost anything else, can be brought. The time for medical malpractice suits is relatively short, often shorter than for other personal injury lawsuits because legislatures have reacted to a perceived crisis—and the powerful medical profession with effective lobbyists. Having a fewer number of lawsuits is considered a good result.

This is called tort reform.

Popular with legislators everywhere.

Limit the greedy plaintiffs and their even more avaricious lawyers; protect our innocent doctors, hospitals, and HMOs.

After a study showing that medical malpractice awards have been larger in the past few years, some legislatures place a cap on damages awards.

After a study showing that one in eight people are seriously injured during their hospitalization by acts of medical personnel, most legislatures do nothing.

As for medical insurance, any legislative action is viewed as tantamount to communism.

My medical insurance refused to allow me to see a doctor "out of network." Even after the oncologists at the famous cancer center had dismissed me as hopeless and I had learned of another cancer center having great success with my type of cancer.

"There are forty thousand oncologists in our network. What makes you think you're so special you need to go elsewhere?" the nurse caseworker assigned to my difficult case asked me.

"I'm dying," I replied.

She suggested hospice.

"I'll fight this," I vowed.

"You don't seem to understand you have a difficult case."

I went out of network. I went out of state. I would have gone out of this world. I filed the insurance claims and figured if the company didn't pay, I'd appeal. I'd resort to credit cards with high interest rates, figuring that if I died, I wouldn't care, and if I lived, I'd be happy to worry about something as survivable as debt.

The doctors at the out-of-network cancer center saved my life.

The doctors at the out-of-network cancer center may think I am a difficult case, but they also seem to realize that I am a person who does not want to die. They do not smirk at me, although I am bald and my elbows are like arrows. They do not seem squeamish when faced with my little notebook of questions.

As if they have read my notebook, the first question the doctors at the out-of-network cancer center ask me is: "Why haven't you had surgery?"

I am so stunned that the only response that forms in the cage of my mind has something to do with the First Amendment cases I have taught about Jehovah's Witnesses, Christian Scientists, and faith healers refusing medical treatment. Luckily, this does not escape my mouth.

The surgeon at the out-of-network cancer center is a talented, careful, and knowledgeable specialist in sarcomas. I am certain that the surgery he performed was far better than any surgery that would have been performed by the surgeon at the famous cancer center who couldn't recognize a hemangioma on a CT scan and who had his secretary make his unpleasant phone calls.

This makes my prognosis, not to mention my life, much better.

This makes my legal case more difficult.

My out-of-network surgery and hospitalization cost less than my chemotherapy regimes had cost, less than a prolonged hospice would have cost. My insurance company denied my claims. I appealed. I lost. I appealed again. After a hearing at the World Trade Center, the company agreed to pay the expenses associated with saving my life, even though they were incurred out of network.

When the World Trade Center buildings collapsed, I was at the out-of-network cancer center having a follow-up CT scan performed.

Strapped into the massive white doughnut of a machine, I prayed the images it produced would be tumorless.

Mesmerized by the television sets in the waiting rooms, I prayed the images they transmitted were exaggerated.

The last section of the complaint is called the "prayer for relief."

If I decided to sue, my damages would be measured by a damages award; my injuries would be compensated with monetary relief.

Money.

I could not ask for an injunction. I could not request that the doctors go back to medical school or receive further training in cancer or compassion. Or that they be administered adriamycin or ifosfamide.

I would never receive an apology. And nothing I could prove would ever mean that the famous cancer center would be ordered to cease and desist its boastful advertisements.

One of the principles of medical malpractice is that the monetary awards will act as deterrents. The theory is that litigation which results in compensation ensures that medical professionals will find it more economically advantageous to avoid future careless injuries to patients than to keep paying damage awards.

If I believed this—if I believed there were enough money in the world to accomplish this—I know I would sue in an irregular heartbeat.

I confer with a colleague who is a torts professor. She has already urged me to sue, but I want to ask her about the possibility of change at the famous cancer center. Would a lawsuit be an actual deterrent? Or would the cancer center, now a defendant, simply circle the wagons as I'd seen other defendants do, not changing policies, practices, or personnel lest this be viewed as an admission of wrongdoing. She is less than hopeful about the prospects of reform.

I finally consult an attorney. Reputed to be the best "med-mal" attorney in the state and by fortuity employing one of my former students.

My former student is pleased to see me.

Alive.

"When I heard what you had, I thought for sure you were a goner."

Obviously, it is not only members of the medical profession who could benefit from an infusion of compassion.

Or at least tact.

She excitedly tells me about an eight-million-dollar settlement for a patient whose stomach was wrongly removed.

I become dizzy and nauseous. My throat burns and my mind recedes. I must look pale, because she offers me a chair.

When she asks me how I am, I respond that I am great. Fine. Recovered completely.

We review the medical records.

"You should see a heart specialist so we can determine the permanent damage. And a neurologist for nerve damage. Do you have any symptoms?"

No. No. No. No. No. No.

She frowns.

An airtight case on liability, no difficulties there. But we need some permanent damages to make the case more lucrative.

"You look good with short hair," she says as I leave.

Just as I researched my cancer, leading me to the out-of-network doctors, I research malpractice, hoping I will be led to a decision.

The failure to diagnose. The lost-chance doctrine, allowing some recovery for terminally ill patients. Community or national standards of care. The constitutionality of damages cap statutes. *Res ipsa loquitur.* The admissibility of certain hospital records. The enforcement of a gag order.

What would my gag order provide?

That I, as a condition of settlement, agree

not to publicly criticize the defendant doctors, medical personnel, or organization, or anyone associated therewith;

not to disclose the terms of the settlement either privately or publicly; and

not to publish or cause to be published any work related to the litigation or the events underlying the litigation, in any form or manner whatsoever, in perpetuity.

To agree—forever—not to talk or write about what happened to me is more unthinkable than what happened to me.

I will not be silent.

I will not be sick.

I let the statute of limitations lapse.

I celebrate by going out to dinner.

How wonderful the food tastes.

How lucid the conversation.

How good not to be a case, legal or medical, difficult or otherwise.

But I live with this terrible knowledge: that if I had been a little less stubborn, a little more awed by authority, a little less economically privileged, a little more charmed by tranquilizers, a little less able to research my own disease, or simply unlucky, I'd be dead now.

And you would not be reading this.

Case closed.

RUTHANN ROBSON ON *"Notes from a Difficult Case"*

Facts are always refracted through particular prisms. In this piece, I was interested in viewing the same set of circumstances through the lenses of two professional epistemologies—the legal and the medical—and simultaneously through the lens of embodied and emotional experiences seeking an epistemology. I intended the contradictions and disparities, but did not expect an ending in which one viewpoint would so forcefully assert its dominance.

Paradoxically, I find myself turning to the genre of creative nonfiction, both as a writer and as a reader, when I am most resistant to the "facts" as conventionally understood. It is nonfiction, at its most creative and convincing, that can describe the Chekhovian gun in act one and then successfully subvert our expectations that it must fire. The practice of such a subversive art requires work, risk, more work, and, of course, joy.

Adventures in Celestial Navigation

PHILIP GERARD

. .

N: *Proving Yourself Wrong*

You begin by pretending you know exactly where you are.

You begin with a fiction.

On a chart of the inshore ocean—or on a blank universal plotting sheet you've laid out with penciled straight lines that represent the curved reality of Earth (another fiction)—you mark your position, a dark point on blank water.

You call this your *DR* position—for *ded reckoning*. You draw a semicircle above the point, so that it looks like an astonished eye.

Ded reckoning has nothing to do with mortality—the *ded* comes from *deduced*, what you think you know based on history: the history of the boat you're sailing in. Where she (all ships are

. .

PHILIP GERARD is the author of three novels and four books of creative nonfiction, most recently *Secret Soldiers: How a Troupe of American Artists, Designers and Sonic Wizards Won World War II's Battles of Deception Against the Germans* (Dutton/Plume). He teaches in the creative writing department of the University of North Carolina at Wilmington, where he lives with his wife, Kathleen Johnson.

feminine, after Minerva, the Roman goddess of navigation)—
where she was when you last knew for sure. How fast she has been
moving since, and in what direction. You draw a line along your
true course to reflect that projected path: five hours, say, at 6
knots equals 30 nautical miles of distance along that course line
from your last known position. You don't know yet what the tidal
set and the currents have done to her. Or leeway—her tendency
to slide a little sideways as she moves forward. As we all do.

So this point 30 nautical miles along your true course from
your last position is the place where you think you are now. This
is what you believe in, but not too hard. Up until this moment, it
has been the basis for all your decisions regarding the voyage, yet
you are utterly willing to abandon it now.

You open your navigator's tool kit—your magician's bag of
tricks: star finder, hand-bearing compass, chronometer, parallel
rules, dividers, triangular protractor, nautical almanac, sight
reduction tables, pencil, stopwatch, and the queen of all navigation devices, the sextant.

And you set to work.

Before you do anything else, you must observe the sky—not
casually, like an idling passenger or a romantic dreamer, but
accurately and with precision. Unless you're shooting the sun—
sighting on it with your sextant—in broad daylight, you must
make your observation at dusk or dawn, in the crepuscular light
of a day dying or being born—during what's called civil or nautical twilight, depending on how many degrees the sun lies below
the horizon. You search the sky in a certain compass direction
and at a certain altitude, looking for some specific heavenly body
such as the planet Venus or the star Hamal, and recognizing it
when you see it. Or else you work the problem from the other
end: shooting it and, by means of its compass bearing and altitude,

figuring out later which body it was—noting the time down to the exact second.

Seconds matter. In navigation, time means distance in all sorts of ways. Four seconds' error in recording time results in an east-west position error of a whole nautical mile.

You aim the sextant by peering through a telescopic eye-piece. The sextant does something very simple and very difficult: it measures the angle between the navigator's eye and the celestial body being observed. It does this by rotating a mirror mounted on what's called an *index arm* along a curved and calibrated semicircular frame called the *main arc* until the body being shot is reflected exactly into another mirror, level with the horizon, called the *horizon mirror*.

In simple terms, with the sextant, you create an optical illusion in your eyepiece: placing a star or planet or the sun exactly on the horizon—otherwise known as *bringing down the body*. You have to love the language—full of absolute metaphor. All the other calculations depend on this first one, so the sextant must be reliable, precise, and accurate to a fine tolerance.

You have just augmented a convenient fiction with a precise optical illusion.

Then, through applied science, spherical trigonometry, simple arithmetic, the accumulated wisdom of master navigators long in their graves, a nautical almanac, sight reduction tables, and a little magic, you prove yourself wrong: you're not where you thought you were.

You prove your boat is actually someplace else—if you're a good navigator, not too far from where you thought you were. Half a dozen miles, perhaps. Enough to make a difference.

You prove.

In an age of endless equivocation, the denial of absolutes,

the wholesale refusal to believe anything for sure, the new academics' stubborn contention that all facts are relative, that nothing can be known for sure, that history is mostly a matter of point of view, not incontrovertible fact, you prove yourself wrong.

And in proving yourself wrong, you prove something else: exactly where you are.

It is not a matter of opinion. It is not open for debate. It is not arguable or biased by gender or ethnicity or influenced by national regimes or political agendas. It is not personal: you either miss the reef or you hit it. You either find the sea buoy that marks the entrance to your harbor or you pass it by in the night. You make landfall or you don't.

That's the beauty of navigation: it is unequivocal.

To set out from one harbor and arrive safely at a chosen destination is its own proof of success. And it carries with it the right to be at the new place—the place you found, without road signs or fixed highways. Hardly anything on earth is as exhilarating as sailing into a new harbor at sunrise after a nighttime passage offshore across open water.

Not long ago, we sailed into Cape Lookout Bight, formed by a sandy crescent on the North Carolina coast, just as the sun rose purple behind the eastern mare's-tail cirrus and the water was studded with scores of floating humps—great loggerhead turtles come to mate in the protected waters under the lighthouse. We glided by them silently, and a few adopted our sloop as we anchored, and floated alongside us all day.

What is it like to sail on the ocean out of sight of land? That's the question most often asked by people who have never been out of sight of land, except perhaps in an airplane. One answer: navigating on the ocean is just like driving your car—if all the road signs were taken down and Earth's surface were flooded to a depth of at least one foot so that all features and contours were invisible under a flat glassy surface—or under a wind-whipped surface full of swells and breaking waves—with of course rivers and lakes and canyons remaining as deep as they are and all other obstacles—rocks, fences, tree stumps, ditches, railroad tracks, and so on—remaining in place.

Finding the hidden roads, keeping from the submerged hazards, dodging tractor trailers and trains and buses coming from all directions and passing you on all sides at varying speeds and with varying degrees of skill and caution and courtesy—without any headlights, if it is night—and using as your reference not easy-to-follow signage but the mathematics of plotting your course, that would be a like challenge.

Celestial navigators most often rely on the sun, and if they shoot stars or planets or the moon, they must do so in a narrow window of opportunity at dusk or dawn—when the bodies are visible but there is also enough ambient light to power the monocular lens of the sextant.

For the navigator, the world is a sphere with a diameter of 6,888 nautical miles. When you achieve a celestial fix on that sphere, gridded into degrees, minutes, and even tenths of minutes of latitude and longitude, you are fixed for that instant, the solution to a complex exercise in mathematics. You are the variable that has been solved for.

NE: Steering by the Stars

A common misconception is that the celestial navigator shoots a star or planet and plugs the sextant reading into a formula and voilà! A perfect fix. But it isn't quite so simple. What you find after shooting one body and working out the math is a line— what's called a *line of position*, or *LOP*. You know you are somewhere on this line. And to make matters more complicated, that line actually represents a small segment of a very large circle.

Remember, we're trafficking in fictions in order to approach reality.

Imagine you are sailing around in utter darkness looking for a little island with a lighthouse on it in the middle of the ocean. You have no compass—and thus no idea whether that island is north or south or east or west from you. Then you spot it. The chart tells you that the light is a hundred feet high.

You know—don't ask me how—that there's an easy way to calculate how far away you are from the light: First you take the square root of its height plus 14 percent. The square root of 100 is 10; 14 percent of 10 is 1.4. So the sum is 10 plus 1.4, or 11.4 miles. But wait—you also have to add your own height of eye—height above the water. Say that when you stand on deck, your eye is about 10 feet above the water. So the square root of 10 plus 14 percent is 3.6. Add that to 11.4 and you realize you should be able to see the lighthouse at a distance of 15 miles in clear weather.

But since you don't know which direction you are from the lighthouse, all you know is that you are somewhere on a circle with a radius of 15 miles with the lighthouse at its center.

Now pretend that that lighthouse is a star and that a straight line runs from the star to the center of the Earth—an imaginary tower on which the starlight is mounted.

The point where that line pierces Earth's surface is the *geographical position*, or GP, of the star—the imaginary island on which the light is located. Only this light is very high, so high you must measure its height by determining its angle above you with a sextant—remember, that's what a sextant does—which will give you degrees, minutes, and tenths of minute of arc. Arc translates into distance at a rate of 1 mile per minute of arc.

Since there are 60 minutes of arc to the degree, the circle you would draw around the star's geographical position based on the angle of that body to you would be hundreds, maybe thousands, of miles in circumference.

For example, if you measure the star at 40 degrees of arc, then its geographical position is 40 times 60, or 2,400 miles away from you. That's the radius of the circle on which you are located, which must therefore have a circumference of over 15,000 miles (δ times the diameter of 4,800 miles).

Hence you must reduce the scale of the problem—reduce the circle to a segment. Reduce thousands of miles to a few dozen. This is why it's called sight *reduction*. All the calculations and tables allow you to do just that. And remember the fiction that anchors all this: You began by pretending to know exactly where you are—your ded reckoning position. If where you think you are is at all close to where you really are, you have narrowed the large circle to a small segment.

In any case, once you have two sights calculated, you plot them as two lines that—if the bodies were separated by an angle greater than 30 degrees and ideally greater than 60 degrees— should intersect. The point of intersection is your fix.

If you can shoot three stars or planets, even better: now you have the classic triangle of a three-star fix, and you are inside that little triangle—a space about as big as a city block.

E: Celestial Baseball

So the celestial navigator fixes a position with reference to the stars, including our sun, and the planets; the location of the ship is reckoned in the context of moving but predictable bodies in the heavens. Those heavenly bodies have complex relationships with the ship's tiny point of location on Earth—the sun, moon, each planet and star is assigned a geographical position for every hour and second of every day of every month and year: the point at which it would, theoretically, splash down on the surface of the Earth on its gravitational plunge toward the center of the Earth.

There is no fudging.

It is exhilarating and humbling to fix your location under the stars—a totally accidental use for the firmament, yet so compellingly precise that the imagination begs for the hand of a Supreme Being to have created such a remarkable instrument of absolute context.

Even the term testifies to this: *celestial*, as in *residing in the heavens*.

It would be like emerging from the steaming jungle and discovering a perfectly formed fossil baseball diamond in the wilderness of prehistory, eons before *Homo sapiens* prowled the Earth and the game of baseball was invented—with the pitcher's mound exactly 60 feet 6 inches away from home plate, the bases 90 feet apart, all the mathematical relationships true, waiting for the day millions of years in the future when mammals would evolve into prosimians and at last primates and humans, and a Civil War general would invent a baseball, a bat, and a book of rules to codify the mathematical and geometrical relationships into a dynamic and meaningful experience.

You'd have to wonder if that baseball diamond were placed there by design, and if so, by whom?

And if so, why?

Now look up at the night sky and imagine that discovery of order on a scale so vast even levelheaded scientists cannot comprehend its scope.

The celestial navigator exists in perfect context with the universe—which is more than most of us can ever claim for even a brief instant in life.

SE: Errors and Imperfections

All the above—of course—assumes you have computed accurately and made no errors—a very big assumption. The odds are very good that your sextant reading is off by a hair. After all, you are sighting a distant object from the deck of a pitching boat and trying to mark the exact hour, minute, and second of the sighting. You may have forgotten to correct for the two kinds of errors common to sextants, especially well-used ones.

You can misread the arc of the body—its angle above the Earth—off the sextant scale. You can mistime the sight, or neglect to corroborate it properly with Greenwich Mean Time—the universal clock located on the prime meridian, the 0 degree of longitude, in Greenwich, England. The tables by which you extrapolate your position require rounding off and then interpolation to correct for rounding off. You might forget whether you are dealing with true degrees or magnetic, or add a correction instead of subtracting it. You might make a simple mistake in arithmetic—forget you are adding degrees, which contain 60 parts, and do the math in base 10, as you normally would, and wind up in the middle of a continent.

If you have made such mistakes, you will find out, and usually quickly.

There are all sorts of ways to check your work.

One way is to turn on your GPS—Global Positioning System—and let the satellites judge your calculations. Until about the year 2000, the military deliberately introduced an error into the civilian GPS signal—to thwart terrorists and rogue nations possessing guided missiles—so it was accurate to only half a mile or so. And in the spirit of true American can-do, the Coast Guard spent millions of dollars every year broadcasting a correction. Now the signal is accurate to 12 meters—the length of a smallish racing yacht—but, of course, the Coast Guard is still broadcasting a correction, so that the corrected signal is accurate to 3 feet.

Three feet. The span of your arm. You can stand up, extend your arm straight out in front of you, spin slowly, and touch your exact position.

Don't mind the technology—once, the sextant was the most modern gadget on the block—and any honest navigator will use every trick he can to find his way across the blank ocean.

Or you can work out all your sights and compare—you'll look at your plot and see one line that goes off on its own and doesn't intersect the others, and you cast it aside. Working out that sight, you just went a-glimmering. Gremlins got into the works. The Imp of the Perverse.

Or you can let your gut tell you. The great circumnavigator Joshua Slocum, the first man known to have circled the globe alone aboard a sailing ship, always maintained he could tell which ocean he was in and what latitude simply by the color, feel, and taste of the water under his keel.

Even I can tell from the surface of the sea when we've moved beyond 20 miles offshore, lost the continental shelf, or sailed into the Gulf Stream. Such information, the sensory residue of experience, is stored in your body—in your ears and stomach and eyes and probably even your blood, the way your immune system remembers diseases and how to survive them. The roll of the boat feels different. The color of the water turns from Atlantic gray to tropical aquamarine. The wave shapes are different, playing a different tune against the cutwater, as is the way rain squalls form on the horizon.

Sometimes the navigator at sea just feels an odd sixth sense operating—something doesn't feel right. It's not logical; there's no science to the feeling—at least none we know of yet—but for thousands of years the great navigators trusted their intuition as much as their instruments, and contemporary sailors are no different. Whatever the instruments say, if it *feels* wrong, it probably *is* wrong.

Sailors who make solo passages across oceans must sleep from time to time, and they report time and again how they rely on intuition to wake them in the event of trouble. After weeks at sea, they become tuned to their natural context in a way that is scarcely possible on land. With no landmarks, no artificial noise or distraction, listening day after day to the soughing whisper of wind, the creak of rigging, the slap and chirrup of waves against the hull, they can recognize at once the slightest variation in pitch and timbre and tone. They acquire an intuitive, overwhelming sense of exactly where they are, like Eskimo, who recognize the subtle and familiar variations in what to us would seem a blank expanse of snow and ice.

S: *Divine Aspiration*

Now, here's the glorious part, the part the Knights Templars might have understood: celestial navigation is an exact science, but it is also an art.

That is to say, the math offers a perfect answer to your position, but you are unlikely ever to achieve perfection in your practice of it. You will, as you get better and better, approach perfection. There is an unequivocally exact right answer, but you can navigate a lifetime and never reach it. The best you can hope for is an approximately right answer, equally unequivocal, approaching perfection.

In celestial navigation, there is an element of aspiration to the Divine.

A very accomplished navigator will be able to fix his position within a mile's range; an inexperienced navigator may be 5 miles off.

Once in a long voyage, a gifted navigator may place the vessel exactly where reality has her and be able to prove it.

SW: *Magical Captains*

In the great days of sail, the captain of a ship was a figure of awesome authority.

His word was absolute law, enforced by the petty officer's knout, the master-at-arms' lash, and the hangman's noose. In the British navy, which ruled the oceans from the time of the first Spanish Armada until the turn of the twentieth century, the crews were made up of the sweepings of the assizes and jails and taverns—landsmen—along with seamen impressed against their wills from the merchant ships of a dozen nations. The captain remained physically aloof from these crewmen and often nearly as aloof from his officers. When the captain emerged from his cabin onto the quarterdeck, all officers retreated from the windward side to allow him private space. Except on ship's business, they dared not speak to him unless spoken to. More often than not, he dined alone. The loneliness of command was more than a cliché—it was an essential social and psychological buffer: the captain might at any time order his men and his fellow officers into catastrophic battle in which a third or more would routinely be killed or mangled.

The contingent of royal marines aboard each of His or Her Majesty's vessels was there as much to guard the captain and his officers from their own crew as to fight the enemy, and one marine always guarded the captain's door with drawn sword.

Yet the crews rarely rose in mutiny—though on a ship of the line, the main fleet battleship, they might number three or four hundred, including men shipped as replacements awaiting the inevitable deaths of scores of their shipmates, as against a dozen officers and fifty marines. For the captain was not only the legal dictator of their daily lives, their judge and jury when they committed infractions; he also held the magical power of the sextant.

Many officers could navigate, more or less, and the teenage midshipmen, future lieutenants and with luck captains, were gathered every morning on deck for lessons in celestial trigonometry, passing around the sextant, and working out their sights with chalk and slate. In later times, ships even had skilled navigators specifically assigned to them, as coastal pilots are today put aboard in shoal waters or harbors.

But the captain was the genius of navigation. A captain who could navigate well commanded the trust of his crew—even if they hated him. The captain held the real key to their destiny—whether they could find their way through storm, hazard, and enemy fleets home to England.

C. S. Forester's fictional Captain Horatio Hornblower—a composite based partly on two real-life naval heroes, Lord Horatio Nelson and Lord Thomas Cochrane—performs heroic feats of navigation in nearly every adventure. In one book, he is commanded to sail from England to the west coast of Central America without coming within sight of any land or any other ships—using only sextant and compass and slate board.

Think about that—the faith, the arrogance, that requires.

With his food and water all but depleted, he makes landfall exactly where he plotted it, exactly on time. As did the real captains Cochrane and Nelson, time after time.

On a schooner or merchant ship, the captain might be the only man on board who knew the art and science of navigation. To lose the captain to illness or death or mutiny—or madness, an occupational hazard—was to lose their way, literally, on the vast untracked oceans of the world.

Christopher Columbus's crew came close to mutiny on his first outbound voyage, not because he was flogging them—he didn't dare—but because they lost confidence that he knew where he was going.

So the tools of navigation, especially the chronometer and sextant, took on a magical quality and were treated with the reverent care usually reserved for sacred relics: secreted in a chest in the captain's cabin inside elaborately carved and inlaid hardwood boxes, protected from salt and sea and rough handling. Even today, if you buy even a moderately priced metal sextant, it will come in a hardwood box or a bulletproof valise.

Imagine the illiterate sailor with no education in astronomy or mathematics, little sense even of the world's geography since he had probably never seen a globe, sailing along for weeks at a time with no land in sight in any direction. It must have seemed magical indeed that a man could put his eye to a strange metal contraption, scribble some queer numerical formulae on a slate, draw lines on a piece of paper, then tack his ship toward an invisible harbor, arriving there exactly as predicted.

A man who could do that, a captain, must be partly divine.

W: M. Thibault and the Greenwich Hour Angle

All my life, I have wanted to know how to plot a course under the stars.

Since my earliest days of reading Robert Louis Stevenson and Jack London—who taught himself celestial navigation during a Pacific voyage—the sextant carried a mysterious power. The trigonometry daunted me, though—the slide rule calculations. Words like *azimuth* and *intercept* and *horizontal parallax* and *meridian passage*. I studied trig in high school, even studied calculus, but the principles eluded me. And other matters took precedence—I didn't own a sextant, didn't know anyone who owned one, did not intend to become a sea captain for my life's work.

And anyway, by the time I became a sailor, electronic navigation had made the sextant obsolete as a primary means of navigation. For years now I have gotten along fine with GPS, which relies on a grid of satellites to locate a boat's position. A unit that fits into your pocket can be had for about a hundred bucks. Entering a harbor in fog or in the dead of night, I can also plot the contours of the land, locate the channel markers, and steer clear of other vessels using radar—like the GPS, another fruit of the military-industrial complex.

But as I took to sailing on the ocean, I felt something of a fraud. It was time to do the things I had always yearned to do. My wife, Kathleen, bought me a celestial navigation class for Christmas. I finally had an excuse to buy a sextant, and promptly sent away for one from a navigation supply house, along with a star finder and a radio-controlled clock that automatically sets itself to the naval observatory clock in Fort Collins, Colorado, and is accurate to the second. I already had parallel rules, dividers, and a hand-bearing compass—staple tools of ded reckoning navigation. I bought a nautical almanac and sight reduction tables, as well as a pad of blank universal plotting sheets and work forms for keeping the math straight while working out sights on stars, planets, and the sun.

Before I ever set foot in the classroom, I read the textbook twice, taking my time, taking months, in fact. Doing every problem twice. Doing the difficult problems again and again until I got them right. The focus, the need to slow down and concentrate, was good for me. Celestial navigation, even reduced to formulae that I could mimic, did not come easily. There was nothing intuitive about it. It was an initiation into mystery, and you arrived at the mystery by numbers.

I found myself making simple errors of arithmetic over and over again. Mistakenly subtracting degrees, which contain 60 minutes, as if they contained 100. Entering the tables through the wrong coordinate. Plotting sun sights that were off by 50 miles. I knew they were off by that much because when I took them, I was standing in the driveway of my own house.

I read a paragraph about determining the Local Hour Angle from the Greenwich Hour Angle of the heavenly body, and my eyes glazed over and I heard a buzz inside my head, so I read it again, and again, and after a while it began to work—the way repetition on those foreign-language tapes in high school gradually resolved into basic sense.

M. *Thibault va à l'épicerie*.

M. Thibault goes to the grocery store.

To obtain Local Hour Angle, in west longitude subtract the ded reckoning longitude from the Greenwich Hour Angle of the body. If your DR exceeds the GHA, place a minus sign before the difference and algebraically add 360 degrees to the result.

Translation: Since we know—and the tables tell you—the longitude of the heavenly body to find out your own true longitude, you need to compare your assumed longitude with it. You will compare the sextant reading you took at this assumed longitude to the one you should actually have obtained if you were in fact at that longitude, and you will find this number by entering the sight reduction tables with the Local Hour Angle, which expresses that comparison.

To pass the American Sailing Association's Celestial Navigation Certification exam, the student navigator must be able to do the following—among many other tasks:

- Convert longitude into time;
- Apply the corrections for index error, dip of the horizon, and total correction to convert sextant altitudes of the sun, stars, planets, and moon to true altitudes;

- Determine the latitude at twilight by means of the polestar;
- Determine the approximate azimuths and altitudes of the navigational stars and planets at twilight;
- Calculate the time of meridian passage of the sun;
- Calculate and plot the lines of position obtained from several celestial bodies at twilight and thus fix the boat's position;
- Find the boat's position using a running fix of the sun—that is, two or more lines of position from sun shots taken at different times.

The test takes the form of a simulated voyage across the Pacific, so that every answer depends on the accuracy of the previous answer's calculations, which means you can't advance to the next question until you have answered the previous question correctly. Every error compounds the next.

A mathematically inclined student can complete the exam in three hours. It took me seven.

NW: *Ships in the Night*
Navigation isn't all about stars.

Most navigation is more worldly.

Sometimes navigation is basic.

You're sailing, say, up the East Coast from Charleston, South Carolina, to Wilmington, North Carolina, broad reaching on a starboard tack, so the wind is more behind you than in front, and you're coming up on the sea-lane for the harbor at Georgetown, maybe 40 miles offshore. It's a black night, full of rain squalls and choppy, breaking seas running 6 and 7 feet, with a wind that has increased steadily from a breezy 10 knots to almost 25—just under 30 miles per hour.

You started off in the fairway of Charleston Harbor in bright sunshine flying a spinnaker—one of those big multicolored balloon-shaped sails. Now conditions are more challenging, and since there are only two of you on board, you've shortened sail and you're sledding along under a triple-reefed main and a hand-kerchief jib with the wind behind you and to the right. Off your starboard bow, you spy lights. Because the sky is suffused with water vapor, the lights twinkle, and the pitching and rolling of the boat—*heeled* at, say, 25 degrees—make it hard to sight on the lights with binoculars.

After a few minutes of hard watching, you make out three lights: on the left, a red light; on the right, not far from the red light, another red light over a white one.

Fishing trawler, you decide. A 50-foot boat crossing ahead. No problem.

With your handheld compass, you take a bearing. In which direction is it located relative to your boat? Every two minutes, you take another. After ten minutes, the bearing hasn't changed a single degree, and you recall the simplest maxim of navigation: *If the bearing of two approaching vessels doesn't change over time, they are going to collide.*

You try the binoculars again. The other vessel is closing, and this time you see not three lights but five. Two were obscured by the halos—what navigators call the *loom*—of the other lights. Now the vessel is showing the same red light on the left but *four* lights—not two—stacked vertically on the right: red-white-red-white, in ascending order.

It is not a 50-foot trawler but an 800-foot container ship, and the reason it didn't look very long on first sighting is the result of an optical illusion: the ship is heading to cross your path at an acute angle, so you're seeing a foreshortened version of its hull.

You do some quick mental arithmetic. You are sailing along at 9 knots—a little more than 10 miles per hour. The container ship is doing over 20 knots. In less than three-quarters of a mile ahead—1,320 yards—your courses will converge.

He will run you down—a vessel bearing down on you is always a "he," from long nautical usage.

Your vessel is 32.5 feet long and displaces about 5 tons. The container ship displaces 50,000 tons and is seven stories tall. If you do collide, chances are very good he will not even know it. You and your boat and your sleeping crew will, of course, disappear in a lather of sundering fiberglass and twisted aluminum spars and boiling water. Whatever his bow bulb doesn't crush will be atomized by his gargantuan propellers.

Distance equals time: you have about six minutes to get out of his way. On a sailboat, six minutes is an instant. Even if the container ship were to stop all engines at this exact moment, the great vessel could not stop in time to prevent it from crossing your path.

And that path is wide and fraught with hazard. Even if he misses you, the suction of a great vessel steaming along will draw your boat toward his hull. If you don't smash into him too hard, you will scrape along his hull and might be sucked into the vortex of his great thrashing propellers. Even if he passes 100 yards off, he will throw a wake at you that can roll you onto your beam ends.

You call down the companionway—once. All you have to say is "Ship," and your crew, your buddy, turns out on deck at once from a sound sleep, dressed in foul-weather jacket over sleeping sweats. Your buddy is a good shipmate, which means that when you call down the companionway in the middle of the night, he does not question, does not hesitate, does not complain, but simply turns out on a cold wet deck swiping the sleep from his eyes and already grabbing the right lines to do the ship some good.

You bring the boat hard up into the wind and go close-hauled—sailing as close to the wind as you possibly can. The boat leans over hard from the added pressure of wind on sails. A wave breaks over the bow, spume scuds over the cabin top and drenches you, and the ride gets suddenly rougher.

But the bearing changes, and it keeps changing, as the massive black hull of the container ship sweeps by off the port bow, close enough to hit with a slingshot. You can hear the great engines thrumming, hear the machine noise leaking out the open ports of her towering superstructure, see rows of buttery cabin lights.

On the VHF radio, in halting English, her captain hails Georgetown for a harbor pilot, repeatedly, and Georgetown doesn't answer. He's oblivious to you, as you suspected all along.

But it doesn't matter now. You're safe.

You just solved a very basic navigation problem. It is not a matter of opinion.

Her blunt stern moves off piled three-high with containers, your sailboat shoulders across the big ship's wake, your crew disappears wordlessly into the black hole of the companionway and sleep, and you ease the sheets and resume course, waiting for the clouds to clear off and the polestar to come out and the other stars to blink on one by one in a perfect map, until they're smeared across the firmament from water to water, and they dissolve into the orange loom of sunrise.

PHILIP GERARD ON *"Adventures in Celestial Navigation"*

The germ of the essay lay in the experience in dodging a container ship on a voyage from Charleston, South Carolina, to Wilmington, North Carolina. As usual when things get tense at sea, the incident occurred in the middle of the night. The darkness flattens out your vision so you lose depth perception—lights that may be miles apart seem to float side by side. The horizon has bleared, so the sky and sea meld together and leave you feeling a kind of vertigo. Piloting—navigating by landmarks ashore or buoys—becomes tricky, sometimes impossible. You navigate by instruments— Global Position System (GPS) and radar—marking your progress on a chart.

But you're really also relying on your gut, the knowledge of your environment that comes from your body: the sound of wind and waves and hull, other sounds that don't belong, sharp smells, the motion of the boat on the water, and a sixth sense that alerts you when something is not right. Being at sea on a small sailboat for even a few days puts you in touch with some essential and very primal part of yourself, the part that acts instinctively, the part that is sharply tuned to the physical world, the part that has been hard-wired into us since the first humans ventured out into the open savanna. This is what, I think, drives sailors back to the sea, time and again: the sense of physical aliveness that we lose indoors.

As I meditated on the ship-dodging incident—and several others like it I have experienced on other passages—I began pon-dering the whole art of navigation, especially celestial navigation, which has long fascinated me, though I am only an enthusiastic amateur navigator. Navigation, at its heart, relies on fiction and illusion to discover absolute truth. It struck me that there is a near perfect parallel between a navigator's attempt to discover his exact position and the writer's attempt to express in an exact way what is so clear in his imagination, the perfect truth about being human, but which never survives intact onto the page.

Both the navigator and the writer can never reach perfection, can never really achieve the exactness which is their ideal—the world simply creates too much friction and possibility for error. Yet the art of both navigating and writing lies in approaching that ideal, which requires an act of faith in yourself and in the craft. Of course you must proceed from the assumption, which I do, that there does indeed exist a perfect truth. Just as a navigator knows his vessel can be pinpointed to a specific location on the globe but can prove it only approximately, I believe there are certain absolute truths in the world, though we can comprehend and express them only approximately. Some of the truths are trivial and others quite profound. I don't believe that all reality is a matter of opinion or perspective.

For me an essay usually begins with a few fixed points, and this one was no exception. A real container ship on a dark ocean. The art of taking sun and star sights and then "reducing" them on a plotting sheet to find a line of position. A sextant and a compass I could hold in my hand. Then the parts began to take shape, and finally an order seemed to impose itself on those segments.

Organizationally, I wanted the essay to follow the compass rose, since the compass is the navigator's most valuable instrument. And a compass tells a subtle lie—true north on any compass is not where the needle points but is figured by a formula that takes into account deviation (error caused by the compass itself or its proximity to large metallic objects) and variation (error caused by the differing magnetic fields of the Earth). Once you understand that the compass tells only part of the truth—though nothing but the truth—it functions as a wonderful, humbling reminder not to trust simple solutions. As the essay comes round full circle from the theoretical to the actual event, we have "boxed" the compass—followed it around through its four cardinal and four intercardinal points.

The mariner's compass is such a powerful symbol for me of the writer's search for a true direction that I keep one on my desk, salvaged from a boat I lost in a hurricane. It reminds me, among

other things, that every story, like every voyage, must have movement and direction.

In a fictional story, the movement and direction arise from
dramatic imperative—a character in motion toward the fulfillment
of a desire or to escape danger. Desire and fear, often the two
together, drive most great novels. Nonfiction often achieves its
momentum not just through narrative—telling the story—but also
through the meditative intelligence behind the story, the author as
narrator thinking through the implications of the story, sometimes
overtly, sometimes more subtly.

This thinking narrator who can infuse a story with shades of
ideas is what I miss most in much nonfiction that is otherwise quite
compelling—we get only raw story and not the more essayistic,
reflective narrator. Fiction doesn't need such a narrator, usually—
the interior lives of the characters furnish the moral, political, and
social arguments. But of course in telling nonfiction stories we
can't as writers know anybody's interior life but our own, so our
interior life—our thought process, the connections we make, the
questions and doubts raised by the story—must carry the whole
intellectual and philosophical burden of the piece.

We don't write what we know—we write what we are passionate to find out. And that process of discovery is what we must share
with the reader, however we do it.

For a long time in the American literary tradition, too much
nonfiction writing was confined to simply stating dry facts, reporting information, stating abstract ideas. Then a corps of gifted writers revived the craft of telling true stories using the fiction writer's
tools—creating memorable characters, delicious suspense, and dramatic conflict out of real people and actual events. For me the
future of creative nonfiction lies in striking that noble balance
between storytelling and ideas—presenting a crackerjack tale with

intelligence and wit, so that the dramatic struggle becomes also a struggle of ideas and the story has staying power, weight, and intellectual heft. The writer has enlarged it with a new dimension, the domain of ideas behind the action, the ultimate source of desire and fear.

Leaving Babylon: A Walk Through the Jewish Divorce Ceremony

JUDYTH HAR-EVEN

. .

Two years after Cyrus, King of Persia, conquered the Babylonian Empire, he allowed the Children of Israel to return to their land. The year was 537 BCE. Two thousand five hundred and thirty-six years later, I walk down his street in Jerusalem, on my way to get divorced at the district rabbinic court. The travel agencies on Cyrus Street are not advertising group tours to Iraq, not yet. Nonetheless, Babylon is on my mind. By its rivers we sat

. .

JUDYTH HAR-EVEN (a pseudonym) teaches creative writing in Israel. Currently she organizes writing retreats around the country (www.writeinisrael.com) for Israelis and tourists. For nineteen years she wrote personal essays for Israeli newspapers. Her writing has appeared in the *Kenyon Review, Hadassah Magazine, Lilith, Reform Judaism,* and Jewish newspapers in the United States and Canada. She holds an MFA in creative nonfiction from Goucher College, a certificate in psychotherapy from the Israel Institute of Psychoanalysis, a BSW from the Hebrew University of Jerusalem, and a BA in American culture from the University of Michigan. She has lived in Jerusalem since 1967.

down and wept when we remembered Zion and wondered how we could sing the Lord's song in a strange land. I wept and wondered, too, for twenty-seven years of married life. Now, just as the Children of Israel walked back to their homeland, their freedom, I am walking to mine.

If all goes well at the courthouse this morning, I will receive my *get*, a Jewish writ of divorce. I already have a civil-divorce document, signed and stamped by an Israeli judge from the district family court. But to remarry in Israel, where I live, and to have "Divorced" rather than "Married" written on my identity card, I need the *get*. Only this document states categorically that I am divorced according to the Law of Moses and Israel.

The civil divorce derives from the decree of a civil court. The Jewish divorce derives from a ceremony steeped in tradition, played out by husband and wife in a rabbinic court. Friends have told me that the *get* ceremony, to which I am walking, is demeaning, primitive, and meaningless.

Demons flitter and play along the narrow hallways of Jerusalem's rabbinic court. They are waiting to snatch a soul. Rabbinic legend claims that when people—women, especially— are in transition from one stage of life to another, demons get restless. Since the rabbinic court is the venue for changing one's personal status, the building is a playground for demons. Watch out, the Talmudic sages warned. Break a glass at weddings; walk around the groom seven times; read Psalms; wear amulets— anything to keep away the evil spirits.

I weave my way through the hallways and arrive intact at the waiting room of Hall A. Other than Psalms, there are no instructions for the soon-to-be-divorced, save for two signs on the door to the courtroom: TURN OFF YOUR CELLULAR PHONE, and DRESS MODESTLY. I pick up Psalms, open it randomly to number 13, and read:

> *How long will I have cares on my mind, grief in my heart*
> *all day?*
> *How long will my enemy be exalted over me?*
> *Look and hear me, O Lord my God:*
> *Restore the luster to my eyes, lest I sleep the sleep of*
> *death . . .*

I am wearing a long black skirt, a white blouse with sleeves that cover my lascivious elbows, and a black sun hat. When my husband enters the room and sees me dressed in uncharacteristically ultramodest garb, reading Psalms, he chides, "Who the fuck are you kidding?"

I am sitting at home by myself, reading the newspaper by the light of one lamp. There is a knock at the door. It is snowing outside, but I can't see the snow because black paper is still taped to the windows. The Yom Kippur War has been over for two months. My husband, a paratrooper, is still stationed in Goshen. Before the war we were trying to make a baby, but now with him being mobilized, there is no chance. My eggs escape unnoticed, untouched. The snow has closed all the roads to Jerusalem.

The knocking persists.

All day I work with bereaved families. As a volunteer social worker for the Ministry of Defense, I help mothers mourn their sons, widows their husbands, children their fathers. I am afraid to open the door, because I know it could be a team of soldiers saying to me, "Your husband is dead."

The knocking persists. I walk to the door. I open it. A man stands there in a green uniform covered with mud and snow. He holds an M16 in one hand and ten red roses in the other.

"Ovulate yet?" he asks.

An usher calls out our last name and escorts us into the chamber. Opposite the door, towering above us, is a long Formica desk. Behind it, three rabbinic judges sit ensconced on cushioned chairs. They wear costumes—black jackets, white shirts, gray beards, and black hats with flat rims. The rabbi on the left is immersed in reading a tome and does not look up when we enter the courtroom. The rabbi on the right is sucking his thumb. He avoids my incredulous stare, which he would have to interpret as lecherous, versed as he must be in rabbinic wisdom. The judge in the middle looks at my husband and me as if our whole sad history is incised on our foreheads.

To the left of the long desk is a small green Formica desk with a computer. Here sits the court secretary. He is a kindly-looking man, bald, with a skullcap.

"Has your w-w-witness arrived?" the attentive rabbi asks.

"Yes," I respond.

"Tell her to come in and then be seated."

I do as I'm told. Nechama, my witness, is an observant Jew from my hometown in the United States. She has played this role for other divorcing friends.

Act One: The Name

"Do you know this woman's f-f-father?" the rabbi asks Nechama.

"Yes. I knew him."

The rabbi listens as if this is the most important information he has heard since his political party became the second largest in Israel.

"Was he a C-C-Cohen?"

"I don't know."

Now the rabbi leans over his desk to question me.

"Did your father ever tell you he was a C-C-Cohen?"

My thoughts race to Moses, the prophet who stuttered. I repress a smile. My father didn't even know what a Cohen was.

"Never," I say.

We are both surprised at the discrepancy in the religious documents. Apparently my name on the *ketubah,* the marriage contract, says I am the daughter of a Cohen. The marriage certificate, however, issued by the Ministry of Religious Affairs after the wedding, says I am a daughter of Israel.

For the purposes of personal status, Jews are divided into two categories: Cohen, the priestly class, and Israel, the rest. I always thought I was one of the rest, but now it appears I may belong to the priestly class.

"What name was used when your father was called up to the T-T-Torah?" the rabbi demands.

A Jewish name, for purposes of marriage and divorce, consists of a given name, the given names of one's mother and father, and the father's religious class, that is, Cohen or Israel. This is why we are spending twenty minutes trying to figure out who I am. Judyth! Judy! Yehudit! Cohen! Israel?

My precise name and lineage is of the utmost importance because the writ of divorce has to be written specifically for me. The legal principle that the *get* be written for a specific wife on a particular day derives from interpretations of the first two verses in chapter 24, Deuteronomy:

> *When a man has taken a wife and married (possesses) her and it comes to pass that she no longer finds favor in his eyes, because he has found some unseemly thing in her, then let him write her a bill of divorce and give it in her hand and send her out of his house. And when she is departed out of his house, she may go and be another man's wife.*

This passage offered fertile soil for reams of rabbinic free associations and legalities, which were ultimately woven together in Tractate Gittin of the Babylonian Talmud, compiled in 500 CE. Talmudic sages deduced at least nine legal principles from the passage in Deuteronomy:

1. *A man must divorce his wife of his own free will.*
2. *A woman must be divorced in writing.*
3. *The get must be a document that states clearly that it severs all ties between husband and wife.*
4. *The husband must give the get to the wife. She cannot take it.*
5. *He must put it in her hand. The woman is not divorced until the get comes into her possession.*
6. *The document must state that he sends her out.*
7. *The get must be given in the presence of two or three witnesses. (This is based on a common word—davar— "thing," which appears in Deuteronomy 24:1–2 and 19:15, where it refers to witnesses.)*
8. *The get must be given immediately after it is written. (For instance, if a husband goes bowling after he writes the get or obtains it from a scribe, and then delivers it, the get is invalid, unkosher.)*
9. *The get must be given only for the purpose of divorce; it cannot be used as a threat.*

"Was her father a C-C-Cohen?" the rabbi pleads again.

It is one hour before the wedding. The men are sitting around a table with the officiating Orthodox rabbi filling in the details of the ketubah. *The rabbi turns to my father.*

"What was the name you gave your daughter at birth?"

"She was christened Judy."

The other men, including my husband-to-be, cannot believe their ears. They motion my father to shut up.

"Christened?" the rabbi repeats, eyebrows raised.

"Yes. At birth we called her Judy."

"But . . . was she christened?"

"Oh, I don't know. That's what we called her."

"Was she christened?"

"What the hell difference does it make? You think every word is important? Let's just get her married, for Christ's sake."

"Who was the rabbi who officiated at your w-w-wedding?" This rabbi is desperate for details, where, some believe, God dwells.

"Rabbi Natan," I reply, "an Orthodox rabbi from Jerusalem." I emphasize this last point so he will understand that someone in his own Orthodox establishment screwed up in 1972.

The talking rabbi looks at the reading rabbi, who points at his watch and urges him to proceed.

The rabbi decides that I am an Israel, thanks my witness, and dismisses her. Then he calls my husband's witness. The man is a jerk. He makes light of my husband's many nicknames. The rabbi reminds him this is serious business, chooses two names among the many, and sends him away after a ten-minute interrogation.

At this juncture a cellular phone in my husband's briefcase rings. The judges and court secretary take cover, as if a knife-wielding terrorist has burst into the room.

"Didn't you read the sign?" the rabbi yells. "Turn that thing off. A little respect for the court, please."

I wonder if Moses lost his stutter when he reprimanded the Children of Israel.

Act Two: The Players

The rabbi calls in two *shlubs*. Their shirttails hang over their black trousers, and their black skullcaps dangle from the sides of their heads. Tweedledee and Tweedledum are full-time employees of the Ministry of Religious Affairs, two of six men who play the role of witness at divorce proceedings. They enter from a side door like extras on a movie set, their only task to stand up, pay attention, and say "Yes" or "No" when asked. My taxes pay their salaries.

The two witnesses stand between the court secretary and the rabbis. Then the talking rabbi calls in my husband's emissary. Enter the Torah scribe. He is a short man wearing a white shirt with a frayed collar and a black skullcap placed on his bald head like a dot over an *i*. He takes up his position opposite my husband. His props are a piece of parchment made from the skin of a kosher animal, a *kulmus*, or reed pen, and a small bottle of ink. The ink is made of crushed sap, pomegranate skin, gallnut, and soot from burnt grapevines, all brewed in water for twelve hours. The exact recipe has been passed down from generation to generation for the past sixteen hundred years, give or take.

The drama begins when the rabbi tells the scribe to give his writing instruments to my husband.

"These are now y-y-yours," says the rabbi, looking at my husband. "Repeat after me: 'These are my writing implements.'"

My husband swallows his pride and intelligence to get out the sentence. "These are my writing implements."

"Speak up and take the gum out of your mouth."

My husband takes the gum out of his mouth and holds it in his right hand. Then he repeats, "These are my writing implements."

The rabbi swivels toward the witnesses and asks if they heard.

"Yes," they chirp.

Then he swivels back.

"Now give your writing implements to the Torah scribe and say, 'I am giving you my implements, and you will write the *get* for me.'"

"I am giving you my implements, and you will write the *get* for me," my husband whispers as he hands the writing materials to the scribe.

The rabbi turns to the scribe and asks, "Did he just give you these writing m-m-materials?"

Well versed, the scribe produces a clear "Yes." Then the rabbi instructs the scribe, my husband, and the two witnesses to retire to a separate room to write the *get*, the writ of divorce. I am dismissed for intermission.

A scribe writes the *get* on a parchment marked with a stylus. The text consists of twelve lines of Hebrew and Aramaic, 12 being the numerical value of the Hebrew letters *gimmel* and *tet*, which spell *get*. The exact wording was finalized by the Babylonian sages of the fourth century CE, who also laid down strict details for its calligraphy. The *get* could only be written in a city or town with a source of water.

This is the standard Jerusalem text, which my husband and the two witnesses watched the scribe write with his reed pen:

On the——— day of the week, the——— day of the month ———, in the year——— of the creation of the world, according to the number of years we count here in Jerusalem, on the waters of the Siloam Spring and by cistern waters, I, called——— ———, son of———, called———, standing today in Jerusalem, the city which has cisterns for water, do hereby consent with my own free will, without any duress, to free and release and divorce you, my wife, called———, daughter of———, called———, standing today in Jerusalem, who has previously been my wife,

*and now I release and send away and divorce you so that you will
be free to go and govern yourself and be married to any man you
desire and let no person oppose you from this day and forever and
behold you are permitted to every man. And this shall be for you
from me a bill of divorce and an epistle of sending away and a bill
of release according to the Law of Moses and Israel.*

————, *son of*————, *witness*
————, *son of*————, *witness*

The Mishna, the code of Jewish law edited by Judah the
Prince in Zippori, Lower Galilee, around 2000 CE, says that a
husband can write the writ of divorce on the horn of a bull, but
then the husband must hand his wife the whole bull. A husband
or his scribe can write the prescribed lines on the hand of a slave,
but then the wife gets the living, full-bodied slave. The rabbis
argued over whether the writ of divorce could be written on an
olive leaf. I think about these disputes as I wait for the final act of
my *get* ceremony. My tradition often seems bizarre, ludicrous, and
surreal. These are the qualities that my friends warned me about,
interpreting the ceremony as demeaning, primitive, and meaningless. But this strangeness stems from the ceremony being
rooted in a time when Jews owned slaves and scribes wrote on
horns. Though part of me chuckles at the antics of the three rabbis this morning, another part acknowledges that the tradition is
larger and richer than those rabbis who claim to be its guardians.
Standing in front of the politically appointed rabbinic judges, I
look beyond them and see the Israelites who walked out of Babylon and those who left Egypt. The Israelites came home from the
north and from the south at different periods in my history. They
came from the east and from the west throughout the centuries,
all yearning to create a new life in a promised land.

We are all players in the same story. It is an ancient tale, told and retold, and though the ceremony this morning in 1999 seems absurd, I love it for the continuity it affords. Each jot and tittle holds me in place against torrents of upheaval. When pieces of my life shatter like shards, the tradition binds. Moreover, the same sages and texts that prescribe my Jewish divorce determined the ceremony in which I was wed, that in which my sons entered the Covenant and those that I enact every Sabbath and on holidays. It is that tradition, that Jewish sanctification of time, that provided the scaffolding for holding my family together for twenty-seven years. Ironically it is that same tradition that allows me an out.

Jewish tradition accepts divorce as a necessary evil, evil because ideally a marriage parallels the eternal covenant between God and Israel. The prophet Malachi admonishes, "Let no one break faith with the wife of his youth. For I detest divorce, said the Lord, the God of Israel." Being human, however, the Talmudic sages recognized the difference between the ideal and the real. They understood that divorce was sometimes necessary, but they did not want to make it an easy procedure.

A kosher divorce cannot be derived by a simple public statement of "You are no longer my wife." A valid divorce cannot be derived from one action—a husband sending out his wife from their home. The sages determined that a divorce, according to the Law of Moses and Israel, is valid only if a specific document is written in the presence of two witnesses and given to the wife in the presence of those same witnesses. The Talmudic sages hoped that the husband, while going through the involved process, would reconsider and not divorce.

Whereas God was present in my wedding ceremony, He is absent from the divorce proceedings. His name is neither mentioned nor invoked. I imagine Him off in a corner, sulking, and for good reason. What, after all, has God been doing every day since the creation of the world? According to the Babylonian Talmud, He has been running a dating service, matchmaking, a task more difficult, the sages claim, than splitting the waters during the Exodus.

My tradition is the palace in which I play out universal themes. Encountering it here in the rabbinic court on a summer morning at the end of the second millennium, I feel as if I have been catapulted back to my roots. The penchant for detail springs from these rock-bottom roots.

I am fortunate that my husband is cooperating in granting me a *get*. Thousands of Jewish women are not so lucky. Called *agunot*, they are locked in unwanted, often violent marriages because their husbands refuse to grant them a *get*. For them the tradition is a prison. For me it is an ancient palace, rising out of a chaotic sea, a palace I visit at the most meaningful transitions of my life.

Act Three: The Walk

After twenty minutes my husband returns with the scribe and the witnesses. They are not smiling. The five of us walk back into the chambers.

The rabbi asks my husband if he is giving me this divorce of his own free will or if somebody is forcing him to do so. In Jewish tradition only the man can grant the woman a divorce. Even if the woman initiates the divorce, the man must say that he is willingly granting it. I hesitate. My husband could balk. He could scream, "It's all *her* idea. *She's* the one who left *me*. *She's* the one who's always taking the initiative. *I* didn't want to get married in the first place. It was *her* idea. It's all *her* fault."

The ambivalence in my heart would like him not to cooperate, at least for a minute. I would like to hear a refusal because it would be an acknowledgment that he cares. But he acquiesces, albeit softly.

"I can't hear you," the rabbi bellows.

"Yes, my own free will. Nobody is forcing me." He barely opens his lips.

We are standing under the wedding canopy in 1972. It is a warm May evening—Lag B'Omer, the thirty-third day of the counting of the barley offering in Jerusalem two thousand years ago, and the only date between Passover and the Feast of Weeks when Orthodox Jewish weddings can take place. Two witnesses and my mother stand with us under the canopy. Tears squat in the corners of my mother's eyes. I see them when I walk around my fiancé seven times. After the seventh circle, I stop next to my man. He looks like a child who has been praised by his kindergarten teacher. He lifts my veil to give me a sip of wine. It is sweet and sanctified. Then he opens his lips slightly, just slightly, and takes a sip. God is crossing His fingers.

The rabbi turns to the witnesses. "Did you hear him?"

"Yes," they chant.

The scribe hands the parchment to my husband, who hands it to the rabbi, who folds it into sixths and hands it back to my husband. The parchment is like a hot potato. Nobody wants to hold it because it is human evidence that God failed. And if His matchmaking is faulty, what about His other interventions?

The rabbi tells my husband to say the following words to me: "Behold, this is your *get*. Accept it, for with it you will be divorced from me from this moment and be permitted to all men." My husband follows the rabbi's orders. He looks straight into my eyes.

"Behold, this is your *get*. Accept it, for with it you will be divorced from me from this moment and be permitted to all men."

The words freeze in the hot July air. I cannot believe he is letting me go, sending me out to copulate with other men. We were enmeshed for so many years. How can he do this to me?

It is the first year of our marriage. Every night, I lie on top of my husband, who lies on the living room couch and watches television. We are one flesh. Eventually I want to sit up. I even want to go into the other room to read a book. I go.

For weeks he does not respond when I talk to him. Over the years we try five marriage counselors. Nothing works. One night after twenty-four years of marriage, he throws a damp towel onto my desk.

"This was out of place," he shouts.

I ask him to leave.

"If you don't like it, lady, you know where the fuck you can go."

Now the rabbi tells me to hold my arms out toward my husband and cup my hands together, with my thumbs slightly inside the cups. I do as I am told.

"No, do not move your thumbs. Do not grab," he admonishes. "You are a vessel. Let the parchment fall into your hands. He must give it to y-y-you."

Now he directs my husband. "Hold the folded parchment about half a meter above her h-h-hands." My husband obeys.

"As soon as he drops it," the rabbi instructs me, "I want you to grasp it with two hands, like this." He holds his hands in the position of Christian prayer.

We both do as we're told. My husband drops the writ of divorce into my hands. I clutch the folded parchment.

"Did you see that?" the rabbi turns to ask the witnesses, who are still awake.

"Yes," they yawn.

"Now hold your hands in front of you, grasping the writ, and walk over th-th-there," he tells me, pointing to the far side of the room.

I am a good walker.

It is a Friday night, the Sabbath. We are seated at either end of the dining room table, flanked by our three children. I have blessed the Sabbath candles; my husband has blessed the wine; our youngest son has blessed the bread. This is the only time during the week we sit together as a family. I want it to be pleasant, so I make conversation and encourage the children to speak. My husband watches the TV weekly news roundup. I hope he won't explode this week, when the wine spills on the tablecloth. I want it to be pleasant, a blessing.

As my fourteen-year-old daughter and I clear the soup plates— homemade vegetable barley—she says to me, "Don't you see he doesn't love you?"

I control the tears through the homemade apple strudel and then run out the door, down the sixty-four stairs, up seven blocks, down two hills, over three neighborhoods, halfway to Bethlehem. I walk fast, tears streaming down my cheeks, arms swinging violently.

By the time I return to the living room an hour later, everyone is sitting in silence in front of the TV, watching the latest terrorist attack.

In the courtroom I take large, powerful strides, but the room, being small and crowded, is big enough only for three. I would crash through the wall if the rabbi told me to, but when I come up against the corner, he says to turn around and come back. I walk. I stand below the three rabbis, the folded parchment between my palms. The rabbi looks at me and says, "You are now a divorced woman. You are permitted to any m-m-man, and you can get married in ninety-two days. Please give me the parchment."

I hand the rabbi the document. He tears it slightly to assure that another couple with our exact names will not use this *get* today.

I say "Thank you" and "Goodbye." The reading rabbi closes his book; the sucking rabbi extracts his thumb; and Moses wishes us good luck in our new lives.

When I say "Thank you" and "Goodbye" to my ex-husband, his silent armor glistens.

Downstairs, outside, a smile breaks forth. It stretches from Cyrus Street to King Solomon Road. I walk over to King David Street and think what a pity these kings are dead, now that I am available and my self-esteem can handle royalty. Marriage, however, is not on my mind, despite the rabbi's mention of those ninety-two days. According to the calculations of the Talmudic sages, that is how long it will take to determine if I am pregnant. This is important, in order to determine the hypothetical fatherhood of the hypothetical fetus.

The King David Hotel on King David Street is bustling with activity. U.S. envoy Dennis Ross is in town trying to help Israelis and Palestinians piece together a separation agreement. Tourist buses block the road. I am glad I am not a tourist. The only place I want to go to is the land of self-respect, the land of my freedom. My feet will take me there. I turn onto Hebron Way. Cars, buses, and ambulances race by as I walk out of bondage, leaving Babylon.

For our first anniversary, I want to buy him something special. He doesn't like jewelry. In fact he doesn't even wear a wedding ring. I choose the Encyclopedia Judaica and buy it on installments. I imagine my husband will be proud to own this rich compendium of Jewish knowledge.

On the eve of our anniversary, he opens the carton, looks, hesitates, and then closes it. He turns to me with disappointment.

"You really don't know who I am, do you?"

I turn onto Ein Gedi Street, where I live with solitude in a garden apartment. Suddenly, the earth whimpers; a soft hiss rises from the ground. From the north an unnatural dampness saturates the street. Sniffles and staccato breaths ride the hot July air. I stop. I wipe tears from my cheeks and rub my fingers on the amulet around my neck.

I will miss Babylon, where I stayed too long. Even in a strange land, one learns to sing.

Like shards, the final words from Tractate Gittin scatter before me on the damp pavement. I pick them up and reconstruct the ancient truth, "When a man divorces the wife of his youth, even the altar sheds tears."

JUDY HAR-EVEN ON *"Leaving Babylon"*

I wrote "Leaving Babylon" during my first year in the low-residency MFA program in creative nonfiction at Goucher College. Lisa Knopp, one of the program's excellent mentors, had given a presentation about libraries and research techniques for personal essays. The idea of researching anything for a personal essay astounded me, because for years I had written personal essays simply because they demanded, or so I thought, no research. Lisa's ideas were challenging and, ultimately, liberating.

At the time, I was reading the anthropologist Victor Turner on pilgrimage and I thought the *get* ceremony, which I had recently experienced, offered a wealth of research possibilities. But as much as I wanted to explore the ancient ceremony, I also wanted to express the personal pain, for which I needed no library.

I read books on Jewish divorce, all of which referred to the Talmud, of course. I knew I would have to overcome my fear of opening this humbling compendium of Jewish law and lore which until recently only Jewish men studied. In less than a week, I leafed through an English translation of the Aramaic/Hebrew text of Tractate Gittin, over which others spend years. I constantly had to tell myself, *It's okay to superficially leaf through the Talmud. You're not a Torah scholar. Just a divorcée looking for enlightenment.*

The next guilt barrier to overcome was that toward my ex. *How dare you take our marriage and make it public?* my conscience battered. I overcame this barrier by using a pseudonym, which respects the family's right to privacy. I also restrained myself from telling all. Instead, I chose a few scenes to be emblematic of the relationship.

In the first draft, my ex-husband turned out one-dimensional. Phil Gerard and Diana Hume George, my mentors at Goucher that year, reminded me that there must have been good reasons why I married this man. Show them. Their pushing forced me to confront the pain, and thereafter I was able to put it on the page. I like the fact that the last line of a complicated Talmudic text expresses that personal pain in an impersonal way, so I appropriated the line for my ending. The image of these words being written on shards scattered on the tear-soaked pavement came to me when I sat still and imagined.

Once I realized there were three elements in the essay that I had to juggle, or balance, I was on my way: the description of the ceremony; the story of the couple; and the biblical and Talmudic background. Each element demanded its own development and voice. For the description of the ceremony, I tried to let the facts speak for themselves, but editorializing did creep in. Flashback scenes of the couple's marriage, placed associatively in the text, proved a fruitful way to describe the deteriorating relationship.

The most difficult element was the researched background. How to make that interesting and not boring? I tried to simplify and use clear language, relevancy always my compass. I did not want to sound like a teacher; more like a participant in the discovery of material, which I found fascinating.

I write poetry, fiction, journalism, and nonfiction because the world is too rich for only one genre and the human soul has multifarious needs. Poetry, with its strict attention to word choice and rhythm, has been the strongest influence on my creative nonfiction.

When I finished "Leaving Babylon," I started to follow my passions in a less solipsistic way, for which I am grateful. When the writer probes history, others, and texts, in addition to her own heart, she can shed light in a deeper, richer, more meaningful way. And that, I feel, is the purpose of writing: to light up the darkness.

Gray Area: Thinking with a Damaged Brain

FLOYD SKLOOT

. .

I used to be able to think. My brain's circuits were all connected and I had spark, a quickness of mind that let me function
well in the world. There were no problems with numbers or
abstract reasoning; I could find the right word, could hold a
thought in mind, match faces with names, converse coherently
in crowded hallways, learn new tasks. I had a memory and an
intuition that I could trust.

All that changed on December 7, 1988, when I contracted a
virus that targeted my brain. A decade later, my cane and odd
gait are the most visible evidence of damage. But most of the

. .

FLOYD SKLOOT's work has appeared in the *Atlantic Monthly*, *Harper's*,
Poetry, the *American Scholar*, *Utne*, and many others. He is the winner
of numerous awards, including the 2004 Pushcart Prize for his essay "A
Measure of Acceptance," which originally appeared in *Creative Non-
fiction* 19, Diversity Dialogues. His most recent book, *In the Shadow of
Memory*, was the third-place winner of the Barnes & Noble Discover
Great New Writers Award and one of two finalists for the 2004 PEN
Award in the Art of the Essay. He lives in a small round house in the
woods with his wife, Beverly Hallberg.

damage is hidden. My cerebral cortex, the gray matter that MIT neuroscientist Steven Pinker likens to "a large sheet of two-dimensional tissue that has been wadded up to fit inside the spherical skull," has been riddled with tiny perforations. This sheet and the thinking it governs are now porous. Invisible to the naked eye but readily seen through brain-imaging technology, are areas of scar tissue that constrict blood flow. Anatomic holes, the lesions in my gray matter, appear as a scatter of white spots like bubbles or a ghostly pattern of potshots. Their effect is dramatic; I am like the brain-damaged patient described by neuroscientist V. S. Ramachandran in his book *Phantoms in the Brain*: "Parts of her had forever vanished, lost in patches of permanently atrophied brain tissue." More hidden still are lesions in my self, fissures in the thought process that result from this damage to my brain. When the brain changes, the mind changes—these lesions have altered who I am.

"When a disease process hits the brain," writes Dartmouth psychiatry professor Michael Gazzaniga in *Mind Matters*, "the loss of nerve cells is easy to detect." Neurologists have a host of clinical tests that let them observe what a brain-damaged patient can and cannot do. They stroke his sole to test for a spinal reflex known as Babinski's sign or have him stand with feet together and eyes closed to see if the ability to maintain posture is compromised. They ask him to repeat a set of seven random digits forward and four in reverse order, to spell *world* backwards, to remember three specific words such as *barn* and *handsome* and *job* after a spell of unrelated conversation. A new laboratory technique, positron emission tomography, uses radioactively labeled oxygen or glucose that essentially lights up specific and different areas of the brain being used when a person speaks words or sees words or hears words, revealing the organic location for areas of behavioral malfunction. Another new technique, functional

magnetic resonance imaging, allows increases in brain blood
flow generated by certain actions to be measured. The resulting
computer-generated pictures, eerily colorful relief maps of the
brain's lunar topography, pinpoint hidden damage zones.

But I do not need a sophisticated and expensive high-tech
test to know what my damaged brain looks like. People living
with such injuries know intimately that things are awry. They see
it in activities of daily living, in the way simple tasks become
unmanageable. This morning, preparing oatmeal for my wife,
Beverly, I carefully measured out one-third cup of oats and.
poured them onto the pan's lid rather than into the bowl. In its
absence, a reliably functioning brain is something I can almost
feel viscerally. The zip of connection, the shock of axon-to-axon
information flow across a synapse, is not simply a textbook affair
for me. Sometimes I see my brain as a scalded pudding, with fluky
dark spots here and there through its dense layers and small
scoops missing. Sometimes I see it as an eviscerated old TV console, wires all disconnected and misconnected, tubes blown, dust
in the crevices.

Some of this personal, low-tech evidence is apparent in basic
functions like walking, which for me requires intense concentration, as does maintaining balance and even breathing if I am
tired. It is apparent in activities requiring the processing of certain fundamental information. For example, no matter how
many times I have been shown how to do it, I cannot assemble
our vacuum cleaner or our poultry shears or the attachments for
our hand-cranked pasta maker. At my writing desk, I finish a
note and place the pen in my half-full mug of tea rather than in
its holder, which quite obviously teems with other pens. I struggle to figure out how a pillow goes into a pillowcase. I cannot
properly adjust Beverly's stereo receiver in order to listen to the
radio; it has been and remains useful to me only in its present

setting as a CD player. These are all public, easily discernible malfunctions.

However, it is in the utterly private sphere that I most acutely experience how changed I am. Ramachandran compares this to harboring a zombie, playing host to a completely nonconscious being somewhere inside yourself. For me, being brain-damaged also has a physical, conscious component. Alone with my ideas and dreams and feelings, turned inward by the isolation and timelessness of chronic illness, I face a kind of ongoing mental vertigo in which thoughts teeter and topple into those fissures of cognition I mentioned earlier. I lose my way. I spend a lot of time staring into space, probably with my jaw dropping, as my concentration fragments and my focus dissolves. Thought itself has become a gray area, a matter of blurred edges and lost distinctions, with little that is sharp about it. This is not the way I used to be.

In their fascinating study, *Brain Repair*, an international trio of neuroscientists—Donald G. Stein from America, Simón Brailowsky from Mexico, and Bruno Will from France—report that after injury "both cortical and subcortical structures undergo dramatic changes in the pattern of blood flow and neural activity, even those structures that do not appear to be directly or primarily connected with the zone of injury." From this observation, they conclude that "the entire brain—not just the region around the area of damage—reorganizes in response to brain injury." The implications of this are staggering; my entire brain, the organ by which my very consciousness is controlled, was reorganized one day ten years ago. I went to sleep *here* and woke up *there*; the place looked the same, but nothing in it worked the way it used to.

If Descartes was correct, and to Think is to Be, then what happens when I cannot think, or at least cannot think as I did, cannot think well enough to function in a job or in the world? Who am I?

You should hear me talk. I often come to a complete stop in mid-sentence, unable to find a word I need, and this silence is an apt reflection of the impulse blockage occurring in my brain. Sitting next to Beverly as she drives our pickup truck through Portland traffic at 6 p.m., I say, "We should have gone for pizza to avoid this blood . . . " and cannot go on. I hear myself; I know I was about to say "blood tower traffic" instead of "rush hour traffic." Or I manifest staggered speech patterns—which feels like speaking with a limp—as I attempt to locate an elusive word. "I went to the . . . *hospital* yesterday for some . . . *tests* because my head . . . *hurt*." Or I blunder on, consumed by a feeling that something is going wrong, as when I put fresh grounds into the empty carafe instead of the filter basket on my coffeemaker, put eyedrops in my nose or spray the cleaning mist into my face instead of onto the shower walls. So at the dinner table I might say "Pass the sawdust" instead of "Pass the rice," knowing even as it happens that I am saying something inappropriate. I might start a conversation about "Winston Salem's new CD" instead of Wynton Marsalis's or announce that "the shore is breaking" when I mean to say "the shower is leaking." There is nothing smooth or unified anymore about the process by which I communicate; it is disintegrated and unpredictably awkward. My brain has suddenly become like an old man's. Neurologist David Goldblatt has developed a table which correlates cognitive decline in age-associated memory impairment and traumatic brain injury, and the parallels are remarkable. Not gradually, the way such changes occur naturally, but overnight, I was geezered.

It is not just about words. I am also *dyscalculic*, struggling with the math required to halve a recipe or to figure out how many more pages are left in a book I'm reading. If we are on East

Eighty-second and Third Avenue in Manhattan, staying with my childhood friend Larry Salander for the week, it is very difficult for me to compute how far away the Gotham Book Mart is over on West Forty-seventh between Fifth and Sixth, though I spent much of my childhood in the city.

Because it is a place where I still try to operate normally, the kitchen is an ideal neurological observatory. After putting the leftover chicken in a plastic bag, I stick it back in the oven instead of the refrigerator. I put the freshly cleaned pan in the refrigerator, which is how I figure out that I must have put the chicken someplace else because it's missing. I pick up a chef's knife by its blade. I cut off an eighth of a giant white onion and then try to stuff the remainder into a recycled 16-ounce yogurt container that might just hold the small portion I set aside. I assemble ingredients for a vinaigrette dressing, pouring the oil into an old olive jar, adding balsamic vinegar, mustard, a touch of fresh lemon juice, and spices. Then I screw the lid on upside down and shake vigorously, spewing the contents everywhere. I stack the newspaper in the woodstove for recycling. I walk the garbage up our 200-yard-long driveway and try to put it in the mailbox instead of the trash container.

At home is one thing; when I perform these gaffes in public, the effect is often humiliating. I can be a spectacle. In a music store last fall, I was seeking an instruction book for Beverly, who wanted to relearn how to play her old recorder. She informed me that there were several kinds of recorders; it was important to buy exactly the right category of book since instructions for a soprano recorder would do her no good while learning on an alto. I made my way up to the counter and nodded when the saleswoman asked what I wanted. Nothing came out of my mouth, but I did manage to gesture over my right shoulder like an umpire signaling an out. I knew I was in trouble, but forged ahead anyway, saying, "Where are the books for sombrero reporters?" Last summer in Manhattan, I routinely exited the subway stations and led Beverly in the wrong direction, no matter which way we intended to go. She kept saying things like, "I think west is *that* way, sweetie," while I confidently and mistakenly headed east, into the glare of the morning sun, or, "Isn't that the river?" as I led her away from our riverside destination. Last week, in downtown Portland on a warm November morning, I stopped at the corner of Tenth and Burnside, one of the busiest crossings in the city, carefully checked the traffic light (red) and the traffic lanes (bus coming), and started to walk into the street. A muttering transient standing beside me on his way to Powell's Books, where he was going to trade in his overnight haul of tomes for cash, grabbed my shoulder just in time.

At home or not at home, it ultimately makes no difference. The sensation of *dysfunctional mentation* is like being caught in a spiral of lostness. Outside the house, I operate with sporadic success, often not knowing where I am or where I'm going or what I'm doing. Inside the house, the same feelings often apply and I find myself standing at the top of the staircase wondering why I am going down. Even inside my head there is a feeling of being lost, thoughts that go nowhere, emptiness where I expect to find words or ideas, dreams I never remember.

Back in the fall, when it was Beverly's birthday, at least I did remember to go to the music store. More often, I forget what I am after within seconds of beginning the search. As she gets dressed for work, Beverly will tell me what she wants packed for lunch and I will forget her menu by the time I get up the fourteen stairs. Now I write her order down like a waiter. Sometimes I think I should carry a pen at all times. In the midst of preparing a salad, I stop to walk the four paces over to the little desk where we keep our shopping list and forget "tomatoes" by the time I get there. So I should also have paper handy everywhere. Between looking up a phone number and dialing it, I forget the sequence. I need the whole phone book on my speed-dial system.

Though they appear without warning, these snafus are no longer strange to me. I know where they come from. As Dr. Richard M. Restak notes in *The Modular Brain*, "A common error frequently resulting from brain damage involves producing a semantically related word instead of the correct response." But these paraphasias and neologisms, my *expressive aphasias*, and my dyscalculas and my failures to process—the rapids of confusion through which I feel myself flailing—though common for me and others with brain damage, are more than symptoms to me. They are also more than what neurologists like to call *deficits*, the word of choice when describing impairment or incapacity of neurological function, as Oliver Sacks explains in his introduction to *The Man Who Mistook His Wife for a Hat*. These "deficits" have been incorporated into my very being, my consciousness. They are now part of my repertoire. Deficits imply losses; I have to know how to see them as gains.

Practitioners of neuroscience call the damage caused by trauma, stroke, or disease "an insult to the brain." So pervasive is this language that the states of Georgia, Kentucky, and Minnesota, among others, incorporate the phrase "insult to the brain" in their statutory definitions of traumatic brain injury for disability determinations. Such insults, according to the Brain Injury Association of Utah, "may produce a diminished or altered state of consciousness, which results in an impairment of cognitive abilities or physical functioning." The death of one Miles Dethmuffen, front man and founding member of the Boston rock band Dethmuffen, was attributed in news reports to "an alcoholic insult to the brain." The language used is so cool. There is this sentence from the web site

NeuroAdvance.com: "When there is an insult to the brain, some of the cells die." Yes.

Insult is an exquisitely zany word for the catastrophic neurological event it is meant to describe. In current usage, of course, insult generally refers to an offensive remark or action, an affront, a violation of mannerly conduct. To insult is to treat with gross insensitivity, insolence, or contemptuous rudeness. The medical meaning, however, as with so many other medical words and phrases, is different, older, linked to a sense of the word that is some two or three centuries out of date. *Insult* comes from the Latin compound verb *insultare*, which means "to jump on" and is also the root word for *assault* and *assail*. It's a word that connotes aggressive physical abuse, an attack. Originally, it suggested leaping upon the prostrate body of a foe, which may be how its link to contemptuous action was forged.

Though "an insult to the brain" (a blow to the head, a metal shard through the skull, a stroke, a viral "attack") is a kind of assault, I am curious about the way *contempt* has found its way into the matter. Contempt was always part of the meaning of insult and now it is primary to the meaning. Certainly a virus is not acting contemptuously when it targets the brain; neither is the pavement nor steering wheel nor falling wrench nor clot of blood nor most other agents of "insult." But I think society at large, medical scientists, insurers, legislators, and the person on the street do feel a kind of contempt for the brain-damaged with their comical way of walking, their odd patterns of speech or ways in which neurological damage is expressed, their apparent stupidity, their abnormality. The damage done to a brain seems to evoke disdain in those who observe it and shame or disgrace in those who experience it.

Poet Peter Davison has noticed the resonant irony of the phrase "an insult to the brain" and made use of it in his poem

"The Obituary Writer." Thinking about the suicide of John Berryman, the heavily addicted poet whose long-expected death in 1972 followed years of public behavior symptomatic of brain damage, Davison writes that "his hullabaloos/of falling-down drunkenness were an insult to the brain." In this poem, toying with the meaning of the phrase, Davison suggests that Berryman's drinking may have been an insult to his brain, technically speaking, but that watching him was, for a friend, another kind of brain insult. He has grasped the fatuousness of the phrase as a medical term, its inherent judgment of contempt, and made use of it for its poetic ambiguity.

But I have become enamored of the idea that my brain has been insulted by a virus. I use it as motivation. There is a long tradition of avenging insults through duels or counterinsults, through litigation, through the public humiliation of the original insult. So I write. I avenge myself on an insult that was meant, it feels, to silence me by compromising my word-finding capacity, my ability to concentrate and remember, to spell or conceptualize, to express myself, to think.

The duel is fought over and over. I have developed certain habits that enable me to work—a team of seconds, to elaborate this metaphor of a duel. I must be willing to write slowly, to skip or leave blank spaces where I cannot find words that I seek, compose in fragments and without an overall ordering principle or imposed form. I explore and make discoveries in my writing now, never quite sure where I am going, but willing to let things ride and discover later how they all fit together. Every time I finish an essay or poem or piece of fiction, it feels as though I have faced down the insult.

In his book *Creating Mind*, Harvard neurobiologist John E. Dowling says "the cerebral cortex of the human brain, the seat of higher neural function—perception, memory, language, and intelligence—is far more developed than is the cerebral cortex of any other vertebrate." Our gray matter is what makes us human. Dowling goes on to say that "because of the added neural cells and cortical development in the human brain, new facets of mind emerge." Like the fractured facet of a gemstone or crystal, like a crack in the facet of a bone, a chipped facet of mind corrupts the whole, and this is what an insult to the brain does.

Though people long believed, with Aristotle, that the mind was located within the heart, the link between brain and mind is by now a basic fact of cognitive science. Like countless others, I am living proof of it. Indeed, it is by studying the behavior of brain-damaged patients like me that medical science first learned, for example, that the brain is modular, with specific areas responsible for specific functions, or that functions on one side of the body are controlled by areas on the opposite side of the brain. "The odd behavior of these patients," says Ramachandran, speaking of the brain-damaged, "can help us solve the mystery of how various parts of the brain create a useful representation of the external world and generate the illusion of 'self' that endures in space and time." Unfortunately, there is ample opportunity to observe this in action since, according to the Brain Injury Association, more than two million Americans suffer traumatic brain injury every year, a total that does not include damage by disease.

"Change the brain, change the person," says Restak in *The Modular Brain*. But how, exactly? No one has yet explained the way a brain produces what we think of as consciousness. How does the firing of electrical impulse across a synapse produce love, math, nightmare, theology, appetite? Stated more traditionally, how do brain and mind interact? Bookstore shelves are now filled with books, like Steven Pinker's brilliant 1997 study *How the Mind Works*, which attempt to explain how a three-pound organ the consistency of Jell-O makes us see, think, feel, choose, and act. "The mind is not the brain," Pinker says, "but what the brain does."

And what the brain does, according to Pinker, "is information processing, or computation." We think we think with our brain. But in doing its job of creating consciousness, the brain actually relies upon a vast network of systems and is connected to everything—eyes, ears, skin, limbs, nerves. As Dowling so dourly puts it, our mental function, our mind—memory, feelings, emotions, awareness, understanding, creativity—"is an emergent property of brain function." In other words, "What we refer to as mind is a natural consequence of complex and higher neural processing."

The key word is *processing*. We actually think with our whole body. The brain, however, takes what is shipped to it, crunches the data, and sends back instructions. It converts; it generates results. Or, when damaged, does not. There is nothing wrong with my sensory receptors, for instance. I see quite well. I can hear and smell; my speech mechanisms (tongue, lips, nerves) are intact. My skin remains sensitive. But it's in putting things together that I fail. Messages get garbled, blocked, missed. There is, it sometimes seems, a lot of static when I try to think, and this is the gray area where nothing is clear any longer.

Neurons, the brain's nerve cells, are designed to process information. They "receive, integrate and transmit," as Dowling says, receiving input from dendrites and transmitting output along axons, sending messages to one another across chemical passages called *synapses*. When there are lesions like the ones that riddle my gray matter, processing is compromised. Not only that, certain cells have simply died and with them the receiving, integrating, and transmitting functions they performed.

My mind does not make connections because, in essence,

some of my brain's connectors have been broken or frayed. I simply have less to work with and it is no surprise that my IQ dropped measurably in the aftermath of my illness. Failing to make connections, on both the physical and metaphysical levels, is distressing. It is very difficult for me to free-associate; my stream of consciousness does not absorb runoff or feeder streams well, but rushes headlong instead. Mental activity that should follow a distinct pattern does not and, indeed, I experience my thought process as subject to random misfirings. I do not feel in control of my intelligence. Saying "Pass me the tracks" when I intended to say "Pass me the gravy" is a nifty example. Was it because *gravy* sounds like *grooves*, which led to tracks, or because my tendency to spill gravy leaves tracks on my clothes? A misfire, a glitch in the gray area that thought has become for me, and as a result my ability to express myself is compromised. My very nature seems to have altered.

I am also easily overloaded. I cannot read the menu or converse in a crowded, noisy restaurant. I get exhausted at Portland Trailblazers basketball games, with all the visual and aural imagery, all the manufactured commotion, so I stopped going nine years ago. My hands are scarred from burns and cuts that occurred when I tried to cook and converse at the same time. I cannot drive in traffic, especially in our standard transmission pickup truck. I cannot talk about, say, the fiction of Thomas Hardy while I drive; I need to be given directions in small doses rather than all at once, and need those directions to be given precisely at the time I must make the required turn. This is, as Restak explains, because driving and talking about Hardy, or driving and processing information about where to turn, are handled by different parts of the brain and my brain's parts have trouble working together.

I used to write accompanied by soft jazz, but now the least

pattern of noises distracts me and shatters concentration. My entire writing process, in fact, has been transformed as I learned to work with my newly configured brain and its strange snags. I have become an avid note taker, a jotter of random thoughts that might or might not find their way together or amount to anything, a writer of bursts instead of steady work. A slight interruption—the movement of my cat across my window view, the call of a hawk, a spell of coughing—will not just make me lose my train of thought, it will leave me at the station for the rest of the day.

I have just finished reading a new book about Muhammad Ali, *King of the World*, by David Remnick. I anticipated identifying a bit with Ali, now suffering from Parkinson's disease, who shows so strikingly what brain damage can do, stripped as he is of so many of the functions—speech, movement, spontaneity—that once characterized him. But it was reading about Floyd Patterson that got me.

Patterson was a childhood hero of mine. Not only did we share a rare first name, we lived in neighboring towns—he was in Rockville Center, on Long Island, while I was five minutes away in Long Beach, just across the bridge. I was nine when he beat Archie Moore to take the heavyweight championship belt, almost twelve when he lost it to Ingemar Johansson and almost thirteen when he so memorably won it back. The image of Johansson's left leg quivering as he lay unconscious on the mat is one of those vivid memories that endures (because, apparently, it is stored in a different part of the brain than other, less momentous memories). That Floyd, like me, was small of stature in his world, was shy and vulnerable, and I was powerfully drawn to him.

During his sixty-four professional fights, his long amateur career, his many rounds of sparring to prepare for fights, Patterson absorbed a tremendous amount of damage to his brain. He's now in his sixties, and his ability to think is devastated. Testifying in court earlier this year in his capacity as head of the New York State Athletic Commission, Patterson "generally seemed lost," according to Remnick. He could not remember the names of his fellow commissioners, his phone number or secretary's name or lawyer's name. He could not remember the year of his greatest fight, against Archie Moore, or "the most basic rules of boxing (the size of the ring, the number of rounds in a championship fight)." He kept responding to questions by saying, "It's hard to think when I'm tired."

Finally, admitting "I'm lost," he said, "Sometimes I can't even remember my wife's name, and I've been married thirty-two, thirty-three years." He added again that it was hard for him to think when he was tired. "Sometimes, I can't even remember my own name."

People often ask if I will ever "get better." In part, I think what they wonder about is whether the brain can heal itself. Will I be able, either suddenly or gradually, to think as I once did? Will I toss aside the cane, be free of symptoms, have all the functions governed by my brain restored to smooth service, rejoin the world of work and long-distance running? The question tends to catch me by surprise because I believe I have stopped asking it myself.

The conventional wisdom has long been that brains do not repair themselves. Other body tissue, other kinds of cells, are replaced after damage, but "when brain cells are lost because of injury or disease," Dowling wrote as recently as 1998, "they are not replaced." We have, he says, as many brain cells at age one as we will ever have. This has been a fundamental tenet of neuroscience, yet it has also long been clear that people do recover—fully or in part—from brain injury. Some stroke victims relearn to walk and talk; feeling returns in once-numb limbs. Children—especially children—recover and show no lasting ill effects from catastrophic injuries or coma-inducing bouts of meningitis.

So brain cells do not get replaced or repaired, but brain-damaged people occasionally do regain function. In a sense, then, the brain heals, but its cells do not.

In *Confronting Traumatic Brain Injury*, Texas bioethicist William J. Winslade says, "Scientists still don't understand how the brain heals itself." He adds that although "until recently, neuroscientists thought that much of the loss of capabilities due to brain damage was irreversible," patients recover spontaneously and rehabilitation programs "can restore cognitive and functional skills and emotional and experiential capacity, at least in part."

There are in general five theories about the way people might recover function lost to brain damage. One suggests that we do not need all of our brain because we only use a small part of it to function. Another is that some brain tissue can be made to take over functions lost to damage elsewhere. Connected to this is the idea that the brain has a backup mechanism in place allowing cells to take over like understudies. Rehabilitation can teach people new ways to perform some old tasks, bypassing the whole damaged area altogether. And finally, there is the theory that in time, and after the chemical shock of the original injury, things return to normal and we just get better.

It is probably true that, for me, a few of these healing phenomena have taken place. I have, for instance, gotten more adept at tying my shoes, taking a shower, driving for short periods. With careful preparation, I can appear in public to read from my work or attend a party. I have developed techniques to slow down my interactions with people or to incorporate my mistakes into a longer-term process of communication or composition. I may not be very good in spontaneous situations, but given time to craft my responses, I can sometimes do well. But I still can't think.

A recent development promises to up the ante in the game of recovery from brain damage. The *New York Times* reported in October of 1998 that "adult humans can generate new brain cells." A team at the Salk Institute for Biological Studies in La Jolla, California, observed new growth in cells of the hippocampus, which controls learning and memory in the brain. The team's leader, Dr. Fred Gage, expressed the usual cautions; more time is needed to "learn whether new cell creation can be put to work" and under what conditions. But the findings were deemed both "interesting" and "important."

There is only one sensible response to news like this. It has no personal meaning for me. Clinical use of the finding lies so far in the future as to be useless, even if regenerating cells could restore my lost functions. Best not to think about this sort of thing.

Because, in fact, the question of whether I will ever get better is meaningless. To continue looking outside for a cure, a "magic bullet," some combination of therapies and treatments and chemicals to restore what I have lost, is to miss the point altogether. Certainly if a safe, effective way existed to resurrect dead cells, or generate replacements, and if this somehow guaranteed that I would flash back or flash forward to "be the person I was," it would be tempting to try.

But how would that be? Would the memories that have vanished reappear? Not likely. Would I be like the man, blind for decades, who had sight restored and could not handle the experience of vision, could not make sense of a world he could see? I am, in fact, who I am now. I have changed. I have learned to live and live richly as I am now. Slowed down, softer, more heedful of all that I see and hear and feel, more removed from the hubbub, more internal. I have made certain decisions, such as moving from the city to a remote rural hilltop in the middle of acres of forest, that have turned out to be good for my health and even my soul. I have gained the love of a woman who knew me before I got sick and likes me much better now. Certainly I want to be well. I miss being able to think clearly and sharply, to function in the world, to move with grace. I miss the feeling of coherence or integrity that comes with a functional brain. I feel old before my time.

In many important respects, then, I have already gotten better. I continue to learn new ways of living with a damaged brain. I continue to make progress, to avenge the insult, to see my way around the gray area. But no, I am not going to be the man I was. In this, I am hardly alone.

Winner of the Creative Nonfiction Award for Best Essay on the Brain

Floyd Skloot on "Gray Area: Thinking with a Damaged Brain"

I believe that if I can write about living with brain damage well enough to communicate what it's like, to discover what it means and how it plays out in a person's life, then I will also be able to understand it well enough to live with it, to make an honest life that incorporates it, and to make it clear for others. I hope that my readers will see and think freshly about a subject that they may have previously ignored or found disturbing. And I hope that some will be cheered by my writing, that they will find my work ultimately hopeful.

I have had to become a jotter of random thoughts . . . a writer of bursts instead of steady work. I constructed the foundation of "Gray Area" a paragraph at a time. I have learned to trust that when I am jotting down isolated thoughts or episodes during the period of time that I'm thinking about an essay, those pieces will eventually belong somewhere in that essay or one of the others I'm engaged with then, because they all tend to emerge from the same emotional state of mind or complex of feelings. I wrote the scenes of buying a recorder for my wife and traveling in New York as separate jottings, which I later recognized as pieces that belonged to the essay.

I'm a poet. I didn't write essays until I got sick, oddly enough, and have gradually, in the fifteen years since getting sick, slowed and perhaps stopped writing fiction altogether. Creative nonfiction offers the engagement of good narrative fiction, with its emphasis on character, setting, and story; the intimacy, compression, and precision of poetry; information and fresh ideas as in good nonfiction; personal revelation as in memoirs; and the immediacy of journalism. It can be as tight or as baggy as the subject requires. It is a flexible, endlessly fresh form for the individual voice to explore.

I encourage young writers to read across genres and revel in research. One of my first and most powerful responses to being ill was to read as much as I could about neurology, cognitive science, virology, immunology, and related fields to build a deeper understanding of what was happening to me. Tangents that emerged during the writing of the essay required new research. It can be tempting to forget that an essay or creative nonfiction piece must have shape and density, must be well written rather than spewed, and must lead somewhere other than the mirror.

But I also like keeping the reader off-balance. Since I never know what's going to pop out of my mouth next, why should the reader?

Joe Stopped By

ANDREI CODRESCU

■ ■

When I handed her the phone, Laura looked like I was taking her to the dentist. Her father was in town and threatened to come over. I had met the guy twice. The first time we stood on the lawn of Laura's old place on Myrtledale, and he looked on me suspiciously, like he must have looked on all her boyfriends since she started bringing them home around the age of sixteen. He complained about his truck and the lack of rain on his pecan trees, and I told him that the publishing industry was going to the dogs. Nice conversation. Mutual incomprehension. Lasted about five minutes.

Next time I had the pleasure of Joe's company was the day

■ ■

ANDREI CODRESCU immigrated to the United States in 1966 from Romania, where he was born in 1946. He is a poet, novelist, essayist, screenwriter, and columnist for national and international publications. He is a regular contributor to National Public Radio, MSNBC, *Nightline*, the *New York Times*, and others. He is the MacCurdy Distinguished Professor of English at Louisiana State University. He lives in Baton Rouge, where he edits the online literary journal *Exquisite Corpse*. His most recent book is *Wakefield*, a novel.

after Christmas. He called and said that he'd be over in two hours. We had just cleaned up after the Christmas dinner the night before. Laura's mother, Laura's two sons, and a couple of friends had come over to eat. We were still hung over, and there were a lot of dirty dishes. The timing wasn't great. Two hours later, Joe showed up with his wife, Carolyn; Laura's sister, Susan; Susan's husband, Lloyd; and Susan's daughter. Joe plunked himself down in an armchair in the front room and declared the excesses of Christmas bankrupt and insufficiently mindful of Christ. Carolyn, who agreed with everything her husband said, added that in their church people were against materialism and that godless TV was turned off during the holidays so people can have a nice, non-alcoholic dinner and praise the Lord. They lived in Jigger, a small town in northern Louisiana near the Mississippi border. They had moved there after Joe's second triple-bypass surgery. He'd given up his wife, drink, cigarettes, and the law and taken up Carolyn, Jesus, and farming. He'd been a prosecutor in West Baton Rouge Parish and a ward heeler for Dixiecrats running for state offices. He gave up all that.

The Christmas visit wasn't so bad because Joe was kind of hemmed in between Laura and Susan and couldn't express himself very clearly. His daughters knew him too well and anticipated nearly every one of his yarns with a detouring quip. And then there was Carolyn. Once Carolyn's shrill voice launched forth the battleship of a story, there was no stopping her. She churned the waves at top speed, and there was nothing anyone could do except get out of the way and let the parable subside. Her stories were all parables. One of her sons had bad grades for a year; then he found himself and did well. The moral of that was that everybody has their own timetable. That was a placating parable for liberals like me, offered in penance for one of Joe's unfinished stories about educational problems among the darker-skinned folk. Joe's story had been ruthlessly chopped to pieces by the whirring blades of Laura and Susan's daddy-choppers, but Carolyn figured that enough of it had gotten out to offend the liberal establishment—me.

Joe had seen action in Japan and wasn't going to buy anything Japanese if his life depended on it. "I'd rather shave with broken glass than the best Toyota shaver they got," he announced. That was how far he got that time in the land of diversity. His daughters were quick to point out that you couldn't tell the difference anymore between what the Japanese and the Americans made, because they were all mixed up together, from management to actual parts in cars and electronics. That nearly got him, because if there was anything he couldn't abide, it was this mixing. He had views on that and on miscegenation, but they never saw the light of day. His girls saw to that.

After they left we felt a residual weirdness, like another kind of hangover. We tried to analyze it. He had gotten Laura all worked up, which was, she said, "his specialty." The former prosecutor had been a formidable dinner-table presence in her childhood. She had honed fearsome debating skills to resist the onslaught of her father's provocations. He had used the family as practice for the court. They all felt like lawyers and criminals, always on the alert for another burst of eloquence, sure to be defeated but not allowed to give up before putting up a good fight. Laura's mother had reacted by creating a passive-aggressive resistance that was intricate, mute, and so "feminine" the prosecutor couldn't get in. It was like going into a women's bathroom. He was a gentleman. He drew the line there. His daughters adopted different strategies. Susan also played the feminine card and wriggled and winked and brought up matters of esoteric hormonal import that were worse than trespassing into the ladies' room. Joe flirted with her for self-preservation. Laura, on the other hand, met him head-on, on his own turf. She countered and parried his arguments, got the better of him, didn't quit until he admitted defeat, which he never did. Outside the home Joe played rough and dirty for his candidates. Laura went after him in the field. She played dirty. She seduced daddy's law partner. She was only fifteen. When Joe found out, he was ready to shoot somebody, but who was he going to shoot? He made a lot of belligerent noises. Did he admit defeat? No. He had a heart attack instead. Left her mother. Took up Jesus. Well, not in that order, but this was the order that Laura saw at the time. No amount of grown-up reason could later dislodge it. She'd felt personally responsible for all the disasters subsequent to her victory, and it had put her in an untenable position. She learned that victory over daddy is a terrible thing but that daddies can be defeated using female wiles. Her insurgent sexuality was a match for any man's posturing, including her invincible daddy's. Is there a worse thing to learn in your adolescence? Of course the son-ofabitch had invited it. He had challenged and challenged, prodded and poked until she had gotten her back up. Was he surprised? Of course. It had been only a game for him. He never expected to be taken seriously.

On the other hand, I'm a man. How am I supposed to take this? Here I am living with a woman who is both a skilled debater and a guilt-ridden daddy-killer. I say guilt-ridden because that is what I attribute her extreme sensitivity to. Laura under attack is a lot like an aroused lynx. She did in the king; who am I to oppose her? But her guilt is also her weakness. If she makes too bold a move, she throws herself, weeping, into my arms. I hold her there; then I seduce her. She gives all of herself. She never wanted anything else. She only wanted daddy to admit defeat and then hold her. I never admit defeat, but I hold her. I am a man, just like her daddy, but I cannot be killed because I am her lover, like her daddy's enemy whom she seduced at fifteen. I am both daddy and anti-daddy. We get along just fine.

The third time Joe came to visit, he gave no more notice than he did before. But there was something different this time, and he made a mistake being casual. Laura and I had gotten married the month before. Joe knew, but he didn't say a word. He didn't call or write the whole month. And now he was coming over on two hours' notice.

Carolyn was right behind him, chatty like a sparrow on a fence post. Joe made a dash toward the commanding post of the first armchair, but I beat him to it. He had to sit next to his daughter on the couch. Carolyn took the other armchair. Between us was a table, on which sat a fine chess set with figures that looked sculpted by Brancusi, my conational, who made ovoids. It was a birthday present from Laura. Carolyn showed off the carved ivory piece around her neck. She had matching earrings.

"An ivory orchid," said Laura. "Isn't ivory illegal?"

"It's fossil ivory!" gloated Carolyn. "My friend found it in Canada and had the craftsman carve it into an orchid. It's a birthday present from Joe."

Laura pointed to the chess set. "That's my birthday present to Andrei."

"Do you play chess?" Joe asked, as if he was asking if I was homosexual.

"Yes," I said. "The best chess players are in jail and in Eastern Europe."

"Five-year-old Hungarian girls!" Laura said. "Masters."

"The only thing I'd know to do with a chess set is take out my gun and shoot the queen," said Joe.

"That wouldn't be very useful," I said.

Carolyn sensed danger. "Did you see it snowed in Shreveport at New Year's? We were at the church playing dominoes after the New Year's meal and heard the radio announce snow, so everybody went home. The kids were disappointed."

"Our people," Joe said, "the Scotch-Irish, Anglo-Saxon people . . . "

Laura was ready. Carolyn was ready. I was waiting.

"Our people," Joe said, enjoying the suspense, "have a whiskey problem, so the preachers and the bootleggers got together and declared the town dry. In the old days, women couldn't walk down the main street without being shouted at. There were gunfights. They outlawed it, and the drinking moved outside the town limits. Jigger is peaceful now."

Everybody laughed. What a relief. Joe was being self-mocking. Then he sighed and said, "Burnt cork! Burnt cork!"

"Yes," he continued when he saw bafflement, "the dark-skinned ones all got fifty thousand dollars from the government because they were discriminated on past loans. I need to get some burnt cork to rub my face with and get myself fifty thousand dollars, too."

"We don't have enough money for our seniors' hot-meal program," said Carolyn, as if there was a connection.

Joe said that the two counties, theirs and the neighboring one, received unequal money for the seniors' program, even though they were exactly the same size. When I asked why, Joe said it was because of the two representatives in the statehouse in Baton Rouge. One got the money; the other didn't.

I stared at the chess set. I didn't want to know what colors these representatives were. Joe didn't push it.

"Did you hear about that county in Florida—Palm Beach, I think it was—where they tried to make Spanish mandatory? They were going to outlaw English."

"Like in Quebec," agreed Carolyn.

"Indeed," said Joe, "Carolyn won't eat in any of those damn restaurants in Quebec. If they can't print their menus in English, no do-re-mi for you!"

"Too bad," I said. "You'll be missing some fine French food. We eat from French-only menus right here in Baton Rouge. Paté. Croissants. Étouffé. Sauté."

"That county in Florida," Joe said, "where they had all those poor illiterates—that's where they tried to outlaw English."

"My mother lives there," I said, "and her English is fine."

"And she didn't vote for Buchanan, that's for sure," laughed Laura. "She voted for Gore."

"They showed that Florida ballot in a nursing home in New York. Everybody figured it out. One woman said, 'They've been out in the sun too long in Florida.'" Joe stopped to laugh to himself and lifted his hand, warning of the coming of a joke. "They asked Barbara Bush why people thought Dubya wasn't too smart, and she said, 'Who's smarter? Dubya, who has an MBA from Harvard, or Gore, who dropped out of divinity school?'"

Joe and Carolyn laughed. We did, too. Laura said, "Gore left divinity school to go to Vietnam. And no mother's going to say her son is dumb. We are still waiting to see how dumb he is."

"Nobody goes to divinity school," I said, "to make good grades. They go there to think about serious issues."

"I went to get an eye exam in Florida," Joe said, "and the optician was a retired Canadian who had sold seven optical shops in Canada before he retired. He couldn't stay put, so he built himself another one in Palm Beach. He couldn't stand it, he said, because of all those whiny, pushy New York Jews. He was moving back to Canada."

"That's just how they are—pushy," agreed Carolyn.

"He couldn't have been a very good optician because nobody

could read that spaghetti ballot," I said. Some of my good humor
was beginning to fray around the edges. So far Joe had gone after
nearly everything he suspected I was: a Jew, a liberal, a Spanish-
speaking something . . . but of course there was more. In our
three encounters so far, he had not asked me once where I was
from. I would have told him. Transylvania. Southern Romania.
Ex-Commie country. He knew all that but not from me. When
Carolyn said later, "You're a teacher. You know what I mean,"
apropos of something or other, I realized that of all my identities
and possible places of origin, they had settled on "teacher" as the
least offensive. A teacher might marry Joe's daughter, but all
those other things—ex-Commies, writers, Transylvanians—they
had no right.

"It can be argued," Joe said in a sort of prosecutorial manner
that had Laura half out of her seat, "that the Southern states are
still under occupation."

"By whom, pray," laughed his daughter, "with a Southerner
in the White House, and a Republican Congress?"

"By the armies of Northern aggression. . . . " Joe intoned
gravely.

"That would be Wal-Mart," I said.

"Yup," agreed Laura, "occupied by Sam Walton."

Carolyn thought that it was time to intervene for reasons of
balance. "I hate Wal-Mart," she said. "We had a nice little store
with everything—children's, women's, men's. It's gone now.
There was another little store one town over. Gone. Wal-Mart's
the only store in fifty miles."

"The bankers are bankrupting the farmers," said Joe. "The
New York bankers."

Carolyn followed on the footsteps of that with a detailed
account of the disasters wrought on farmers by Wall Street. Their

own thirty-five acres of pecans were not in question; the soul of the country was.

"Where is all that booming economy Bill Clinton was talking about? I don't see any money." Joe looked angry.

For once I agreed with him. "It's funny how that booming economy left with Clinton."

"Everybody around Clinton dies mysteriously," Joe said, having had enough of making nice. "Just like that. They found a guy shot in the back of the head. They said it was suicide."

"Must be the Kennedy syndrome," Laura said.

"That was the work of a single gunman," Joe said proudly. "That Jackie Kennedy was one loose woman."

"Her children were probably all by Jack's daddy, Joe," Laura sighed, briefly amused by the game.

Joe laughed, but Carolyn didn't.

I wondered who was left. We had already done the Japanese the first time we met. The Jews, the Hispanics, the Quebecois, and the Catholics had just been disposed of. Joe was in a good mood.

"When Earl K. Long couldn't run for governor anymore, he ran a friend of his. They were campaigning in northern Louisiana, and Earl went to take a leak in the bushes while his man, who was a terrible speaker, kept droning on and on. When Earl came back, an old-timer who didn't understand one word of the speech said, 'Is that guy a Communiss?' Earl laughed. 'No,' he said, 'he's a Catholic. He can't be a Communiss; his brother is a priest.' 'I knew there was sumpthin',' the old man said."

We all laughed, Carolyn the loudest. She was Catholic.

Joe got suddenly serious. "I first voted in 1948. I didn't vote for either Truman or Dewey. I voted for Strom Thurmond. He was running on states' rights."

"A lot of elections since then," I said. "I wish I understood what Strom says when he speaks."

"Sure," Joe said. "How about that Jesse Jackson? Is he going to retire with Jimmy Swaggart and that Tammy Faye Bakker?"

He was being conciliatory. I extended a finger, too. "I can't understand what Jesse Jackson says, either."

"They should have a conversation, Strom and Jesse," laughed Laura.

Joe's mood got visibly cloudy. "I ran a lot of elections . . . I neglected other things for them!" He looked ready to mist over. "I'm seventy-five years old!"

Laura winced. In the past she must have heard some variation of the age thing. But there was more here. He was old, but he was still daddy. Stubborn. His girl may have married, but without his permission, it meant nothing. But it was only a game. He knew that his stubbornness meant nothing. Laura knew that it meant nothing. But it hurt nonetheless. It was between them, half forgotten, still raw. It was everybody's second marriage— Joe's, Carolyn's, Laura's, and mine—but in some alternative universe, none of that had happened.

When they got up to leave, I felt like I'd been in a wrestling match. All my muscles hurt. At the door Carolyn launched into another story. I shook Joe's hand. Laura lingered with Carolyn while I retreated into the room and started playing chess with myself.

Laura looked as if she'd trekked through a swamp.

"That man." She shook her head. "Carolyn told me why they were in town."

"Why? To wish you well in your marriage? Which they haven't mentioned?"

She shook her head. "He's getting operated on. A tumor in his neck."

I shook my head, too. Can't win, one way or another. If the opinions don't get you, life will. Diversity. What a joke.

Andrei Codrescu on *"Joe Stopped By"*

The pleasures of writing this story were as follows: doing something untoward under the noses of everyone present (i.e, making mental notes); wondering how violent disagreement could go hand in hand with empathy; finding some tolerance for the strangeness of people I couldn't help being related to; and seeing my own life under a cold light. In this kind of reporting (there are many kinds) the success of the effort is in how closely you manage to achieve empathy for your subject, or even (in the best of cases) sink below the subject, in humility and abjection. The true oddness of people, or even objects, is never released by authorial hubris, but it yields, occasionally, to effacement. Some of my other nonfictions are driven by glee or malice, but I was so much younger then.

In the Woods

LESLIE RUBINKOWSKI

. .

I.

The day my grandfather saw the naked woman began at dawn. He and his brother Louie had parked the Chevy pickup at the edge of the woods and stepped down between the trees, carrying their rifles. When they lost sight of the road they parted, Louie disappearing deep. My grandfather found a stump, sat down, and waited.

Hours passed with no sign of deer or any other living thing. The middle of the day came but among the trees it was dark and still.

Then my grandfather heard a sound, a shuffling in the leaves. He looked up.

"Louie," he said, "is that you?"

It was not. It was a woman and she was standing before him, naked. She was young and very pretty and shivering in the cold.

. .

LESLIE RUBINKOWSKI is the author of *Impersonating Elvis*. She teaches writing in the MFA program in creative nonfiction at Goucher College. She is currently working on a memoir about her father's family.

My grandfather stared at the woman. She hugged herself, made some small joke. She offered no excuse for her nakedness and it did not occur to my grandfather that she needed one. She smiled at him and the woods fell silent again.

After a long time my grandfather stood, still cradling the rifle in his arms. Then he turned and leaned the gun against the stump. He slid off his jacket and held it up for the woman to see.

"Here," he said. "I got long johns."

"I'll bring it back to you, I promise," she said.

"No," he said. "It's okay."

My grandfather turns to look at me. It is not deer season anymore but a night in July, maybe August. We sit on his back porch. I am fourteen. I know my grandfather wants to see what I am thinking so I lower my eyes and stare at my bare feet. While he talked the sun slumped below the trees just behind the beagle pens at the back of the yard. The sky is purple turning over to blue. In the kitchen behind us my grandmother says, "Oh God." Neither of us move. I scuff my toes on the fake grass carpet. I study my feet. They are huge for a kid my size.

He knows he has me.

I know he is lying.

I hate my grandfather's lies but I love a good story even more. I know this fact will either be my salvation or the reason I will never get a date. But I also know I must hear what happened next. I need to know so much that I might as well be naked. I am too young to understand that I already am. And that this truth is both my future and my everlasting doom.

I look up.

"Then what," I say.

That is where it all starts, doesn't it? *Then what:* that lovely painful pull of the thing you need to know, whether you need to know it or not. One thing follows another and you tell yourself you know all the answers but suspect in the end you are still stupid because you lack the strength to say: Enough. Because you also know that your stupidity can teach you something.

This is a true story about lies. I spent my childhood listening to my grandfather lie. That is not what made me a writer, but it is what made me the kind of writer I am, the kind of person I am. The kind of person who asks too many questions.

Like: Then what?

Like: Did you ever get that jacket back?

Like: Have you ever wanted to know the truth about something so much you made it up?

2.

Some facts about my grandfather:

He was born September 10, 1910, in Phillips, Pennsylvania, to Hungarian immigrants, the second child of six. He dropped out of school in the sixth grade and went to work in the coal mines after his father died. He began smoking around the same time—unfiltered Chesterfields. He met my grandmother at a dance. The first time he saw her she sat at the edge of a dance floor on a wooden folding chair, wearing a white lace dress.

They married on July 31, 1931. They had three children— my mother, who was the middle child, and two sons. My grandfather was a mechanic in the mines and he settled his family into a company house in a neighborhood of other miners and their families in what people called a coal patch. Sometimes he drank. Sometimes he drank too much. On one of those nights my grandmother threw a bottle of ketchup at him and when my mother and her brothers saw the spatters on the wall they thought she had finally killed him. In 1941 a mine ceiling collapsed on him; a sheet of slate shaved off his face and the crush of rock nearly killed him. They rebuilt his face but he was different. After the accident he got softer, stopped drinking. Started telling stories.

He loved professional wrestling. He used to sit in front of the television in his favorite recliner—the armrests sticky from where my grandmother had taped the cracks in the vinyl—and shadowbox while the wrestlers dropped on each other like meat falling out of a grinder. When he swung his recliner lurched, and by the end of the show his knees nearly touched the screen.

He had his teeth pulled around 1945 but hated the way his false set felt so he went around toothless. He used to open a box of chocolates and squeeze each piece to determine which were the creams. Anyone in the house hungry for candy had to decide whether they wanted it badly enough to eat my grandfather's dented rejects.

He wore his teeth only for special occasions like weddings and deaths. At those times he disappeared into his room and emerged wearing a blue suit, white shirt, black shoes. He lingered outside his door, studying the plastic runner in the hall, and when his eyes darted up his smile shone like a burst of flashbulb, an unexpected slice of moon, and from the living room everyone already dressed and waiting would smile back and say how nice he looked, and he would open his mouth a little more and his eyes would get shiny behind his glasses and he would study the runner again, and though I am not a child anymore I still ask myself: What wrong could ever live inside a man bashful about having teeth?

Almost nothing, except that he lied to me every time I saw him—once a week, minimum. Most Saturday nights my parents would drop off my younger brother and me at my grandparents' house and go off ballroom dancing; we would sleep over and they would pick us up in the morning after my grandmother had served us a breakfast of pancakes and hot dogs smothered in homemade syrup that tasted suspiciously like whiskey. I remember those Saturday nights as an improbable cocktail of Lawrence Welk hours and marathon story sessions. Sometimes my grandmother would corner me and explain the recipe for this soup she made that had an omelette floating on top or confide her dream of becoming an accountant, killed when her mother made her quit school in the eighth grade to clean houses. My grandmother never lost the sense that she was destined for better, and she was always trying something artistic. Her garden took up two-thirds of her backyard. While supper cooked one afternoon, she spray-painted every surface in the living room gold. We all had to agree it looked pretty amazing.

Most nights I would try to slink across the side yard into the house but my grandfather would always catch me. "Hey, farmer," he would holler. "Come here. I gotta tell you somethin'." Sometimes I would be padding across the living room with a plate full of nut rolls and a head full of adolescent disco misery and he would say something like, "Boy, I'll bet Mazeroski's cold," which was my signal to sit down and start listening.

Some stories were set in the mines where he worked, tales of horrible accidents involving heavy machinery and rats as big as lunch pails. A few took place in his childhood, like the one about George Washington, a kid in second grade who was so stupid my grandfather sold him his own shoes.

But most of my grandfather's stories unfolded in the woods: infinite possibilities, no witnesses: wilderness. Most people went into the woods and got lost. My grandfather found things. Once he saw a laughing monkey in a tree. Once he stumbled upon a truckload of shih tzus. Once, when he was a boy, he found something in the woods and he didn't know what the hell it was. It bristled with quills just like a porcupine but the quills were more like fur. It had a bill like a duck and beady black eyes.

Like a platypus? I asked when he told me this. I was probably twelve.

He looked at me as if to say: Shut up. "We put it in a bucket and filled it full of water," he said. "We called the game warden. He came over and looked at the thing. 'I don't know what the hell that is,' he said. He took the bucket and left, and that's the last we heard of him."

As I am writing this, I realize that I am lying to you. I am telling stories that I know to be untrue. And I am filling them with memory, the clumsiest editor of all. I don't remember my grandfather's exact words. I do remember the color of the summer night sky, though maybe time has simply convinced me this is true. But in one thing I am honest: I accept that in some ways I am no better than my grandfather. Writers lie all the time, even when they deal in fact. We try to sell ourselves as natural-born architects of polished sentences and balanced arguments when bias and doubt force and influence every word. My first draft of this story looked nothing like what you are reading now. In an earlier version I began with a story from another hunting season. My grandfather was sitting on a stump, holding a rifle in one hand and a walkie-talkie in the other.

The walkie-talkie crackled.

"Louie," he said, "is that you?"

"No, John, it's me," a woman's voice said. "You want some pie?"

"What kind?" my grandfather said.

"All kind," the woman said. "I just made 'em. My house is just through the trees."

My grandfather walked for a while. He saw the woman's house. He saw the pies, steaming on a kitchen windowsill. He saw the woman. Good God, she was ugly. My grandfather was not an educated man but he knew he wanted no part of any ugly woman's pie. He slipped back through the trees.

A year later, he was sitting on the same stump. The walkie-talkie crackled.

"Louie," he said, "is that you?"

"It's me, John," the pie woman said. "Where you been?"

When I was a kid, this story would not let me sleep. On nights when I stayed at my grandparents I would lie awake listening to the beagles moan in their pens out back and try to make sense of what I'd heard. How did this woman find my grandfather's frequency? How did she know when he'd return? How in the hell did she know his name? *What kind of pie?*

I was a pretty sad kid.

It was probably inevitable that I grew up to be a reporter.

3.

Three a.m. on a Thursday. I lie in bed in my own home obsessing over a stranger who told me she used to be a star on *Hee Haw*. To be exact, a Hee Haw Honey, one of those women in hillbilly bikinis who pop out of a cornfield and tell awful jokes. My past warns me she is lying; I can feel it. Nothing feels like the feeling I get when I sense I am being lied to, that hot whine behind the eyes, that cold pressure beneath the bridge of the nose. I love that feeling: not surprise or shock but a wash of comfort and relief. People lie. You can count on it.

If she is telling a lie it is a small one and in the scheme of things—in the book I am writing—it means next to nothing.

Rationally, I know this. Truthfully, I don't care. Size is exactly the point. The smaller a lie is the harder I scramble to expose it. Because one tiny lie slides past and then bigger ones follow and then rot sets in and then everything flies apart and because it is 3 a.m. I believe that if this happens I will die. This is how pathetic my life is: this is the tension, the engine that drives my days and wrecks my life. I am never more miserable or more alive than when I lie sleepless, trapped in my past and happy in my pathology.

Her last name sounds like a first name. I tried once, in a bright orange booth at a Waffle House in Erlanger, Kentucky, to see if it was her real name when she pulled out her wallet to pay for her eggs. Instead my eyes went *thwock* on her driver's license photo: postapocalyptic corona of platinum hair. Pillow lips. Eye makeup straight off a cathedral ceiling.

"When I leave this world," she informed me at an Elvis impersonators' contest in Memphis, Tennessee, "first person I want to see is my Lord. Second person is Elvis. I want to touch him. I want to say, Thank you."

We huddled in the back of a nightclub while up front a guy in a jumpsuit popped his hips to a drumroll. She told me about her history and *Hee Haw*, offered vague insinuations about Elvis. I asked if Elvis gave her the TCB necklace around her neck, the kind he gave people, the one she claimed she never removes. She started to weep. She proclaimed she didn't love him as a lover but as a man. She said she has a tapestry of Elvis on her ceiling. "It looks like he is going up to heaven," she said.

In bed, I stare at my ceiling. A car grinds past. My head began to hurt the moment she began to cry. It was all so beautiful I knew it couldn't be true.

I trust nothing but I am prepared to believe anything. This seems to me like common sense. Reporting relies mainly on common sense. This may explain why so many people are so bad at it. So I consult reference books. The dates the woman says she appeared on *Hee Haw* don't jibe with her account of the year she met Elvis. I feel wronged. I feel wonderful.

The show is no longer in production, but at the time it ran in syndication on the Nashville Network. I ask the TV listings editor at the newspaper where I work if she has a phone number for the network. She hands me a fat binder full of numbers. I fish one out. I make a call.

A receptionist ships me to a public relations woman's voice mail. I identify myself, explain my dilemma. She calls back. I explain my dilemma in more detail. It occurs to me I sound like a nut. I don't care. Reporting also relies on the willing suspension of self-loathing. She tells me the name of a woman in the *Hee Haw* office who knows everyone who's ever been on the show. She will call her and get back to me.

A day later, she calls back and leaves a message: No person by the name I gave her ever appeared on *Hee Haw*.

I call the self-proclaimed Hee Haw Honey. She has moved, so I get her new number from a couple who take turns checking me out on the phone. The alleged Honey is happy to hear from me. I was so nice to her, she says. She's married now, and happy. I'm glad, I say. Discrepancies, I add. Could she clarify?

Of course. She worked on *Hee Haw* in Bakersfield, California, at a ranch owned by one of the stars. Ah, I say. Again we verify dates, times, years. And again I ask her to spell her name. I have it on tape, but still. One *n* on the last name, right?

No, she says. Two.

I call back the woman from the Nashville Network. Discrepancies, I say. She sounds frightened. Take the *Hee Haw* number, she says. I call Nashville. I love the *Hee Haw* historian as soon as I hear her voice. She finds my drama funny but is happy I'd rather not lie. She will check records, files, and the memory of the show's former star and get back to me. A day later, she does. The show never filmed in Bakersfield, she says. The woman is lying. I ask her, "Why would anyone say they were on *Hee Haw* when it is so easy to find out they weren't?"

A few times a year, she says, she gets calls asking about people claiming they used to come out of a cornfield on *Hee Haw*. After all these years she still has no idea why.

We hang up. I put a picture of the woman wearing a black and gold evening gown and a ring on every finger into an envelope with a letter. Could the historian kindly look at the picture to, without a doubt, verify that this woman definitely never appeated on the show? A few days later, she returns the picture. *I must say I've never seen her before*, she writes, *and she most definitely was not a member of the* Hee Haw *show cast—ever—under any circumstances. You are to be commended for checking the information which is represented as fact.*

I change the passage in what I am writing but still I cannot sleep. At first I decide it's because I'm happy. It takes me a few dream-state days to realize I am miserable. Deep down, I wanted that woman to be a Hee Haw Honey.

I used to think I was trying to expose the same lies that annoyed me when I was young, but as I've gotten older I realize I was lying to myself. There are lies that attempt to hide, and then there are those that reveal. These are the ones that haunt me because of what they say about loss and hope. I could count on my grandfather lying to me the same way I could count on him loving me. He lied to me because he loved me, I think. And because he didn't think he was lying. In his mind he was the guy who rescued naked women in the woods, resourceful and dashing even without teeth, a coal-patch Cary Grant. This is who I am, he seemed to be saying. Never mind that it isn't true. In his lies he offered up his best self, and he taught me the possibility of strange and powerful things. Naked women may not roam the woods, but coal miners with sixth-grade educations can burn with stories and the desire to tell them.

So maybe what I'm looking for aren't lies at all. Maybe what I'm looking for—hoping for—is a happier truth.

Maybe what I'm looking for is the way I felt another summer night, the summer of the year I turned seventeen.

4.

I am standing at the edge of my woods listening to my grandfather meow like a cat. Seventeen years old and I have nothing better to do on a Saturday night than scowl into a stand of trees beyond the garden so my grandfather can prove something.

He seldom repeats stories but for a couple of weeks he has refused to let one of them go. "Hey, Joanne," he says, as always calling me by my mother's name, "I was up in the woods and I hear this sound, and you know what I seen? This Siamese cat. Just like yours. Cried like a baby. When I tried to come up on it, it ran from me."

"Really," I said.

"Honest to God!" he cried.

So I stand next to him while he makes a sound that suggests his foot has been pinned in a trap. The beagles out back believe him; they yelp and throw their shoulder blades against the chicken-wire doors. "Get in there!" he yells at them, then resumes mewing.

I cannot see the moon. My grandfather yowls on behind me,

dressed in his usual plaid shirt and dog-running pants, patches on top of patches. My legacy in action. I regard my unfortunate feet and wonder how it came to be that I am damned. I am a strange child, given to memorizing soliloquies from *Hamlet* and the lyrics of Barry White songs. I wake at 5 a.m. to write poems, all of them containing the word "darkness." Nothing I see this night gives me any hope.

Then I see something coming out of the woods and I don't know what the hell it is. Except that I know exactly what it is. It strolls, shoulders rolling, wet and yowling and with its blue eyes wide. I half expect a naked woman to stroll out of the woods behind it, carrying a pie.

I cannot lie. I do not remember the speed of the wind or the velocity of my shock and bewilderment, though I can still feel it, how everything in the world seemed to lift and spin, and how it seemed perfectly normal that everything was weird, and how in some way I'd always expected it, and how my grandfather leaned forward and shot me one of his bottomless smiles. And I do remember that its fur looked like wet feathers, and when it cleared the woods it walked right past my grandfather and headed straight toward me.

LESLIE RUBINKOWSKI ON *"In the Woods"*

I wrote the first draft of "In the Woods" when I was a graduate student in the University of Pittsburgh's MFA program in creative nonfiction. At the time I also worked as a full-time reporter at the now-defunct *Pittsburgh Press*. After I left daily journalism for teaching, I revisited the essay, interviewing family members and looking through old photographs. I tried to tell it the way my grandfather would tell a story: you think it's leading you down a dark row in a field but suddenly opens up in a clearing, and everything makes sense. It reads to me now like a bridge between the two kinds of writing I have done, connecting the relentless attention to truth that journalism requires and the play of imagination that my grandfather taught me to love and look for.

Some people see an impossible divide between the writing of fact and what they consider more creative endeavors; I just can't. My childhood taught me the astonishment of opposites and unexpected combinations—after all, a coal miner who could barely sign his own name was one of the best writers I'll ever know. Story is possibility: hang out around enough beagle pens and you begin to see.

Sa'm Pèdi

MADISON SMARTT BELL

. .

Someone was screaming so loudly and horribly I shot out of the bed, but the hotel room was too close and absolutely dark for me to see anything at all. The screams were ragged and inhuman, and I had locked somebody's arm—but this person wasn't resisting. He was my friend, with whom I'd flown to Port-au-Prince two days before, then driven to Cap Haïtien in the north of Haiti, and he was now talking to me in a low steady voice, trying to calm me down. As the screams stopped, I realized that they had been coming out of my own body, though not from anything I was prepared to recognize as myself.

. .

MADISON SMARTT BELL is the author of ten novels and two collections of short stories. Born and raised in Tennessee, he has lived in New York and in London and now lives in Baltimore, Maryland. A graduate of Princeton University and Hollins College, he has taught in various creative writing programs, including the Iowa Writers' Workshop, the 92nd Street Y, and the Johns Hopkins University writing seminars. Since 1984 he has taught at the Goucher College creative writing program, where he is currently writer in residence along with his wife, the poet Elizabeth Spires.

I let go of him, apologized, lay back on my bed, and immediately fell into a sleep so wet and thick it felt like someone was smothering me with it. The screaming started up again, and this time I could feel a rip through my whole psyche, like a fingernail tearing down the peel of a banana, that left the screaming thing divided from whatever it was in me that heard the screams. I had been torn out of my skin. I could not get out from under the suffocating blanket of sleep, however, until my friend dragged it off of me.

I apologized some more and lay down with my eyes open. The slats in the wooden doors to the balcony did admit just a little light. Beyond the balcony and the wall protecting the compound of the Hôtel Roi Christophe was a calm June night; the rain had passed earlier in the evening and the air was cool, moist, and still. It was not far from the compound wall to the edge of the city—an abrupt edge, where a narrow twisting alley ascended to become a dirt trail that passed among some makeshift shanties and emerged in an open-air *hounfor* where Vodou ceremonies were performed. Now in the night I could hear a desultory tap of drums, but for the moment observances were in a lull. If they became more concentrated, the drums might drive you out of yourself, dividing the parts of you from one another; you might lose your self, or be freed of it.

That was what had happened to me, it seemed. Now I was in the presence of fear, but the fear was outside of me, moving in the shadows of the room, beneath a table where I'd piled my notebooks, or looming from a hanging plant above my head. The fear wandered patiently as a dog through the room till morning, while the part of me that remained subjective kept its eyes as open as it could.

I had come to Haiti for several reasons, one of which was to see the differences between June 1996, when the foreign military was rapidly completing its withdrawal, and June 1995, when the intervention had been in full force. Also it happened that I had spent the last several years inhabiting an eighteenth-century Haiti composed of imagination and old texts, because I was writing a series of novels about the Haitian Revolution, a sort of tragedy that featured in its central role one of the first Haitian leaders, Toussaint-Louverture. Some politicians in the States like to make it a mystery that Americans should take any interest in Haiti, but I had begun to wonder how Americans could be interested in anything else, because Haiti now appeared to me as a crucible of all the forces that created our own society, beginning like ours as a colonial system that incorporated both African slavery and essentially genocidal programs against the indigenous people, but which was then suddenly injected, between 1776 and 1791, with a lot of powerful liberation ideology. In the American and the French Revolutions, freedom was proffered to white people only, and in the States at least we all still have to struggle with the consequences of that fact. In the Haitian Revolution things had played out quite differently. Haiti is the only nation on earth founded by black slaves who freed themselves. By 1804 there were, officially, no whites left in the country at all. Jean-Jacques Dessalines, Haiti's first emperor, declared that to be a citizen of Haiti was to be nèg, or black. To this day, Haitians regard all foreigners, whatever their melanin levels, as *blancs*.

Haiti is a convenient place for the student of history, because time doesn't exist there, and no one ever really dies. Whether anyone approves or not, Vodou (conflated to varying degrees with Catholicism) is the religion of the vast majority of the Haitian people, and in Vodou, death is not a departure but a translation of state. At death the spirit is understood to join *Les*

Morts et Les Mystères, a sort of aggregate Vodou oversoul that includes everyone who has ever died in Haiti, and from this oversoul a pantheon of gods is formed: the *loa*, who return to possess the believers who feed and serve them. The drumming of Vodou ritual builds to a crisis of possession in which the individual element of the soul vacates the body to make room for one of the *loa* to manifest itself. A depth psychologist might say that archetypes still walk the earth in Haiti; a mystic might say that Haitians still have the honor of meeting their gods face to face. Possessed bodies may speak in tongues or scream weirdly at the moment of crisis; it is a fearful thing to fall into the hands of a living god.

It was convenient for me to believe in Vodou because the ever-presentness of dead souls in Haiti made it more conceivable for me to reach the eighteenth-century personages who were the subject of my work. I had come to further my own particular ambitions, but I also had a yearning to have my individual ambitions self-obliterated; this, however frightening at times, remained a strong temptation.

Our program was to tour the country in a wide circle, driving up the coast road from Port-au-Prince and crossing the mountains to Cap Haïtien. From Le Cap we would drive eastward along the north coast, then turn south again to the Citadelle, Haiti's most magnificent mountain fortress, and afterward continue south into the interior, up onto the central plateau, through Hinche and Mirebelais, finally completing the circle by returning to Port-au-Prince. This was the plan, but fixed agendas aren't worth much in Haiti.

Dawn finally did leak into the hotel room where I was lying with my eyes jammed open, and as the light came in the fear went out. The first setback was that my companion woke up completely incapacitated with dysentery. I handed over the sack of medicaments we'd brought for such a case and started off toward the Citadelle in the Nissan four-by-four we had rented, with the guide who'd come with us from Port-au-Prince riding shotgun.

The first blockade was just beyond the left fork of the Y intersection where the road for Port-au-Prince divides from the road for Fort Liberté. We thought nothing of the delay at first, being accustomed to Haitian traffic jams, which include goats, pigs, chickens, dogs, small children, and adult pedestrians scattering like schizophrenic pinballs among the overloaded *tap-taps* and motorbikes and livestock trucks and small wizened witch-women riding donkeys. Driving in this sort of mayhem requires a global paranoia. If you collide with livestock you have only to pay a disadvantageous price, but if you run over a child the people are likely to drag you out of your car and cut your head off on the spot; Haitians are very fond of children. Today the traffic was complicated by a lot of black smoke, which proved to come from tires burning in an improvised blockade; visibility was poor, and people were circling through the smoke, shouting angrily and waving fists in the air.

"*Les gens chaché ajan,*" the guide said, speaking a blend of French and Haitian Kreyol. "*Parce ké, la vie est chère. Les gens chaché ajan. Laisse-moi voir.*" We had brought him principally as a translator, since outside of major cities most Haitians speak only Kreyol. Now he got down from the car and disappeared into the general swirl. I was now alone, and I felt a little lonely, because I could no longer see the guide and because although there were people swarming all over the car and a number of young men angrily signaling me to lower my window, I was unable to oblige them. Haitian weather, along with Haitian roads, is hard on sensitive machinery, and the overcomplicated electric system for the Nissan's windows had crashed somewhere between Gonaives and Cap Haïtien, leaving my window permanently shut. The windows in the back, on the other hand, were jammed half open, which would make it more convenient for the people whirling around outside to come in whenever they felt like it. I opened the door and explained in French that the window was not operational and that I was waiting for a Haitian friend in the crowd. More Kreyol speakers understand French than can speak it in reply, and my words seemed to calm the youths, who pinwheeled off into the crowd somewhere.

The guide returned, having negotiated a price of 25 gourdes to cross the *blocus*. I paid, and someone began hauling chunks of old engine blocks out of the barricade so that the Nissan could pass. The next *blocus*, about twenty yards beyond the first, involved a lot more burning tires and a lot of angrier-looking people. The tires reminded me unpleasantly of the Haitian practice of "necklacing," which means they put you inside the tires before they light them.

I wondered aloud how many barricades there were likely to be along our route. *"Laisse-moi voir,"* the guide said, and got down to approach a farouche-looking youth who was capering about with an air of authority. He wore a yellow *mouchwa-tèt* and a pair of pink denim trousers intentionally chewed through with regular small holes, which gave them the look of lace. This peculiar costume, along with his whirling eyes and air of a Vodou *possédé*, distinguished him even against the general anarchy of the scene. His name turned out to be Ouayé Jean-Pierre when I made his acquaintance (enchantedly) in the backseat of the car, and he agreed to take us through all the barricades between us and the airport for the sum of 100 Haitian dollars. Prices went up, I noticed immediately, once you had a barricade behind you as well as in front.

The basis for Haitian currency (as for many other aspects of Haitian life) is not to be found in the material world. All prices are marked in dollars, but no bills exist to represent these dollars, because all Haitian currency is printed in gourdes. In the world of pure ideas, 5 gourdes are worth one Haitian dollar, while 2.8 Haitian dollars are worth one American dollar. The resulting calculations are so complicated that we already had made a number of very bad deals, and now seemed as good a time as any to reverse the game, except that Ouayé was not amused when I pretended to believe that 100 gourdes were equal to 100 Haitian dollars. The end result of this negotiation was that I gave him all of my American cash as well, to dissuade him and his friends from smashing the Nissan's windows and perhaps overturning and burning it. On the road from Port-au-Prince to Cap Haïtien we had passed the scorched hulk of a car formerly belonging to a *zenglendo,* or Haitian bandit, who'd had his head summarily hacked off in a different popular uprising. I paid Ouayé with reasonably good grace, for the road ahead of us seemed to be clear, but within ten minutes of our parting from him, we had struck another blockade.

I got out of the car. It occurred to me that I should be afraid, but I wasn't; the fear that had lain beside me in the room all night had now gone off somewhere else. The morning was clear. Inland, the hulk of Morne du Cap seemed to block off half the sky; two hundred years ago thousands of revolted slaves, many of them possessed by the *loa,* had swept down off the mountain to sack and burn the city. Within six years Le Cap had been rebuilt to an even higher level of opulence by blacks organized by Toussaint-Louverture. In ten years it had been burned to the ground again by the same black men who had rebuilt it—so that

Napoleon's invading army would be denied its use. At the moment, amid the smoke and the stench of burning rubber and the shouting and boiling of the people, the cycle still seemed to be repeating itself.

"On peut se retourner," the guide said. *We can turn back.* I nodded, since we were out of money. When a Haitian tells you that you can do something it means that you might succeed or you might fail or you might die in the attempt, and the distinctions between these options often seem to be of small importance. As it happened, the demonstration had calmed somewhat by the time we began recrossing the barricades (the *zenglendo* element had already gone off somewhere to spend the money, we imagined), and attention had shifted to a march full of drummers maintaining a hypnotic beat with sticks on pot lids or scraps of tin—flowing down from all the *hounfors* that circle Cap Haïtien just beyond the city's boundaries and gathering more people as it went. Now the people no longer seemed to see us, and the march parted around the car, then flowed back in upon itself as smoothly as a wave.

Cap Haïtien, *described* during the days of French dominion by phrases like "the Pearl of the Antilles," is in fact a very small town, surrounded, on the sharply rising slopes of Morne du Cap, by little shanty villages and their *hounfors*. Today's demonstration was repeating a venerable pattern. From colonial times through the present, popular uprisings in Haiti have tended to start in the mountains and flow toward the plain, flooding from the interior out toward the coast. Often they are inspired and nourished by Vodou as well. Vodou certainly can whip up the warrior passions, but also the Haitian Revolution was able to use the interlinked structure of *hounfors* to establish a countrywide network very similar to those recommended by twentieth-century revolutionary manuals; that structure is still in place today. For such reasons, the leaders of Haiti from Toussaint-Louverture on up have publicly suppressed Vodou, usually while privately practicing it themselves. François Duvalier worked artfully to reinforce the popular belief that he himself was a *bokor*, or Vodou sorcerer, and his terrorist network of *macoutes* appeared to be interlaced with the black-magic underside of Vodou and its secret societies. Within Vodou, Bizango reflects Ginen as Satanism reflects Christianity; the bokors of Bizango work to harm others and consolidate their own power, as the *houngans* of Ginen work to heal others and serve the community. The overthrow of the Duvaliers was to some extent reflected by a reform movement within the religion, as suggested by song lyrics of the popular populist ensemble Boukman Eksperyans: *"Ginen pa Bizango."* For better or worse, Haitian culture is thoroughly integrated with itself; religion will not come separate from politics.

Once the guide and I had turned back from the Citadelle, we found no blockades on the road toward Port-au-Prince. Near the village of Haut du Cap we stopped and climbed a little staircase to get a closer look at a revolutionary monument near the village of Haut du Cap. At the foot of the statue a boy sat with a schoolbook open on his knees, reciting his lesson in a loud voice and staring fixedly into nowhere. Three little girls came up the stairs and stared at my white skin in utter amazement, then smiled and passed in single file along a curving path toward the cluster of tin-roofed houses in the crease beyond the colline where the monument was raised. Then an older toothless man appeared and fell into conversation with the guide from Port-au-Prince. When Haitians meet at backcountry crossroads they may begin to speak as if they had known each other all their lives; this possibility is supported by the structure of Kreyol, which sometimes uses the same word to express both "you" and "we."

This newcomer, it developed, could guide us to the remains of French colonial architecture on the mountain; such buildings are difficult to find since most were burned and razed to the ground in the Revolutionary period between 1791 and 1803. He led us first to a cluster of half-finished resort hotels that the Duvalierians of the region had begun; like a lot of Haitian constructions, they had never been finished. Even in Port-au-Prince it's usual to see rusty iron rods protruding hopefully from cinderblock structures already in use, in case someday the funds might come to build another story. These hotels, however, had been utterly abandoned since the fall of Baby Doc. Amidst them stood the delicate remnant of a complicated colonial brick vault, and on its inner curve the fire-blackened outline of a Corinthian pilaster. *"Icit sé ancien maisê français,"* the mountain guide said. It was apparent that its builders hadn't prospered.

He led us next to a boggy terrain on the other side of the southbound road where all sorts of cinderblock structures were under construction—a team of UN military engineers was supervising the raising of a building. We passed. I listened to the monotonic thrum of the Kreyol conversation between the city guide and the mountain guide and learned that this terrain had belonged to a *grand bourgeois* under the Duvaliers, had been controlled by the *macoutes* during the Cédras coup, and had finally been seized by the people with the return of Aristide. Now they were making houses for the people here. But there had been no vengeance against the *macoutes*, who had been allowed to leave with their lives and had gone into exile, no one knew where. Such was the policy of Aristide's return, enacted, perhaps, under pressure of the international occupying forces. Yet for whatever motive, Aristide is the first Haitian leader to attempt such a strategy of reconciliation since Toussaint-Louverture was deported from the country in 1802; Toussaint had effected a workable peace with wealthy proprietors from the epoch of slavery, who soon enough betrayed him. Since Toussaint fell until Aristide's election, power has always changed hands in Haiti via assassination or military coup. Since Magloire took power in 1950, the winners of whatever political struggle have always done whatever they can to murder all the losers.

We passed the clanking steam shovel and continued some fifty yards further to the ruin of an old brick factory that survived from the colonial period; the chimney was completely intact and something of the interior vaults remained. I stooped and went inside. A couple of piglets were sheltering in the shade, and a sow, tied to a column, slept on her side in the vegetation that pushed up through the brickbats and rubble of old mortar. Beyond, a stream pulled torpidly, through the swampy land. . . .

"*Il a dit,*" said the city guide, translating the mountain guide's Kreyol into French to be sure I understood, "that here was the *abattoir* of the *macoutes* of that time. Here they brought each person who had contact with foreigners to be killed. The *macoutes* killed many, many persons here."

I nodded. The mountain guide took off his hat. There was nothing in the way of bloodstains, no clear evidence of what had taken place. I imagined that the killers might have rolled the bodies down the gentle slope from the brick oven into the stream. Hogs will eat almost anything, I reflected, including human flesh. The father of the city guide had been murdered by Duvalier for belonging to the wrong political party, and when we had made the passage through the arid land on the coast road just north of Port-au-Prince, he took pains to point out the killing grounds of Papa Doc and Baby Doc in the whitely scarred hills under the blinding sun. "Here they killed many persons." As for the leaders of the military coup, they had preferred Morne Cabrit, a mountain on the road toward Hinche from Port-au-Prince. "Each night they killed many persons there," the city guide said. "This was done by Cédras, by Namphy, and Michel François. They killed men and women and left their bodies in the bush for dogs to eat. This was done by Cédras and Michel François and Namphy." The city guide leaned over from the backseat of the Nissan and pointed at my notebook. "Write their names."

Now we put on our hats again and began picking our way over the swampy hummocks back toward the car. At the new construction, the steam shovel huffed and slobbered mud. The city guide paused and addressed the military engineers in his severely limited English. "Thank you," he said. He shook their hands. "Thank you."

My *friend* was still seriously ill when I returned to the Hôtel Roi Christophe. After what for him was a very monkish dinner, I went out alone. The state-supplied electricity was working for the moment, which was a sign of progress, but I didn't like it much because it meant that other people could see me. The previous June, the streets of Cap Haïtien had been ink black after nightfall, which afforded me better privacy. This year it seemed that an unescorted unofficial white person abroad after dark was a truly remarkable sight. Fear was not operating from inside me, but roaming elsewhere like a pariah dog; still it seemed practical to get off the street as soon as possible; I didn't want the fear to find me. At the close of that evening it also seemed practical to climb the suddenly locked gate of the hotel compound rather than remain waiting outside with the people who had followed me there. Progress or not, the prevailing mood seemed grimmer than it had the year before, and the sentiment toward foreigners was beginning to turn sour.

Those people in the demonstration, said the stranger at the Bon Dieu Bon hotel bar, *are like the living dead. They have no hope. Nothing has changed. The Americans destroyed the old system here but now that they are leaving, they leave nothing in its place. Haiti cries to the outside world like a baby cries for its mother, but the mother must take care of the baby for fifteen years before it knows how to take care of itself. A child does not like to go to school because the masters are too strict, but the parents must make him go, so he will learn.* The stranger smiled and adjusted his cap. Economic status in Haiti can often be judged by body weight, and by this measure I could guess my interlocutor belonged to the middle class. *I myself have nothing to do with politics*, he said. *It would be unwise to do so. But those people in the demonstration are like the living dead. In Haiti, one must die ten times to win one's life.*

To *stay sane* in Haiti you must remember that if what you intended cannot take place, something else certainly will. Therefore on the following day I found myself climbing Morne du Cap toward an area called Pont Français. People kept passing me, both coming and going: schoolgirls balancing stacks of books on their heads, and women balancing huge swollen baskets of vegetables, and ancient crones balancing sacks of charcoal or unthreshed peas. The path itself was very narrow and alternated between mudslide and rockslide. Its angle was seldom more than ten degrees off the vertical. Whenever I was overtaken from below, whether by small children or by people old enough to be my grandparents, I would haul myself off the trail by clinging to some clump of vegetation. *Passez, passez*, I said.

"*Blan swe anpil,*" said the mountain guide, and it was true that I was as sweat-drenched as if I had just crawled out of a ship-wreck. They stood together, the mountain guide and the city guide whom we had brought from Port-au-Prince, and watched me pant and drip. The mountain guide took out some scraps of leaf tobacco and a shred of glossy paper from a magazine and rolled himself a cigarette the size of a baby's arm. He lit it and inhaled voraciously and began scampering effortlessly up the path again. . . .

After Toussaint-Louverture lost power, these terrains belonged to his successor, the Emperor Jean-Jacques Dessalines, who was assassinated before he had very much time to enjoy his empire and was succeeded, in the northern department, by King Henri Christophe. (If these titles sound absurdly grandiose one must also remember that they were strictly imitated from the titles used by the leaders of France at that time.) When I had to stop and double over to try to regulate my breathing and my heart-beat, I could turn (clinging to a tree) and look eastward across the ravine toward the inner mountain range miles in the dis-tance and see Christophe's fortress, the Citadelle La Ferrière, crowning the highest peak. I would get no closer to it, this time, but it meant something to see it at such a distance. If you imag-ined constructing an Egyptian pyramid or a Gothic cathedral on a summit of the Rocky Mountains it would give you some idea of the labor involved and the astonishment of its effect. But the fort was useless to Christophe in the end, unable to protect him from internal enemies; he too was swept from power by a coup.

Now a little horse came up the trail, setting hooves carefully on the stones, followed by a twelve-year-old boy driving a pair of diminutive long-horned cows. Livestock in Haiti tends to be small and anxious-looking; animals wait for humans to finish before they eat. These animals were marked along their flanks with the foot-high initials of their owners, cut with the blade of a hot machete. They passed, and a file of schoolgirls followed, whispering *"Blanc, blanc"* and giggling as they passed me. They wore the brown and cream uniforms of the state school at the foot of the mountain, crisp and neat and perfectly clean and without even a vestige of a sweat stain.

I sat down, just for two minutes, on a mud hummock under shade; my shirt hung like a drenched dishcloth and even my trousers were sweat-soaked to the cuffs. That evening when I returned to the Hôtel Roi Christophe I discovered that my two-ply leather belt had been sweated through from one side to the other, so that when I twisted it, beads of water appeared at the seam. I sat with my dysentery-racked friend on the balcony, feeling the weight of the air increase. Crows flew urgently from the trunks of one palm to another, shrilling in something that sounded much like Kreyol. One snatched up a last lizard in its beak. Haitian crows have learned to hunt live food, as carrion is rare. A little warning wind began, and the palm leaves stirred, tossed slightly, but the rain was slow when it began, a gentle whisper. I lay on my back on a scrolled daybed, limp and exhausted and half in a daze, counting the shifts in tempo of the rain like the gear ratios on a hot sports car. Between fifth and sixth, lightning smashed down so loud and hard we thought a mortar round had landed in the courtyard. It was the season for storms and cyclones; the solar power system at the Citadelle had been toasted by a similar thunderbolt the night before. Now the rain became a torrent beyond measure, simply a wall of water, and all over the countryside it would be ripping earth from the eroded mountains, and the path we had climbed up Morne du Cap that day would have become a waterfall. The streams were tearing down from all the mountain villages, called *lakou*, from the heights of all the mountains, joining to form a flood, or, as

Aristide once expressed it, "from an infinity of little streams was born the torrent, *lavalas.* . . . "

This was the flood that brought Aristide to power; Lavalas, the political party, poured out of the mountains and the interior toward the cities of the coast, replicating the pattern of move-ment of the Haitian Revolution and of most internal power struggles ever since then. The Haitan defense system, from the time of the runaway slaves who were called maroons, has always depended on the inaccessibility of the mountains and the inte-rior. In colonial times, this tough terrain meant that large num-bers of slaves could escape and never be recaptured; maroon communities thus became quite sizable, and in the mountain *lakou* they formed, they bore their children in freedom.

During the Revolution, the maroons tended to function as a separate faction from the slaves revolting from the plantations; after independence their descendants evolved into "Cacos," whose periodic insurgencies played a part in a hundred years' worth of coups in the capital. The invention of *macoutisme*, which infiltrated those remote mountain communities partly via the networks of Bizango and the more sinister Vodou secret societies, was what allowed Papa Doc to hold power so much longer than his predecessors ever had. But after the fall of the Duvalier regime, those old maroon communities poured them-selves into Lavalas, and as a part of that process, Ginen believ-ers revolted against the grim stranglehold of Bizango. *Dechoukaj*, or "uprooting," left a good many *macoutes* strung from lampposts in the days following Baby Doc's flight. Of course the founder of Lavalas is a priest, a charismatic Christian, but that presents no problem to the sunny, Ginen side of Vodou. The *serviteurs* see no contradiction between Vodou and the Catholicism they practice along with it; Vodou ceremonies typically begin with Catholic prayers.

Lavalasien euphoria was thoroughly dampened by the coup, where Duvalierists, soldiers and *macoutes* reasserted their power with a bloody iron fist. *Apre bal, tanbou lou* is a Kreyol proverb used as a title of a 1996 book by Christophe Wargny and Pierre Mouterde, which details a theory of American duplicity during the coup and its aftermath; *after the dance, the drums are heavy.* It's highly likely that the left-leaning Aristide was never the favorite candidate of the United States; still, however ambivalently, the United States did sponsor his return to his elected office—thus making it possible for Aristide to become the first Haitian head of state since the Revolution to relinquish his post peacefully and at the end of his appointed term. But the drums are even heavier now.

Due to the misfortune of his exile, Aristide never had the opportunity to deal directly with the problems that his successor, René Préval, has now inherited. Before Préval's election he was popularly thought to be as close to Aristide as two fingers on a hand; fading Port-au-Prince graffiti still cheerily proclaims: *Vote for Préval, it's Aristide for four years more!* In fact Préval and Aristide have (with a few episodes of friction) continued to support each other publicly, but Préval was never as personally popular as Aristide, and the strictness of his economic policy had cost him in that area. Both friendly and hostile observers of his administration tended to agree that Préval was doing what he must—to satisfy foreign lenders and investors and the IMF—but it involved a lot of belt-tightening, and there's not a lot of slack in the average Haitian belt. The demonstration I'd witnessed in Cap Haïtien was sparked by a state hike in the price of gasoline, which infallibly led to a jump in the price of just about everything else: *The people are looking for money,* the city guide had said as he went to investigate, *because life is so dear.* Along with being a political gesture, the Cap Haïtien demonstration had functioned as a cross between an ad hoc fundraiser and semiorganized highway robbery, but you could hardly blame *les morts vivants* if all they were trying to finance were their next few meals.

The inaccessibility of the interior was still holding up nicely, we concluded. Given the shaky condition of the car, the probability that the evening rains had turned the deteriorated mountain roads into mudslides, and the dysentery of the better driver, the route through the Central Plateau no longer seemed feasible. Then there were certain security issues: although advice in Port-au-Prince had said that there were no such hazards on the road via Hinche, advice in Cap Haïtien said that there was considerable *zenglendo* activity around both Vallière and Morne Cabrit. I was further discouraged that long segments of the road we'd meant to take were marked, on the Air Force map I was using, as "nonexistent." We would return the way we had come.

The coast road from Cap Haïtien curves around Morne de Cap and La Baie d'Acul, then passes Limbé and begins the steep ascent of Morne Lafleur. From Limbé upward, the terrain is lush, cool as the morning mist lifts off the mountain and damp from all the vegetation that presses every side of the road. People come streaming down from the mountains, carrying produce balanced on their heads or on pack saddles on their donkeys, and the cultivations in the impossibly steep mountainside fields look orderly and successful. Haiti remains an astoundingly fertile country— everything grows, and in the ascent of Morne Lafleur and beyond we could believe that an environmental salvation for this land might still be within the realm of possibility. On the southern slopes of the hills above Plaisance were signs of an erosion-control project begun between last summer and this—the terraces looked as if they had been built up by hand, and there are millions of hands available to do such work in Haiti. A program of reforestation might succeed in areas like Morne Lafleur, and with reforestation comes more rain, less drought, and cleaner water in the streams. . . .

At the peak of Morne Pilboreau we reached a market on the frontier between the rich green northern mountains and the bone-dry peaks south toward Gonaives. Here people sell manioc and cassava bread and soursops and pineapples and green lemons and fresh bananas and everything else that grows so abundantly to the north of this crossroads—and the reason why is obvious, as further to the south the mountains turn visibly to desert. The city guide stopped to buy cassava bread; prices here for all food-stuffs are about a quarter of the prices in Port-au-Prince. Beyond this last-chance market, the mountains on the way to Gonaives are parched and eroded beyond retrieval, worn down to the bare bones of the rock. Because of overfarming and clear-cutting of the mountain rain forests, erosion has been a problem in Haiti since colonial times, remarked by eighteenth-century travelers, and a flyover shows how dreadfully far the damage has progressed since then. If it is to be reversed, the work must begin quickly.

Between this summer and the last, the crazy quilt of lethal potholes between Gonaives and Saint-Marc had been repaired sufficiently to save two hours from the trip, yet here and in most of the other stretches the repairs were already deteriorating. The macadam is laid too hastily, using large stones instead of sand and fine gravel, so that any hole enlarges quickly once begun, especially when assisted by torrential rains. Also the people break the roads themselves, to force travelers to slow or stop for markets along the way, for restaurants or businesses—it's common enough to find a ragged trench hoed across the road directly in front of a tire repair shop. In the bad old days, the *macoutes* and Duvalierist *chefs de section* maintained foot-high concrete blockades topped with metal gates to exact a semiofficial tribute from any car that passed. Those barriers have been torn down now, but the system persists, one way or another, among the people: *blocus* after *blocus* after *blocus*.

In this manner fortunes were made by a few in Haiti, under Papa and Baby Doc and under the generals who led the coup, for after the land had been ruined beyond much further capability to produce real wealth, the get-rich-quick schemes that could still succeed were drug smuggling and diversion of international aid. Historically, gifts of food and clothing and medicine have been converted somewhere along the road into merchandise for sale here, and gifts of money have been simply embezzled, demands renewed at each roadblock until nothing remains; the *paysans* and the truly needy here get the mango seed after it's been sucked dry of flesh and juice. This corrupt system might have been razed by the foreign intervention, but still it seemed unfortunate (as remarked by my acquaintance at the Hôtel Bon Dieu Bon) that the foreigners were leaving without putting anything in its place.

At a restaurant somewhere between Gonaives and Saint-Marc, we chanced onto a pair of business partners with a good idea: to export certain craft items made with local materials by artisans in the mountains. The European partner was voluble at first (what businessman would lose a chance to promote his enterprise to the public?) until the Haitian partner shut him up. *You will never hear anything about any business here that does anything good for the people,* he said, *because once the affair is known, someone comes to take a bite out of it.* The notion of the *loupgarou*, or vampire, is alive and well in Haitian Vodou; they suck just a little more blood at every crossroad, *blocus* after *blocus* after *blocus*. . . .

At the Hôtel Oloffson in Port-au-Prince, a small green lizard walked the concrete balustrade outside Graham Greene's old room, stalking a prosperous black housefly with infinite caution and infinite desire. There was a ridge at the center of the balustrade and the lizard was using this for cover. The fly was on the other side of the ridge, buzzing, content and insouciant as the lizard moved nearer, limbs working in oily slow motion, round suction-cup toes gripping the concrete. Every so often the lizard could just raise its head to check the position of the fly across the ridge, but then it was me he saw, some chance movement I had not intended. I froze too. The lizard's golden eye rolled toward me, black ogive of the pupil focusing. He remained motionless for a long time, balancing hunger against risk. Nothing moved of him except his eye. Somewhere in the coconut palms of the hotel courtyard, a crow was waiting for him too.

This was Haiti: everyone was hungry and angling for position. The gossip among the human beings on the Oloffson gallery was also all about predation. Unrest was general, though its source was unclear. Almost everyone seemed to agree that the UN disarmament effort had failed more or less completely, with the result that the various underground factions were now better armed than the newly invented Haitian police. The theory of the foreign intervention was to create a police force incapable of carrying on terrorism, but perhaps this theory failed to foresee that such a police might well become a target of terrorism. Several police officers had been victims in a recent rash of killings.

Who exactly had control of all that underground weaponry was a matter of some dispute on the gallery. Members of the Haitian *haute bourgeoisie* believed that a left-wing terrorist movement existed, influenced and perhaps armed by outside

Communist agitators, based in the Port-au-Prince slums of Cité Soleil and La Saline, and winningly titled "L'Armée Rouge." Others claimed that the whole notion of an armed left-wing faction was actually a fabrication of the right—and certainly the title "Red Army" had the odor of shopworn right-wing propaganda. No doubt whatsoever, though, that a right-wing faction, made up of former military and *macoutes* was still present and still distressingly well armed. As before the rains, the weather smelled like trouble.

In Haiti, where Vodou allows events in the unconscious to be experienced as outside forces, such changes in ambience are almost physically tangible. By summer's end, when I had left the country and was getting my Haitian news through the Internet, it seemed much clearer that outbreaks like the August 19 attack on the Presidential Palace and the Port-au-Prince police headquarters came from the quarter of the *macoutes* and former military; if any armed and organized "Armée Rouge" existed, it had taken no action whatsoever, although there had been some populist manifestations, complete with tire burning and machete waving. In Cap Haïtien that night in June, I had been breathing the same charged air as the people in the demonstration, and hindsight gave me a better idea about where the fear that embodied itself in my room had come from.

Precisely because so little had changed in Haiti since the revolution two hundred years before, there was now a chance to build a new Haitian society directly on its eighteenth century foundation—on the ideas and ideals that also informed the American Revolution, but in a situation where the race issue, which still gnaws at the roots of our own society, had been, quite radically, done away with. This opportunity seemed significant not just for Haiti but, symbolically if in no other way, for the whole Western Hemisphere, but it was a fragile opportunity, and looked as if it might be missed. As the delicacy of the situation increased, so did a palpable sense of dread.

By the time we returned to Port-au-Prince from the north, I had come to the point of feeling these things viscerally, rather than understanding them in the conventional, intellectual fashion. My thinking self had disappeared somewhere. I didn't miss it. Dissolution of the self is a Haitian speciality; the experience can be euphoric, as in Ginen, or terrifying, as in Bizango. *Sa'w pèdi pou sa?* asks a Boukman Eksperyans lyric. *What do you lose for this?* Your panicking individual identity answers that it's your very self you're losing, but the singers insist that in losing your individual life you will gain eternal life, as *serviteurs* in the crisis of possession exchange their personal identities for union with the *loa* and with *Les Morts et Les Mystères*. In Haiti it was still forever, but in leaving Haiti I would lose all this; it would become *sa'm pèdi*—what I've lost. The obliteration of one's boundaries is always overwhelming and yet one remembers it like an addiction. Afterward, when I met other *blancs* who had been in Haiti, it would be like talking to people who had been in the same war. In the end one always came to the same question: *Do you still have those dreams?*

MADISON SMARTT BELL ON *"Sa'm Pèdi"*

My Haitian essays began in a fairly tortured way, as an effort to fulfill commercial magazine assignments I had taken on, partly to pay my expenses there, and partly to air some truth about the country, its culture, and its current political situation. The task presented real difficulty since I found my personal attachment to the subject was so great that I was very unwilling to adapt (distort) the stories to conform to the expectations of the Stateside slick magazine market. It was also very difficult at first to write up the material in a way that seemed just, since my usual linear ways of proceeding seemed to be inapplicable.

As for surprises during the writing, the ballooning of the length was a big one. "Sa'm Pèdi" ought to have been about 20 some pages long and went to 65. "Action de Grâce" exploded to over 100 pages. When I got to "Namn nan Boutey" I had accepted that I was inadvertently writing a book, so I first did a short version for the magazine assignment and then expanded it from the inside to my own satisfaction.

Finding a form for the material was difficult and I don't think I hit on it till "Action de Grâce." The solution came from a sculpture I saw in the studio of Patrick Vilaire, which portrayed a woman suspended in a webwork of wire. Each intersection of the wires was meant to be marked with a brass bead. This image connected with my nascent belief that Haitian thinking, Haitian culture, the whole Haitian experience really, is absolutely nonlinear. At all levels of Haitian culture it is the intersections, crossroads, that are important. The lines between them are not.

In writing "Action de Grâce" and "Namn nan Boutey," I tried to make each modular subsection function like a Haitian crossroads, or *kalfou,* where one or more ideas would connect. These vertices could potentially be arranged in many different orders, and I did not begin to put them in order until most of the "Action de Grace" sections were already written. So I came to a nonlinear method of work, since the linear approach had been a very frustrating failure.

I'm mainly a fiction writer. This writing about Haiti is my most extended foray into nonfiction (other than literary journalism of some kind). I use the same descriptive tactics I would use in fiction, without making anything up. In terms of the pattern of the narrative, the facts obviously cannot be fudged but can be arranged extrachronologically to alter the emphasis and the total effect of combination . . . this too is a fictional device.

I think the term "creative nonfiction" is a new term for an old phenomenon. Back when, Norman Mailer and Truman Capote tried to get everyone to call it the "nonfiction novel." The term "new journalism" embraced nonfiction writers as diverse (and creative, to be sure) as Tom Wolfe and Gay Talese. John McPhee taught a course at Princeton in the seventies called "The Literature of Fact." Hemingway's *Death in the Afternoon* and *Green Hills of Africa* could certainly be called "creative nonfiction." I'm sure you could find the genre in other centuries if you looked.

What's different about today's "creative nonfiction" has to do with a shift in the academy, and also with the pressure of market forces. The genre is moving out of journalism programs toward creative writing programs, and is thus being academically institutionalized in a different way. For the past few years I've heard literary agents saying that nonfiction sells a good deal better than fiction . . . at a time when the creative programs have produced a large oversupply of trained fiction writers. I suspect the growth of creative nonfiction in the academy is a response to these factors.

My advice for young writers? Don't quit your day job.

Going Native

FRANCINE PROSE

■ ■

Several years ago at an elementary school Christmas play in upstate New York, I sat behind three fourth graders from the most remote and poorest section of the rural school district. In all likelihood the boys had never seen an actual African-American person except on television and on rare trips to Kingston, forty miles away. Nonetheless they wore their version of authentic gangsta attire: huge windpants, baggy sweatshirts, baseball caps turned backward. During one confusing scene—

■ ■

FRANCINE PROSE is the author of ten highly acclaimed works of fiction, including *Bigfoot Dreams, Household Saints, Hunters and Gatherers, Primitive People*, and *Guided Tours of Hell*. Her work has appeared in *The New Yorker*, the *Atlantic Monthly, GQ*, and the *Paris Review*; she is a contributing editor at *Harper's*, and she writes regularly on art for the *Wall Street Journal*. The recipient of numerous grants and awards, including a Guggenheim and a Fulbright, Francine Prose is a director's fellow at the Center for Scholars and Writers at the New York Public Library. She has taught at the Iowa Writers' Workshop, the Sewanee Writers' Conference, and Johns Hopkins University. She lives in New York City.

something about Santa looking for his elves—one of the boys turned to his friends and said, "Yo, man, whassup? What that mothafucka be saying?"

For these little boys, the identification with inner-city kids ran deeper than a taste for rap music and the urge to make a fashion statement. In their secret hearts, they were the black kids who—had they actually met them—would have ignited their prejudices and their secret fear of flesh-and-blood (as opposed to fantasy) African-Americans. For these isolated white kids, victims of a rural poverty more hidden and less readily acknowledged than its urban counterpart, the African-American musicians they saw on MTV were saying something that they felt but could not express for themselves—voicing their alienation, their disenfranchisement, their sense of being exiled to the fringes of a society that would prefer they didn't exist. Likewise the appealing young men and women in Alan Parker's film *The Commitments*—poor Northern Irish kids without a lot of career prospects who form a soul band specializing in the greatest hits of Aretha Franklin and Otis Redding—are drawn to the music for reasons that go beyond the music, and the gifted young performers joke about their identification with the poverty, alienation, and disenfranchisement of African-Americans.

Something of this sort—but stranger and more complex—is currently going on among the white working class and rural poor who attend regional powwows and decorate their homes with images representing a sort of airbrushed, mythical, Disneyfied version of the Native American experience. Every summer I visit the same flea market in central Tennessee, and each year there are more stands selling clocks, rugs, paintings, and countless household items depicting beautiful Indian maidens and muscular braves in buckskins and feathered headdresses.

Of course cartoonish images of Native Americans have long

adorned cultural artifacts ranging from heroic, commemorative historical paintings to the hoods of automobiles to the logos of football teams. But what seems to have changed is that the people most drawn to these symbols have increasingly convinced themselves that they *are* Native Americans, or close to it. With just a little cultural fantasizing, whites—conveniently ignoring the fact that the land their flea market stands on originally belonged to Native Americans—can see themselves as the authentic, self-sufficient, proud people, close to the land and valiantly defending traditional ways against the incursions of the Other: rich, white, urban, or, alternately, immigrant or African-American.

So for the past several years, a small community in New York's Hudson Valley has been severely divided and damaged by a conflict over whether to retire the Indian that serves as the local high school's logo. Much of the pressure to get rid of the hideous, racist cartoon has come from the more politically liberal elements of the Onteora school district, which includes families who have moved up from Manhattan and the suburbs, as well as the area's few minority and immigrant families. But conservatives—more likely to be older retirees and working people, economically embattled and fearing political disenfranchisement—have fought bitterly to retain the image, which on some level they sincerely believe to be an image of themselves. If the symbol disappears, they feel that a link to their past will be taken away. So what if it's not *their* past, exactly? The logo makes them feel part of a larger community with a braver history than their own; they're the Iroquois Nation, just as their kids imagine themselves as the gangstas in the Wu-Tang Clan.

"Going native" embraces a myth of what a culture represents and makes it one's own myth—a handy process when at the moment there isn't a viable myth to explain our experience or to make us feel better about ourselves. If for example the American dream no longer describes the arc of our personal history or seems like a possible goal, we must seek another fantasy—an altered notion of who we are or who we might become. The desire or the need to go native reminds us of how much about our most basic identity is subject to a certain slippage—particularly in certain individuals who for personal reasons require the equivalent of cosmetic psychic surgery. They need not only to surround themselves with the Other; they need to become the Other.

The trouble arises, of course, when the person or people who have gone native lose sight of the actual lives of the actual group they imagine they are. They fail to acquire any special sympathy for the people with whose culture they identify (why do I doubt that the kids at my school's Christmas play are going to grow up to be campaigners for civil rights?) and may even resent the group for actually existing and thus spoiling the fantasy of the gone-native. It's one thing to have a Big Chief air freshener hanging from your dashboard; it's quite another to believe that the Native Americans are entitled to all the profits from the bingo casino in your county.

For many reasons, going native is frequently unattractive, and our distaste often expresses itself in ways that combine the visceral and the esthetic. Our feelings about the Hare Krishna movement are not unaffected by the fact that pink and orange are unflattering colors for white kids so wan and pale they look nearly transparent. Our image of the gone-native evokes, more often than not, the tubby, middle-aged white guy in a sarong in a thatched hut, snacking on some local delicacy cooked by his beautiful child bride.

Part of our unease stems from the fact that going native has traditionally involved a certain amount of sexual colonialism and imperialist exploitation. It is hard not to feel protective of the very young men whose photos turn up (with captions like "My loyal guide, Fariq") in the biographies and travel journals of such legendary voyagers as Wilfred Thesiger and T. E. Lawrence, in anthropological studies, and in accounts of American expatriate artists—for example in the social circle surrounding the Beats and Paul Bowles in North Africa. In the popular imagination, going native often invokes an element of hands-on anthropological research. This response is partly what Conrad is trading on in *Heart of Darkness:* the notion of the white man who has left the clean light of day to tunnel deep into the jungly nether regions of sex, death, and God knows what else.

Perhaps the most famous cultural figure to have gone native is Paul Gauguin—a beloved figure almost as adored as van Gogh, or maybe more so. In our own mythology, he's the big, life-loving, Anthony Quinn character, leaving his chilly French middle-class life, lighting out for paradise, from where he dispatches idyllic telegraphs from a world of luminous color, populated by graceful, mysterious, beautiful women perfectly in tune with their surroundings.

His journal, *Noa Noa*, tells a somewhat different story. Arriving in Papeete on an "artistic mission" which the local governor assumed to be espionage, Gauguin was soon dissatisfied with the port city—so full of Europeans!—and resolved to go inland. His Papeete *vahini*, Titi, had a lot to recommend her: "The amorous passion of a Maori courtesan is something quite different from the passivity of a Parisian cocotte—something very different! There is fire in her blood, which calls forth love as its essential nourishment; which exhales it like fatal perfume." But she also had an insurmountable flaw, and soon enough he left her because her ancestry, he felt, would prevent her from initiating him in the cultural or sexual mysteries which he fantasized experiencing with a lover of purer extraction: "It was her half-white blood. . . . I felt that she could not teach me any of the things I wished to know, that she had nothing to give of that special happiness which I sought."

After Gauguin had been in his inland village long enough to get lonely, his neighbors brought him a "large child" on whom "two swelling buds rose on the breasts." Worried at first that the girl has been forced into marriage by her mother, the artist was reassured "when I saw in the face of the young girl, in her gestures and attitude the distinct signs of independence and pride which are characteristic of her race." Despite age, cultural, and language differences, the artist and his wife, Tehura, fell deeply in love, and she was the last thing he saw as he sailed back to France for a two-year stay, after which he returned to Tahiti, where he would die in 1903. "She had wept through many nights. Now she sat worn-out and sad, but calm, on a stone with her legs hanging down and her strong, lithe feet touching the soiled water. . . . The flower which she had put behind the ear in the morning had fallen wilted upon her knee."

Such accounts only reinforce our discomfort with the solipsistic romanticization, the racism and exploitation involved in going native, with the narcissistic projection, the frequent inability to see the actual human beings behind (and possibly contradicting) the myth. How, for example, did Gauguin ascertain that his child bride had decided to marry him of her own free will when, at least at the beginning, neither spoke the other's language? But are there cases which seem to us nonexploitative, in which we intuit that something not merely beneficial but essential transpires for the individual and for the community in which an old identity is traded for a new one?

Since there are, as we now know, transsexuals—men and women who grow up knowing instinctively and beyond persuasion that they have been doomed to inhabit a body with a different gender from their brain and heart—surely there must be transculturals—people who have been born in the wrong society and for whom going native represents the equivalent of a surgical correction.

For a while I believed that about myself. From 1969 to 1970, I spent almost a year in India, from which I returned convinced that I should have been born there. Everything about Indian society—the bad as well as the good—seemed preferable and more sensible than the one I had left, in Cambridge, Massachusetts. The colors were brighter, the people handsomer, the culture richer. I was happier there than I'd ever been—and certainly happier than I'd been in Cambridge in graduate school, living with the college boyfriend I'd married during my senior year at Radcliffe. I was miserable, and after months spent attending one class every morning and watching TV for the remaining hours, I began to think that I was losing my mind. Eventually I asked my husband—a graduate student in math—where he could take his fellowship and still get academic credit. I skimmed the list he brought home and realized that the Tata Institute of Fundamental Research in Colaba, Bombay, was as far as I could possibly get from Harvard Square.

Ten months later we landed in India. I didn't sleep for three nights. In the dark when I closed my eyes, my mind replayed choppy silent films from the day: naked *sadhus* with tridents, covered with ash and feathers; bony cows, like tent poles with skin, freely grazing the vegetable stalls; men in white holding hands, drifting over the dusty maidan; the dust that coated everything, the homeless families living on the sidewalks, at the station, sleeping on string cots, cooking on camp stoves.

Much of what I saw terrified me, yet I was intensely happy, perhaps because my fear was the closest thing I'd felt in months to a genuine emotion, but also because I'd already fallen in love with the excess, the overabundance: too many people, too much to see, too much noise, too many bright colors. It seemed less like overload than replenishment after the sensory-deprivation tank in which I'd been living.

This new world around me was dizzying and chaotic. And I recovered my mental health within a matter of days. I knew what pleased me (the smell of *bidi* cigarettes, of burning cowshit, of curry, the children's kohl-rimmed eyes, the brilliant saris and bangles, the little pyramids of spices and lapidary dyes in the market) and what saddened and enraged me (the cruelty of the caste system, the bleating of the lepers, the glassy stare of the beggar women's babies, the families living in drainage culverts).

I was too ironic, too much of a snob to wear a sari, which makes European women look so awkward and awful. But I did pick up a trace of an Indian accent and the ability to shake my head *no* to mean *yes*, a language of intonation and gesture that made it easier to communicate with my neighbors in Bombay. I wore embroidered Indian shirts and let the sun darken my face until I could pass for Indian, especially among people who didn't know any better. Traveling back to the United States, I stopped in London and was secretly pleased (when, for example, my unfamiliarity with the British monetary system inspired some racist mumbling from a woman in a tobacco shop) to be taken for a different sort of foreigner than I actually was.

When I returned to America, I imagined that I would stay just long enough to get my life in order, long enough to arrange for a speedy turnaround, after which I would go back to my real country—India. But of course things didn't work out that way. Life, as they say, intervened. Seven years passed before I returned, as a tourist—and knew that was what I was.

In my case going native represented the equivalent of a

reversible operation. Some of the effects on me were permanent. I had learned the obvious lesson that things were different else-where, that disparate cultures could view the world in entirely dissimilar ways. And I like to think that, for me, the experience helped to enlarge the tiny little prison of the self to which we are mostly confined.

But there are instances of going native that are more final, life-changing, and irreversible, capable of curing a sense of dislocation, the unhappy conviction of having been born in the wrong place. Surely for some individuals, going native constructs or reconstructs the person who should have been born in the adopted home.

Probably the most striking example is that of Lafcadio Hearn. Born in 1850 in Greece to a local woman and an Irish Protestant surgeon in the British army, Hearn was brought as a child to Dublin, where he was abandoned by his parents and raised by a great-aunt. His physical appearance—he was extremely short and nearly blind from a childhood accident—contributed to his sense of alienation, homelessness, and exile. After sojourns in Ohio and New Orleans, where he worked as a reporter, and an early marriage to a half-black woman named Alethea Foley, Hearn left for Japan in 1890. There he found a succession of jobs as an English instructor, a journalist, a transla-tor, and finally as a teacher at Tokyo and Waseda Universities.

Soon after arriving in Japan, he wrote to a friend, "I only wish I could be reincarnated in some little Japanese baby, so that I could see and feel the world as beautifully as a Japanese brain does." And from the beginning, he felt that he had come home, that (after a lifetime of believing that he was doomed to peripatetic solitude) he finally comprehended and was capable of being accepted by the world around him. He described a sort of existential déjà vu—a sense of being surrounded by "strange Gods. I seem to have known and loved them before somewhere."

Not long after his arrival, Hearn entered into an arranged marriage with a Japanese woman, with whom he had four children. He became a Japanese citizen and assumed a Japanese name. He took financial responsibility for his wife's extended family and evolved into a beloved and revered patriarch—a position in society which could hardly have been more different from his lonely, marginal existence in England and the United States.

In Japan Hearn discovered not only his subject (his best books are redactions of Japanese folktales) but also a literary aesthetic; he abandoned his formerly elaborate prose style and pursued "perfect simplicity." His most basic values shifted to reflect those of his adopted culture: "I have nine lives depending on my work—wife, wife's mother, wife's father, wife's adopted mother, wife's father's father, and then servants, and a Buddhist student. . . . You can't let a little world grow up around you, to depend on you, and then break it all up—not if you are a respectable person. And I indulge in the luxury of 'filial piety'—a virtue of which the good and evil results are known only to us Orientals." He looked back with wonder and more than a little horror on his "old self as of something which ought not to have been allowed to exist on the face of the earth—and yet, in my present self, I sometimes feel ghostly reminders that the old self was very real indeed." And he succumbed—with deep pleasure and gratitude—to the rewards and domestic satisfactions of his life as a Japanese husband and father: "I should find living away from all Europeans rather hard, if it were not for the little world I have made around me. . . . [A]t home I enter into my little smiling world of old ways and thoughts and courtesies. . . . It has become Me."

So what are we to make of this case in which going native is not a process of self-obliteration but of self-discovery, not a matter of colonialism and sexual or cultural exploitation but of genuine appreciation of—and contribution to—a society that proves in every way more congenial than the world that has been left behind? First it is a salutary reminder that our responses to the questions of assimilation and diversity (how much we should contribute to and take away from the melting pot) are as various, unpredictable, and endlessly mysterious as every other aspect of human behavior. And finally it is a warning against easy judgments and facile formulations on the subject of cultural politics, and about the ways each of us stitches together an identity from the scraps we are able to collect from the world just outside—and far beyond—our doorstep.

On *"Going Native"* by Francine Prose

Francine Prose may be best known for her fiction, especially *The Blue Angel*, her searing satire of American academic life. But she has worked for many years as a journalist, inspired by her short stint as the author of "Hers," a column of personal essays in the *New York Times*.

"I discovered that I liked reporting," Prose told an interviewer. "It takes me out into the world and makes me see things and meet people whom I wouldn't ordinarily have met. And it's a good source of material for a fiction writer."

Her *Lives of the Muses*, which reexamines the lives of nine women and the artists they inspired, is meticulously researched and dazzlingly written. Starting sometimes with just an image, like Lewis Carroll's portrait of young Alice Liddell, who was the inspiration for Alice in Wonderland, her narratives spiral in ever-widening circles, until each chapter has unfolded for the reader not only a woman's life but also the world in her time. In "Going

Native," which originally appeared in *Creative Nonfiction* 19, Diversity Dialogues, Prose weaves cultural analysis with memoir and self-reflection to plead the case of transculturals—those of us who "grow up knowing instinctively and beyond persuasion" that we have been "born in the wrong society." For Prose herself, moving to India early in her career seemed, at the time, "the equivalent of surgical correction."

Prose says that she tries to write every day, but because she writes so many different things it's a challenge to stay focused and organized. "On an ideal day I would work on fiction in the morning, when I'm really fresh, and then on reviews or journalism in the afternoon. . . . I used to tell my students to write every day, but I no longer say that. It turns out to be destructive advice. You tell people to write every day and they're consumed with guilt when they don't. So forget that. I do tell people to be careful about whom they show their work to in its early stages. It must be someone you trust, who has your best interest at heart. Reading constantly and carefully is also very important. Finally, be observant. Watch what's going on around you. Listen to people. You need to listen to people's voices, to how they tell their stories." —*Jessica Mesman*

Chimera

GERALD N. CALLAHAN

. .

Last Thursday, one of those gray fall days when the starlings gather up and string between the elms around here, my children's mother—dead ten years—walked into a pastry shop where I was buttering a croissant. She ignored me, which she always does,

. .

GERALD N. CALLAHAN is associate professor of immunology/public understanding of science in the Department of Microbiology, Immunology, and Pathology as well as the Department of English at Colorado State University. His work has appeared in *Nature*, the *Journal of Experimental Medicine*, the *Journal of Immunology*, *Emerging Infectious Diseases*, *Science and Spirit*, *turnrow*, *Puerto del Sol*, *Rhino*, *The Bridge*, the *Cream City Review*, the *Midwest Quarterly*, *Southern Poetry Review*, *The MacGuffin*, *Atlanta Review*, and others. Callahan is science editor for *turnrow* magazine, scientific adviser for the International Foundation for Ethical Research, and along with his wife, Virginia Mohr-Callahan, was for five years a food writer for the daily *Fort Collins Coloradoan*. This essay, "Chimera," is included in Callahan's most recent book, *Faith, Madness, and Spontaneous Human Combustion: What Immunology Can Teach Us About Self-Perception* (Berkley Books, 2003), which was a finalist for the Colorado Book Award for Nonfiction in 2003.

368

ordered a plain bagel and an almond latte, picked up her food, and, without a glance at me, walked out. The starlings chittered, the day frowned, and I went back to buttering my croissant.

Just after her suicide, I saw this woman often—in towns where she never lived, walking her Airedales in the park, eating poached eggs at Joe's Cafe, sweeping grass clippings from her walk on Myrtle Street, stepping off the Sixteenth Street bus. We get together less often now. But when we do, like this morning, her image is as vivid as it ever was—her dark eyes as bright, her odd smile just as annoying.

I'm not crazy.

I know it isn't her, this woman I see. After all, she's dead, and I myself gave her ashes to my son. So it is another, a stranger, transformed by some old film still flickering through the projector inside my head. I know that. But every time I see her, it takes all that I have to stay in my chair or my car, to hold on to myself and not run after her calling out her name.

Some of this I understand. When something or someone is suddenly stripped from us, it seems only natural that our minds would try to compensate. Minds do that. If they didn't, we might be sucked into the vortex ourselves. That part, I grasp. I'd have thought, though, that in a year or two, the films in my mind would fade and break, and the tear in my life would scar and close like any other wound. And I expected, as the fissure closed, that my first wife would disappear.

I was wrong.

All the pieces of human bodies fit (more or less) into eleven systems—endocrine, musculoskeletal, cardiovascular, hematologic, pulmonary, urinary, reproductive, gastrointestinal, integumentary, nervous, and immune. So there are a limited number of places where someone could hide something inside a human body. And so far as we know, only two of the body's systems, immune and nervous, store memories—fourth birthdays or former wives. That narrows it even further.

Most of us don't for a moment associate immune systems with hopes and fears, emotions and recollections, we don't imagine that anything other than lymph—the pale liquid gathered from the blood—is stored inside of thymuses, spleens, and lymph nodes. The business of immune systems is, after all, not hope, but immunity—protection against things like measles, mumps, whooping cough, typhus, cholera, plague, African green monkey virus, you name it.

But immune systems do remember things, intricate things that the rest of the body has forgotten. And the memories stored inside our immune systems can come back, like my first wife, at unexpected moments, with sometimes startling consequences.

My grandmother had a penchant for saving things. She had grown up in a very poor family and believed nothing should be wasted. On the plywood shelves of her closets, Mason jars that once held apple butter or pickled tomatoes were filled with buttons, snaps, paper clips and strips of cloth, seashells, rubber bands, pebbles, bobby pins, and cheap, shiny buckles—everything she'd ever come across that she thought might be useful someday.

Immune systems do that, too—believe that most everything they come across will be useful again someday. Grandmother used Mason jars, immune systems use lymph nodes. Immune systems collect bacteria, parasites and fungi, proteins, fats, sugars, and viruses—the stuff that falls through the cracks in our skin.

Human skin is like nothing else in this universe. It tastes of sea salt and the iron inside of men and women. Its touch arouses us. Skin is cream, sand, teak, smoke, and stone. But mostly, skin is what keeps us apart from everything else on this planet, especially everything that might infect, infest, pollute, putrefy, and possess us. First and foremost, it is our skin that allows us to be here as individual men and women in a hungry world. Skin keeps things out—things that would eat us for lunch. And skin keeps things in—things we couldn't live without.

But skin can break down, get punctured by knives and needles or scraped off by tree limbs and tarmac. When that happens, we'd die without our immune systems—abruptly. Immune systems deal with the things that crawl through the holes in our skin. They label the intruders as dangerous, round them up, and destroy them. And immune systems never forget the things they've seen beneath our skin because they believe that one day those things will be back.

That's how we get to be adults—immunological memory. That's also how vaccines work. Until a few years ago, children in this country were regularly injected with cowpox, also know as vaccinia virus. Vaccinia virus is very similar to the virus that causes smallpox, with one important exception. Vaccinia virus doesn't cause the disfigurement, illness, and often death caused by smallpox. But as Edward Jenner discovered in the 1700s, people (in Jenner's case, milkmaids) who have been infected with cowpox don't get smallpox. A miracle. Immunity to cowpox protects a child from smallpox. That's because, even though their personalities are very different, smallpox virus and vaccinia virus have a lot of physical features in common. Immune systems that have learned to recognize and destroy cowpox virus also recognize and destroy the look-alike smallpox virus before it can do harm.

And immune systems remember. They remember each and every miracle, and remember them for a lifetime. A child vaccinated against smallpox virus will make a much more rapid and specific response on a second encounter with that virus than will an unvaccinated child. And the rapidity and specificity of that second response is what saves the vaccinated child's life.

Immunological memory is a simple memory of a tiny virus, but a memory powerful enough to have ended the devastating disease of smallpox on this planet. In essence it is no different from the memory that pulls our hand from the flame a little faster the second time, the memory that guides the cleaver beyond the scars on our knuckles or the memory of a first love lost.

The way immune systems do this is extraordinary. Lymph nodes are little filtering stations strung throughout the human body. Lymph nodes monitor the fluids of the body—mainly lymph and plasma—for infections. When something out of the ordinary is detected, it is usually the lymph nodes that remember and initiate an immune response.

Every time we are infected, a little of the bacteria or virus that infected us is saved in the lymph node where it first arrived. By the time we're adults, lymph nodes are filled with a bit of most everything we've ever been infected by; our lymph nodes are the repositories of our infectious histories. Just like my grandmother's jars but our immune systems sort this growing mass of memorabilia and remind themselves of what they've seen before, what they are likely to see again, and what they mustn't forget.

Mustn't forget, but mustn't hold too close to the surface, either. Because, just like some of the memories lurking in our brains, an inappropriate recollection can hurt or blind us, sometimes even kill us. Those things we suppress.

Some viruses and bacteria stored inside our bodies are intact and alive. The only thing keeping us from having the same diseases all over again is the constant vigilance of our immune systems. Through that vigilance, all of those things hanging around inside us are kept in check, are suppressed to the point where they can help us remember, but cannot cause disease. Memory with a mission, selective recollection and suppression.

Lots of things can distract immune systems, though—drugs, malnutrition, stress, age, infection. When these things happen, immune systems can forget for a moment all those deadly things packed away inside of us. Then, like minds in panic, immune systems can become confused, forget which memory to recall, which memory to suppress, and the past can flare inside of us. When that happens, our very survival depends on our ability to regain our balance, to enhance some recollections and suppress others. A particularly pernicious example of this is shingles—a severe chicken pox–like rash that usually appears across the ribs beneath the arms, but may also grow in the eyes and lungs. It is most commonly a disease of the elderly.

People can't get shingles if they weren't infected with chicken pox, usually as children. Shingles and chicken pox are caused by the same virus—varicella zoster virus. When we get chicken pox, our immune systems and (interestingly) our nervous systems store a few leftover varicella zoster viruses for future reference. Later, when age or illness or depression distracts our immune systems, the virus begins to multiply again. Then the virus may blind us, may even kill us. This is shingles—a blazing memory of chicken pox, a childhood disease—a thing we wish we could forget.

So immune systems, like minds, are filled with memories— vivid, painful, sometimes fatal memories. The fragments of a life lived, bits and pieces of the past. And sometimes immune systems lose control of this smoldering wreckage and old flames flare anew.

Within me, then, is there a woman living in this ruin, a woman who walks and speaks exactly like my first wife? It is, of course, impossible to answer that question. No one understands nearly enough about wives and immune systems. But it isn't, as it might seem, an entirely stupid question. Among the things we regularly trade with our wives (and the rest of our families for that matter) are viruses—colds, flus, cold sores, to mention only a few.

Enveloped viruses—like those that cause flu, cold sores, and AIDS—are so called because they carry with them an "envelope" of lipids and proteins taken from the host cell (the cell they grew up inside of). And many viruses also carry within them a little of the host cell's nucleic acids—DNA or RNA—the stuff of genes. Some of that DNA or DNA made from that RNA clearly gets incorporated into our chromosomes and begins to work inside of us. That means that each time we are infected with one of these viruses, we also acquire a little of the person who infected us, a little piece of someone else. Infection as communication. Infection as chimerization. Infection as memorization.

Perhaps that seems trivial—a bit of envelope here, a little DNA there. But over the course of an intimate relationship, we collect a lot of pieces of someone else. And a little of each of those pieces is stored in our lymph nodes and in our chromosomes.

Until. Until the person we've been communicating with is gone, and we stop gathering bits of someone we love. For a few days or weeks, everything seems pretty much like it was. Then one day, a day when, for no apparent reason, our defenses slip just a little, and a ghost walks through the door and orders an almond latte.

Nervous systems don't appear to store memories in the same way immune systems do. Most neurologists and neurochemists

believe that memory within the nervous system involves something called long-term potentiation or LTP—a means by which
certain nerve pathways become preferred. Because of LTP a particular trigger—a picture of Aunt Helen—becomes likely to
stimulate the same nerve circuit—the smell of cheap perfume—
every time. But in general, how nervous systems store and recall
memories isn't very well understood.

Human memory has been divided into two broad categories—declarative memory (explicit, consciously accessible
memory: what was the name of the cereal I had for breakfast?)
and emotional memory (often subconscious and inaccessible:
why was I so frightened by that harmless snake I saw today?). But
there is evidence for a third kind of memory as well, something
I'll call phantom memory, memories that come from someplace
beyond or beneath declarative and emotional circuits.

I'm pretty confident that declarative memory had nothing to
do with my first wife walking in on me as I was buttering my
croissant last Thursday. I'm less certain about emotional memory.
And I am deeply intrigued by phantom memory.

People who have had arms and legs removed often experience phantom limbs—a sensation that the arm or leg is still
there, sometimes a very painful sensation. This feeling is so real
that people with phantom hands may try to pick up a coffee cup
just as you or I would. People with phantom legs may try to stand
before their declarative minds remind them they have no legs.
The missing limbs seem completely real to these people and as
much a part of themselves as any surviving appendage—even
when the phantom limb is a foot felt to be dangling somewhere
below the knee with no leg, real or phantom, between the ankle
and a mid-thigh stump.

Some of those who have studied phantom-limb sensations
argue that these are only recollections of sensations "remem-

bered" from the days before amputation. But children born without limbs—children who've never experienced the sensations of a normal limb—experience phantom limbs. Clearly, these phantoms are not simple recollections of better days. Instead, the presence of phantom limbs in these children suggests that some sort of prenatal image—some template of what a human should look like—is formed inside our fetal minds before our arms and legs develop, before even our nervous systems are fully formed. If at birth our bodies don't fit this template, our minds or brains attempt to remake reality, twist it until it fits what our minds say it ought to be.

No one knows where phantom memories reside. Often, phantom limbs are exceedingly painful, so physicians have tried to locate the source of the sensations and eliminate them. Spinal cords have been severed, nerve fibers cut, portions of the brain have been removed. Some of these sometimes caused the pain to disappear, but it usually returned within a few months or years. And none of these treatments routinely caused phantom limbs to disappear.

Occasionally over time phantom limbs will disappear on their own, though almost never permanently. The limbs usually return—in a month or a year or a decade. And when they do, they are just as real as the day they first appeared, or disappeared.

Phantom memories aren't always memories of limbs either. People who've lost their sight describe phantom visions: not recollections, but detailed images of sights they've never seen—buildings, burials, forests, flowers. Similarly, some people who've lost their hearing, Beethoven being one, are haunted by complex symphonies blaring in their ears.

No one knows how much of our reality comes to us from the physical world and how much "reality" we create inside our own minds. If we were to analyze, using something like a PET scanner all the nervous activity occurring at any given moment inside a human body, no more than a fraction of a percent of this activity would be directly due to input from the senses. That is, only a tiny portion of what our nervous systems are occupied with, and by inference only a tiny portion of our thoughts, are direct results of what we see, hear, taste, smell, or touch. The rest of it, the remainder of our mental imaging, begins and ends inside of us. How that affects our "reality" isn't clear.

But it is clear that much of what originates within us is powerful enough to fill our mental hospitals with people who see and hear things that aren't there. Among the sights and sounds that originate within us are our images of ourselves and our realities—our archetypes. Such images are powerful icons, nearly immutable. These are the images of our dreams, our poetry, our theaters, our psychoses.

If physical reality, the outside world, changes abruptly, it may not be within our power to so abruptly change such deep-rooted images of ourselves and our worlds. When that happens, reality itself becomes implausible. Then our only way out is through a phantom, a bit of virtual reality that reconciles our world and the real world.

Are the dead, then, living within my neurons—inside my own pictures of me?

Images of ourselves—some apparently older than we are—are obviously deeply etched into the stones of our minds. Powerful things that resist change, particularly sudden change. But even these archetypal portraits of ourselves aren't without seams or cracks. And inside those seams and between those cracks, small forces working over years can introduce change. Time, in an intimate and powerful relationship, may reshape even our images of ourselves. The changes would be little ones at first, a tiny fissure unmortared here or there, room to include in our self-portraits parts of other men or women, a first vision of ourselves as something more. Later, larger pieces of us might be lifted and replaced by whole chunks of another. Husband and wife begin to speak alike, know what the other is thinking, anticipate what the other will say, even begin to look alike. Until one day, what remains is truly and thoroughly a mosaic, a chimera—part man, part woman; part someone, part someone else.

And then, if that man or woman is amputated from us, clipped as quickly and as cleanly as a gangrenous leg, our minds are suddenly forced into a new reality—a reality without the other, a reality in which an essential piece of us is missing. At that point, our declarative minds would be at odds with our own pictures of ourselves. To rectify that, to reconcile the frames flickering inside with the darkness flaming outside, we conjure a phantom, a phantom to change our worlds. We force a bit of what is inside out there into the real world, to create someone or something that will help us slow the universe for a moment while we repaint our pictures of ourselves with a very small brush on a very large canvas.

There is a painting by Pierre Auguste Renoir which I first saw at the National Gallery in Washington, D.C. This painting, titled *Girl with a Watering Can*, is filled mostly with the off-whites and intense blues of the impressionist painter. But in the girl's hair, there is a blood-red bow. I've often wondered about that bow and why Renoir put it there. I've imagined the bow was a symbol of the death that begins at each of our births; I've imagined it as an omen of sexual maturity—its pain and its promise; I've even imagined it was nothing more than a schoolgirl's red bow.

But just now, I think the red bow is the other one inside of us, the red one who is probably at first mother—physically, immunologically, and psychologically. The one, too, who is later so many others—grandmother, friend, severed limb, or lost wife.

Renoir placed the bow in the girl's hair, near her brain. I don't imagine, though, that by that placement he intended for us to ignore all the other spots where bits of men and women gather in us.

Today, sitting on the redwood deck behind my house, the air smells of cinnamon and rainwater. For reasons I can't recall, those smells remind me of the Brandenburg Concertos, coffee on Sunday mornings, and the intricate paths of swallows.

Somewhere inside of me, there is a woman. But where she lives and who it was that led her into that pastry shop last Thursday, I've no way of knowing. For one part of me, that ignorance is a gnawing blindness. For another part of me, it is enough to simply know for certain that I will see her again.

Gerald N. Callahan on *"Chimera"*

When I was twelve years old, my brother Michael gave me his old Gilbert chemistry set as he left for school in Ohio. I loved the smell of acetic acid, the swirls of the Bohr atom, and the taste of potassium chloride. The moment I opened that old blue box, I was a chemist. Nothing would ever change that.

But when I wasn't blowing holes in the backyard or asphyxiating my sisters, I read everything I was allowed to, and then some. I read Edgar Rice Burroughs, Robert Heinlein, Robert Louis Stevenson, Isaac Asimov, Jules Verne, H. G. Wells, D. H. Lawrence, Jack London, and later Melville, Rilke, Dostoevsky, Dos Passos, Loren Eiseley, Huey Newton, and Pablo Neruda. I was enraptured by pictures painted with words and the worlds beneath them. Saturday mornings I filled with library books and pipe bombs.

It was a great time in my life. It ended too soon. And it would be thirty-five more years before I found my way back. For me, I came back to where I began with the essay "Chimera." This was the first essay in which the schizophrenic halves of my life once again fused. Science and literature on the same pages, and neither seemed too much the worse for the company.

The essay began, as many of my essays do, from a poem. The poem was not mine. It might have been Sharon Olds'. I really don't remember now. In the poem, the author steps onto a bus and meets a dead relative. I was struck by the image and how often we see the dead here and there. Especially if we have just lost someone we love. I wanted to write about that. So I did, and the first few paragraphs came quickly—my ex-wife, the coffee shop, the look on her face.

In the beginning, that was all I had in mind, no science, just a scene. But once that scene was on paper, I became intrigued with where we store memories, especially our memories of the dead. Most people, I think, assume everything is stashed inside our heads. But as an immunologist, I knew that wasn't true. So I wanted to explore that as well, to consider all the unexpected places memories might be buried. The rest just fell into place. I didn't expect that. I didn't expect the clear connection between our visions of the dead and phantom memories, or the parallels between immunological and neurological memories. But the more I researched, the more that was handed to me—immunity and memory, amputation and vision, and the smell, and the feel, and the look of the dead—all seemed to fall in my lap as the tale took on a life of its own.

Creative nonfiction, some people argue, is an oxymoron. Either, it has been said, it is creative or it is nonfiction. It cannot be both. I don't agree. But neither do I agree with those who define creative nonfiction in terms of some form of absolute truth or fact.

What we put in, what we leave out, the words we choose, the metaphors we build on, change everything. None of it is "real" in any absolute sense.

Clearly, the facts get muddled in creative nonfiction. That's how humans are. Conversations get constructed from ten-year-old memories, scents and scenes are rebuilt from imperfect neurons, tastes are retasted and touches are refelt. None of that is done with absolute accuracy.

That doesn't, in my opinion, detract from what we call creative nonfiction. Rather it adds. Creative nonfiction is about human experiences, real human experiences—the ways we recall things, the ways we revise things, the ways we relive things. And creative nonfiction fills a niche that will never be filled by either fiction or traditional nonfiction. An important niche about the things that happen to people in real time and the ways those things change us a day or decade later.

For me, that is the great allure of creative nonfiction—working with the world as we find it. Piecing together a moment when it seems the world offered a glimpse behind the curtains and we saw, for an instant, some sense in it all.

Writing is an unusual occupation. There are no rules, at least none that is written down anywhere or agreed upon by more than a handful of writers. There are many more paths to oblivion than to success, and no one can tell you with any certainty which is which. Beyond that, writing is a dangerous job. People have died from it.

All of my career, I've watched writers with much greater talent than mine simply disappear. I am still here, I think, more because of endurance than talent. I am still here pushing these keys because, to me, success and oblivion are nearly the same, as long as I have an hour or two, a keyboard, and an idea.

Mixed-Blood Stew

JEWELL PARKER RHODES

. .

It was an old document. Rough parchment, yellowed and withered. I was all of ten, on the threshold of womanhood, digging in my mother's closet, trying to find clues about why my mother abandoned me when I was an infant, why she returned to claim me when I was nine. On this sweltering summer day, I found a

. .

JEWELL PARKER RHODES is the Virginia G. Piper Chair in Creative Writing and artistic director of the Virginia G. Piper Center in Creative Writing at Arizona State University. She is the author of two writing guides, *Free Within Ourselves: Fiction Lessons for Black Authors* and *The African American Guide to Writing and Publishing Nonfiction*. She has written three novels: *Voodoo Dreams, Magic City,* and *Douglass' Women*. *Douglass' Women* was the winner of the 2003 American Book Award, the Black Caucus of the American Library Association Award, the 2003 PEN Oakland Josephine Miles Award, and was a finalist for the PEN Center USA Award in Fiction and for the Hurston-Wright Legacy Award. She has received a Yaddo Creative Writing Fellowship, the National Endowment of the Arts Award in Fiction, and several distinguished teaching and mentoring awards.

treasure trove of documents—birth certificates, Social Security cards with various names, paycheck stubs, and blurred photographs of my mother with strangers. But I knew I'd discovered something special when I uncovered the fragile sheet sandwiched between cardboard and tissue paper.

SLAVE AUCTION

Various goods and animals to be auctioned,
including one healthy male, a woman (good cook), and child.
WRIGHT PLANTATION
Respectable offers only

"What are you doing?"

My hands trembled, but rather than retreating, I asked, "What this?"

"I don't like you going through my things." She took the package from my hand and laid it on the bed.

"That your family?" I asked. Of course they were my family, too. But Mother had been gone so long I couldn't help thinking of her as separate from me.

Almost whispering, Mother traced the dulled letters with her fingers. "The good cook. She was my great-grandmother. The man, her husband. The child, my grandmother. Master Wright sold them like cattle. When slavery ended, my folks claimed Master's name because they were his kin."

Kin, I knew, was a code word for rape. Race-mixing. Miscegenation. The child was mulatto. The "healthy male" who raised her wasn't her father. Nonetheless, the small family, lucky to be sold together, took Wright's name and created another, darker limb of his family tree.

For a brief moment, I thought Mother would slap me. Or ground me. Or scream, making me cower, cover my ears.

"This is mine," she said, and layered the auction sheet beneath tissue paper and taped the cardboard shut.

But I knew she was wrong—it was mine, too—part of my blood. I reached out to give her a hug, but Mother pulled away. "Don't touch my things again."

After Mother left I had a vision of a handsome black man and woman riding on a wagon perch with a yellow-brown girl between them. When the child's hand clasped a parent's, did she ever wonder about her lighter skin? About the faces stirring inside her blood?

Mother had the auction sheet framed but never hung it. Until her death it remained shelved in a closet—a buried reminder of what my mother considered a secret. What was worth hiding from neighbors' and her children's eyes. Wipe away roots. Mother created herself full-blown, sprung from the head of Zeus. Mother was all charm, respectability; in her mind her people arrived on the *Mayflower*, never anchored belowdecks in a slave ship's hold.

I'd always known mysterious people were stirring in my blood.

During the nine years of my mother's absence, my paternal grandmother raised me. Raised me in the A.M.E. Methodist Church and in a community with its own special rainbow. Red-toned Miss Chalmers, sandy-faced Willie, black-beyond-midnight Reverend, and ivory-skinned Mrs. Jackson. Dozens of words described our myriad colors: *Chocolate. Coffee. Café au lait. High yellow. Indigo. Bronze.* Street-corner boys whistled at the parade of sepia girls. Proud churchwomen declared our deacons "fine, righteous black men." And on Easter Sundays, with pastels adorning black and brown bodies, I knew each and every one of us was beautiful.

"African-American people, like all people, be rich within themselves," my grandmother said. We grandkids—my sister, Tonie, my cousin Aleta, and I—sitting on porch steps, sucking on salted ice or feeding grass to lightning bugs trapped inside a jar, would listen as Grandmother, her voice rising and falling like a sermon, told us tales of ourselves.

"We come from Georgia. Before that—Africa. White folks didn't understand there be thousands of tribes. Each with its own history. Slavers thought anybody with black skin be ignorant, be blank slates for them to write upon and breed. Foolishness."

"Hun-hunh," we testified, drawing people with white chalk, printing our names in block letters. If it was especially hot and humid, we'd pretend we were in church and fan ourselves with newspapers folded like accordions.

"Once black folks could fly. They came from a special tribe with magic words. One day when Master worked them too hard, beat them too long, they played their bodies like drums. Foot-stomping. Hand-clapping. Chest- and thigh-beating. Sent the message, 'Tonight. We fly.'

"Come midnight, when day blends into the next, they strapped their babies on their backs, whispered their magic, and lifted off the ground like crows. Blackbirds in the sky. Sailing high across the fields and above the seas."

"How come we couldn't fly?" I asked.

"Somebody needed to tell the tale. Like I be telling you. Like one day you be telling your children." .

Tonie giggled. "I ain't marrying."

I elbowed my sister, declaring, "I'll tell."

Tonie rolled her eyes, stuck out her tongue.

Grandmother laughed, patting my back, making me feel special.

"White folks used to say one drop of black blood makes you a

slave. Made it a law, too. Sheer foolishness. Pepper in the pot
makes everything taste better. Can't use just salt."

"You saying we a stew?"

"Yes. The best kind. Mixed-blood stew."

Then Grandmother, noticing the sky filled with twinkling
stars and a crescent moon, shooed us to bed and dreams of clouds
cradling us. Dreams of ancestors flying, filling a pot with laughter
and love.

Grandmother's tales were better than my mother's silence.
Cross-racial diversity didn't imply any shame, only grace.

One summer Grandmother blessed us with a vacation trip to
Georgia. We grandkids frolicked, skipped across grass, marveling
at homes made of wood rather than brick. Marveling at one-story
houses with acres of pecan and orange trees. Our three-story home
had an L-shaped yard of concrete and just enough dirt for a rose-
bush, which rarely bloomed.

Blood memories of that Southern visit still stir me. I remember
glimpsing my great-grandmother, half Seminole, half black, sitting
in the middle of her bed, wearing a white flannel gown. She was so
frail I thought her a ghost. So silent I thought her mute.

I stood in the doorway watching her brush, over and over
again, her long strands of black silk. Hair so long she could sit on
it. Hair so dark it gleamed like polished rock.

For three days I watched her with each setting sun. Finally I
asked, "Why does she do it, Grandmother? What for?"

"She's afraid water will make her catch cold. So she brushes
away the dirt. Stroke by stroke."

"Hmmm," I murmured, my eyes sparkling.

"Don't you think it," answered Grandmother, knowing I
dreaded shampoos and the hot comb pressing my kinky hair flat.

Grandfather, not to be outdone by Grandmother's line, had his own stories to tell.

"Seminole be all right. But I got Choctaw and Irish in me."

Sunday afternoons he'd be in his familiar spot, sitting at the head of the dining room table, smoking a pipe and sipping Iron City beer. He'd grab anyone who passed by and tell his ancestral stories.

"In the twenties, Irish come to the Pittsburgh steel mills. Stood the heat 'like niggers,' some say. I say they stood the heat like men who appreciated an extra dollar at the end of the day." Then he'd jab his pipe. "Negroes got fifty cents.

"My Irish granddad, nearly bald, freckled all over, fell in love with my grandmother, who had some white in her from a generation before. She had Choctaw, too. Warrior blood. My grandmother's mama already had several of Master's children. One year, to spite him, she got pregnant by an Indian. Master was fit to be tied."

"So what all that blood makes me?"

He laughed, his mouth wide like a neighing horse. "Someone smart. Someone with the best of the best."

"Oh," I exhaled while Grandfather slapped his leg, his laughter ending in a fit of coughing.

As decades passed, our ethnic group kept changing, shifting, melding into more beautiful and varied gumbos, mixed-blood stews. Each marriage, each baby born, yielded new blood.

White Americans insisted our bloodlines were uncomplicated. "One drop of black blood" had historical resonance.

In contemporary terms "one drop" meant bigots and Klansmen, thickheaded policemen and ignorant folk could kick, beat, lynch, verbally abuse you, regardless. There was no measure for diversity.

It was always white versus black.

Even when whites confronted a technically Anglo/Irish/ Choctaw/Cherokee/African girl. A nigger was a nigger was a nigger . . . even when she, like me, was an assistant professor at the University of Maryland walking home from educating young minds, enjoying the sunshine and startled into fury at being called a nigger by the frat-house boys.

I always wanted to know the bloodlines of my tormentors. How white was their whiteness? What secrets lived in their veins? Did delving into generations yield Asian, Pacific Islander, Hispanic, and African, too? And if we went back to the beginning, the early dawn of our species, wasn't Lucy their mother, too?

In 1954 I was born and Emmett Till, fourteen, was murdered for speaking slang ("Bye-bye, baby") to an adult white woman. His mother insisted his coffin be open so everybody could see the battering of her baby boy.

Till's death sparked the birth of the civil rights movement. African-Americans demanded justice. Unity was our strength. But like wily and gifted tricksters, proud marchers knew they embodied "the other," embodied, in each and every one of them, some drop, *one drop*, of Anglo-American blood.

Even a child knows there is no pure color. Everything comes from a mix. And like artists African-Americans have always embraced the mix, even when some of our blood mirrored our tormentors'.

Living in my grandmother's house, I often dreamed about the faces inside my blood. As a child, stepping onto the bathtub rim, leaning against the bathroom sink, I'd stare into the mirror, pinching my skin. Freckles sprinkled across my nose—Irish?

Black, slightly slanted eyes—Seminole? Hair curled tight about my face—African? For hours I tried to account for how each part of me revealed the light and dark shadows in my blood.

In school I learned about Dick and Jane (who came to America from nowhere) and read all the tales about white families, rural and urban, rich and poor, living happily ever after in white houses with white picket fences. Fences that kept children like me out. Literature, I had discovered, was only about white lives. I smiled, kept reading nevertheless, for I knew my own joy and happiness being a brown girl raised in my grandmother and grandfather's house. One afternoon after my eighth birthday, I passed the dining room table. A newspaper cutting lay in the center of it.

"That's your father's daddy," said Grandmother, coming to stand behind me.

"That's Grandfather Thornton?"

"No. I was married before. This is your father's daddy."

"He's white."

"He's dead."

A sad-eyed man seemed to stare right through me. He was in a naval uniform, handsome, with a high forehead like mine and a squared-off chin like Daddy's. Name given: "Lieutenant J. Parker." Bold headline: "Served Valiantly in the War." Plain print: "Age 56, survived by his wife and four kids."

"My grandfather's white?"

"Or else so light he passed. It wasn't clear. One time he told me he was French-Canadian. Another time he said he was colored. Another time, Southern white."

I exhaled, excited by the revelation.

Grandmother turned away from the photo but left it on the dining room table. I could see her down the short hallway, opening our freezer and pulling out Grandfather's (should I still call him that?) white shirts, all balled up and half frozen. "They iron better this way," Grandmother always told me.

I watched her lumber down the hallway, then into the living room to set up her ironing station. She turned the TV to the afternoon movies. Both Grandmother and I liked to watch Bette Davis in *Jezebel*, Bob Hope in *Going Down to Rio*, and Lon Chaney in *Abbott and Costello Meet Frankenstein*.

Steam hissing from the flatiron, I asked, "Why you stopped being married to him—the other man?"

"In a way I didn't. He left. Said a sailor couldn't be an officer unless he be white. So he chose white."

"He passed?"

"Maybe."

"Did you divorce him?"

"Didn't have the money. I had two kids to raise. Your grand-father—the real one, your Grandfather Thornton—and I jumped the broom."

I puffed my cheeks out. This was better than the movies.

"His other wife. She white?"

"Yes." Grandmother turned the shirt over. "And his kids, all white. They live about thirty miles from here."

"No lie."

"Watch your mouth."

"I'm sorry."

Grandmother paused. "Sorry be as sorry does." The shirt was near to burning. "The white Parkers don't want to know you," she said flatly, and began moving the iron back and forth again.

Chin cupped in my palms, I tried to imagine the white Parkers who'd never lay claim to me or my father. That year, 1961, Daddy went to court to prove he was the eldest son. He wanted the flag from his father's military coffin. He wanted his white brothers and sisters to see and acknowledge him.

Much later I found out Lieutenant Parker died of liver failure. Drank himself to death.

When my mother came to claim me, I didn't want to go. But since she and my father were trying marriage one more time, I had little choice. We were the only African-American family in a suburban white community. The community was fine. But Mother, unfortunately, was skittish that we'd seem too rowdy, which meant, in her mind, too colored. The first night, she laid down rules, soft yet insistent commands about propriety, about being pretty in a dull, not-flamboyant way. "Be charming. Be gracious," she said.

At sixteen I grew rebellious. I was both a hippie and a power-to-the-people child. *"Times, they are a-changing"* . . . *"Say it loud, I'm black and I'm proud."*

I painted my bedroom red and black, hung fishnets from the ceiling, propped African spears and masks against the wall. A strobe light flickered in the corner, making every movement seem like two. Jimi Hendrix and Jefferson Airplane blared from my stereo. I was celebrating my bloodlines, and for me, a black flower child was not a contradiction. I wore a bushy Afro and leopard prints with love beads and a lei. My Huey Newton print scared my mother more than the incense. My support of the Olympians' black-power salute frightened her more than the potential of my doing hard drugs at a pool party in a neighbor's backyard.

Mother kicked me out of the house. "Go," she said; Father said nothing. I flew from California back to Pittsburgh, to my birthplace, to Grandmother and Grandfather Thornton.

I think now that my mother couldn't accept herself. It was as though her shame that her family came from a plantation, that her grandmother was a mixed child of rape, still unsettled her. There was no lens to make the past less frightening, less upsetting to her sense of decorum. She wasn't an Uncle Tom or a white wannabe. Rather, she was proud of her racial heritage, but her pride was bound up with the etiquette of a white world that was a figment of the fifties. Like Booker T. Washington, Mother thought if she worked hard enough, adopted the tastes of white middle-class culture, then she would be accepted. This desire for acceptance was her weakness, an insidious insecurity, an illogical belief that what she was—a mixed-blood New World African-American—was something to be ashamed of.

I say what she was was just fine. A special mix of humanity shaped my mother as it shaped and continues to shape us all. Mother's fears wouldn't let her embrace all the recesses and twists of her blood. Instead she established categories that contradicted themselves: Being black was fine; being a descendant of slaves was not fine. Being lovely like Lena Horne was fine; being descended from a white master wasn't. If she could she would have suppressed half the blood that made her.

Sometimes I dreamed Mother and I were sitting on the bed, side by side, reflected in a wardrobe mirror. "See," she'd say to me. "You look just like me."

And I would nod, saying, "There's plenty of good ghosts in our blood."

"Yes," she'd answer, and just like in a child's (a Native American's?) ritual of bonding, we'd prick our fingers, press them flesh to flesh, blood to blood, swearing, "Always." Swearing our ties couldn't be unbound. But I woke knowing Mother would have preferred purity. Being of mixed blood was too complicated for her. From either racial side, she thought she was being judged, could never be at ease. Her behavior became more and more rigid. Friendships, familial relations became a trial.

Mother surfaced periodically in my life, most memorably when she questioned the wisdom of my marrying a white man (Lucy's pale child from the North: British, Norwegian, and Scotch-Irish). "Think of the children," she said.

True to form, Mother did not call or write to congratulate me when I gave birth to a daughter. Nor did she call or write to congratulate me when I gave birth to a son.

One child light. One child dark.

My greatest fear is that one day someone will shout out to my son, "Nigger, what are you doing with that white girl?"

In the meantime I tell them to celebrate rivers, the roar of people, faces, histories stirring in their blood.

My census category is African-American. It always has been. Yet this category doesn't deny all the people in my blood, my genes, bubbling beneath my skin. I pass it all on. That's what Grandmother taught me.

In the 2000 census, millions of Americans checked more than one ethnic category. Native American. Hispanic. Anglo. Pacific Islander.

I think this is a good thing. All blood runs red.

JEWELL PARKER RHODES *on "Mixed-Blood Stew"*

I write historical fiction taking grains of truth and embellishing them with my imagination. Through fiction, I try to present the "emotional truth" of what it felt like to be a nineteenth-century voodoo queen in New Orleans, what it felt like to be swept up in the violence of the Tulsa race riot of 1921, what it felt like to be the white mistress and black wife of the great abolitionist and ex-slave Frederick Douglass. All my fictions have "me" inside them, but none of my fiction has ever been able to capture the facts, details, and emotional truth of my childhood. My first novel, *Family Lies*, was my creative dissertation at Carnegie Mellon University, written in 1979. This novel is essentially about my childhood and family. It is bleak and, essentially, a failed fiction.

It's taken me more than twenty years to begin mining my childhood memories again, and only through creative nonfiction have I gained a measure of satisfaction. Somehow the announcement of these memories as "truth," as nonfiction, liberates me in ways no fiction ever has. Yet I'm fully aware that my creative nonfiction is distorted by the fictional lies of memory and perception.

Trying to write about myself and my family within the context of plot didn't reveal the myriad layers of meaning in my life. Creative nonfiction, on the other hand, allows me to scratch at emotional sores with depth, passion, and, I think, with a full awareness that I'm still searching to understand my life and the interconnections between my grandmother, my mother, myself, and my children, and my children's children-to-be.

"Mixed-Blood Stew" wasn't easy writing; nonetheless, the process was deeply satisfying. It means something when the hurt child can put herself front and center inside the tale, and through memory, the passage of time, weave a bit of healing. Maybe that's why this particular creative nonfiction is so satisfying to me—it means I've survived. It signifies hope. I belong in the world and the world is alive—inside me.

Why I Ride

JANA RICHMAN

■ ■

The fear begins to subside as soon as I'm out of town. The speed of the open road should cause greater fear, but the whir of the engine lulls me into a false sense of safety. A slight vibration from the foot pegs seeps into my toes, travels though my legs and around the curve of my butt, settling in my lower back. I squeeze the grips to send another tremble through my hands and into my elbows to dwell in my chest and shoulders. The unseasonably cool Arizona summer morning air slips up my sleeves and twirls inside my zipped jacket. I pop up my face shield, take the blast full on my face; sunglasses flutter with the force. The wind enters at my temples, roars past my ears, and exits at my neck. The pavement slides under me, and I'm stunned, always, to see it so close. My brain tells me it is rough and hard, but in my eyes, it shimmers and glides. The weeds on the side of the road beckon me to reach out and brush my hand over their fluffy tops. I resist.

■ ■

JANA RICHMAN's essays and articles have appeared in numerous magazines and journals. She is writing a book about motorcycling the Mormon Trail, to be published by Crown in 2005. She lives in Tucson, Arizona.

I am strikingly aware of even the slightest change in temperature. And here at this point, all intuitively begins to make sense— here, where wind, steel, flesh, asphalt, rubber, blood, speed, bone, plastic, and muscle coalesce. Here I might begin to understand my motives. But a rabbit hops across the road, and I hit my brakes with a little too much force, causing the back tire to skid just a tiny bit. In that moment the illusion shatters; the elements separate.

I didn't grow up dreaming of speed and power. I didn't collect miniature models of motorcycles and didn't have a crush on a James Dean-type rebel roaring slowly by on his Harley-Davidson. A hip father didn't tote me to school on the back of a spit-polished classic Triumph—in fact quite the opposite. Whenever my father began to guide his Oldsmobile into a parking space only to find it occupied by a motorcycle, his words were something like, "Those goddamned ridiculous contraptions ought to be outlawed." But while my father's outright disdain worked at me from one angle, something much more surreptitious worked at me from another.

I enter the curves north of Winkleman on Highway 77 and hit the throttle to blow off any lingering shreds of trepidation. The road climbs through steep rock walls bearing the jagged red scars of dynamite blasts on their slate-gray interiors. I crave a glimpse of the murky green waters of the Gila River, which I know to be in the grassy gorge below, but I dare not look long enough to locate it. I keep my eyes up, turn my head to look as far as I can through the first curve, tip my bike so it rests on the left side of its tires, and roll on the throttle.

Trust your tires. Words spoken by Will, my husband, when he caught me kicking my tires as the bike stood in the driveway. Trust my tires? Place my trust in strips of grooved rubber wrapped around a thin steel belt strapped to aluminum alloy? Francis Scott Key thought we might place our trust in God; Francis Bacon put his trust in old friends; Goethe suggested that we trust ourselves. I can't recall anyone who trusted tires. But leaning into a curve at 65 mph, supported only by physics and a pavement/rubber-contact width of about two inches, it is no time to contemplate the trustworthiness of tires. I trust Will, so upon his words, I put my faith in my tires.

The bike slowly straightens as I come out of the first curve and begins to lean to the opposite side as I enter the next. I no longer see shades of green and beige along the road. Everything is black and white. *Get your motor runnin'. Get out on the highway. Lookin' for adventure. And whatever comes my way. Booorrrn to be wiiillld.* My horrendous singing voice reverberates in my helmet.

Look. Lean. Roll. The simple instructions for riding through a curve repeat themselves in my head. But halfway through the fourth turn, something feels wrong. I've lost focus, or I've hit the curve hot—my entry line too tight. Hitting the brakes while leaning over would take me down. More lean would pull me back into the curve, but I don't have the stomach for it. I roll off the throttle, cross the double yellow, and end up halfway into the opposite lane before I slow enough to pull it back to the right. Had a car been coming in the opposite direction, the driver would not have seen me in time to stop. Had I been in a left-hand curve, I would have wiped out on the right shoulder. A stupid mistake, a lucky outcome. My knees quiver against the tank, but I keep riding, knowing that if I get off the bike, it will be hard to get back on.

I am going to Utah to attend the Hatch family reunion—the reunion of my mother, her seven brothers and sisters, my thirty-two cousins and their two hundred and forty offspring—which I have attended every year for the past ten years. The Hatches have held the reunion every year for at least forty years, but its importance in my life has only recently become apparent.

I was born Jana Richman but never felt like a Richman, a family ruled by amplification. Whoever yells loudest—usually obscenities—is in charge. I like to think of myself as a Hatch, a family of strong but gentle men and quietly independent women.

I don't always understand the independence of the Hatch women and, for a very long time, did not recognize it at all. At first glance they are typical Mormon women accepting the role the church outlines for them: subordination. Each of them married in the L.D.S. Temple and took on the role of wife and mother with gusto, as if there were no other option.

Aunt Agatha, the oldest, used to take my sister and me to her dairy farm in Cove, Utah, every summer. I roamed the vast woods and fields, free to eat raspberries off the bushes growing around the farmhouse, while she baked bread and pies, made her own ice cream, and bottled peaches. She was the perfect aunt, the perfect mother, and the perfect Mormon housewife. Ten years ago when her husband had a stroke, people expected her to fall apart. She did not. She washed and fed him every day until he died two years later. Shortly thereafter, when someone mentioned that she might want to remarry, she said no, she no longer chose to take care of others. Instead she sold the farm and at age eighty embarked on a mission for the Mormon Church.

Right around that time, I realized the possibility that my mother and my aunts were in fact making choices. Until then I had assumed that the Mormon Church was dictating the facts of their lives, that they were simply too weak to extricate themselves from a Mormon legacy that runs deeper than the Great Salt Lake.

Their great-great-grandfather, Ira Sterns Hatch, was in Nauvoo, Illinois, with Mormon prophet Joseph Smith when Smith was assassinated. His son, their great-grandfather, Orin Hatch, helped settle the Salt Lake Valley with Brigham Young. When Young asked Hatch to help settle Carson Valley, Nevada, Hatch's young wife, Elizabeth, refused to budge. Young suggested that Hatch take a second wife for the job, and with the blessing of Elizabeth, he chose Maria Thompson, a sturdy eighteen-year-old, my great-great-grandmother. When Orin and Maria returned to Utah, Orin moved back home with Elizabeth while Maria lived with her father and raised her eight children. Maria was a leader in the Relief Society, the women's organization of the Mormon Church; she was also a leader in the suffragette movement in Bountiful, Utah.

I head for the Texaco on the south side of Globe because Will and I have stopped there more than a dozen times on previous rides. I want the familiarity. Years of riding experience allow Will to scan a parking lot in the few seconds it takes him to drive in, register the layout, and maneuver accordingly. I'm not so astute. If I pull forward into a parking place that appears to be level but in fact has a slight forward slope, I'm rendered helpless. Ready to ride, my bike weighs 517 pounds. Add to that 90 pounds of saddlebags, tank bag, and duffel bag, and you get this picture: a 115-pound woman straddling a 600-pound machine attempting to push it backward up a tiny hill with only the use of her two skinny legs.

Parking lots present more than just slope problems. Making U-turns on a motorcycle requires a unique mix of enough speed to keep the bike upright and enough lean to get the bike turned. A skilled rider can make a U-turn easily in the space of a single traffic lane. I can make a U-turn not so easily in the space of three traffic lanes. I'm told that my particular bike has excellent "rake and trail." In engineering terms that means nothing to me, but in riding terms it means it is the perfect bike to make tight U-turns, which should make me feel better but does not. My instincts are wrong when it comes to U-turns. If Will gets into trouble and the bike begins to tip, he instinctively hits the throttle, which pulls him upright and out of trouble. I instinctively hit the brakes, and my bike and I both end up horizontal on the pavement.

When I was growing up, my father considered reading and writing to be a waste of time when there was "real work" to be done. *Get off your ass and do something, for Christ's sake!* When I heard my father stomping down the hallway toward my closed bedroom door, intent on catching me in petty pursuits, I jumped up, shoved my book under the bed, and busied myself with dusting the dresser. At times my mother quietly intervened. Sometimes the footsteps retreated; other times I cowered behind the closed door, listening to the venom she received on my behalf.

Because I like my mother better than my father, I've always attributed everything good about me to her and blamed everything bad about me on him—a simple system that has served me well for more than thirty years but is beginning to fall apart. I realize now, much to my consternation, that my father taught me to dream and, even more, to follow those dreams. Lord knows he didn't do it on purpose. He stressed practicality. He talked me into going to business school and becoming a CPA. But while I studied balance sheets, he vigorously chased his dream of being a cowboy like his father and his grandfather.

When I was ten years old, my father mortgaged everything he owned to buy a rundown ranch with fifty head of scraggly Hereford cows and one bull, putting our family into a financial spiral. But he dressed up in a cowboy hat and boots, bought himself a horse, a truck and trailer, and saddled up. Twenty-two years later, his daughter quit her high-paying Wall Street job, moved to the desert to write, and bought a motorcycle. He thought she had lost her mind.

That wasn't the first time. He also thought I was crazy when I left Utah for New York three years earlier, intent on landing that Wall Street job. He never thought a Western girl, a rancher's daughter to boot, had a chance in hell of surviving there. Once he found out how much money I made, however, he became a proud father. But he was right about one thing—a Western girl can't survive in Manhattan. At least this one can't. It's not the breakneck pace or the cutthroat business dealings—I adjusted to that stuff. And I didn't see much difference between herding fifty cows through a three-foot wide gate and shoving my way through an open subway door during rush hour. It's the lack of dirt that got to me. I mean real dirt—not the kind that comes off commuters' shoes or the tires of a bus—the kind you can dig into for a foot or two and find nothing but more dirt. And it's the lack of mountains that soar from earth to sky so splendidly as to remind me that the activities of Wall Street are only a game with winners and losers. I need reminders in my life. A year after I married Will, a New Jersey native, I brought him home to the West.

The dazzling blue water of Roosevelt Lake on my right undulates in absolute dissonance with its barren desert shores, each gently pushing the other to gain just a little more ground. Will and I have ridden this road dozens of times, but the unrelenting heat along this stretch always ambushes me. I expect the body of water that's next to me for more than twenty minutes to cool the air, but it is no match for the ruthless Arizona sun. I unzip my jacket, looking for a little relief, but find none. I could remove it altogether, but a leather jacket works like health insurance—you only need it when you don't have it. The idea of making contact with pavement that can peel layers of skin down to the bone is unappealing in any case but more so without my leather insurance policy. The dozens of gnats splattered directly in front of my eyes tell me that popping the face shield for extra airflow might not be wise, either. So I sweat.

Less than two hours out on a six-hour first-day ride, my body begins to ache. I take my feet off the pegs one at a time, straighten my legs, and shake the kinks out of my knees. They scream at me for doing this, shooting jolts of pain to my brain in an attempt to remind me of my age. *Yeah, yeah,* I tell them. I remind them about Mary, a seventy-eight-year-old woman I met two years ago in Flagstaff. I remind them that she walked with a cane and had to have someone help her on and off her motorcycle, but she had just ridden several hundred miles, solo, from New Mexico, leaning into a windstorm. I inform them that I will be doing the same when I am seventy-eight and they should toughen up and stop complaining. After several miles of this, I realize I am talking to my knees out loud, my voice echoing in my helmet.

I shake out both hands, which have started to cramp. Beneath my gloves my hands are beginning to look like my mother's. Her hands look like those of her sisters, whose hands look like those of their mother. It is the arthritic claw of Ethel Gooch Hatch, my grandmother. My mother gave her Hatch hand in marriage to my father forty-nine years ago in the Logan, Utah, L.D.S. Temple. Soon after the wedding, my father abandoned the church and forbade my mother to wear her temple garments (the underclothes worn by members of the Mormon Church who have gone through a temple ceremony) because he did not find them sexy. He stopped short of forbidding her attendance at church, but he ridiculed her and hindered her from taking on church responsibilities that might interfere with her duties as a wife. My mother was torn in half, loving the church more than she loved her husband, at the same time try-ing to follow church doctrine that taught her to worship him and respect his wishes. She sought guidance from her sisters, who, operating under the same principles, encouraged her to stand by him, believing always that God would guide my father back to the church.

Thirty-six years later, when God still hadn't intervened, my mother donned her temple garments, walked past my father on her way to church, and threatened to leave him if he stood in her way. Most of her life now revolves around church activity and commitments. She feels liberated and fulfilled. I asked her once if she didn't see the irony in finding liberation in an organization that grants men master status among women, in finding fulfill-ment as a woman in an institution that sees priesthood as the highest honor possible—an honor never to be bestowed upon a woman. I asked her if she didn't see the irony in finding freedom in an organization whose doctrine kept her in a difficult marriage for almost fifty years. Yes, she supposed there was a bit of irony there, and she laughed softly. But my mother shines in her work with the Relief Society. I have seen her organize twenty women into a legion of caretakers, chefs, chauffeurs, financiers, and diplomats when tragedy strikes a local family. I have seen her drive forty miles through a blizzard to get to the Salt Lake City Temple to do church work. I have seen her share a meal with a reclusive woman who won't let anyone else walk through her front door. Since my mother's return to the church, I have seen her face change; I have seen lines fall away and return in exquisite softness. I have seen her at peace.

I don't know the source of her peace—the church or the reclamation of a life. But watching the Hatch women, I am beginning to understand that there might be as many roads to fulfillment and freedom as there are women to take them.

I called Mom the day before I left and told her not to expect me for another three days. "I'm taking the bike, and I don't want to push it."

"You're not going to camp, are you?"

"No. I don't want to pack a tent and a bag."

"Where will you stop?"

"Flagstaff the first night, Panguitch the second. I'll be there early afternoon on Saturday."

"You'll call me every night?"

"Sure. Don't worry; I'll be careful."

"I know. I love you."

"See you Saturday."

I wanted to say something to alleviate her fear but had nothing to offer. My mother is one of a handful of people who have not asked me why I ride a motorcycle. Although Will has been riding for more than twenty years, he seldom hears this question. Surprisingly, the admonishments usually come from my own gender. Those who ask point out the obvious dangers, as if they were an oversight on my part, and once I recognized them, I'd come to my senses. I curse every person—and they number in the dozens—who, on learning I ride a motorcycle, is compelled to tell me about a cousin who was killed on a bike, a friend who is now in a wheelchair because of a motorcycle accident, or a brother who now maintains vegetable status. *I would never ride a motorcycle,* they say with a certain wisdom I obviously lack. Everyone within hearing distance nods knowingly in agreement. I'm thankful Mom does not ask because I have no ready answer. But I get the feeling she doesn't ask because she already knows.

I walk out of the hotel in Flagstaff at 7 a.m. and find my motorcycle resting on its side. Voices rush into my head. *That bike's too big for you. You shouldn't ride a bike if you can't pick it up when it falls.* That's always been the big question: Could I pick the bike up if I had to? I've never been tested on this. I've dropped a bike, but Will was there to pick it up for me. My bags fall from my hands, and I sit down next to them and stare at the bike. My heart pumps more rapidly than usual, and sweat beads emerge on my forearms inside my leather jacket. I tell myself this is an irrational thing to panic over—no danger involved, nothing really at stake. I stand, take hold of the grip closest to the ground with one hand and reach just beneath the seat with the other, bend my knees and prepare to lift with my legs. The muscles in my arms and legs engage in one unified movement. The bike doesn't budge.

"Want some help?" The voice comes from behind me—a young man watering petunias in pots with a hose.

"Yes," I say. "I want help."

"It's a big bike," he says as he lifts it without my assistance and rests it on its side stand.

"Yes, I know."

I ride a BMW R1100R. Someone once told me it looks like a pregnant guppy. The 5.5-gallon fuel tank puffs out into a pregnant stomach, and down below the cylinder heads stick out on either side like fins. It has a top speed of 133 mph and a 0-to-60 acceleration time of 3.98 seconds. But none of that is the reason I ride this particular bike. I ride it because it has horizontally opposing pistons and a Telelever front end. In my language, that means the bike will forgive a novice rider; it will hug even the roughest road—bumps and ruts and railroad tracks—and it will minimize "diving" when the rider on its back pounces too strongly on the front brake. My bike has a low center of gravity and an adjustable seat that allows me to put both feet flat on the ground when I come to a stop. In spite of its size, it is a popular bike among women riders.

This is not my first solo motorcycle trip. Last summer I rode the bike to a monastery in northern New Mexico. Everything about that trip felt right; I never questioned it. I headed north out of Tucson, then east on Highway 70 across the San Carlos Apache Indian Reservation because I wanted to spend the first evening soaking in a mineral bath in Truth or Consequences, New Mexico. It was a straight shot from San Carlos to Safford—the kind of curveless empty road that real motorcyclists hate. I twisted my cruise-control knob, set the needle right at 90 mph, spread my face into a smile, and watched the miles fly by. I didn't think about the animals that might dart in front of me, the cars that might pull out, the rough road surface that might suddenly appear. Pondering any of these things at any speed is a foolish game. It makes me shudder, makes my hands shake, makes me incapable of riding.

Critic Robert Hughes wrote of the Guggenheim motorcycle show, "Bikes mean a lot of things, but the main one is raw, unprotected speed, and there is little point of owning one unless you are prepared to go somewhat out on the edge." I never drive my car at speeds of 90 mph or more. On a bike, though, the edge is so close, so enticing, unencumbered by airbags and seat belts and headrests. I suppose most would liken riding to flying, but to me it is more like floating, faceup, spread-eagle in the middle of the ocean, with your ears submerged. You feel vulnerable because the water is more powerful than you, and your senses have been dulled. But you can hear your own breathing and your own heartbeat, and that is worth the risk.

I arrived at the monastery with a two-inch band burned around each of my wrists. Exposed to seven hours of desert sun, the skin between my gloves and my shirtsleeves blistered and peeled, and the markings stayed with me for months. When I explained how they got there, a woman sitting next to me reached over, placed her cool hand around my hot wrist, and squeezed gently, with tears in her eyes. She told me later it had taken every bit of courage she could muster to drive 180 miles to the monastery by herself.

The mesas of the Navajo reservation north of Flagstaff playfully run alongside me, their eroded shapes changing colors from lavender to burnt orange and back again as the clouds move about the sky and cast their shadows. But the 8 a.m. sun is already hot, and after eighty miles or so of straight road, with no relief in sight, the mesas begin to mock me: *It doesn't matter how fast you ride; nothing will change; you aren't going anywhere.*

The land below the mesas looks as if an enormous dump truck came through centuries ago, leaving hump after hump of gray dirt. Grass has tried to grow on some of them and has succeeded in a few cases. From time to time, the gray earth blends with red that flows from the mesas, as if an irrigation head gate has been opened. I scan the mounds, looking for an old sheepherder on a horse, anything to take my attention from counting the mile-marker posts. Chief Yellow Horse advertises Navajo jewelry, blankets, and phone cards—one-stop shopping. As I pass the shockingly yellow roadside stand, a sign tells me: TURN AROUND. NICE INDIANS BEHIND YOU! Each rickety booth along the road glitters with silver laid out on a white sheet, and I tell myself the same thing every time I take this road: *One of these days I'm going to stop and do some shopping.* A passing motorcyclist waves to me, and I wave back.

I let out a little yelp for joy at the 89A turnoff, a hundred miles out of Flagstaff, which will soon take me into the shadows of the imposing Vermilion Cliffs—where I will quickly come to feel like a flea on the underbelly of a Clydesdale—then into Kaibab National Forest, with a promise of pine aroma and dappled, shady roads.

Once I thought I saw you in a crowded, hazy bar/Dancing on the light from star to star/Far across the moonbeams, I know that's who you are/I saw your brown eyes turning once to fire. I have decided unequivocally that any Neil Young song has the perfect tone to sing inside my helmet, but the words come most easily to this one. As I round the first curve, happy to have a curve after a hundred miles of straight road, I launch into the chorus in my loudest Neil Young, nasal whine: *You are like a hurricane/There's calm in your eyes/And I'm getting blown away . . . to someplace safer where the feeling stays/I want to love you but I get so blown away.* A large bug whacks my helmet with the force of a small projectile and puts an end to my singing.

The jagged mesas travel with me until I rumble over the Colorado River on the Navajo Bridge. The narrow two-lane road stretches into an elongated V in front of me. To my left: acres of barbed-wire-enclosed crusty yellow fields cut into irregular pieces by deep, red gullies. I search for grazing cattle, for life of any kind. Nothing. To my right: looming formations of rounded rock the brownish red color of dried blood. The rocks look as if they were purposefully arranged by giant prehistoric people with magnificent tawny bodies of muscle and stature. I am completely alone, riding on an uninhabited planet. I have no one expecting me, no place to go. I am possibly the only human alive at this moment. I find peace here. I ride only to ride.

I spent most of my childhood shrinking in fear and lying low in corners, avoiding the Richman men. I remember the first time I said I wanted to be a writer; I must have been about nine. My father was in the mood to mold a personality, and this particular day he picked me. We—my mother, father, brother, and sister— were driving to Paradise, Utah, for a picnic. It was the town of my father's youth, a two-and-a-half hour drive each way from where we lived.

"So, Jana," he said, "what do you want to be?"

I knew, even at that age, it was a setup, but I must have been feeling courageous.

"A writer," I replied.

I vividly remember the top of his hairless head when he threw it back to laugh.

"You're being silly. What will you write?"

I didn't reply. He reached behind the seat and gripped my leg just above my ankle.

"What will you write?"

"Nothing."

I gas up at Jacob's Lake in Kaibab National Forest near the north rim of the Grand Canyon, take a break, and chat for a bit with two gnarly Harley dudes—bandannas, chains, oil-stained fingers and hair. Five years ago I would have walked a circle around them to get into the lodge; now I feel an instant camaraderie, an unspoken understanding.

"Which way ya headed?" one of them asks me as he adjusts the bandanna on his head.

"North," I say. "How about you guys?"

"We're going down to Flag."

"How do you like your boxer?" the other one asks me.

"I love it."

"Yeah, they're good bikes. I used to have an R69."

We chat for a while longer and part.

"Have a good trip," one says.

"Thanks."

"Keep the shiny side up," says the other.

"Yeah, you too."

Just north of Fredonia, I spot the WELCOME TO UTAH sign. Though I still have 450 or so miles to go before I reach home, I feel immediately among friends and family, as if I could stop at any house now along the way and they would invite me in to supper, as if they were damn glad to see me. Every muscle—from my little toe to one solid strip of pain running up my back and into my head—aches. I want to stop at the nearest house and test my theory, but I ride on.

In Kanab, I meet up again with Highway 89. The red rock turns to yellow as I enter the rolling green valleys north of the Zion National Park turnoff. I slow down, let hurried travelers pass me, and open my face shield to get the full impact of the beauty surrounding me. This stretch of road—no matter how many times I drive it—stuns me with its subtle magnificence. I daydream about a little house here tucked carefully into the hills, surrounded by murmurs of creeks cutting their paths through green pastures, flashes of pink summer roses, smells of lilac drift ing through the air, and quiet—so much quiet that you could hear a cat stroll through tall grass. I pass through the familiar little towns of Mount Carmel, Orderville, and Hatch, a town settled by the brother of my great-great-grandfather, where my mind insists on making life simple and happy.

My daydreams carry me to Panguitch, where I pull into the empty lot of the motel and begin the methodical process of de-kinking every joint in my body while removing gloves, glasses, helmet, and jacket. I shake out my hair (which insists on clinging to my head as if frightened to let go) and glance in my rearview mirror. I look worse than roadkill. The front desk is unattended, but I hear a television in the back. "Hello?" I call out. A short nondescript woman shuffles out and smiles to greet me. I place my helmet on the desk to free my hands. She takes a look at it, then at my bug-splattered jacket, then glances out the window at the bike, the only vehicle in the lot. "We're full up," she tells me. I smile smugly. I tell her I have a reservation.

I love riding—I love the feel of hot wind colliding with my body. I love the smell of wildflowers, pine trees, diesel fuel, and sagebrush rushing at me, one after another. I love the clarity of colors that have not been dimmed through a plate-glass window—like the place where a faultless blue sky touches a bronze earth with such crystallinity that I'm certain of reaching that spot before sundown. And I love speed.

I am not a classic thrill-seeker. I have not been bungee jumping, skydiving, rock climbing, or helicopter skiing. Motorcycling is not a passing fancy until the next bigger and riskier thrill comes along. And I don't have a death wish.

Will owned a motorcycle when I met him, and occasionally I went for a ride with him. Nothing about those rides on the backseat engaged me. But he was passionate about bikes, and I was passionate about him, so I kept trying. At a roadside stand, we once struck up a conversation with a couple in their seventies. The woman said, "I have a BMW R65 for sale; do you want to buy it?" At the time, I knew nothing about motorcycles. "Yes," I said, "I want to buy it." I purchased the bike and had Will drive it home for me; I had no idea how to operate a motorcycle. A month or so later, after taking some lessons, I started the R65, backed it out of the driveway with much trepidation, and drove it around the block—never exceeding 30 mph. From that moment on, I knew what it meant to have a personal sense of power.

Initially Will was adamantly against the idea of my riding. He claims this had less to do with my being a woman and more to do with the particular woman I am. I am a klutz. Around the house I run into walls, knock my elbows on doorframes, stub my toes on chair legs, bang my knees on table edges, and drop heavy objects on the tops of my feet—all on a regular basis. My body sports no fewer than four or five good-sized bruises at all times. Will naturally assumed I would be an oncoming disaster on a motorcycle. But as it turns out, the instincts needed to ride a motorcycle are not the same as those needed to maneuver safely around the house, and with the exception of U-turns, I'm a pretty good rider. *Better than most guys who ride,* Will now brags.

But I felt uneasy about this trip from the beginning. Coworkers had asked me for documents they might need in case I never returned. Friends who have known me for years had asked me: *Is that a wise thing to do?* Even Will, my bedrock of strength and support, had lapsed into obvious concern a few times before my departure.

We had planned to ride together to the family reunion, but

problems with Will's job changed our plans. He decided he couldn't take the time; instead he would fly up for the weekend. The day before I left, I started complaining about not having enough room on the bike for three weeks' worth of clothes in addition to the extras required: rain suit, tool kit, spare fuses, spare taillight and headlight bulbs, bike cover, first-aid kit, leather jacket, jacket liner, chaps, gauntlet gloves in case it gets cold, lightweight gloves in case it stays hot. I sat in the living room with it spread all around me and dreamed of dumping it all in the back of the car without another thought. Will walked out and popped the hood on the Isuzu. I followed.

"What are you doing?" I asked.

"Checking the oil."

I turned away and looked at my bike.

"I'm going to take a quick ride."

The sun was barely down and the leftover monsoon clouds gave the sky vast sweeps of pink, lavender, and orange. I turned into Sun City, where wide roads and broad curves provide the perfect short ride. I scanned for golf carts, leaned into the first turn, and let the bike take over. I pulled into the driveway as Will slammed the hood on the Isuzu.

"I checked everything. It's all set," he said as I pulled off my helmet.

"I'm taking my bike."

"I never doubted it for a minute."

The day I left, Will circled the bike, tugging on the straps holding the duffel bag in place. "Make sure you check these every time you stop."

"I will."

"When you stop for the night and reload your gear, make sure you strap to the frame, not to the saddlebags."

"Okay. I took the air pressure gauge out of the car."

"Your tires are fine. Leave 'em alone. You're just going to let the air out of them if you check them all the time."

"I won't."

"Be careful when you go up the drive at the hotel in Flag. It's steep, and there's a sharp turn at the end where you can't see cars coming. Work your clutch and keep your revs up."

"Okay."

"Call me when you get to Flag."

I can count in single digits the times Will has slipped into caretaker mode in our thirteen years of marriage. For this reason I treasured the moment. Our relationship works as a mix of accommodation and recklessness. I think of him as an open-minded, thoughtful, politically liberal man with an undercurrent of Latino machismo and Marine Corps-induced virility. He thinks of me as a tough-minded, opinionated, feminist woman barely coating the inner shell of a quivering, insecure little girl. There are moments when I want to be pulled in by him and given reassurances that he'll take care of things. Out of respect for me, he does not accommodate these moments.

I spend the third morning snaking through alfalfa fields and tiny farm towns on Utah back roads as I make my way north. I find the roads purely through instinct and submerged childhood memories of family car trips. I never make a wrong turn. I stop for gas in Nephi midmorning, then head west to find the old road that will take me to Jericho Junction. As far as I know, the road has never been assigned a road number and is barely maintained. But I'm so close to home I can smell the pot roast, and this road provides the shortest route. Robert Hughes defines riding as an odd mix of aggression and vulnerability, requiring a degree of both abandonment and intense focus. I think about this as I note the weather damage to the road in the years I've been away. In places there is barely a road at all; I steer through crumbled chunks of pavement. Again I am completely alone in the world. But this time I'm left haunted.

The thought of seeing the Hatch women draws me on. I try to remember any one of them talking to me about what it means to be a woman—about the things women do and the choices they make. I know this never happened. Still, somehow I felt their encouragement to step out, to push myself beyond my fears.

Each of them lived a life different from and similar to the others. Aunt Agatha found joy in the kitchen of her farmhouse while her husband milked the cows and kept her laughing with his stories; Aunt Carrell baked her bread in the kitchen of a sprawling ranch house in an exclusive Denver suburb—the wife of a successful businessman; Aunt Leona looked from her kitchen window to see a city view of her beloved Ogden, Utah, one year, the dark faces of African natives the next year and the Pacific Ocean the next, as she followed her wandering husband around the globe; my mother made tuna sandwiches while listening to a herd of bawling calves and the constant swearing of my father.

They have in common their commitment to the Hatch family and to the Mormon Church, which most times seem one and the same. I hope the commitment to both is voluntary—a choice made with full awareness—but I find it difficult to tell where the legacy ends and the choice begins. Nevertheless the Hatch women have wordlessly given me their blessing to stray from the Mormon Church and the strength to make my own choices. The one thing I do remember their saying is, "Take a backseat to no one." I doubt they meant this literally.

All is familiar—every rut, every curve, every side road—these back roads are seared into my memory. But just after the Eureka turnoff on State Road 36, an unfamiliar sight. Up ahead the road turns to a deep brownish red and stays that way for a good hundred yards. I slow down and keep my eyes on the anomaly; it begins to move. I downshift and crawl toward it. About twenty feet away, I check my mirrors for traffic (although I have not seen a car in over two hours) and stop in the middle of the road. Whatever is in front of me is alive. I cannot turn back; I'm less than fifty miles from home, and any detour would be hundreds of miles. A few renegades have broken from the group and have crawled next to my front wheel. They look a little like crickets, but they are too large—about an inch in diameter—and too red. They are also too strange and ugly to contemplate any longer. I try to pick a path of minimal destruction, hope to hell they don't fly, shift into gear, duck my head behind the windshield, and head home.

I pull into the driveway of my childhood home, stiffly swing one leg over the duffel bag, and gratefully lean the bike onto its side stand. Mom and Dad come out to meet me. Mom hugs my bug-splattered body with tears in her eyes. Dad says to put the bike in the garage before the neighbors see it. I ask Mom about the bugs on the road. Mormon crickets, she tells me. They've returned. They are supposedly the same strain of cricket that almost wiped out the Mormons in the spring of 1848, shortly after they arrived in Utah. After the Mormons tried battling the crickets, to no avail, with fire, water, and brooms, seagulls from the Great Salt Lake swarmed the fields, ate the crickets, and saved the crops.

"We'll pray for gulls later," my father says.

Mom asks if I am going to ride my bike to Cache County to the reunion. No, I say. I'll go with you. I'll sit in the back.

JANA RICHMAN ON *"Why I Ride"*

This essay began as an earnest attempt to answer the question that was asked of me often: why do I ride a motorcycle. Few people ride and of those who choose to do it, less than 10 percent are women. So what was it that enticed me, and what about my background, my character, let me be totally seduced by riding—an act that, as so many point out, can be a little dangerous.

The unexpected element that emerged in this essay was the realization of the staggering impact the Mormon Church, along with many generations of Mormon women in my family, has had on the formation of who I am, the values and beliefs I hold, the way I think. The success of this essay is that it honestly sets out to discover and disclose, and I think it accomplishes that. The shortcoming of the essay is that the length of this form doesn't allow a deeper exploration. But it sparked a journey to understand what happens when a woman begins to chip away at the foundation of her life. This essay led to a 2,000-mile motorcycle trip following the Mormon Trail in an attempt to understand Mormon history, personal faith, feminism, and breaking from family traditions as well as motorcycling and community among bikers. The journey resulted in a book tentatively titled *In the Shadows of Saints* to be published by Crown in 2005.

In addition to creative nonfiction, I write some fiction and playwriting, but my background is journalism. A creative writing instructor once told me that the journalism training had probably "ruined" me for any kind of "real" writing and I should just stick to journalism. Fortunately, I chose not to believe him. Journalism taught me to care about the details, taught me to ask the right questions, and taught me to recognize and question my own biases.

I don't think creative nonfiction *is* an emerging genre in American literature; I think it's simply an emerging genre in MFA programs. Twain and Thoreau were writing in the 1800s what would now be called creative nonfiction; H. L. Mencken, James Thurber, James Baldwin, and others were writing creative nonfiction throughout the 1900s. My favorite creative nonfiction writer, E. B. White, was just finishing up his fifty-year career in 1976, about the time I graduated from high school. Creative nonfiction has a rich history. I see no reason to ignore it and pretend we are breaking new ground with a new kind of literature.

Two pieces of advice have served me well as a writer: the first is to read a lot; the second is to write a lot (and don't assume your creative writing instructors have all the right answers).

Delivering Lily

PHILLIP LOPATE

■ ■

Ever since expectant fathers were admitted into delivery rooms a few decades ago, they have come armed with video cameras and awe. Before I became a father, I often heard men describe seeing the birth of their baby as "transcendental," the greatest experience in their lives. They would recall how choked up they got, even boast about their tears . . . it sounded very kitschy, like the ultimate sunrise. Being a nontranscendentalist, with suspicions, moreover, about my affective capacities, I was unsure how I would react. I had seen birthing scenes often enough in movies: how much more surprising could the reality be? I wondered, as someone who used to pass out at the sight of my own blood filling syringes, would I prove useless and faint? Or would I rise to the occasion, and be so moved in the bargain that at last I could retire those definitions of myself as a detached skeptic and accept the sweet, decent guy allegedly underneath?

Whatever reactions would befall me, I prepared myself for a

■ ■

PHILLIP LOPATE's recent books include *Getting Personal: Selected Writings*, *Waterfront: A Journey Around Manhattan*, and *Rudy Burckhardt*.

minor role. The star of any birth is the mother, her costar, Baby, her supporting leads, the medics. At nativity, every father feels himself a Joseph.

September 16, 1994, around four in the afternoon, I came across my wife, Cheryl, lying on the couch. She said she had "spotted" earlier, and wondered if this teaspoon's worth of sanguinous discharge could be what the books referred to, more scarletly, as "the bloody show."

I had already made a date with a friend—poet and fellow Brooklynite Harvey Shapiro—to attend the end of Yom Kippur services at the local temple, after which I was to bring Harvey back to our house to break fast together. Harvey would supply the traditional challah bread and herring, and Cheryl the rest of the meal. I promised her I would return with Harvey no later than seven.

At the Kane Street Synagogue, the rabbi was taking her own sweet time, and I knew Cheryl would be annoyed if her dinner got cold, so I prevailed on Harvey to leave the service early. Just as well. We were sitting around the table, getting ready to enjoy Cheryl's lamb and baked potatoes, when she pointed mysteriously to her belly.

"What's up?" I asked.

"I think it's starting."

She smiled. If it was indeed starting, she could skip her appointment the following week for an artificial induction. The fetus was at a good weight, and the doctors hadn't wanted to take the chance of the placenta breaking down, as happened often with overdue deliveries. Cheryl had felt sad at the thought of being artificially induced—missing the suspense of those first contractions—but now the baby seemed to be arriving on her due date, which meant we were in for the whole "natural" experience after all.

First-time parents, we had wondered whether we would really be able to tell when it was time. Would we embarrass ourselves by rushing off to the hospital days early, at the first false quiver? How to be sure whether the sensations Cheryl reported were the contractions? As instructed, we began timing them. Meanwhile, our downstairs neighbor Beth popped in, and stayed to witness potential history.

Harvey, a man in his late sixties and a grizzled veteran of parenthood, distracted us with stories of his boys' infancies while I kept my eye on the second hand. The contractions seemed to be spaced between five and seven minutes apart. We phoned our obstetricians. The office was closed for the Jewish holiday, but the answering service relayed the message to Dr. Arita, who was on call that night. Dr. Arita told Cheryl not to come into the hospital until contractions began occurring regularly, at five minutes apart, and lasted a full minute.

As soon as we had clocked two one-minute contractions in a row, I was impatient to start for the hospital. I had no wish to deliver a baby on the kitchen floor. Cheryl seemed calmer as she described her condition to Dr. Arita. It was now 10 p.m., and he told her she would probably be coming into the hospital "sometime that night." This phraseology sounded too vague to me. I marveled at my wife's self-possessed demeanor. Cheryl was manifesting her sweet, lovely, modest, cheerfully plucky side—the side she presented to my friends and to outsiders; it was not a lie, but it gave no hint of her other self, that anxious, morose perfectionist she often produced when we were alone.

At ten-thirty the contractions began to arrive five minutes apart, and with more sharpness. Arita, beeped, said to come in. I pulled together a few last items (rubber ball, ice pack) on the checklist of what to take to the delivery room, and, saying good-bye to our guests, had gotten halfway to the door when I noticed Cheryl was, as usual, not quite ready to leave the house. She decided she had to water the mums.

For months, we had debated which neighborhood car service to call for the hour-long trip from Carroll Gardens to Mount Sinai Hospital, on the Upper East Side of Manhattan. Cheryl, a superb driver with no faith in my own lesser automotive skills, had even considered taking the wheel herself when the time came. Now suddenly she turned to me and said, "You drive. Just don't speed."

I maneuvered the car with caution over the Brooklyn Bridge, then up the FDR Drive, while Cheryl spoke happily of feeling empowered and in control. The contractions, she said, were not that painful: "I like these intense experiences that put you in contact with life and death." Premature bravado, I thought, but kept this to myself, glad to have her confidently chatting away; it meant she wouldn't have as much chance to find fault with my driving.

We parked the car in the hospital's indoor lot. Cheryl began walking very slowly up the ramp, holding her back. "I can't walk any faster," she snapped (the first sign of a change in mood?), as if responding to an unspoken criticism she sensed me making about her pace, when in fact I was stumbling all over myself to support her.

It was close to midnight as we entered the eerily quiet Klin-genstein Pavilion. I approached the security guard, busy flirting with a nurse's aide, for directions. We had preregistered weeks before to avoid red tape at zero hour. After signing in, we were directed down a long creepy corridor into Birthing Room C. Mount Sinai Hospital has one of the largest maternity wards in the country, which is one reason we chose it; but suddenly its very magnitude made us uneasy. We felt no longer dramatic or special, but merely one more on the assembly line, popping babies up and down the hall.

The expectant couple was deposited in Room C, and left alone. It would be difficult to describe Room C except in regard to absences: it was not cozy, it was not charming, it was not tiny, it was not big, it was not even decrepit, it had nothing for the eye to fasten on. It was what you expected, more or less, of an anonymous hospital room with a quick turnover; but Cheryl, I sensed, had hoped for more—more ambience, amenities, *something* for the money. A visual designer by trade, she could, I knew, be preternaturally sensitive to new environments. Like a bride who finds herself in a nondescript wedding chapel, Cheryl may have long nurtured a fantasy of the ideal first-time birthing chamber, and something told me this was not it.

Often I allow myself to be made captive of my wife's moods, registering in an instant her first signs of discontent and trying (usually without success) to gentle her out of it. I suspect that this catering to her anxiety—if only by playing the optimist to her pessimist—is really laziness on my part: It saves me the trouble of having to initiate emotions on my own.

Cheryl was given a hospital gown to wear. The moment she put it on, her confidence evaporated. She became an object, a thing to cut open. I cast about for ways to regain the light mood we had had in the car, but it was no use. "Let's get out of this room. It gives me the willies," she said.

We went for a walk around the ward, opening doors and peering inside like naughty children. Our best discovery was a conference room, dark and coffee-machined and air-conditioned —freezing, in fact—which suited her just fine. We hid out for fifteen minutes in this nonmedical haven. But her contractions eventually drove us back to Room C.

Cheryl lay down. She took an instant dislike to her berth, saying, "I don't like this bed!" and fiddling with the dials to raise and lower it (an aversion, I thought, to proneness itself, which brought with it the surrender of her last sense of control). I turned on the TV to distract her. The second half of *Working Girl*, with Melanie Griffith, was on; Cheryl said she didn't want to hear the dialogue, so I was just to keep the sound loud enough to provide a background of "white noise." This was certainly a temperamental difference between us: if I had been giving birth, whatever the ordeal, I think I would have wanted the dialogue as well as the visuals of the movie on television. But I obliged; besides, we had already seen it.

For some reason, I had imagined our being swamped by medical personnel the moment we entered the hospital. We had not anticipated these quarter hours of waiting alone, without instructions. We sat about like useless tourists who arrive in an economy hotel after a long trip, too tired to attempt the streets of a foreign city, yet too hemmed in by the unlovely room to enjoy a siesta.

How glad we were to see Dr. Arita walk in! A silver-mustached, suavely Latin, aristocratic type, he was one of Cheryl's favorites on the team. (She had been instructed to "establish a rapport" with all four obstetricians, since you never knew who was going to be on call during the actual delivery.) Cheryl had once admitted to me she thought Arita handsome, which made me a little jealous of him. He wore the standard green cotton scrubs with "Property of Mt. Sinai Hospital" printed on the material (still wrinkled, pulled straight from the dryer, no doubt: in former times, they would have been crisply ironed, to maintain authority and morale) and, improbably, had on a shower cap, which suggested he had come straight from surgery; this fashion accessory, I was happy to see, reduced somewhat his matinee-idol appeal.

It was Dr. Arita who had, months before, performed the amniocentesis, which ascertained among other things that our baby was to be a girl. Dr. Arita had a clinical terseness, never taking five words to say what four could accomplish. He asked Cheryl if she wanted Demerol to cut the pain and help her sleep.

Cheryl had her speech all ready. "No, I don't want Demerol. Demerol will make me groggy. It'll turn my brain to mush, and I hate that sensation."

"All right. If you change your mind, let me know." With those succinct words, he exited.

From time to time a nurse would see how Cheryl was getting along. Or the resident on the floor would pop in and say, "You're doing great, you're doing great!" Increasingly, Cheryl wasn't. Her contractions had become much more intense, and she began making a gesture with her hands of climbing the wall of pain, reaching her arms toward the ceiling. Finally she cried out:

"Painkiller. Painkiller. DEMEROL."

I ran to fetch the resident.

"I'd give it to my wife," he said, which seemed to soothe Cheryl somewhat. Exhausted by her pain, she had entered a cone of self-absorption, and only a doctor's or nurse's words seemed able to reach her. She had tuned me out, I thought, except as a potential irritant—a lowly servant who was not doing his job. "More ice," she said, rattling the cup as though scornful of the lousy service in this joint.

During prenatal Lamaze pep talks, the husband was always being built up as an essential partner in the birthing process.

This propaganda about the husband's importance, the misapplied fallout of equal sharing of domestic responsibilities in modern marriage, struck me as bunk, since the husband's parturient chores appeared menial at best. One of my spousal duties was to replenish the ice that Cheryl sucked on or rubbed across her forehead. Throughout the night I made a dozen of these ice runs, dashing into the kitchenette and filling the cup with chips. Back in the room, Cheryl would cry out "Ice," then "Ice, ice!" with mounting urgency, as though the seconds between her request and my compliance were an eternity marking my bottomless clumsiness. I was rushing as fast as I could (though I must confess that when someone yells at me to fetch something or perform any manual action, it releases a slight physical hesitation on my part, perhaps no longer than 1.5 seconds, but this 1.5-second delay was enough to drive Cheryl wild. It is, you might say, the 1.5-second factor that makes conjugal life so continuously absorbing). Also, if I gave her a piece she deemed too small or too large, she would berate me in tones of "How could you be so stupid?" This went on for hours.

Her underlying reproach seemed to be that I was not hooked into her brain—was not able to anticipate her needs through ESP or heightened sensitivity—and she would have to waste precious breath articulating them. I would occasionally try to ease the tension by giving her a neck rub or caressing her hand, all recommended consolations by the Lamaze instructor. She shook me off like a cockroach. We husbands had been instructed as well to make "eye contact" with our wives: but whenever I tried this, Cheryl acquired the look of a runaway horse made acutely distressed by an unwanted obstacle in her path.

Sadly, I was not sufficiently generous to rise above feelings of being unfairly attacked. Days later, it surprised me to hear Cheryl telling people I had been wonderful during labor: "like a rock."

Why, if this was so, I asked her, had she been so mean to me at the time? She explained rather reasonably that she was just taking her pain and putting it on me as fast as possible.

Sometimes, during contractions, she would literally transfer her pain to me by gouging my leg. Mistakenly thinking she was attached to my foot, I offered it to her, only to have it pushed away. "No, not the foot, I don't want the foot, I want the hand!" she screamed. (Being abnormally sensitive to smells all during pregnancy, she had picked up an unpleasant odor from my socks.)

What she liked best, it turned out, was to grip my trousers belt and yank hard. Eventually we worked out a routine: as soon as she started climbing a contraction, I would jump out of my chair, which was on her left side, run over to her right side, and stand beside her as she pulled and thrashed at my belt for the duration of the spasm. All the while I would be counting off every five seconds of the contraction. I was not entirely sure what purpose I served by counting aloud in this fashion; they had told us husbands to do so in Lamaze class, in connection with certain breathing exercises, but since we had thrown those exercises out the window soon after coming to the hospital, why, I wondered, was it necessary to keep up a count?

I should explain that we had never been ideal Lamaze students. Too preoccupied with our lives to practice the breathing regularly at home, or perhaps unable to overcome the feeling that it was a bit silly, when the actual labor came, it was so unremitting that we could not be bothered trying to execute these elegant respiratory tempi. It would be like asking a drowning woman to waltz. Cheryl continued to breathe, willy-nilly; that seemed enough for both of us. (I can hear the Lamaze people saying: Yes, but if only you had followed our instructions, it would have gone so much easier. . . .) In any event, I would call out bogus numbers to please Cheryl, sensing that the real point of this exercise was for her to have the reassurance of my voice, measuring points on the arc of her pain, as proof that I was equally focused with her on the same experience.

In spite of, or because of, this excruciating workout, we were both getting very sleepy. The wee hours of the morning, from 2 to 6 a.m., saw the surreal mixture of agony merging with drowsiness. Cheryl would be contorted with pain, and I could barely stop yawning in her face. She too would doze off, between contractions: waking suddenly as though finding herself on a steeply ascending roller coaster, she would yowl Ooowwwww! I'd snap awake, stare at my watch, call out a number, rush to the other side of the bed and present my belt for yanking. When it was over I would go back to my chair, and nod off again, to the sound of some ancient TV rerun. I recall Erik Estrada hopping on a motorcycle in CHiPS, and Hawaii Five-O's lead-in music; and early morning catnap dreams punctuated by a long spate of CNN, discussing the imminent invasion of Haiti; then CBS News, Dan Rather's interview with the imperturbable dictator Raoul Cedras, and "Ice, ice!"

During this long night, Cheryl put her head against my shoulder and I stroked her hair for a long while. This tenderness was as much a part of the experience as the irritation, though I seem to recall it less. It went without saying that we loved each other, were tied together; and perhaps the true meaning of intimacy was not to have to put on a mask of courtesy in situations like these.

Demerol had failed to kill the pain: Cheryl began screaming "PAINKILLER, PAINKILLER, HELP," in that telegraphic style dictated by her contractions. I tracked down the resident and got him to give her a second dose of Demerol. But less than an hour after, her pain had reached a knuckle-biting pitch beyond Demerol's ministrations. At six in the morning, I begged the doctors to administer an epidural, which would numb Cheryl from the waist down. "Epidural"—the open sesame we had committed to memory in the unlikely event of unbearable pain—was guaranteed to be effective, but the doctors tried to defer this as long as possible, because the numbness in her legs would make it harder to push the baby out during the active phase. (My mind was too fatigued to grasp ironies, but it perked up at this word "active," which implied that all the harsh turmoil Cheryl and I had undergone for what seemed like forever was merely the latent, "passive" phase of labor.)

The problem, the reason the labor was taking so long, was that while Cheryl had entered the hospital with a membrane 80 percent "effaced," her cervix was still very tight, dilated only one centimeter. From midnight to about five in the morning, the area had expanded from one to only two centimeters; she needed to get to ten centimeters before delivery could occur. To speed the process, she was now given an inducement drug, Proactin—a very small amount, since this medication is powerful enough to cause seizures. The anesthesiologist also hooked Cheryl up to an IV for her epidural, which was to be administered by drops, not all at once, so that it would last longer.

Blessedly, it did its job.

Around seven in the morning Cheryl was much calmer, thanks to the epidural. She sent me out to get some breakfast. I never would have forgiven myself if I had missed the baby's birth while dallying over coffee, but Cheryl's small dilation encouraged me to take the chance. Around the corner from the hospital was a Greek coffee shop, Peter's, where I repaired and ate a cheese omelette and read the morning *Times*. I can't remember if I did the crossword puzzle: knowing me, I probably did, relishing these quiet forty minutes away from the hospital, and counting on them to refresh me for whatever exertions lay ahead.

Back on the floor, I ran into Dr. Raymond Sandler, Cheryl's favorite obstetrician on the team. Youthfully gray-haired, with a melodious South African accent and kind brown eyes, he said the same things the other doctors did, but they came out sounding warmer. Now, munching on some food, he said, "She looks good!" Dr. Sandler thought the baby would come out by noon. If so, delivery would occur during his shift. I rushed off to tell Cheryl the good news.

Momentarily not in pain, she smiled weakly as I held her hand. Our attention drifted to the morning talk shows. (Cheryl had long ago permitted me to turn up the volume.) Redheaded Marilu Henner was asking three gorgeous soap opera actresses how they kept the zip in their marriage. What were their secret ways of turning on their husbands? One had the honesty to admit that ever since the arrival of their baby, sex had taken a backseat to exhaustion and nursing. I liked her for saying that, wondering at the same time what sacrifices were in store for Cheryl and me. Marilu (I had never watched her show before, but now I felt like a regular) moved on to the question, what first attracted each woman to her husband. "His tight buns." The audience loved it. I glanced over at Cheryl, to see how she was taking this: she was leaning to one side with a concentrated expression of oncoming nausea, her normally beautiful face looking drawn, hatchet-thin. She seemed to defy the laws of perspective: a Giacometti face floating above a Botero stomach.

We were less like lovers at that moment than like two soldiers who had marched all night and fallen out, panting, by the side of the road. The titillations of the TV show could have come from another planet, so far removed did it feel from us; that eros had gotten us here in the first place seemed a rumor at best.

Stubbornly, in this antiseptic, torture-witnessing cubicle, I tried to recover the memory of sexual feeling. I thought about how often we'd made love in order to conceive this baby—every other night, just to be on the safe side, during the key weeks of the month. At first we were frisky, reveling in it like newlyweds. Later, it became another chore to perform, like moving the car for alternate-side-of-the-street parking, but with the added fear that all our efforts might be in vain. Cheryl was thirty-eight, I was fifty. We knew many other couples around our age who were trying, often futilely, to conceive—a whole generation, it sometimes seemed, of careerists who had put off childbearing for years, and now wanted more than anything a child of their own, and were deep into sperm motility tests, in vitro fertilizations, and the lot. After seven months of using the traditional method, and suffering one miscarriage in the process, we were just about to turn ourselves over like lab rats to the fertility experts when Cheryl got pregnant. This time it took. Whatever torment labor brought, we could never forget for a moment how privileged we were to be here.

"You've got to decide about her middle name!" Cheryl said with groggy insistence, breaking the silence.

"Okay. Just relax, we will."

"Elena? Francesca? Come on, Phillip, we've got to get this taken care of or we'll be screwed."

"We won't be 'screwed.' If worse comes to worst, I'll put both names down."

"But we have to make up our minds. We can't just—"

"Well, which name do you prefer?"

"I can't think straight now."

A *new nurse* came on the day shift: a strong, skillful West Indian woman named Jackie, who looked only about forty but who told us later that she was a grandmother. As it turned out, she would stay with us to the end, and we would become abjectly dependent on her—this stranger who had meant nothing to us a day before, and whom we would never see again.

At nine centimeters' dilation, and with Jackie's help, Cheryl started to push. "Pretend you are going to the toilet," Jackie told Cheryl, who obeyed, evacuating a foul-smelling liquid.

"She made a bowel movement, that's good," Dr. Sandler commented in his reassuring way. Jackie wiped it up with a towelette, and we waited for the next contraction. Jackie would say with her island accent, "Push, push in the bottom," calling to my mind that disco song, "Push, Push in the Bush." Cheryl would make a supreme effort. But now a new worry arose: the fetal monitor was reporting a slower heartbeat after each contraction, which suggested a decrease in the baby's oxygen. You could hear the baby's heartbeat amplified in the room, like rain on a tin roof, and every time the sound slowed down, you panicked.

Dr. Sandler ordered a blood sample taken from the infant's scalp, to see if she was properly aerated (i.e., getting enough oxygen). In addition, a second fetal monitor was attached to the fetus's scalp (don't ask me how). My poor baby, for whom it was not enough to undergo the birth trauma, was having to endure the added insult of getting bled while still in the womb.

The results of the blood test were positive: "Not to worry," Dr. Sandler said. But just in case, he ordered Cheryl to wear an oxygen mask for the remainder of the labor. This oxygen mask frightened us, with its bomb shelter associations.

"How will the baby be delivered?" Cheryl asked as the apparatus was placed over her face. "Will they have to use forceps?"

"That will depend on your pushing," answered Dr. Sandler,

and then he left. I did not like the self-righteous sound of this answer, implying it was ours to screw up or get right. We had entrusted ourselves to the medical profession precisely so that they could take care of everything for us!

Often, after a push, the towelette underneath Cheryl was spattered with blood. Jackie would swoop it up, throw it on the floor, kick it out of the way, raise Cheryl's lower half from the bed, and place a fresh towelette underneath. The floor began to smell like a battleground, with blood and shit underfoot.

"Push harder, push harder, harder, harder, harder," Jackie chanted in her Barbados accent. Then: "Keep going, keep going, keep going!" Cheryl's legs were floppy from the epidural; she reported a feeling of detachment from her body. In order for her to have a counterpressure to push against, I was instructed to lift her left leg and double it against the crook of my arm. This maneuver, more difficult than it sounds, had to be sustained for several hours; a few times I felt that my arm was going to snap and I might end up hospitalized as well. It was probably the hardest physical work I've ever done—though nothing compared, of course, to what Cheryl was going through. I feared she would burst a blood vessel.

Around eleven, Jackie went on her lunch break, replaced by a nurse who seemed much less willing to get involved. A tense conversation ensued between Dr. Sandler and the new nurse:

"This patient is fully effaced," he said.

"My other patient is fully, too."

He sighed, she shrugged, and the next minute they were both out the door. Left alone with a wife buckling in pain, I felt terrified and enraged: How dare Jackie take a food break now? Couldn't we page her in the cafeteria and tell her to get her ass back? It was no use, I had to guide Cheryl through her contractions as if I knew what I was doing. This meant watching the fetal monitor printout for the start of each contraction (signaled by an elevating line), then lodging her leg against my arm and chanting her through the three requisite pushes per contraction, without any firm idea exactly when each was supposed to occur. The first time I did this I got so engrossed pressing her leg hard against me that I forgot the cheerleading. I have a tendency to fall silent during crises, conserving energy for stocktaking and observation. This time I was brought up short by Cheryl yelling at me: "How am I supposed to know how long to push?" I wanted to answer: I'm not a trained medic, I have no idea myself. The next time, however, I bluffed, "Push, push in the bottom!" doing my best Jackie imitation until Jackie herself came back.

Sometime near noon, Dr. Sandler made an appearance with his colleague, Dr. Schiller, and began explaining the case to her. Cheryl had never felt as confident about Laura Schiller as she had about Dr. Sandler and Dr. Arita, either because Dr. Schiller was the only woman on the team (not that Cheryl would have agreed with this explanation), or because Dr. Schiller had a skinny, birdlike, tightly wound manner that did not immediately inspire tranquillity, or because the two women had simply not had the opportunity to "develop a rapport." With a sinking sensation, we began to perceive that Dr. Sandler was abandoning us. Actually, he probably would have been happy to deliver Lily, if only she had arrived when he had predicted, before noon. Now he had to be somewhere else, so he turned the job over to his capable colleague.

Dr. Schiller brought in a younger woman—a resident or intern—and they discussed whether the baby was presenting OA or OR (whatever that meant). Now they turned to the expectant mother and got serious. Dr. Schiller proved to be a much tougher coach than Jackie. "Come on, Cheryl, you can try harder than that," she would say. Cheryl's face clouded over with intense effort, her veins stood out, and half the time her push was judged effective, the other half, not. I could never fathom the criteria used to separate the successes from the failures; all I knew was that my wife is no shirker, and I resented anyone implying she was. If some of Cheryl's pushes lacked vigor, it was because the epidural had robbed her of sensation below, and because the long night of pain, wasted on a scarcely increased dilation, had sapped her strength.

Over the next hour, doctor's and patient's rhythms synchro-nized, until something like complete trust developed between them. Dr. Schiller cajoled; Cheryl responded. We were down to basics; the procedure of birth had never seemed so primitive. I couldn't believe that here we were in the post-industrial era, and the mother still had to push the fetus by monstrously demanding effort, fractions of an inch down the vaginal canal. It was amaz-ing that the human race survived, given such a ponderous child-bearing method. With all of science's advances, delivering a baby still came down to three timeworn approaches: push, forceps, or Caesarean.

This particular baby, it seemed, did not want to cross the per-ineum. "If the baby's no closer after three more pushes," Dr. Schiller declared, "we're going to have to go to forceps."

Forceps would necessitate an episiotomy—a straight surgical cut of the pubic region to keep it from fraying and tearing fur-ther. An episiotomy also would leave Cheryl sore and unable to sit for weeks. Knowing that I would probably be accused of male insensitivity, and sensing my vote counted marginally at best, I nevertheless expressed a word in favor of forceps. Anything to shorten the ordeal and get the damn baby out. Cheryl had suf-fered painful contractions for eighteen hours, she was exhausted, I was spent—and I was dying with curiosity to see my little one! I couldn't take the suspense any longer—obviously not a legitimate reason. Cheryl worried that the forceps might dent or misshape the baby's skull. Dr. Schiller explained that the chances of that occurring were very slight, given the improved design of modern instruments.

Cheryl pushed as hard as she could, three times, with a most desperate look in her eyes. No use.

"I always try to give a woman two hours at best to push the baby out. But if it doesn't work—then I go to forceps," Dr. Schiller said authoritatively. Cheryl looked defeated.

"Okay, we'll try one more time. But now you really have to push. Give me the push of the day."

The Push of the Day must have felt like a tsunami to Lily, but she clung to the side of her underwater cave.

They readied the scalpel for an episiotomy. I turned away: some things you can't bear to watch done to a loved one. Dr. Schiller, kneeling, looked inside Cheryl and cried out, "She's got tons of black hair!" Standing over her, I could make out nothing inside; the fact that someone had already peeked into the entranceway and seen my baby's locks made me restless to glimpse this fabled, dark-haired creature.

The last stage was surprisingly brief and anticlimactic. The doctors manipulated the forceps inside Cheryl, who pushed with all her might. Then I saw the black head come out, followed by a ruddy squirming body. Baby howled, angry and shocked to find herself airborne in such a place. It was such a relief I began to cry. Then I shook with laughter. All that anguish and grief and triumph just to extract a writhing jumbo shrimp—it was comic.

The doctor passed the newborn to her mother for inspection. She was (I may say objectively) very pretty: looked like a little Eskimo or Mexican babe, with her mop of black hair and squinting eyes. Something definitely Third World about her. An overgrown head on a scrawny trunk, she reversed her mother's disproportions. A kiss from Cheryl, then she was taken off to the side of the room and laid on a weighing table (seven pounds four ounces) and given an Apgar inspection by Jackie, under a heat lamp. Lily Elena Francesca Lopate had all her fingers and toes, all her limbs, and obviously sound vocal cords. She sobbed like a whip-poor-will, then brayed in and out like an affronted donkey.

Abandoned. For, while Cheryl was being stitched up by Dr. Schiller (who suddenly seemed to us the best doctor in the world), Lily, the jewel, the prize, the cause of all this tumult, lay on the table, crying alone. I was too intimidated by hospital procedure to go over there and comfort her, and Cheryl obviously couldn't move, and Jackie had momentarily left the room. So Lily learned right away how fickle is the world's attention.

Dr. Schiller told Cheryl she would probably have hemorrhoids for a while, as a result of the episiotomy. Cheryl seemed glad enough that she had not died on the table. She had done her job, delivered up safely the nugget inside her. I admired her courage beyond anything I had ever seen.

Happy, relieved, physically wrung out: these were the initial reactions. For hours (I realized after the fact) I had been completely caught up in the struggle of labor, with no space left over for self-division. But that may have had more to do with the physically demanding nature of assisting a birth than with any "transcendental" wonderment about it. In fact it was less spiritually uplifting than something like boot camp. I felt as if I had gone through combat.

That night, home from the hospital, I noted in my diary all I could recall. Consulting that entry for this account, I see how blurred my understanding was—remains—by the minutiae of medical narrative. What does it all "mean," exactly? On the one hand, an experience so shocking and strange; on the other hand, so typical, so stupefyingly ordinary.

When people say that mothers don't "remember" the pain of labor, I think they mean that of course they remember, but the fact of the pain recedes next to the blessing of the child's presence on earth.

Odd: what I remember most clearly from that long night and day is the agitated pas de deux between Cheryl and me, holding ourselves up like marathon dancers, she cross at me for not getting her ice fast enough, me vexed at her for not appreciating that I was doing my best. Do I hold on to that memory because I can't take in the enormity of seeing a newborn burst onto the plane of existence, and so cut it down to the more mundane pattern of a couple's argument? Or is it because the tension between Cheryl and me that night pointed to a larger truth: that a woman giving birth finds herself inconsolably isolated? Close as we normally were, she had entered an experience into which I could not follow her; the promise of marriage—that we would both remain psychically connected—was of necessity broken.

I remember Cheryl sitting up, half an hour after Lily was born, still trembling and shaking.

"That's natural, for the trembling to last awhile," said Dr. Schiller.

Weeks afterward, smiling and accepting congratulations, I continued to tremble from the violence of the baby's birth. In a way, I am still trembling from it. The only comparison that comes to mind, strangely enough, is when I was mugged in the street, and I felt a tremor looking over my shoulder, for months afterward. That time my back was violated by a knife; this time I watched Cheryl's body ripped apart by natural forces, and it was almost as if it was happening to me. I am inclined to say I envied her and wanted it to be happening to me—to feel that intense an agony, for once—but that would be a lie, because at the time, not for one second did I wish I were in Cheryl's place. Orthodox Jews are taken to task for their daily prayer, "Thank God I am not a woman." And they should be criticized, since it is a crude, chauvinistic thought; but it is also an understandable one in certain situations, and I found myself viscerally "praying" something like that, while trying to assist Cheryl in her pushes.

Thank God I am not someone else. Thank God I am only who I am. These are the thoughts that simultaneously create and imprison the self. If ego is a poisonous disease (and it is), it is one I unfortunately trust more than its cure. I began as a detached skeptic and was shoved by the long night into an unwilling empathy, which saw Cheryl as a part of me, or me of her, for maybe a hundred seconds in all, before returning to a more self-protective distance. Detachment stands midway between two poles: at one end, solipsism; at the other end, wisdom. Those of us who are only halfway to wisdom know how close we still lean toward the chillness of solipsism.

It is too early to speak of Lily. This charming young lady, willful, passionate, and insisting on engagement on her terms, who has already taught me more about unguarded love and the dread meaning of responsibility than I ever hoped to learn, may finally convince me there are other human beings as real as myself.

PHILLIP LOPATE ON *"Delivering Lily"*

What pleases me most about how "Delivering Lily" turned out is that I finished the essay at all. It also has some moments of uncomfortable honesty that please me. I'm not sure I succeeded in welding a narrative and an analytical piece: I felt too much at the mercy of reporting the "facts" and can't tell if the power of the event comes through on the page.

I initially thought I would write a much longer essay on Lily's first year. Her birth was supposed to be a prologue, but took over. Also, I hadn't known I would reach the conclusion I did about solipsism. Maybe I feel more comfortable writing essays than poetry or fiction because I don't have to work myself into quite as emotional or "inspirational" a state; I can be cooler, more rational, and trust more to analysis than invention. I've written about the emergence of creative nonfiction in my anthology *The Art of the Personal Essay*. As a form, it is obviously drawing a lot of interest: more memoir pieces than Montaignean reflections, alas. In my own writing, I use all the literary techniques I can: scenes, dialogue, conversational address to the reader, humor, philosophy, sensuous detail. Anything that will bring the piece alive.

My advice to young writers is that if you can't *not* write, go to it. But don't quit your day job.